Natural Enemy,
Natural Ally

Natural Enemy, Natural Ally

Toward an Environmental History of Warfare

edited by
Richard P. Tucker and Edmund Russell

Oregon State University Press
Corvallis

The paper in this book meets the guidelines for permanence and durability of the Committee on Production Guidelines for Book Longevity of the Council on Library Resources and the minimum requirements of the American National Standard for Permanence of Paper for Printed Library Materials Z39.48-1984.

Library of Congress Cataloging-in-Publication Data
Natural enemy, natural ally : toward an environmental history of warfare / edited by Richard P. Tucker and Edmund Russell.-- 1st ed.
    p. cm.
 Includes index.
 ISBN 0-87071-047-8 (alk. paper)
 1. War--Environmental aspects. I. Tucker, Richard P., 1938- II. Russell, Edmund, 1957-
  TD195.W29N38 2004
  333.72--dc22
                          2004007872

Oregon State University Press
101 Waldo Hall
Corvallis OR 97331-6407
541-737-3166 • fax 541-737-3170
http://oregonstate.edu/dept/press

Contents

Preface and Acknowledgments

When we began work on this project eight years ago, we found this book impossible to produce. Our own work on the history of forests (Tucker) and chemical weapons and insecticides (Russell) had led us to conclude that war had shaped the natural environment in important but underappreciated ways. Editor Mary Elizabeth Braun invited us to put together a collection of essays on the topic. We agreed. We had noticed that environmental historians occasionally mentioned war in their narratives, just as military historians often discussed the natural settings of their subject, but the two groups had virtually no contact with each other. All we had to do, we hoped, was pull these threads together by asking authors to elaborate on the relevant parts of their stories. What could be simpler?

But it turned out that nothing was simple. Almost no historians had set out to understand the relationship between war and the environment in any systematic way, which meant that very few had collected enough data for a substantial essay. Although frustrating, this pattern was also inspiring because it increased our sense that a book on the history of war and the environment would address a major need.

As a first step, we organized panels at conferences of the American Society for Environmental History (ASEH). We found that several historians had unpublished drafts. A wave of interest appears to be developing. In 2002, for the first time, the program of the ASEH meeting featured two panels on war and the environment. More Europeans are now joining this interdisciplinary discussion. And increasingly scholarship on war and the environment has appeared in fields other than history, as we indicate in chapters 1 and 2 of this volume.

In 2002 this collection finally came together. Our work would have been impossible without help. Mary Elizabeth Braun, first at University of Wisconsin Press and then at Oregon State University Press, was a steadfast source of inspiration and guidance. Several other environmental historians have helped us in important ways, notably Colin Duncan, John McNeill, and two anonymous readers for the OSU Press. Cheryl Oakes searched the Environmental History bibliography and photograph collection at the Forest History Society in Durham, North Carolina. Vitally important, several members of the military history seminar at the University of Michigan gave rigorous analytical support to the evolving discussion; without them, this collection would not be as strong. Contributions by Russell were supported by sabbatical leave from the University of Virginia and a grant from the National Science Foundation (SES-0220764). Any opinions, findings, and conclusions or recommendations expressed in this material are those of the author(s) and do not necessarily reflect the views of the National Science Foundation. Finally, our families (Lia Frede and Lucy, Anna, and Margaret Russell) steadfastly supported our efforts throughout this book's long gestation and birth.

A condensed version of Chapter 2 can be found in the *Encyclopedia of World Environmental History* (New York, NY: Routledge, 2004). Chapter 7 first appeared in slightly different form as Edmund Russell, "'Speaking of Annihilation': Mobilizing for War against Human and Insect Enemies, 1914-1945," *Journal of American History* 82 (March 1996), 1505-29 (© Organization of American Historians; reprinted with permission). Some of this material also was published in Edmund Russell, *War and Nature: Fighting Humans and Insects with Chemicals from World War I to Silent Spring* (New York: Cambridge University Press, 2001). Chapter 9, "Landscapes in a Dark Valley: Toward an Environmental History of Wartime Japan," by William Tsutsui, was first printed in *Environmental History* 8 (April 2003), 294-311, published jointly by the American Society for Environmental History and the Forest History Society, Durham, North Carolina (www.foresthistory.org/ehmain). We thank the publishers for permission to include those pieces.

Richard Tucker
Edmund Russell

Introduction

Edmund Russell and Richard Tucker

Nature's faces are legion. Environmental historians have studied many ways in which people have envisioned nature: as a collection of resources, a threat, a holy place, a source of beauty and artistic inspiration, a refuge, a playground, a location for rites of passage, an object of scientific discovery, and a source of employment.[1] Rarely, however, have we studied nature as a soldier.[2] And rarely have we explicitly considered the ecological consequences of warfare as a central, distinctive element of humans' historically evolving relation to the natural world. This is somehow the case in spite of our increasing awareness that twentieth-century wars have made momentous contributions to the global environmental stress and deterioration of our contemporary world. Thus we have little long historical understanding of either the patterns or the recent acceleration of warfare's environmental impact.

Other historical disciplines have also failed to consider how warfare, central to relations between societies and between states, has changed the natural world. Although military historians have long portrayed nature as a set of strategic or tactical obstacles—especially in the form of terrain and weather—they have rarely discussed the impact of warfare on that same terrain.[3] While war has figured with increasing prominence in histories of science and technology, the impact of wartime ideas and tools on nature has retained a low profile. And although cultural historians have illuminated many ways in which war has shaped domestic social relations, they have rarely extended their studies to include relations with nature.[4]

Why have historians neglected this linkage? Tradition has surely played a role. At least since Isaiah contrasted swords with plowshares, we have seen war and control of nature (exemplified by agriculture) as belonging to separate categories. In the nineteenth century, Clausewitz declared war to be a human endeavor in which the number of soldiers was the primary determinant of victory. Directions of scholarly fields have also been important. The trend away from seeing history as "war and politics" has reduced interest in military history. Environmental history's roots in the history of conservation focused attention on civilian rather than military affairs.[5]

Recently, though, interest in the environmental effects of warfare has surged, as scholars have watched global events unfold. The Vietnam War, which saw the destruction of forests with herbicides, laid the groundwork for more widespread concern. The strength of the environmental movement before and during the Persian Gulf Wars increased this interest and, perhaps for the first time, debates about the propriety of going to war featured environmental concerns. Iraq's torching of Kuwaiti oil wells in the first Gulf War, and its intentional release of oil into the Gulf to foul ships, confirmed environmentalists' fears that war would increase pollution. In 2001, the United Nations declared 6 November of each year to be the International Day for Preventing the Exploitation of the Environment in War and Armed Conflict.[6]

Developments within the academy have also been important. Scholars in a number of fields have come to view issues through the lens of environmentalism, so it was likely that this concern eventually would encompass warfare. As environmental history has broadened beyond its base in American history, scholars concerned with other parts of the world have begun to bring recognition of war's frequency and impact to their work. Thinking about international relations, rather than domestic issues alone, also encourages thinking about military relations among nations.

One purpose of this volume is to argue for the importance of understanding war as a major and distinctive force in environmental change, as well as the environment as a force in shaping warfare. Intellectually, this means merging two prime fields: environmental history and military history (not to mention related fields such as historical anthropology and geography). In environmental history, it entails seeing war as an important force in environmental change. In military history, it entails understanding the role of environmental consequences of warfare, as well as the traditional concern for the ways terrain and weather have shaped the planning and course of wars. The practical value of the inquiry may be that those interested in the environment, and in war, should understand how interaction has operated in the past. These influences have not always been obvious or direct.

A second purpose is to illustrate emerging trends in scholarship. The next chapter is a preliminary survey or overview of the subject as it now stands; the remaining chapters complement the breadth of that chapter with in-depth analyses of particular topics. These chapters illustrate not only the significant and sometimes surprising result of this sort of research, but fruitful types of sources and methods as well.

A third purpose of the book is to encourage further research. Scholars have only scratched the surface of this topic. We hope legions of historians will dig more deeply and broadly. As they do, our understanding will become more balanced as well as more sophisticated. The need for a greater range of studies came home forcefully for us as we sought essays for this volume. We began with the goal of including essays that ranged across the continents from north to south and east to west, and across periods from the ancient world to the present. For a long time it was hard to find enough essays at all. When we finally had the essays published here in hand, it was clear that the majority of work in this nascent field has focused on the twentieth century, with an emphasis on the Northern Atlantic powers.

We emphasize, then, that we see this volume as a sample of early initiatives, not as an exhaustive review of what the field will become.

When research on this topic grows enough to fill a sprawling mural of scholarship, what aspects of that mural will stand out? At this stage, we can only sketch broad outlines of a few important elements. Chapter 2 gives a chronological overview of findings already in hand. Here, drawing primarily on examples from the case studies in this volume, we emphasize angles from which researchers might approach the historical interaction between war and the environment.

Before we do, a brief word on terminology is in order. We use "war" and "warfare" in a broad sense. Preparations for war, related events on the home front, and the aftermath of war are included in this usage, along with battles and campaigns. Many historians prefer to describe their work as "military" history. In common usage, though, "military" implies a narrow concern with armed forces, and our concern is wider. Also, here we use "nature" and "environment" as shorthand for elements of the world other than humans. We are fully aware that humans are part of nature and the environment, but that awareness does not negate the usefulness of having terms to refer to things other than humans.

Now let us turn to angles of approach. Here we emphasize that the effects of war have been direct and indirect, immediate and long term, enduring and ephemeral, harmful and beneficial, and local and regional. These themes weave through the discussion below.

Most of us interested in the topic of this book find our attention drawn first to the wounds battles have carved on the landscape. The book's cover photograph captures one vivid example from World War I, when bullets, bombs, and gas at the battles of Ypres left behind a ghost forest of trees stripped of branches and leaves. The soil, bereft of cover, became muck requiring duckboards for those who wanted to walk over it. This sort of landscape became a postwar icon bespeaking revulsion at the war's waste of lives and resources.[7] Nearly every battle leaves scars: bomb craters, trenches, foxholes, dead vegetation, polluted water, and even a new ground cover of corpses.

In today's parlance, this sort of damage would be called collateral, since nature got caught in the crossfire rather than being the intended target of attack. Most battles of the American Civil War, World War I, and World War II were not waged to destroy forests and farms, but farms could not get away from bullets, bombs, and troops. Military engineers leveled islands and mined coral reefs in the Pacific in World War II not because they wanted to eradicate plants and animals, but because they wanted to create landing strips for their planes.

In other cases, wars have changed nature less through weapons or sculpting battlefronts than through demand for resources. Sometimes armies and their followers in the field have extracted the resources directly. Stewart Gordon recounts in chapter 3 that Mughal armies resembled mobile metropolises with an insatiable maw. Relying on harvest and plunder of the surrounding countryside, an army that camped in one place for a few months created circular deserts forty miles across. As Mark Fiege shows in chapter 5, armies continued to depend on the surrounding countryside for sustenance well into the modern period (in that case, during the American Civil War). Wartime shortages have also forced civilians to tax nature more heavily than in peacetime. Japan, as William Tsutsui shows in chapter 9, captured millions of songbirds in World War II for food and feathers. By war's end, only crows and a few sparrows survived to greet the armistice.

The extent of an army's footprint on the landscape has depended on transportation. In the American Civil War, as Mark Fiege shows in chapter 5, soldiers and horses in the Confederate army relied largely on the food and fodder they could scour from the countryside surrounding wherever they happened to be. Local areas rarely could support entire armies for long, so soldiers and animals slowly wasted away. Union troops and animals, on the other hand, benefited from an extensive railroad system that enabled the nature of one region to fortify armies in other regions. Superiority of resources and transportation, rather than of military acumen, dictated the result of the war. Richard Tucker shows in chapter 6 that shipping each World War II American soldier to Europe required 500 board feet of lumber. Keeping him fighting demanded another 50 board feet per month. America's ally, Britain, had few timber resources on the home island. Both countries mobilized tropical forests—far from battlefronts and often without a soldier in sight—to feed the furnace of war.

Transportation can be a curse as well as a blessing, for it can abet natural enemies as well as allies. In chapter 10, Judith Bennett demonstrates that ferrying cattle among Pacific islands in World War II spread parasites and diseases as well cows. She blames ignorant and cocksure Americans, who ignored the advice of more experienced experts from the Antipodes, for the severity of the problem. Without World War II, which drew Americans into new regions and created a sense of urgency, the biogeographic map of Pacific cattle diseases might well look different today.

These examples remind us that war has shaped, and so should be studied, on a variety of geographic scales. Some effects of war have been narrowly local, as in the case of a crater created by a single bomb dumped in a remote place by a plane on its way back to base, though such events have often been repeated in large numbers. Battles have reshaped landscapes on a larger, but still often local, scale. Other effects are regional, such as the clear-cutting of forests for navies (chapter 6) and the transmission of cattle diseases in the Pacific (chapter 10). Others are national, as in the extirpation of songbirds in Japan (chapter 9). Still others are global, as in the contribution of military activities to international lumbering and to greenhouse gases.

The very usefulness of nature to one side of a conflict has often made it the enemy of another. Armies have at times salted the earth and poisoned the wells of their enemies to deprive them of sustenance.

General George Sherman's march to the sea in the American Civil War, still infamous in the Southern United States as an example of Northern excess, did not target civilians directly. It relied instead on destroying food and other Southern natural allies, which in turn invited malnutrition and disease to follow in its wake. Similarly, in South Africa, Lord Kitchener's forces burned thousands of Boer farms while leaving most of the human population alive in concentration camps. During the Vietnam War, American forces used herbicides to destroy vast forests thought to be shielding North Vietnamese soldiers from view.[8]

These examples illustrate the dynamic highlighted in the title of this book. "Natural ally" emphasizes that nature has long been an ally of peoples at war, providing the raw materials for food, clothing, and shelter that underpin military success. "Natural enemy" emphasizes the other side of the coin. Being the natural ally of one side has made nature the natural enemy of the other, converting normally benign organisms such as food, trees, shrubs, and grass into the targets of bombing, burning, poisoning, and looting. Flipping the coin again, the title's reference to "natural enemy" also highlights nature's role as a direct threat to armies, which in turn has made it the target of "attack." Chapter 7 describes the anti-malaria program in the Pacific during World War II. That campaign grew out of the recognition that malaria-bearing mosquitoes posed a far bigger threat than Japanese soldiers to Allied soldiers; for every one soldier knocked out by Japanese troops, malaria felled eight. The island-hopping campaign across the Pacific depended as heavily on effective malaria control (a capacity the Allies developed during the war) as it did on guns. Flipping the natural enemy-natural ally coin once again, this campaign eventually turned a natural enemy into a natural ally. By protecting their own soldiers from malaria while keeping the techniques secret, the Allies enlisted malaria as a powerful legion against the Japanese.

Allied troops were not the only beneficiaries of enemy-to-ally reversals. As Chapter 6 shows, Japan captured enormous supplies of lumber in World War II when it took Burma from the British. Imagine a quartermaster's smile upon learning that 15,000 tons of sawn teak, 1.2 million tons of teak logs, 75,000 tons of sawn hardwoods, and 250,000 tons of hardwood logs had suddenly become his.

Some natural enemies are attacked because they represent indirect as well as direct threats. Because mosquito-borne malaria threatened workers in factories (as well as soldiers in training) in the southern

United States during World War II, the federal government launched a massive mosquito-control program that succeeded in all but eradicating the disease.[9] Nature has also become a target even when it has had little or no military significance. One example appears in Chapter 11, in which Kurk Dorsey notes that whales became targets of depth charges in World War II because they resembled submarines.

So far we have focused on ways in which war has changed nature "in the raw." Environmental historians have found it useful to distinguish first nature (organisms and geology) from second nature (the built environment). That distinction is useful in thinking about ways in which war has changed nature. Like first nature, second nature—here, especially technological systems that have converted nature into usable forms—have become military targets throughout history. In the ancient Fertile Crescent, the Assyrian army wrecked complex irrigation systems that had increased the enemy's agricultural productivity.[10] More recently, when the United States entered World War II, its theory of strategic bombing emphasized destruction of enemy technology (factories, railways, and ports) rather than enemy civilians.[11] Recognition that one's natural allies could "switch sides" has also led to destruction of nature-transforming technology. In 1942, for example, the Dutch destroyed sawmills and lumber camps on Java rather than allow them to fall into Japanese hands.[12]

Widening the circle from nature to humans, the civilians operating machinery converting nature into usable forms have also become targets of attack. One of the rationales for firebombing civilians (a strategy embraced by the United States later in World War II) was that it would destroy the enemy's ability to supply its army. We have relatively little to say in this volume about the effect of war on humans. That is not because we are unconcerned, nor because we underestimate the moral, political, economic, and social effects—often tragic—of war. In our other work, we have looked closely at such effects. Our focus in this volume is on a different dimension of warfare.

War has been able to increase its demands on natural resources by changing institutions. Chapter 6 shows that belligerents in World Wars I and II relied heavily on forestry services and companies to supply the timber on which their forces floated and flew. Where forestry institutions and infrastructure did not exist, war encouraged their founding. Where they already existed, they flourished. Similarly, the same wars led warring nations to create new, and accelerate the growth of existing, scientific and technological organizations. It also created or strengthened ties between such institutions, often by tying military science closely to civilian science. Chapter 7 describes examples from the world of chemical warfare.

Harder to measure, but clearly important, has been the effect of war on ideas about nature. Because winning a war has often become an overriding national priority, other priorities often have found themselves shuffled lower in the deck. In chapter 10, Judith Bennett shows that military demand for beef torpedoed peacetime programs designed to limit the spread of cattle parasites and diseases. Chapter 7 suggests that describing efforts to control nature as war has implied the existence of an immediate and serious threat, with a need for quick and forceful action, increased government intervention and authority, decreased individual autonomy, and mobilization of large resources. In this way, viewing insects as inveterate enemies in need of eradication has implied something different from seeing them as costs of production that are worth killing only if they became so numerous that the benefit of spraying outweighs the cost.

Nature has also shaped ideas, such as by teaching humans how to wage war. Roger Levine's essay on southern African warfare in the early nineteenth century (chapter 4) argues that different environments have created different military strategies. He compares the landscapes in which Zulu speakers and Xhosa speakers lived and their ways of hunting and fighting, and how these differences affected their ability to adapt to fighting Europeans with more advanced technology.

Ideas about nature have also contributed to war by helping propagandists. Students of propaganda have long emphasized the role of dehumanization in reducing moral qualms about attacking other humans. But dehumanization—moving people out of the category of human—is only half the process. The other half is reclassification, or moving people into new categories. (If dehumanization alone were sufficient, calling enemies chalk, flowers, toasters, or toothbrushes would be as effective as calling them wolves, rabid dogs, rats, or lice.) Chapter 7 argues that existing ways of thinking about and interacting with nature supply ready-made templates for thinking about and treating enemies.

Along with helping or hurting the conduct of warfare, nature can also provide causes. Access to natural resources is often the purpose of war (rather than interest in defeating people themselves). The fruits of victory have usually included access to more such treasures. These effects can be interlinked, as Stewart Gordon's chapter on eighteenth-century India in this volume illustrates. War was not some externality that intruded upon peaceful farmers; it was an integral part of "business as usual." In the Mughal and Maratha empires, militarized elite families controlled much of the strategically important Malwa plateau. These families looked on control as "an entrepreneurial activity that involved war, colonization, conquest, and bestowal." Militarized families had the obligation to find cultivators and open new areas to agriculture, and intermittent military campaigning was one of their tools.

The effects of war often have continued—sometimes lingering, sometimes thriving—after the end of hostilities. The short-term effect of battles in the American Civil War and the two world wars, as Mark Fiege, Richard Tucker, William Tsutsui, and Simo Laakkonen show in this volume, was to produce barren, haunted landscapes. But now, except where preserved as battlefields, many of these sites once again look like neighboring farms and forests. Contrast those short-term effects on vegetation to the long-term effects of unexploded ordnance. Canisters of poison gas and explosives from World War I remain in the earth. For the unlucky few who happen upon them, these weapons sometimes are just as lethal today as they were nearly a century ago.

It is probable that long-term environmental transformations resulting from warfare, in which neither nature nor human effort can restore the natural or managed ecosystem to the level of productivity it formerly had, are usually caused by soil erosion, disruption of water regimes, or (in the industrial era) severe pollution, far more than the more obvious damage to flora and fauna. Several papers in this collection suggest this, and ecologists might assert that we should expect just that. But clearer conclusions on this vital issue must await more focused research in specific cases.

Some of the most important long-term environmental consequences, including those resulting from economic, technological, or institutional changes, arise in the aftermath of war. Emergency acceleration of the timber industry in both world wars gave the industry the expanded capacity to meet enlarged civilian demand in postwar years, beginning with the vast international need for immediate reconstruction of war-torn zones. World Wars I and II and the Cold War stand front and center as causes of rapid expansion of chemical industries. Government subsidies, government investment in research, civilian use of arsenals as factories, and increased knowledge gained from conquered foes helped power the explosive growth of the American chemical industry in the twentieth century.

Aftereffects on ideas and values have also been profound. In Chapter 8, Simo Laakkonen suggests that the attitudes engendered by World War II influenced postwar thinking about Finnish forests. "After the war, it seemed that the forest industry opened a new front," he writes, "to kill its natural enemies and save useful collaborators in order to maximize production and profit." In chapter 11, Kurk Dorsey argues that geopolitical changes wrought by World War II deeply influenced the shape of postwar whaling. During the war, the United States favored the creation of a strong institution that would rely on science to regulate whaling. After the war, though, Britain and the United States began to see whaling regulation not as an isolated issue, but as part of a larger effort to create international institutions (such as the World Bank and United Nations) to promote peace and prosperity. But for the countries that continued whaling, protection of national sovereignty trumped conservation.

Antecedents to war deserve as much attention as aftereffects. In the American Civil War, Mark Fiege (chapter 5) argues, the North and the South entered the conflict with different abilities to tap natural resources. The continuation of that differential underpinned the North's ultimate victory. As Richard Tucker demonstrates (chapter 6), wars of colonial conquest set the stage for World War I by equipping nations with varying levels of timber access. Britain's enormous empire enabled that nation to import timbers from around the globe. Germany and France lacked well-developed colonial administrations, and they had to rely on domestic production. This experience in turn led Germany to make the capture of eastern European forests a prime objective in World War II. Edmund Russell (chapter 7) notes that Germany's strength in chemical manufacturing before World War I made possible its initiation of gas warfare in 1915.

Although damage is the image that usually leaps first to mind when thinking about war and the environment, benefits have also been significant. As Simo Laakkonen shows in chapter 8, World War II cut water pollution in Finland by diminishing pulp and paper production. These and other benefits served Finnish forests so well, Laakkonen provocatively suggests, that war might have been an "ecological alternative for peacetime."

Similarly, military bases have often been de facto nature preserves. By building up small areas while leaving most of the base open for training and maneuvers, bases sometimes have created well-guarded sanctuaries for species. Colorado's Rocky Mountain Arsenal is one of the most polluted sites in the world, having hosted manufacturing of nerve gases and pesticides, but the unpolluted areas of the arsenal preserve a prized piece of high plains ecology and host rare species. Bombing ranges, mined areas, and "no-man's lands" have served the same purpose by keeping away civilians who otherwise would have destroyed the habitat. The occasional deer has blown itself up on a land mine, but, from a population perspective, the cost has been low compared to the benefits of preserving habitat. The demilitarized zone of Korea, guarded against intrusions by soldiers on both sides, has become one of the most important bird sanctuaries in East Asia. Absent its military value, the zone probably would have (and still may) become tracts of housing offering little habitat for migrating wildfowl.[13]

We raise these examples not to argue that one should create bases and bombing ranges in order to preserve wildlife, but to highlight the complex, surprising, and often ironic ways in which war and nature interact.

This sort of counterintuitive finding reminds us how much more we need to learn about this topic. How do wars in other regions and periods resemble or differ from those described here? How have preparations for war shaped nature? Can we separate war's effects from those of civilian economies, or are they essential to each other? How do types of wars resemble or differ from each other in their effects? What would ecological accounting reveal about the costs and benefits of war? What parts of nature have been most important in war? Thus our research joins a growing body of work from fields outside history—including law, political science, economics, and science—that is beginning to produce a wide as well as deep body of scholarship.[14]

Overall, the evidence in this book leaves little doubt that modern warfare has accelerated long-term damage to the biosphere, as a direct consequence of the intensifying destructive capacity of military technology. This is an ominous portent for the twenty-first century, and it prompts us to look back over previous centuries for a fuller perspective on where we may be heading.

Notes

1   The literature in environmental history is enormous and beyond review here. Instead, we cite examples of works on various ways of viewing and interacting with nature. For others, see the bibliography in Richard Tucker's global survey which follows this introduction.

On environmental history in general, see Ted Steinberg, *Down to Earth: Nature's Role in American History* (New York: Oxford University Press, 2002); Carolyn Merchant, ed., *Major Problems in American Environmental History* (Lexington, MA: Heath, 1993); Donald Worster, ed., *The Ends of the Earth: Perspectives on Modern Environmental History* (New York: Cambridge University Press, 1988); Kendall E. Bailes, ed., *Environmental History: Critical Issues in Comparative Perspective* (Lanham, MA: University Press of America, 1985); Lester J. Bilsky, ed., *Historical Ecology: Essays on Environment and Social Change* (Port Washington, NY: Kennikat Press, 1980); and the round table in *Journal of American History*, 76 (March 1990), 1087-1147.

On attitudes toward nature in general, see Clarence J. Glacken, *Traces on the Rhodian Shore: Nature and Culture in Western Thought from Ancient Times to the End of the Eighteenth Century* (Berkeley: University of California Press, 1967); Peter Coates, *Nature: Western Attitudes since Ancient Times* (Oxford: Polity, 1998); and Simon Schama, *Landscape and Memory* (New York: A. A. Knopf, 1995).

On aesthetics, see Marjorie Hope Nicolson, *Mountain Gloom and Mountain Glory* (Ithaca, NY: Cornell University Press, 1959). On religion, see Dennis Williams, *God's Wilds: John Muir's Vision of Nature* (College Station: Texas A&M University Press, 2002). On politics, see Samuel Hays, *Beauty, Health, and Permanence: Environmental Politics in the United States, 1955-1985* (New York: Cambridge University Press, 1987). On natural resources, see Arthur F. McEvoy, *The Fisherman's Problem: Ecology and Law in the California Fisheries, 1850-1980* (New York: Cambridge University Press, 1986); Nancy Langston, *Forest Dreams, Forest Nightmares: The Paradox of Old Growth in the Inland West* (Seattle: University of Washington Press, 1995); and Joseph E. Taylor III, *Making Salmon: An Environmental History of the Northwest Fisheries Crisis* (Seattle: University of Washington Press, 1999).

On recreation, see John Reiger, *American Sportsmen and the Origins of Conservation* (1975; third edition, Corvallis: Oregon State University Press, 2000); Louis S. Warren, *The Hunter's Game: Poachers and Conservationists in Twentieth-Century America* (New Haven, CT: Yale University Press, 1997); Karl Jacoby, *Crimes Against Nature: Squatters, Poachers, Thieves, and the Hidden History of American Conservation* (Berkeley: University of California Press, 2001). On nature writing, see Stephen Fox, *John Muir and His Legacy: The American Conservation Movement* (Boston, MA: Little, Brown, 1981). On science, see Michael L. Smith, *Pacific Visions: California Scientists and the Environment, 1850-1915* (New Haven, CT: Yale University Press, 1987); and Donald Worster, *Nature's Economy* (New York: Cambridge University Press, 1977).

2   For exceptions, see Susan D. Lanier-Graham, *The Ecology of War: Environmental Impacts of Weaponry and Warfare* (New York: Walker and Company, 1993); J. P. Robinson, *The Effects of Weapons on Ecosystems* (Oxford: Pergamon, 1979); Ralph H. Lutts, "Chemical Fallout: Rachel Carson's Silent Spring, Radioactive Fallout, and the Environmental Movement," *Environmental Review*, 9 (Fall 1985), 210-25; Avner Offer, *The First World War: An Agrarian Interpretation* (Oxford: Clarendon,

1989); Alfred W. Crosby, *Ecological Imperialism: The Biological Expansion of Europe, 900-1900* (New York: Cambridge University Press, 1986); Albert Cowdrey, "Environments of War," *Environmental Review* 7 (Summer 1983), 155-64; A. Joshua West, "Forests and National Security: British and American Forestry Policy in the Wake of World War I," *Environmental History* 8 (April 2003), 294-311.

3   Harold A. Winters, Gerald E. Galloway, Jr., William J. Reynolds, and David W. Rhyne, *Battling the Elements: Weather and Terrain in the Conduct of War* (Baltimore, MD: Johns Hopkins University Press, 1998); Leon J. Warshaw, *Malaria: The Biography of a Killer* (New York: Rinehart, 1949).

4   Works on links between military and civilian endeavors include William H. McNeill, *The Pursuit of Power: Technology, Armed Force, and Society Since A. D. 1000* (Chicago: University of Chicago Press, 1982); Seymour Melman, *Pentagon Capitalism: The Political Economy of War* (New York: McGraw-Hill, 1970) and *The Permanent War Economy: American Capitalism in Decline* (New York: Simon and Schuster, 1974); Lewis Mumford, *Technics and Civilization* (New York: Harcourt, Brace, and World, 1963) and *The Myth of the Machine, vol. 2: The Pentagon of Power* (New York: Harcourt, Brace, and World, 1970); and John U. Nef, *War and Human Progress: An Essay on the Rise of Industrial Civilization* (New York: W. W. Norton, 1968).

Overviews of environmental and military issues in the history of technology include Jeffrey K. Stine and Joel A. Tarr, "Technology and the Environment: The Historians' Challenge," *Environmental History Review*, 18 (Spring 1994), 1-7; Merritt Roe Smith, ed., *Military Enterprise and Technological Change: Perspectives on the American Experience* (Cambridge, MA: MIT Press, 1985); Barton C. Hacker, "Military Institutions, Weapons, and Social Change: Toward a New History of Military Technology," *Technology and Culture*, 35:4 (1994), 768-834; and Alex Roland, "Technology and War: The Historiographical Revolution of the 1980s," *Technology and Culture*, 34 (Jan. 1993), 117-34.

Works on war and culture include Elaine Tyler May, *Homeward Bound: American Families in the Cold War Era* (New York: Basic Books, 1988); John Morton Blum, *V Was For Victory: Politics and American Culture During World War II* (New York: Harcourt, Brace, Jovanovich, 1976); Paul Boyer, *By the Bomb's Early Light: American Thought and Culture at the Dawn of the Atomic Age* (New York: Pantheon, 1985); Paul Fussell, *The Great War and Modern Memory* (New York: Oxford University Press, 1975).

5   Isaiah 2:4; Karl von Clausewitz, *On War* (O. J. Matthijs Jolles, trans.) (Washington, DC: Combat Forces Press, 1953). The foundation texts of environmental history illustrate this focus on domestic, civilian affairs. They include Roderick Nash, *Wilderness and the American Mind*, 3rd ed. (New Haven, CT: Yale University Press, 1982); Richard White, *Land Use, Environment, and Social Change: The Shaping of Island Country, Washington* (Seattle: University of Washington Press, 1992); William Cronon, *Changes in the Land: Indians, Colonists, and the Ecology of New England* (New York: Hill & Wang, 1983); Donald Worster, *Dust Bowl: The Southern Plains in the 1930s* (New York: Oxford University Press, 1979) and *Nature's Economy: A History of Ecological Ideas* (New York: Cambridge University Press, 1977); Carolyn Merchant, *The Death of Nature: Women, Ecology, and the Scientific Revolution* (New York: Harper and Row, 1980); and Samuel P. Hays, *Conservation and the Gospel of Efficiency: The Progressive Conservation Movement, 1890-1920* (Cambridge: Harvard University Press, 1959).

6   J. B. Neilands, G. H. Orians, E. W. Pfeiffer, A. Vennema, and A. J.
    Westing, *Harvest of Death: Chemical Warfare in Vietnam and Cambodia*
    (New York: Free Press, 1972); United Nations, Dag Hammarskjold
    Library (http://www.un.org/depts/dhl/environment_war/), viewed 24
    March 2004 (this web site has links to many publications on the
    environmental impact of war in general and of specific conflicts, including
    those in Yugoslavia, Kuwait, Chiapas, Afghanistan, and Iraq).
7   Paul Nash painted similar landscapes in *We are Making a New World 1918*
    and *The Menin Road*, both in the Imperial War Museum, London.
8   National Academy of Sciences, *Effects of Herbicides in South Vietnam*
    (Washington, DC: National Academy of Sciences, 1974).
9   Stanley B. Freeborn, "The Malaria Control Program of the United States
    Public Health Service among Civilians in Extra-Military Areas," *Journal of
    the National Malaria Society* 3 (Mar. 1944), 19-23.
10 Chapter 2, this volume.
11 Michael Sherry, *The Rise of American Air Power: The Creation of
    Armageddon* (New Haven, CT: Yale University Press, 1987).
12 Chapter 6, this volume.
13 Rocky Mountain Arsenal Wildlife Society (http://
    www.rmawildlifesociety.org/rma.html) viewed 24 March 2004; White
    Point Nature Preserve (http://www.pvplc.org/land/white_point/
    whitepoint.htm) viewed 24 March 2004; CNN.Com, "War zone to
    Wildlands: The Campaign to Restore Korea," 19 June 2000 (http://
    www.cnn.com/2000/NATURE/06/19/korea.warzone.enn) viewed 24
    March 2004.
14 Jay E. Austin and Carl E. Bruch, eds., *The Environmental Consequences of
    War: Legal, Economic, and Scientific Perspectives* (New York: Cambridge
    University Press, 2000); Thomas F. Homer-Dixon, *Environment, Scarcity,
    and Violence* (Princeton, NJ: Princeton University Press, 1999); Michele
    Stenehjem Gerber, *On the Home Front: The Cold War Legacy of the Hanford
    Nuclear Site* (Lincoln: University of Nebraska Press, 1992); Seth Shulman,
    The Threat at Home: Confronting the Toxic Legacy of the US Military
    (Boston, MA: Beacon Press, 1992); William H. Durham, *Scarcity and
    Survival in Central America: Ecological Origins of the Soccer War*
    (Stanford, CA: Stanford University Press, 1979); Roy A. Rappaport, *Pigs
    for the Ancestors: Ritual in the Ecology of a New Guinea People* (New
    Haven, CT: Yale University Press, 1984); Arthur Westing, *Warfare in a
    Fragile World: Military Impact on the Environment* (London: Taylor and
    Francis, 1980), and *Threat of Modern Warfare to Man and His
    Environment: An Annotated Bibliography Prepared Under the Auspices of the
    International Peace Research Association* (Paris: UNESCO, 1979); Steven
    V. Price (ed.), *War and Tropical Forests: Conservation in Areas of Armed
    Conflict* (Binghamton, NY: Haworth, 2003).

The Impact of Warfare on the Natural World: A Historical Survey

Richard P. Tucker

Introduction: Major Themes

Human impacts on the natural world are roughly as old as *Homo sapiens'* presence on earth, and collective violence seems to have been a typical aspect of human behavior throughout our history. So it is bound to be difficult to sort out how humans' violence toward land and natural resources in the course of collective violence has differed from the environmental impacts of societies in times of peace. The following survey is tentative at many points. It is based largely on historical literature, and is designed to be an illustrative starting point for research rather than an exhaustive account, which would necessarily have to be far longer. It is an attempt at a new historical synthesis, which may help to set a context for a major public issue in our own times. As Edmund Russell, my coeditor, writes, "There is vastly more research waiting to be done on both the synthetic and the case study levels. That project will take many people; we are just shining beams of light on a few aspects in hopes of interesting others."[1]

This essay considers several interlocking themes and trends. Foremost is the acceleration of the capacity of states to inflict violence. Closely parallel has been the acceleration of the destructive capacity of military technology, and its demands on natural resources for the production and use of weapons. This must ultimately entail a broader recognition of the military aspects of societies in peacetime, since the boundaries between warfare and peacetime preparation for future wars have frequently been blurred.

Furthermore, warfare—and its linkages with changes in the natural world—must be understood in terms of its systemic links to broader trends in human history, such as demographic fluctuations and epidemic diseases of both humans and their livestock. This suggests a counter-theme: the recognition that in some circumstances warfare has actually reduced human pressure on nature, enabling other species to recover and flourish at least temporarily. Another paradoxical way that warfare has benefited natural systems has been most pronounced in modern times. Modern wars' enormous consumption of natural resources and destruction of nature have led governments to intensify systems of resource management and protection during and immediately after wartime, especially for resources deemed vital for military use.

In addition, we must recognize that the environmental impacts of war are always specific to the unique characteristics of particular ecosystems. As with all environmental history writing, the goal is to see fully the complex interactions between human and natural systems.

Finally, this essay highlights the environmental impacts of warfare rather than the ecological causes or settings of battle. But a fully integrated discussion would integrate the two dimensions, from the present back through the millennia to early human times when nature shaped human life far more than humans were able to reshape nature, even with their most powerful prehistoric tool, fire.

Hunter-Gatherer and Sedentary Farming Cultures

Collective violence between structured social groups is as old as human societies themselves, and resulting ecological change must have just as ancient a history.[2] What has often been called "tribal warfare" has occurred throughout our history, wherever indigenous cultures have not yet been displaced by modern regimes. In this type of conflict the scale and duration of violence was highly localized, limited by the destructive power of hand tools and the small scale of social organization. Border areas between two communities were perennially contested for control of food sources and other useful resources, and shifts in territorial control were frequent.

Attackers typically raided their enemy's fields and food supplies, both to seize resources and to cripple their foes. This often resulted in high mortality rates and depopulation of conquered areas, for raiders made little distinction between fighting men and the families that supported them. Humans suffered, and so did their crops and water sources. As historical anthropologist Lawrence Keeley expresses it, "Except in geographical scale, tribal warfare could be and often was total war in every modern sense. Like states and empires, smaller societies can make a desolation and call it peace."[3] However, as ecologist Jeffrey McNeeley adds, "The greatest diversity of terrestrial species today is found in forested areas inhabited by tribal and other indigenous peoples, where relatively large areas of 'unoccupied' territory served as a sort of buffer zone between communities that may be embroiled ... in virtually constant warfare."[4]

Many examples of these patterns have been studied in Pacific island groups, tropical forests, and savannas, where ancient history persisted until well into the twentieth century.[5] In the buffer zones where human populations were scarce, game animals multiplied and biodiversity flourished. Though previous human activity had reduced the diversity of vegetation and wildlife, now that trend was reversed, and natural communities tended to revert to species composition closer to the diversity of earlier times. A well-documented example of buffer zones is the western Great Lakes forests of North America, where Dakota and Chippewa hunters contested woodland hunting grounds for deer and other game for many generations. In the eighteenth century, still at an early stage of the European presence in the area, when French and English were not yet dominant, the Chippewa were able to reduce the Dakota presence. In a wide buffer region subsistence hunting of game animals was greatly reduced, allowing game species to increase greatly in numbers.[6]

In the long run, warfare between small communities had inadequate destructive power to cause lasting ecological change, for preindustrial tools had very limited destructive power. The major exception to this was fire, throughout history the most destructive of tools. Its early ecological impact occurred in semi-arid regions, such as Australia, where fire transformed landscapes into stable but species-reduced fire-climax ecosystems.[7] But in tribal settings it is almost arbitrary to distinguish the ecological consequences of collective violence from those of broader social processes, since violent and peaceful times were so closely interwoven. So this essay moves quickly to larger-scale societies and state systems.

Urban Civilizations with State Systems

Here we meet more complex social and political/military organizations, with more sophisticated and powerful technologies that enabled a larger-scale and more protracted duration of warfare, and concomitantly greater impacts on the natural world. The Neolithic era of settled agriculture emerged some ten thousand years ago in the arid lands of the Near East. In the Fertile Crescent of the Tigris and Euphrates valleys, large-scale human labor made possible perennial agriculture through the construction of an elaborate system of irrigation canals that needed constant maintenance. The lowland areas of these arid river basins suffered gradual long-term ecological disruptions such as siltation and waterlogging.[8] But they could also be deliberately damaged. When two states went to war with each other, the enemy's irrigation systems were tempting targets for attack, and the dessicating impact on the land could last for long periods. In an illustrative instance, the Assyrian army destroyed the intricate Haldian irrigation works around 705 BCE, flooding their victims' lands as a sign of their defeat. Soon thereafter, around 695 BCE, King Sennacherib conquered the Assyrians, leveled Babylon, and diverted one of its principal irrigation canals through the devastated city.[9]

This precedent was followed many centuries later during the Mongol conquest of Iran and Iraq in the thirteenth century CE. In the long and varied history of relations between pastoral and sedentary peoples, in peacetime and war, there has never been more appalling cultural destruction than in the Mongols' conquest of other civilizations. But the ecological consequences seem to have been highly variable over the long run. In the well-watered agricultural regions of Iran, Mongol cavalry conquered one city after another in the late 1200s, wiping out or enslaving entire populations. The immediate impact, according to Ira Lapidus, "amounted to a holocaust. The populations of many cities and towns were systematically exterminated. Whole regions were depopulated by invading armies and by the influx of Turkish and Mongol nomads who drove the peasants from the land. The conquerors plundered their subjects, made them serfs, and taxed them ruinously. The result was a catastrophic fall in population, income, and state revenue. ... Substantial territories were turned from agriculture into pasturage."[10] But the long-term consequences for irrigation systems and agriculture were highly variable, for some post-conquest rulers replaced plunder with reconstruction. As early as the Ilkhan regime, from 1295 into the 1330s, Mongol rulers rebuilt cities, repaired irrigation and farming systems and fostered trade.

In Iraq the drama had far more lasting results for both people and the land. There the Mongol invaders raced through the Abassid Empire of Islam's heartland and captured its capital, Baghdad, in 1259, massacring the entire population of the city. As Bernard Lewis summarizes the staggering consequences, "Baghdad and Iraq never again recovered their central position in the Islamic world. The immediate effects of the invasion were the breakdown of civil government and the consequent collapse of the elaborate irrigation works on which the country depended for its prosperity, even for its life. ... In Iraq ruin was unchecked."[11] Ecological, demographic and cultural decline limped hand in hand for centuries thereafter. Throughout the turbulent history of the Middle East since then, irrigation systems have been vulnerable targets for armies. It is startling that they seem to have rarely been actually destroyed, but have been usually left as symbols of the deadly threat of mutual destruction.[12]

Ecological changes that can be clearly linked to warfare appeared in the lands around the northern and eastern Mediterranean basin some twenty-five hundred years ago, with the emergence of the first well-documented city-states. The Mediterranean borderlands are naturally fragile, featuring long hot summers and short wet winters; their topography is mostly mountainous, with soils that are light and easily eroded once natural vegetation is removed. The rulers of the city-states of Greece and adjacent lands raised armies and navies, commanding the human and natural resources they required in order to confront their enemies. In these "command states," as William McNeill has called them, military-political elites organized entire societies around the constant threat of hostile neighbors.[13] They used wood for forging metal and building chariots, battering rams, siege machines, and fortifications, permanently reducing forest cover in many places.

Siege warfare was well developed by the sixth century BCE, and both defensive fortification and the besiegers consumed large amounts of wood.[14] For example, when Nebuchadnezzar besieged Lachish in 588 BCE, the Babylonian army placed great piles of wood from stripped forests against the wooden ramparts and burned them until the fortress collapsed. More broadly, in military campaigns as early as the Persian invasion of Greece in 512 BCE, armies burned their enemies' forests and pillaged their farmlands. Rural people fled to safety in the forest ahead of advancing military columns; if they stayed for any time, the new fields and pastures they created there damaged the fragile woodlands. In the Peloponnesian War (431-04 BCE), which ended the golden age of Athens, when Spartan attacks forced Athenian leader

Pericles to move the farming population of his hinterland into the city, the Spartan army ravaged the countryside, destroying crops in the effort to starve the city into submission. Attacks on nature such as these were the grim precursors of modern "Total War," involving civilian casualties and targets as much as military. Their short-term impacts were obvious to everyone involved; their longer-term environmental results are more difficult to measure.[15]

In the same centuries, naval warfare also caused ecological damage onshore, as the impacts of militarization spread into peacetime. Lumber ports grew up at the mouths of rivers, where ships of all sizes were built: ships of various designs for peaceable trade, and also the great triremes for naval warfare. Woodsmen gradually cleared forested watersheds upriver to meet the shipyards' needs. As local timber supplies ran low, strategic needs demanded control of more-distant stands of timber. In the Peloponnesian War great naval battles between Sparta and its allies on one hand and the Athenian empire on the other destroyed hundreds of triremes; the prime trees of whole forests were lost as the ships burned and sank. This was a bitter irony, since one of Athens' purposes in the long Sicilian Campaign was to capture forests for shipbuilding.[16]

An entirely greater scale of ecological change appeared with the rise of the Roman Empire, which left the most dramatic transformations yet seen in Mediterranean and European landscapes.[17] On maritime shores timber supplies for naval armaments produced deforestation and soil loss. In North Africa Roman armies damaged croplands and water systems in the conquest of Carthage. Looking northward from Italy on land, Rome faced perpetual threats from many enemies, and responded by mobilizing heavy plebeian infantry units to complement its cavalry. As the Roman armies moved northward in the conquest of Gaul and then southern Germany and Britain, they built a system of all-weather roads so superbly engineered that some are still in use today.[18] On the northern frontiers of the empire, as far as frontier lands along the Rhine and Danube, a string of military fortifications sustained garrisons of troops. These military installations were the opening wedge of the domestication of entire landscapes, as the roads and fortifications enabled peasants to clear hundreds of patches of forest for settled agriculture, even in the midst of chronic skirmishes between the Romans and their Germanic adversaries. Villages appeared on cleared forest land, where peasants worked to provide food and fiber for the garrisons of many frontier fortifications.[19]

In the wake of the fourth and fifth century invasions from the north that crippled Rome's empire, urban centers declined and rural medieval Europe slowly emerged in its aftermath. As populations fell, agricultural lands reverted to secondary woodlands until a peaceable era of population growth and forest clearances ushered in the High Middle Ages in the twelfth century.[20]

Warfare was endemic in medieval Europe, interlacing with civilian life on the land. This made the boundaries between war and peace vague indeed. In the early feudal era warriors' weapons were no more powerful than in earlier imperial days, so the major environmental impacts of organized violence revolved around fortifications and siege warfare. Here the importance of social hierarchies in shaping warfare's environmental impact is clear. Lords of the land defended their headquarters by building ever more massive, intricately designed fortifications surrounded by earthen ramparts with wooden palisades. Sieges of these fortresses and fortified towns often lasted for months, even years, devouring both woods and croplands in the process, as peasant levies impressed by their lords swept across farms and woodlands, ripping the sources of subsistence from their adversaries of the moment.[21] And in the twilight zone between mass violence and peaceful times, brigandage (hardly distinguishable from regular soldiering) festered.[22] Peasant populations were terrorized by raids on food and livestock. Lands deserted when rural people became refugees reverted toward natural woodlands and wetlands, with concomitantly increasing species diversity. The short-term damage to partially domesticated landscapes was evident to anyone with eyes. The long-term ecological transformations of the early medieval period are difficult to assess , but it is virtually impossible to generalize about the long-term environmental changes that any particular campaign brought about in any ecological zone, since the long term was a matter of peacetime recovery processes.

Even more problematical is distinguishing the relative importance of collective violence from peacetime trends such as clearing land for agriculture. And both should be seen in relation to rising and falling demographic patterns. Regarding the overall environmental impacts of medieval warfare, it seems reasonable to suggest that warfare often caused disease epidemics that in turn led to population declines, leaving once-tilled farms deserted in the postwar stillness, reverting gradually to secondary woodlands.[23]

One of the major paradoxes regarding the environmental impacts of war appeared in the course of the sixteenth century, during an early stage of the transition to industrial warfare, when the Ottoman Empire first introduced cannon and muskets into its arsenal. The historian of the Ottoman army argues that prior to this time, with far less destructive weapons, campaigns often lasted for an entire season or even dragged on intermittently for years. Typically they involved "sustained raiding, gradual encirclement, harassment of enemy supply lines, embargo, [and] blockade"; in other words, they were wars of attrition. In contrast, in the new artillery age, campaigns were concentrated on major targets and sieges were generally brief, taking only a couple of weeks before the outcome became clear. Hence "warfare of the medieval pattern inflicted greater and more permanent damage" to civilian and economic life.[24] By inference, it seems that ecological stress, at least in the immediate regions of military movements, may also have declined in the sixteenth century.

European societies were by no means the only ones whose mass conflicts produced environmental change in the long centuries before modern times, though statements about the ecological impacts of warfare in non-European civilizations are even more tentative, since historians of other civilizations have hardly begun to address the issue. Yet some suggestions are warranted, as a brief survey of the varied landscapes and climates of Asia indicates. China stands out, with its great river basins draining wide mountain systems, its dense lowland populations, and its long north-south distances. Cycles of stability followed by civil war recurred there for twenty-five centuries, as imperial dynasties struggled to establish and maintain control over regional warlords. Within China's heartland the complex irrigation systems of the Yangtze and Yellow rivers were repeated targets of armies disrupting their enemies' food supplies.[25] Refugees from floodwaters, like refugees from war throughout history, caused additional environmental disruptions as they traveled and camped.[26] And on China's northwest frontier, facing perennial threats from nomadic warriors of the central Asian grasslands, emperors built the Great Wall and other fortifications. They also protected forest zones, to guard against invading cavalry.[27]

South of the great Himalayan mountain barrier, monsoon India presented a very different climatic cycle. In most of the Indian subcontinent the three to four months of heavy summer monsoon rains alternate annually with a long dry season. Over the millennia ecological communities evolved that featured drought-resistant plant and tree species which could survive long droughts, even multi-year failures of the rains. Just as in other parts of monsoon Asia and Africa, human ecologies were also adapted to these natural realities, including the fact that warfare was largely restricted to the dry season.

The Indian subcontinent has been the setting for Asia's longest history of continuous urban civilizations, stretching as long ago as the Indus Valley culture and its decline some fifty-five hundred to four thousand years ago. Recent archeological work has largely discredited the former view that Aryan "invasions" destroyed the twin cities, Mohenjo Daro and Harappa, and their surrounding villages. Hence, the subject of warfare probably has little bearing on that early urban period in the flatlands of northwest India.

Much later, beginning with the Maurya Empire nearly twenty-five hundred years ago, Indian kingdoms, especially in the Ganges basin, developed the capacity to mount extended wars for control of river basins and forested hilly hinterlands, employing weapons essentially similar to those of the Chinese in their destructive power. The increasing scale of military forces gradually became a key element in north Indian warfare. On long campaigns, huge royal armies led by elephant corps slowly devoured the food and fodder resources of the land. In the upper Ganges basin, from 997 CE onward, Muslim conquest states from farther northwest—the Delhi Sultanate and then the greatest of them all, the Mughal empire—mounted sustained campaigns that had widespread environmental impacts. Cavalry swept the countryside, depopulating villages, and the royal elephant corps required massive amounts of fodder. The Mughal imperial army at its apogee, in its late seventeenth century campaigns in central India, was a mobile city of nearly one million fighters, camp followers, and suppliers, who stripped wide areas of the land as they moved.[28] Rural society and its biological base could take years to recover from the disruption. But that process has not been studied in detail; it seems likely that the locally complex and varied impacts of these dislocations on farm and forest were usually short lived. Further local studies might clarify the long-term effects of this ebb and resurgence of the military presence in the countryside.

Throughout the pre-modern world, many conflicts took the form of frontier wars, fought between two non-state societies, two states, or as wars of conquest pursued by an ambitious power on its periphery. Often protracted and intermittent, these wars were similar in many ways to modern guerrilla warfare and counter-insurgency, though they did not produce the devastation that is caused by today's counter-insurgency weapons. They were characterized by seasonal skirmishes and raids, fortified outposts, capture of loot including movable natural resources, and probably most significant, the dislocation of rural populations. Many were fought in mountainous or hilly areas, on forested slopes with easily eroded soils. In one of many instances, in the central Himalayas in the eighteenth century, the armies of the rising Gurkha state based in the Kathmandu valley of Nepal conquered peripheral hill areas of western Nepal and Kumaon. The conquerors destroyed crop terraces and irrigation systems, and cut hardwood timber as booty. In the monsoon climate, this resulted in soil erosion, permanently reducing the agricultural productivity of the land and density of forest cover, even after the British colonial army displaced the Gurkha legions and brought peace after 1815.[29]

In settings where depopulation occurred and human pressures receded, food crops often gave way to increased populations of domestic livestock including cattle, sheep, and goats, for less labor was needed to maintain livestock than to till soil. In the case of Scotland in the mid-eighteenth century, the English army cleared the highlands of its ancient clans in order to suppress political resistance, bring "Christian civilization" to the northern hinterland, and replace the crofters' subsistence farming with more commercially valuable sheep farming.[30] Some of the Scottish countryside reverted to secondary forest vegetation; other lands evolved toward degraded pasture under the pressure of the flocks.

In one frontier war after another, farm and grazing land reverted to secondary woodland, where wildlife flourished and local biodiversity increased in semi-wild habitats. But these changes were usually temporary, for farmers sooner or later renewed agricultural landscapes with the return of peace and security.

Global Empires in the Modern Era

Except for the impacts of regional empires such as Rome, China, and Mughal India, the ecological impacts of wars were largely local until Europe began to extend its hegemony globally in the sixteenth century. Since then the world has changed fundamentally, as the era of the imperial nation-state and large-scale capital and industry accelerated the technological impacts associated with global trade and transport.[31]

The frontier wars of European conquest from around 1500 onward—one of the most momentous dimensions of history, both human and ecological—were the cutting edge. Over a half millennium, in a process that has been largely completed in our own generation, European empires, later joined by the United States, dismantled non-state societies in temperate forests, savanna lands, and tropical rainforests. The Western empires commanded weaponry that gradually, and certainly by the mid-nineteenth century, overwhelmed their pre-modern human prey. Their arms, and their military-bureaucratic capacity to sustain warfare over long periods, undoubtedly had many long-range environmental consequences as well. The most important may well have been the decimation of indigenous populations in the Americas and Oceania, as well as the displacement of defeated peoples in Africa and parts of Asia, rather than the immediate impacts of military campaigns. Analysis of the ecological impacts of Europe's frontier wars has hardly begun, and may be difficult to distinguish from other warfare during the same centuries. Indeed, all of the eighteenth-century cases mentioned above, including Nepal and the Chippewa, as well as the papers in this volume by Gordon and Levine, probably all reflect one degree or another of European contact.[32]

The rise of bureaucratic administration meant increasingly efficient taxation power, the capacity to channel social and economic resources toward systematic violence against enemies. Funding for military research and development inexorably increased in the wars between European states, in accelerating arms races, as the wars between them ultimately engulfed every continent.[33] Early ecological damage outside Europe reflected the navies' needs for construction timber and naval stores. By the 1700s European navies began cutting the hardwood and white pine stands of northeastern North America, the coastal hardwoods of Brazil, and later the teak forests of monsoon Asia, to find substitutes for the depleted English oak and Scandinavian conifers.[34] These environmental costs of naval warfare were confined to the land; the seas themselves suffered little pollution or biological reduction from naval wars until the great wars of the twentieth century.

The most fundamental ecological impacts of Europe's global conquests occurred in the Americas, where Europeans brought with them epidemic diseases that were a holocaust for native Americans. Up to 90 percent of the indigenous American population had died by the late sixteenth century.[35] This depopulation led to widespread abandonment of cultivated lands and reversion to secondary forest, often for long periods. In Latin America even in the 1500s the impacts of conquest registered on lowland coastal zones and riverine forests, the highlands of Mexico and the Andes, where sheep and goats came to rule degraded pasture lands, and the wide natural grasslands where cattle soon prevailed.[36]

In North American woodland ecosystems the impact of endemic frontier warfare was somewhat different. There Europeans were able to follow up their conquests by settling on the land and clearing temperate forests far more readily than they could anchor themselves in tropical rainforest zones.[37] In contrast to Latin America, where populations did not recover to their pre-1492 levels until around 1800, the native populations of North America were fully replaced by North European immigrants in much shorter order.

Wars of the Industrial Era

The great escalation of modern warfare and its impacts began in Europe in the 1790s, when revolutionary France and Napoleon expanded both the intensity of warfare and its continent-wide reach.[38] The Napoleonic wars also disrupted intercontinental transport of food supplies, in one case resulting in a major long-term change in cropping patterns. The British naval blockade after 1805 cut off supplies of cane sugar from the Caribbean to French ports. In response, new techniques of extracting sugar from beets led to an explosion of sugar-beet farming in the heavy soils and cool climate of northern Europe. Meanwhile the former slaves of Haiti turned their work from half-deserted cane plantations in the fertile lowlands to subsistence cropping in the erosive hill woodlands, and Haiti became one of the most degraded landscapes in the Americas. In this way Europe's revolutionary wars had unintended ecological consequences across the ocean.[39]

From the mid-nineteenth century onward Western European and American industry produced a leap upward in destructive capacity, through revolutionary innovations in mass production. By the late1800s highly accurate breech-loading Enfield, Mauser, and Springfield rifles and Maxim machine guns transformed the battlefield, and more powerful explosives began to ravage both urban and rural targets. Moreover, railroads and steamships gave industrialized nations far greater mobility and international reach. In addition to their civilian uses, they moved troops and materiel rapidly, inexpensively, and far, making possible the conquest of the rest of the world.[40] At century's end in South Africa's Boer War, both sides—the British colonial army and the Boers—were armed with the new weapons. The result was savagery on both sides, in campaigns that lasted far longer than anyone had anticipated at first. Finally, as one historian reflects, "to shatter Boer resistance once and for all, Kitchener began systematically to destroy Boer farms. ... Between 1900 and 1902 the British burned thousands of Boer farms and herded their wretched inhabitants into 'concentration camps'." Sixty percent of the entire Boer population, some 120,000 Afrikaners, were moved into those camps, while their farms withered.[41] A careful analysis of the environmental aftermath on those wide lands would be in order.

The U. S. Civil War had already given a grim demonstration of the ecological dangers of the new industrial warfare. When it began in 1861, no one expected the war to grind on for over four years, but its glacial momentum toward exhaustion of the South produced widespread destruction of croplands and fodder resources by Northern armies, extending to deliberate scorched-earth campaigns in its last two years.[42] Seeing that neither army could destroy the other in major battles, General Grant instructed General Sheridan in 1864 to destroy all crops, livestock, and farm buildings in the Shenandoah Valley. Not long after, General Sherman's army torched the earth across Georgia in the war's final campaign of ecological terror. As Grant's biographer wrote, he "was engaged in a people's war, and [...] the people as well as the armies of the South must be conquered, before the war could end. Slaves, supplies, crops, stock, as well as arms and ammunition— everything that was necessary in order to carry on the war, was a weapon in the hands of the enemy; and of every weapon the enemy must be deprived."[43] These strategies were not new in the history of warfare, but their scale and intensity were unprecedented. Ultimately the manpower, economic wealth, and industrial power of the North prevailed. Northern armies could be supplied and supported more consistently by the northern railroad network connecting military movements back to factories and farms. Even so, environmental war against the southern landscape provided the decisive blow. The experience trained northern soldiers to attack and destroy the food supplies of the indigenous tribes in the American West, including their herds of bison, as an "acceptable" strategy in the final conquest of that great frontier.

This war also produced an early example of environmental impacts half a world away from the scenes of battle. The Northern navy's blockade of southern ports and rivers interdicted the South's raw cotton exports to Europe, forcing the English cloth mills to look elsewhere for their supplies as long as the war lasted. On the rich black soils of the Malwa plateau in central India, small farmers responded to a spike in cotton prices in Bombay in early 1862, switching from subsistence food crops to cotton for export to England, tilling even some previously forested land until the war ended in 1865. Though many fields were returned to food crops when prices fell again, Malwa cotton production acreage remained higher than before the North American war, and some forest acreage remained permanently cleared.[44]

In Europe in the same decade, Germany harnessed the industrial revolution to accelerated military mobilization. Rapid victories over the Austro-Hungarian Empire and then France resulted from skillful movement of the German armies over the new railway networks, with communications provided by the new telegraph, while more powerful artillery damaged woodlands and cities.[45] Great Britain, faced with the new challenge from Germany, strove to maintain its control of the seas by producing rapid innovations in naval technology, which required that military planners and industrialists work closely together.[46]

In terms of ecological violence, these mid-nineteenth-century wars and the concomitant arms race were merely overtures to the two world wars that followed, when the environmental impacts of warfare became truly global.

World War I

This was the Great War, in which the military-industrial complex finally matured. The technological scale of warfare had matured so rapidly since 1870 that all combatant economies had to forge close ties between military commanders and industrial designers and managers.[47] The results were daunting. As the first campaigns bogged down in stalemate along hundreds of miles of trenches in Flanders and northern France, munitions were consumed to the furthest extent that each country's factories could produce them. In the course of three years and more, millions of bomb and shell craters left puddles, ponds, and mud where crop fields and woodlands had been before. On both sides of the war, improved long-distance food transport enabled mass armies to be sustained year-round, and battles to be fought almost endlessly. And on a scale greater than ever before, armies deprived both enemy units and civilians of food, fiber, and fodder, by ravaging land and destroying stored crops. In early 1917, as the German armies withdrew from the Somme battlefields, they systematically destroyed nearly every building, fence, well, bridge, and tree over an area sixty-five by twenty miles, to deprive the advancing enemy of sustenance and cover.[48]

The war also saw the first large-scale use of chemical warfare. Germany's chemical industry, which had recently emerged as the world's leader, forged close cooperation with her military, enabling the German army to use massive amounts of mustard gas on Allied troops. By the war's end chemical war produced 1.3 million casualties, including ninety thousand deaths; mustard gas and other chemical agents temporarily poisoned lands on and near the battlefields. It is very difficult to assess the immediate environmental impact because no one tried to record or measure it. Its carryover effect was, however, large. Chemical warfare increased the size of chemical industries, demonstrated the value of scientific research to chemists and governments, and helped inspire postwar pesticides such as chloropicrin, a fumigant. And military aircraft became the backbone of postwar crop dusting, increasing the scale on which pest control was economical.[49]

Moreover, forests came under unprecedented pressures. Seemingly endless bombardments in battle zones shattered forests that had been carefully managed for centuries. Not only that—and this was new in history —for hundreds of miles behind the lines emergency fellings of timber were carried out in France and elsewhere around Europe. Only the great forest zone of Russia escaped heavy exploitation, since imperial Russia's transport system was still rudimentary. But the British, Canadians, and Americans organized large timber imports into Europe from both North America and South Asia's monsoon forests, intensifying the intercontinental mobilization of natural resources for warfare. But this war saw only the beginnings of tree cutting from tropical rainforests, since logging and transport facilities were still in their infancy, even in the colonial forests of British and French West Africa. Perhaps equally important for the longer run, government forestry agencies in many countries took greater control over forest resources during the war. The immediate postwar recovery period saw reforestation programs in both Europe and North America, in which single-species tree plantations replaced the greater variety of species in the former natural forests.

World War II

Further industrialization between the two world wars enabled militarized states from 1939 to 1945 to mobilize far greater resources from around the world than a quarter century before, and impose new levels of destruction. When Hitler launched the war in late 1939, he did not envision a war in which seventy million people would die, and his own country ultimately suffered some of the most total devastation, particularly at the hands of the Allied air forces in their sustained counterattack. By the summer of 1945, British and American bombers had destroyed the Moehne and Eder dams in the Ruhr valley, destroying or crippling over one hundred twenty-five factories and forty-six bridges, and inundating three thousand hectares of cropland. And using incendiary bombs produced by the rapidly maturing chemical industry, the same planes almost totally leveled one hundred thirty German cities, killing some six hundred thousand civilians. The postwar reconstruction, physical as well as social, would be daunting.

In combat zones the forests of Europe were once again badly damaged by fighting. Behind the lines of combat, timber was cut at the most urgent rates that the limited available workforce could achieve, and great forests of Norway and Poland were looted of their timber wealth. This time, even more than in the previous war, the battle zones of Europe, north Africa, and the Middle East could call upon timber resources from other continents. Harvesting machinery and transport networks from forest roads to harbor facilities to oceanic ships were much more highly developed than in the previous war. (Strikingly, the vast forest resources of Asian Russia were still largely inaccessible.) British Columbia was now a leading source of military timber for Great Britain, while Washington and Oregon provided massive amounts of spruce for the Allied Air Forces. Innovations in airplane design, combined with recently acquired knowledge of the tropical forests of the Americas, even led to harvesting balsa, one of the lightest of tropical woods, for experimental aircraft. The postwar impact of these timber harvests was largely the result of the roads that penetrated previously inaccessible forests, encouraging new frontier settlements after the fighting stopped. Once again wartime and subsequent peacetime together produced long-term changes on the land; neither can be understood without the other.[50]

In another dimension, World War II marked a watershed in the history of warfare because, for the first time, more soldiers died in battle than of disease. The control of the environment was key to this transition. One of the more dramatic symbols of this increased scale of control was a new insecticide called DDT, which killed the mosquitoes that transmitted malaria and the lice that transmitted typhus. The surge in manufacturing of DDT, along with its miraculous reputation, created a massive postwar market. Some of the traits that made DDT so useful in warfare also contributed to problems in the postwar environment: its persistence was a wonderful trait when used on a small scale, but when used on a wide scale it built up in the systems of birds and endangered the survival of several species.[51]

The war in the Pacific had impacts on both island systems and the aquatic environment that had no previous parallel in that ocean's web of life. Small islands have limited varieties of plant and animal species, and many have thin or fragile soils; they are exceptionally vulnerable to the impacts of human conflict. On both steep volcanic islands and coral atolls throughout the Pacific, the fighting produced fundamental ecological degradation of forests, watersheds, coastal swamplands, and coral reefs.

Diseases, of both humans and livestock, had spread into the Pacific with traumatic impacts ever since the 1770s, but the Pacific War accelerated the process in some instances. Allied disease-control teams succeeded in containing the spread of malaria from the islands where it was already widespread, but the cattle tick reached New Caledonia, infecting livestock and damaging agricultural systems there. In this war, as in others, the spread of epidemic diseases could accelerate longer trends in human and animal populations. Malaria itself caused nearly ten times as many casualties as battles for the American forces until 1943. But DDT almost totally controlled the disease among the troops before the war's end. No one at the time foresaw the massive environmental damage which DDT would produce in the following peacetime.[52]

For the marine resources of the Pacific, the war had paradoxical effects. Commercial fisheries and whaling fleets were largely destroyed, docked, or transformed into military uses until 1945, leaving fish stocks and marine mammal populations to recover somewhat, though submarine warfare killed some whales, and any increase in their numbers would prove to be very temporary.[53] Overall, this war initiated major environmental damage to the planet's oceans.

In the home islands of Japan, the war had tragic ecological as well as human impacts. The Japanese war machine had attempted to command the mineral and forest resources of Southeast Asia, to compensate for its limited resource base at home, but that effort was brief and limited by the Allied counterattacks. But the domestic damage in Japan was appalling. For Japan's forest resources, the wartime loss of import sources (especially the northwest coast of North America) meant intensive cutting of domestic forests, even ancient stands which had been preserved for centuries, for charcoal, firewood, and construction. In many locations the direct result was loss of soil and damage to water regimes. On Japan's farms food production expanded urgently, especially on marginal lands, and even songbirds were virtually wiped out for emergency food.[54]

American incendiary bombing, following the attacks on German cities, almost totally destroyed Japan's urban areas, which had been built largely of wood. And the ultimate environmental disaster, the impact of nuclear bombs, was also Japan's fate, when Hiroshima and Nagasaki were leveled on August 6 and 9, 1945. The two cities were rapidly rebuilt after the war, and the local flora made a surprisingly rapid recovery from radioactive pollution, yet the human costs of the two bombs are still being counted.

By August 1945 the United States was triumphant, having suffered relatively little long-term damage to its domestic resources and ecosystems or to its additional source areas in Latin America. Its military industry had grown exponentially, and military-industrial coordination had reached high levels. Hence that war sowed the seeds of later disasters, which began to be evident as the Cold War deepened after 1948.

The Late Twentieth Century

The global arms race after 1945 produced incalculable accelerations of every tool of destruction. One of the smallest weapons, though multiplied almost countless times, has been the land mine. Some one hundred million unexploded anti-personnel mines remain around the planet now, littering rural Vietnam, Afghanistan, and many other war-torn countries, and grievously retarding the restoration of postwar farms, pastures, forests, and water regimes. These and a Pandora's box of other weapons have spread through many unstable regions of the post-colonial world—Africa and elsewhere. Grim contributions to wars both civil and trans-boundary, they have also extracted a widespread ecological toll on forests, savannas, and farmlands.[55]

Equally widespread by the time the Cold War ended in 1990, long-term pollution effects of military industry left many locations severely poisoned. Weapons production sites and testing grounds in the United States required massively expensive cleanups of a broad spectrum of toxic wastes. Even more appalling, large areas of Soviet and Eastern European land and air had become virtual wastelands, and even the Arctic Ocean north of Russia was severely polluted.

Chemical warfare reached a new level of destruction in the Second Vietnam War (1961-1975), as the U.S. Air Force applied Agent Orange and other defoliants to the forests of Indochina. In addition to fourteen million tons of bombs and shells, American planes sprayed forty-four million liters of Agent Orange and twenty-eight million liters of other defoliants over Vietnam. The result was serious damage to 1.7 million hectares of upland forest and mangrove marshes, widespread soil poisoning or loss of soil, and destruction of wildlife and fish habitat.[56]

Most potent of all in the post-1945 years, nuclear technology designed for both bombs and power plants became the most ominous environmental threat in history, though its greatest impact resulted from the peacetime armament race rather than from actual war. Until international nuclear-testing freeze conventions came into effect, nuclear-testing sites, such as Soviet sites in Central Asia and Britain's testing grounds in central Australia, became uninhabitable for almost all forms of life. And in the southern Pacific Ocean, islands and their coastal reefs, their civilian populations entirely removed by force, became unfit for life as a result of American and French nuclear weapons testing.[57] Beyond that, in the nuclear industrial complex, many weapons production and storage sites became highly radioactive. In the United States, nuclear facilities in Washington state, Colorado, and elsewhere became radioactive sewers. Soviet nuclear weapons sites were even more highly radioactive.[58]

Finally, twentieth-century warfare has made a major contribution to warming of the global atmosphere. Military establishments consume great amounts of fossil fuels, contributing directly to global warming. The Persian Gulf War of 1991 was the most notorious case of atmospheric pollution in wartime, as the plumes of burning oil wells darkened skies for months far downwind. It now seems that the fires caused less regional and global air pollution than was feared in their immediate aftermath, though they dropped heavy pollution on nearby desert, farmland, and the Gulf's waters.[59]

Recent wars, from Vietnam onward, have received far more detailed analysis of their environmental costs than any previous mass conflicts. Awareness of this fateful dimension of warfare has been slowly, belatedly rising, thus raising the hope that our ability to plan and carry out, or criticize and resist, future wars can become more skillful and more aware of the fateful consequences we face.[60]

War and Nature Conservation: Deliberate and Accidental

As warfare has concentrated power in the hands of the military and the state, it has also enhanced the power of governments to regulate the use of nature. In the twentieth century, warfare has resulted in rapid strengthening of regimes for resource management that have shaped postwar years. Under the United Nations, the Forestry Division of the Food and Agriculture Organization created a global network of professional foresters in the late 1940s. Within member countries, in Europe, North America, and colonial countries, governments' forestry services extended their authority to manage forest reserves, limiting private owners' ability to sell or cut timber for short-term financial gain. But close relations between forest departments and timber corporations have often minimized this distinction: in the United States and Canada, as well as countries newly independent after 1945 such as India, Malaysia, Indonesia, and the Philippines, the enhanced power of governments over timber resources often led to more efficient clear-cutting of forests. Subsequent "reforestation" programs should more clearly be called tree-plantation programs, for they are nearly always intended as commercially valuable tree farms of one or at most a few species.

Wildlife conservation in many countries and as an international movement was almost entirely derailed during both world wars, so the wildlife movement received new organizational momentum after both. In World War I the trauma and disillusionment that people experienced at the devastation of entire landscapes, including their wildlife, led to links between the postwar peace movement and the international wildlife-conservation movement, plus the first major efforts to survey and protect endangered species.[61] World War II brought about decisive new legislation for wildlife protection in many countries, as well as the founding of the International Union for the Preservation of Nature.[62]

This renewed effort expressed many conservationists' agonized awareness of the wanton impact of modern war on wildlife and their natural habitats. Wild species had suffered grievously in and near war zones, especially in World War II, when, for example, warplanes used wildlife reserves such as flamingo marshes in the Caribbean for target practice or dumping unused bombs.

But war also often gives a reprieve to wildlife populations by temporarily reducing the human presence. In the war in Nicaragua in the late 1980s, Contra troops forced rural subsistence hunters to leave Caribbean lowland forests for several years. By 1990 wildlife populations in the rainforest were flourishing, but this was only a temporary reprieve from human pressures, as usually happens whenever populations have been forced off land by war.[63]

Finally, officially delineated demilitarized zones, including the buffer zone that has divided Korea for half a century, have become de facto wildlife reserves. Equally ironic, military reservations such as the severely degraded Rocky Mountain Arsenal Wildlife Refuge in the United States often act as de facto wildlife reserves, in peacetime as well as war, even being managed in part for their wildlife values.

Conclusions

It is often difficult to distinguish between environmental change resulting from the overall presence of humans on the earth and the more intensive impacts of warfare. From the perspective of human institutions, warfare merges into war-related peacetime planning, and that in turn leads to the militarization of peacetime societies in modern times. Each has its distinctive structures. A full assessment of the ecological consequences of warfare and military operations should encompass them all. Furthermore, this spectrum is inseparable from the historical acceleration of technology, both civilian and military; this has probably been the most momentous cause of the modern acceleration of war's impacts on nature. But weapons operate through human hands and minds, and their primary victims are humans. Hence, the history of population changes caused or accelerated by war, and the history of disease (both human and livestock) triggered by war, must be taken into account as links between human conflict and the natural world.

Human warfare has not always been detrimental to the wider webs of nonhuman life. In buffer zones and depopulated areas, species diversity has often flourished, at least temporarily. And institutionally, the great wars of the twentieth century have led to a peacetime follow-up of intensified state-led conservation and management of strategically important natural resources, including forests. And non-state organizations have intensified the conservation of wildlife and even entire ecosystems, as individuals have recognized war's systemic devastation.

From the perspective of natural systems, every war's impact on nature has been specific to its unique ecological setting, for no two natural communities respond identically to human activity. Moreover, it is often difficult to distinguish short-term damage from long-term change or degradation of landscapes and natural resources, or even to articulate the criteria for that distinction. Future studies of the environmental history of warfare must merge the tools of historians with those of ecologists more fully.

In the broad picture, however, we can already conclude that warfare has accelerated processes of ecological degradation that humans were already causing; this has been overwhelmingly true in the twentieth century. Despite the ironies of times when warfare has reduced human impact on natural systems or stimulated people to care more systematically for nature, the heart of this inquiry shows that humans' collective violence toward each other has had a profound parallel with humans' violent disruptions of the natural world. Neither can be fully comprehended without the other.

Notes

1 I am particularly grateful to him, as well as to Jonathan Marwil and two diligent readers for the Press, for their detailed comments on earlier drafts of this paper, though I have been able to integrate their suggestions only in part.
2 For variant treatments of the origins of warfare, see Lawrence H. Keeley, *War before Civilization* (Oxford: Oxford University Press, 1996); Raymond C. Kelly, *Warless Societies and the Origin of War* (Ann Arbor: University of Michigan Press, 2000); and Keith F. Otterbein, *The Evolution of War: A Cross-Cultural Study* (New Haven, CT: HRAF Press, 1970). For the early history of species extinctions see Paul S. Martin and Richard G. Klein, eds., *Quaternary Extinctions: A Prehistoric Revolution* (Tucson: University of Arizona Press, 1984).
3 Keeley, *War before Civilization*, 108.
4 Jeffrey A. McNeely, "Biodiversity, War, and Tropical Forests," *Journal of Sustainable Forestry* 16: 3-4 (2003), 2.
5 For South Pacific societies, see for example, Andrew P. Vayda, *War in Ecological Perspective: Persistence, Change, and Adaptive Processes in Three Oceanian Studies* (New York: Plenum Press, 1976), and B. M. Knauft, "Melanesian Warfare: A Theoretical History, *Oceania* 60 (1990), 250-311. For Amazonia, see for example, R. B. Ferguson, "Game Wars? Ecology and Conflict in Amazonia," *Journal of Anthropological Research* 45 (1989), 179-206. For western North America, see for example, Douglas B. Bamforth, "Indigenous Peoples, Indigenous Violence: Pre-Contact Warfare on the North American Great Plains," *Man* 29 (1994), 95-115.
6 Harold Hickerson, *The Chippewa and Their Neighbors: A Study in Ethnohistory* (New York: Holt, Rinehart and Winston, 1970), 106-119.
7 Tim Flannery, *The Future Eaters: An Ecological History of the Australian Lands and People* (New York: George Braziller, 1994); Stephen J. Pyne, *World Fire: The Culture of Fire on Earth* (New York: Henry Holt, 1995).
8 For the general process, see Thorkild Jacobsen and Robert M. Adams, "Salt and Silt in Ancient Mesopotamian Agriculture," *Science* 128 (November 21, 1958), 1251-58.
9 Peter H. Gleick, "Water, War and Peace in the Middle East," *Environment* 36:3 (1994), 10-11, summarizes the more detailed account in H. Hatami and P. H. Gleick, *Chronology of Conflict over Water in the Legends, Myths, and History of the Ancient Middle East* (Oakland, CA: Pacific Institute for Studies in Development, Environment, and Security, June 1993).
10 Ira Lapidus, *A History of Islamic Societies* (Cambridge, U.K.: Cambridge University Press, 1988), 278-82. For further corroborating detail see I. P. Petrushevsky, "The Socio-Economic Condition of Iran under the Il-Khans," in J. A. Boyle, ed., *The Cambridge History of Iran, vol. 5: The Saljuq and Mongol Periods* (Cambridge, U.K.: Cambridge University Press, 1968), 484-95; Peter Christensen, *The Decline of Iranshahr: Irrigation and Environments in the History of the Middle East, 500 B.C. to A.D. 1500* (Copenhagen: Museum Tusculanum Press, 1993).

11 Bernard Lewis, *The Middle East: A Brief History of the Last 2,000 Years* (New York: Simon and Schuster, 1995), 99.

12 For the threat to water-management systems in more recent Middle Eastern wars, see Peter Gleick, "Water and Conflict: Fresh Water Resources and International Security," *International Security* 18:1 (1993), 79-112; Gleick, "Water, War, and Peace in the Middle East," 6-42.

13 William H. McNeill, *The Pursuit of Power: Technology, Armed Force, and Society since A.D. 1000* (Chicago: University of Chicago Press, 1982), chap. 1: "Arms and Society in Antiquity."

14 For an overview, see Christon I. Archer, John R. Ferris, Holger H. Herwig, and Timothy H. E. Travers, *World History of Warfare* (Lincoln: University of Nebraska Press, 2002), chap. 1: "Warfare of the Ancient Empires."

15 J. Donald Hughes, *Pan's Travail: Environmental Problems of the Ancient Greeks and Romans* (Baltimore, MD: Johns Hopkins University Press, 1994); J. V. Thirgood, *Man and the Mediterranean Forest: A History of Resource Depletion* (London: Academic Press, 1981). For this and later developments in the technologies of warfare, see Martin van Creveld, *Technology and War from 2000 B.C. to the Present* (New York and London: Free Press, 1989).

16 Russell Meiggs, *Trees and Timber in the Ancient Mediterranean World* (Oxford: Clarendon Press, 1982).

17 Archer et. al., *World History of Warfare,* chap. 2: "War and Society in the Classical West."

18 Adrian K. Goldsworthy, *Roman Warfare* (London: Cassell, 2000).

19 Steven K. Drummond and Lynn H. Nelson, *The Western Frontiers of Imperial Rome* (Armonk: M. E. Sharpe, 1994). For French sources on this period, see Albert Merglen, "La forêt germanique contre les armées romaines," and Alain Deyber, "Les Celtes et la forêt pendant la Guerre des Gaules," in Andrée Corvol and Jean-Paul Amat, *Forêt et Guerre* (Paris: Harmattan, 1994), 19-28, 29-40.

20 Clarence Darby, "The Medieval Clearances," in William L. Thomas, ed., *Man's Role in Changing the Face of the Earth* (Chicago: University of Chicago Press, 1956); Norman J. G. Pounds, *An Historical Geography of Europe, 450 B.C. – A. D. 1330* (Cambridge, U.K.: Cambridge University Press, 1973), chap. 3.

21 Maurice Keen, *Medieval Warfare: A History* (Oxford: Oxford University Press, 1999); Roger Beaumont, *War, Chaos and History* (Westport, CT: Praeger, 1994), chap. 2: "Chaos upon Chaos: The Environmental Impact of War."

22 John R. McNeill, *Mountains of the Mediterranean World: An Environmental History* (Cambridge, U.K.: Cambridge University Press, 1992).

23 See William H. McNeill, *Plagues and Peoples* (Garden City, NY: Anchor Books, 1976); Kenneth Kiple, ed., *The Cambridge History of Human Disease* (Cambridge, U.K.: Cambridge University Press, 1993).

24 Rhoads Murphey, *Ottoman Warfare, 1500-1700* (New Brunswick, NJ: Rutgers University Press, 1999), 171-73.

25 Mark Elvin, "Three Thousand Years of Unsustainable Growth: China's Environment from Archaic Times to the Present," *East Asian History* 6 (1993), 30.

26 John R. McNeill, "China's Environmental History in World Perspective," in Mark Elvin and Liu Ts'ui-jung, eds., *Sediments of Time: Environment and Society in Chinese History* (Cambridge, U.K.: Cambridge University Press, 1998), 36-38, 46-47.

27 Nicholas K. Menzies, *Forest and Land Management in Imperial China* (London: St. Martin's Press, 1994), 22, 59-61. Peter Perdue's forthcoming work, tentatively entitled, *China Marches West* (Cambridge, MA: Harvard University Press), will explore in greater detail the ecological aspects of imperial China's strategic operations on the northwest frontier, including the use of grassland fire against her enemies.

28 For the first north Indian Hindu empire, see Thomas R. Trautmann, "Elephants and the Mauryas," in S. N. Mukherjee, ed., *India: History and Thought. Essays in Honour of A. L. Basham* (Calcutta: Subarnarekha), 254-81. For a much later period see Simon Digby, *Warhorse and Elephant in the Delhi Sultanate* (Oxford: Orient Monographs, 1971) and Stewart Gordon, "War, the Military, and the Environment: Central India, 1560-1820," in this volume.

29 Richard P. Tucker, "The British Empire and India's Forest Resources: The Timberlands of Assam and Kumaon, 1914-1950," in J. F. Richards and Richard P. Tucker, eds., *World Deforestation in the Twentieth Century* (Durham, NC: Duke University Press, 1987), 91-111.

30 See, for example, the classic social history, John Prebble, *The Highland Clearances* (London: Secker and Warburg, 1963).

31 Archer, et. al., *World History of Warfare,* chap. 11: "The West Conquers the World."

32 There is a lively debate among historical anthropologists over the changes in indigenous societies in what some call the "tribal zone" in response to European penetration. The papers in R. Brian Ferguson and Neil L. Whitehead, eds., *War in the Tribal Zone: Expanding States and Indigenous Warfare* (Santa Fe, NM: School of American Research Press, 1992), survey that discussion broadly. Enhanced understanding of the ecological consequences of the West's wars of conquest must take this debate carefully into account.

33 Geoffrey Parker, *The Military Revolution: Military Innovation and the Rise of the West, 1500-1800* (Cambridge, U.K.: Cambridge University Press, 1988). For the critically important role of the military in the rise of the nation-state's capacity to command resources, and the closely associated role of civilian contractors and financiers in the commercialization of warfare, see W. H. McNeill, *Pursuit of Power,* chaps. 3-5. For further background, see J. R. Hale, *War and Society in Renaissance Europe, 1450-1620* (London: Fontana, 1985).

34 Robert G. Albion, *Forests and Sea Power: The Timber Problem of the Royal Navy, 1652-1862* (Cambridge, MA: Harvard University Press, 1926); Paul Walden Bamford, *Forests and French Sea Power, 1660-1789* (Toronto: University of Toronto Press, 1956); Shawn William Miller, *Fruitless Trees: Portuguese Conservation and Brazil's Colonial Timber* (Stanford: Stanford University Press, 2000); Graeme Wynn, *Timber Colony: A Historical Geography of Early Nineteenth Century New Brunswick* (Toronto: University of Toronto Press, 1981).

35 The broad patterns are traced in Alfred W. Crosby, *The Columbian Exchange: Biological and Cultural Consequences of 1492* (Westport, CT: Greenwood Press, 1972), and his *Ecological Imperialism: The Biological Expansion of Europe, 900-1900* (Cambridge, U.K.: Cambridge University Press, 1986). On the demographic collapse in sixteenth-century America, see Kenneth F. Kiple, ed., *The Cambridge World History of Human Disease* (Cambridge, U.K.: Cambridge University Press, 1993), 305-33, and several authors' chapters in Kenneth F. Kiple and Stephen V. Beck, eds., *Biological Consequences of the European Expansion, 1450-1800* (Aldershot, UK: Ashgate Publishing, 1997).

36 There are indicative references to these trends in many works, though no one has yet studied the subject systematically. See Carl Sauer, *The Early Spanish Main* (Berkeley: University of California Press, 1966); Elinor Melville, *A Plague of Sheep* (Cambridge, U.K.: Cambridge University Press, 1994); Murdo J. MacLeod, *Spanish Central America: A Socioeconomic History, 1520-1720* (Berkeley: University of California Press, 1973); Warren Dean, *With Broadax and Firebrand: The Destruction of the Brazilian Atlantic Forest* (Berkeley: University of California Press, 1995).
37 Michael Williams, *Americans and Their Forests* (Cambridge, U.K.: Cambridge University Press, 1989).
38 For the transformations of industrial warfare initiated in those campaigns, see Martin van Creveld, *Supplying War: Logistics from Wallenstein to Patton* (Cambridge, U.K.: Cambridge University Press, 1977), chaps. 2-3.
39 For background, see Sidney Mintz, *Sweetness and Power: The Place of Sugar in Modern History* (New York: Viking, 1985); for a summary of the process and its environmental impact, see Richard P. Tucker, *Insatiable Appetite: The United States and the Ecological Degradation of the Tropical World* (Berkeley: University of California Press, 2000), 25-36.
40 Daniel R. Headrick, *The Tools of Empire: Technology and European Imperialism in the Nineteenth Century* (Oxford: Oxford University Press, 1981). See also Roger Levine, "African Warfare in All Its Ferocity," in this volume, and Thaddeus Sunseri, "Forests, Social Rebellion, and Social Control in the Rufiji Region, German East Africa," *Environmental History* (July 2003), 430-51.
41 Geoffrey Wawro, *Warfare and Society in Europe, 1792-1914* (London and New York: Routledge, 2000), 144.
42 See Mark Fiege, "Gettysburg and the Organic Nature of the American Civil War," in this volume; Gerald Linderman, *Embattled Courage: The Experience of Combat in the American Civil War* (New York: Free Press, 1987), chap. 10: "A Warfare of Terror"; Russell F. Weigley, *The American Way of War: A History of United States Military Strategy and Policy* (New York: Macmillan, 1973), 144-52.
43 Quoted in Weigley, *The American Way of War*, 150-51.
44 John F. Richards and Michelle McAlpin, "Cotton Cultivating and Land Clearing in the Bombay Deccan and Karnatak: 1818-1920," in Richard P. Tucker and J. F. Richards, eds., *Global Deforestation and the Nineteenth-Century World Economy* (Durham: Duke University Press, 1983), 68-104.
45 For the broad setting, see Wawro, *Warfare and Society in Europe*.
46 W. H. McNeill, *Pursuit of Power*, chap. 8.
47 Paul A. C. Koistinen, "The 'Industrial-Military Complex' in Historical Perspective: World War I," *Business History Review* 41:4 (Winter 1967), 379-403.
48 Beaumont, *War, Chaos and History*, 140.
49 I am grateful to Edmund Russell for this and later information on the impacts of chemical warfare. For more, see his book, *War and Nature: Fighting Humans and Insects with Chemicals from World War I to Silent Spring* (Cambridge, U.K.: Cambridge University Press, 2001).
50 See Richard P. Tucker, "The World Wars and the Globalization of Timber Cutting," in this volume.
51 Edmund Russell, "The Strange Career of DDT: Experts, Federal Capacity, and 'Environmentalism' in World War II," *Technology and Culture* 40 (1999), 770-96.
52 See Judith A. Bennett, "Pests and Disease in the Pacific War: Crossing the Line," in this volume; also Judith A. Bennett, "War, Emergency and the Environment: Fiji, 1939-1946," *Environment and History* 7 (2001), 255-87.

53 See Kurk Dorsey, "Compromising on Conservation: World War II and American Leadership in Whaling Diplomacy," in this volume. There was a parallel, and equally temporary, resurgence of the cod population in the north Atlantic during the war, when German submarines prevented the Allies' fishing fleets from operating. Mark Kurlansky, *Cod: A Biography of the Fish that Changed the World* (New York: Walker & Co., 1997).

54 See William Tsutsui, "Landscapes in the Dark Valley: Toward an Environmental History of Wartime Japan," in this volume.

55 The most systematic study so far is the recent symposium published as "War and Tropical Forests: Conservation in Areas of Armed Conflict," *Journal of Sustainable Forestry* 16: 3/4 (2003).

56 Asit K. Biswas, "Scientific Assessment of the Long-term Environmental Consequences of War," in Jay E. Austin and Carl E. Bruch, eds., *The Environmental Consequences of War: Legal, Economic, and Scientific Perspectives* (Cambridge, U.K.: Cambridge University Press, 2000), 307. See also the earlier works of Arthur H. Westing, including *Ecological Consequences of the Second Indochina War* (Stockholm: Almqvist and Wiksell International, 1976), and *Herbicides in War: The Long-term Ecological and Human Consequences* (London and Philadelphia:Taylor & Francis, 1984).

57 Stewart Firth, *Nuclear Playground* (Honolulu: University of Hawaii Press, 1987); Bengt and Marie-Therese Danielssohn, *Poisoned Reign: French Nuclear Colonialism in the Pacific* (Harmondsworth, UK: Penguin, 1986); and an updated study, Mark Merlin, "Environmental Impacts of Nuclear Testing around the Pacific," paper prepared for conference of American Society for Environmental History, Victoria, British Columbia, April 2004.

58 Murray Feshbach and Alfred Friendly, *Ecocide in the USSR* (New York: Basic Books, 1992); Ze'ev Wolfson [Boris Komarov], *The Geography of Survival: Ecology in the Post-Soviet Era* (Armonk: M. E. Sharpe, 1994.

59 Samira A. S. Omar et. al., "The Gulf War Impact on the Terrestrial Environment of Kuwait: An Overview," in Austin and Bruch, 316-37.

60 See various authors in Austin and Bruch; also Thomas F. Homer-Dixon, *Ecoviolence: Links among Environment, Population and Security* (Lanham, MD: Rowman and Littlefield, 1998); Thomas F. Homer-Dixon, *Environment, Scarcity and Violence* (Princeton: Princeton University Press, 1999). For a systematic critique of his project's working assumptions, see Nancy Lee Peluso and Michael Watts, eds., *Violent Environments* (Ithaca: Cornell University Press, 2001).

61 Martin Holdgate, *The Green Web: A Union for World Conservation* (London: Earthscan Publications, 1999), chaps. 1-2; Richard Tucker, *The Rise of Tropical Wildlife Conservation*, manuscript in preparation.

62 Holdgate, *The Green Web*, chap. 2. For the new round of centralized planning for natural resources management in Britain, see E. M. Nicholson, *The Environmental Revolution* (London: Hodder & Stoughton, 1970); John Sheail, "War and the Development of Nature Conservation in Britain," *Journal of Environmental Management* 44 (1995), 267-83.

63 Bernard Nietschmann, "Conservation by Conflict in Nicaragua," *Natural History* (November 1990), 42-48.

War, the Military, and the Environment: Central India, 1560-1820

Stewart Gordon

Introduction

Those casually acquainted with India often know Gandhi and the Buddha and extrapolate that India has had a dominant tradition of nonviolence. Nothing could be further from the truth. Many of the earliest Indian texts describe Vedic ceremonies efficacious for success in tribal warfare.[1] Written somewhat later, the two great classical epics of India—the Ramayana and the Mahabharata—are both war epics. The predominant viewpoint on kings in Indian classical texts is that conquest was every bit as important as peace and prosperity. By the beginning of the Common Era, the texts formulated a full ideology of conquest. A king, in order to fulfill his destiny, had to conquer the four "quarters," that is, surrounding kingdoms in the four cardinal directions from his capital.[2]

In spite of overwhelming evidence of very frequent actual warfare for more than two millennia, scholarship on the precolonial period of India has generally viewed war as an unfortunate aberration rather than the norm.[3] Few scholars, to this point, have connected the environment and warfare. This discussion of the military and the environment in precolonial India is, therefore, necessarily preliminary.

To understand precolonial India, we cannot use twentieth-century notions of "war" and "peace." They are too tied to the idea of nation-states and assume a concentration and exclusivity of force that comes from our own time. Nor can we look to Europe of an earlier period and apply general models of "feudalism." These, too, miss

42

important and central features of war and society in South Asia. For this chapter, I plan to stay relatively close to the data and follow a single region, the Malwa plateau, through three empires over about three centuries, 1560 -1850 CE.

The focus throughout will be on the military's impact on the environment. The concluding section considers larger questions of war and the environment in the South Asian context.

The Malwa Plateau

Let us begin with a description of the Malwa plateau, for which a good bit of indigenous eighteenth-century documentary evidence on war and the environment remains. This region whose northern rim is fifty miles south of Agra (see Figure 1) is an oval tableland about one hundred fifty miles across its longer east-west axis and one hundred twenty miles across its shorter north-south axis. It drops off on the north and south edges through hills and ravines to major river valleys. On the east and west, the plateau descends in broad belts of hills. Like all of India, Malwa depends on monsoon rains. Though rainfall is nowhere near as predictable or as heavy as on the coasts, the Malwa plateau has a distinct pattern. Rainfall is heaviest in the southeast corner with 126 cm and drops off in steady northeast -southwest isobars to 80 cm on the northwest rim.[4] Much monsoon rain falls on the hills south and east of the plateau and these areas were, in our period, heavily forested with large timber, much of it teak. The hills beyond Malwa's western rim were also forested. With substantially less rain than the eastern rim, trees were smaller, drought-resistant varieties mixed with shrubs.[5] Large patches of this scrub forest dotted the northwest half of Malwa.[6] Rivers run southwest to northeast and drain into the Chambal and eventually into the Ganges.[7]

Malwa's soil is famous for holding moisture; then and now, an adequate monsoon yields a good single crop in a year. A second food crop is possible where monsoon rainfall is heaviest, on the southeastern portions of the plateau.

Malwa has virtually no areas that could be termed pristine or unaltered by long-term human habitation. Archeologists have discovered many Iron Age settlements in the area. At least one Iron Age city (Ujjein) is widely mentioned in early Buddhist and Hindu texts of the first millennium BCE.[8] Long-term human settlement long

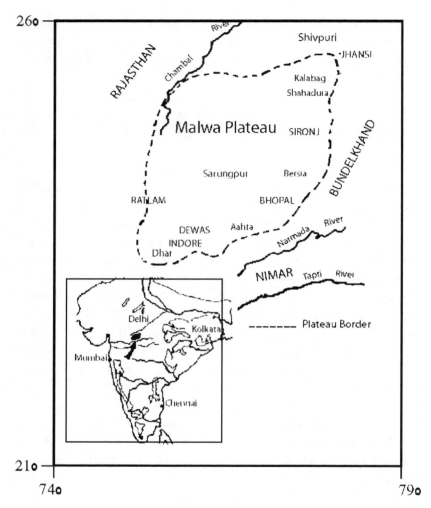

Figure 1. The Malwa Plateau, 1600-1800.

ago shifted the plateau's landscape, possibly originally subtropical forest, to savanna. Smaller trees and brush replaced most large trees (which now seem to be mostly in and around villages and adjacent to shrines).

For more than two thousand years, the area has been crossed by the main trade routes connecting the western coast and the Ganges plains to the north.[9] Politically, the plateau's long-term pattern varied between a core area for major kingdoms and a march area easily invaded from both the north and the south. In the centuries before British colonial conquest, the population was a complicated mix of Hindus and Muslims.[10] Muslims were a small minority, mainly traders, administrators, artisans, and soldiers, who lived in towns. Hindus—representing more than twenty castes—were mainly cultivators, laborers, and local militarized elites. Forest-dwellers, mainly Bhils and Gonds, hunted and gathered in the hilly areas principally on the fringes of the plateau.[11] Periodic induced burning for slash-and-burn agriculture had long altered some of these hilly areas.[12]

Eastern and Western Malwa

Let us look briefly at one of the more "developed" areas of eastern Malwa. Along a main road (connecting the western coast to the Ganges valley) lies a town known as Sironj (see Figure 1). In our period, it was not only a caravan stop but also the administrative center of a group of some 224 nearby villages (also known as Sironj) densely packed into a region of about 45 sq. mi.[13] With more than four villages to each square mile, Sironj region had almost continuous cultivated fields and little forested areas between villages. This matches the observations of W. Smith, who was with a British expeditionary force that passed Sironj in 1778.[14]

Administrative documents of the mid-eighteenth century differentiated between "original" villages (a designation that referred to early Mughal village lists of the 1670s) and "later" villages. Of Sironj's 245 villages in the eighteenth century, more than two-thirds were categorized as "later," that is, colonized in the preceding two centuries.[15] The area had done well during the Mughal period.

Cultivators grew more than twenty-five different crops with the summer monsoon rains.[16] Wheat was the largest crop followed by oilseed, chickpeas, cotton, lentils, and tobacco and sugarcane.[17] Sorghum was widely grown as a non-monsoon season food crop. Clearly, there was a mixture of subsistence food crops and market crops sold in nearby Sironj town.[18] This trade allowed all of Sironj's villagers to pay their taxes in cash, a total of about two hundred thousand silver rupees each year. Sironj town was famous for looming a particular variety of fine white muslin.[19]

Fortunately, local revenue documents show on-the-ground measurement of agricultural land, what was grown, tax receipts, and outstanding taxes due not only for villages in the region, but occasionally for individual cultivators for a decade or more.[20] Irrigated land (termed "garden land") paid the highest rate. Typically, the percentage of irrigated land in a village was small, generally less than 4 percent and often used for opium or sugar cane, both high labor/ high value crops. Monsoon crops paid roughly twice the taxation rate of non-monsoon subsistence crops.[21]

The point of this excursion into micro-agricultural history is that Sironj's pattern is typical of more than a dozen towns along the trans-regional trunk road through eastern Malwa. A colleague and I found the same pattern in the Tapti River valley just south of the Malwa plateau.[22] Towns and hinterlands developed together. Nearby villages sold foodstuffs and raw materials in the town markets. These transactions allowed the villagers to pay taxes in cash. The strength of empires derived from these trade routes, forts that protected them, towns along them, nearby villages, and taxes from sedentary agriculture of villages.[23]

Like other areas of agricultural surplus, eastern Malwa provided several important commodities for larger empires. Wheat went to imperial capitals (Agra and Pune in our period) and armies. Malwa's soil and climate are particularly suited to cotton and its cultivation goes back as far as we can trace textiles. For example, a complex of large and important Buddhist monasteries (Barhut and Sanchi) on Malwa's eastern rim was active in the first millenium CE and used prodigious quantities of cloth both in ritual and the clothing of monks and pilgrims. At the end of the sixteenth century, the *Ain-i-Akbari*, a famous Mughal survey of the empire, says of Malwa, "Cloth of the best texture is here woven" and names the specialty fabrics of several of Malwa's towns and cities.[24] The same source mentions Malwa as a source of betel leaves.

As noted, rainfall gradually diminishes from southeast to northwest on the Malwa plateau. In our period, this climatological fact meant sparser settlement and less prosperous villages on the western half of the plateau. In Dewas (see Figure 1) on the western rim of the plateau, for example, the same land area as Sironj had slightly less than one-quarter the villages. The tax rate on agricultural land was only about two-thirds that of agricultural land in Sironj.[25] Between villages, European observers found large areas of what they termed "jungle."[26]

Dewas was, however, still on a major road. Away from roads, the village and population density dropped even further. Only a few miles west of Dewas, roads stopped, as did large-scale sedentary agriculture and government control. In the hills, a thin population (perhaps only six to eight per square mile) of hunter-gatherers extracted most of what they needed from the forest. Some practiced supplemental small-scale subsistence agriculture.

Overall, we can divide Malwa into three ecological regions. Eastern Malwa, along major roads, was densely populated, tied to trade, and had little forest surrounding its villages. A second region, central and western Malwa, had less-dense settlement, lower rainfall, and substantial areas of scrub forest between villages. And hilly areas on the rim of the plateau had no roads, little central-government control, much dense forest, and a mix of shifting agriculture and hunting and gathering.[27] Now, let us turn to war and the military in this setting.

Conquest and the Environment in Malwa

The largest concentration of force occurred when one major state fought another for control of the whole plateau. In the three centuries preceding British rule, this event happened only twice in Malwa, in the 1560s and the 1730s. The scale of the fighting, however, could be quite large, involving upwards of twenty thousand horse troopers, plus infantry.

Court chronicles as well as many paintings of Mughal armies of the period help us document the 1560 conquest of Malwa. A generation before, Mughal armies had been typical Central Asian war bands, that is cavalry in chain mail on strong Central Asian or Afghan horses using primarily a reverse-curve bow from horseback.[28] This sort of army traveled fast, struck at opportune times and places, and took loot and prisoners. By the 1560s, however, the Mughal war band had changed in the Indian context. For many reasons (including the frequency and importance of forts), the army added early artillery, infantry, and provisioning capacity. The Mughal army had, thus, slowed down and had become—as several observers noted—a moving city, complete with a bazaar, artisans, luxurious tents for the officers, and recreational hunting between battles.[29] As the *Ain-i-Akbari* (c. 1595) put it, "On account of the crowding of camp-followers and the number of troops themselves, it would take a soldier days to find his tent; and how much worse would it be for a stranger?"[30]

The indirect environmental effects of these large armies can only be suggested here. For example, not only did the elite of the army travel by elephant, the animals had been front-line attack vehicles for two millennia. Kautilya's *Arthasastra*, a classical text on statecraft, details the processes of elephant capture, various grades of elephants, and even setting aside kingly territory for the maintenance of herds of wild elephants.[31] These two military uses of elephants—carriage and attack—led to a strong demand for tribute in elephants from forested regions where elephants were found. The *Ain-i-Akbari* lists several areas of Malwa's forested perimeter as prime for the capture of elephants.[32] The Mughal emperor kept approximately five hundred elephants; his nobles each often had a dozen or more. War elephants were also kept in large provincial forts and capitals, and by local militarized families. At any time in our period, we estimate that at least five to ten thousand elephants had been removed from their forest environment, trained, and stabled in forts, towns, and with armies.[33]

The long-term effects of large numbers of military horses were more complex. Because of the warm climate, horses did not (and still do not) breed well in India. They were, therefore, imported in large numbers from Central Asia and the Middle East. Babur, the Mughal conqueror of India, noted in the early sixteenth century that ten thousand horses passed through Kabul each year on route to horse fairs in India.[34] The number was far higher as armies expanded over the following two centuries.

A Mughal army (and its opponents) generally wreaked environmental havoc wherever it went. The path of devastation generally led from the capital to a battle site hundreds of miles away. Every day, foragers from the slow-moving army cut fodder for perhaps forty thousand horses.

> *In the fair season, when there is no pasture, the horsemen and their attendant grass cutters sally forth out of camp to dig up the roots of grass, which are washed and given to the horses as more nutritive than the stems of dried reedy grass.*[35]

Camp woodcutters stripped everything burnable nearby for thousands of cooking fires, as well as forges and bakeries.

At best, professional long-distance grain traders supplied men and horses, but seizing local grain from villagers was a standard practice as frequent government prohibitions suggest. Wise rulers (like Akbar) recognized how devastating large concentrations of forces would be. They dispatched units of the army by separate routes only to assemble when approaching an important battle.

Peasants did not, however, quietly wait to have their grain and valuables seized. Characteristically, they packed their valuables and harvested grain in bullock carts and moved out of the path of the slow-moving army. When army patrols arrived, villages would simply be deserted. Some later correspondence suggests that the villagers did not go far. In most of Malwa, the "forest" was quite close to the village and the villagers moved into dense nearby brush and hid. In other cases, villagers went to relatives ten to twenty miles away.

Longer-term environmental damage occurred only if a large army stopped for several months, for example, jockeying around a battle site, negotiating for allies, or besieging a fortress. Observers noted that the countryside around such a stalled army was stripped of anything eatable (plant or animal) and depopulated for as much as twenty miles in every direction.[36]

Large battles that decided the fate of the plateau were generally one-day affairs with charges and counter-charges, much dust, and considerable slaughter of the losers. The battle was generally decided by the death or flight of one commander, at which time his army fled and the victors looted his camp. This sort of large battle was, however, decisive only if the winning side captured or killed the losing king. If he managed to flee to a fortress or a capital, he could wait, assemble allies, and return to fight the next campaign season. In the Mughal conquest of Malwa, this is, in fact, what happened. The reigning Afghan sultan of the region reassembled an army after monsoon the following year and recovered much of Malwa. It took yet another campaign and another large battle to defeat him decisively.[37]

The Mughal chronicles give us a picture of how "conquest" proceeded after the decisive battle. First, the losing Afghan sultan was brought to the Mughal camp and integrated into the Mughal elite at quite a high level. Some of his nobility likewise became Mughal military commanders. Second, local militarized families that headed groups of villages (defined and discussed shortly) were brought to the Mughal camp, honored, and offered the opportunity to pay homage to the Mughals; if they accepted these terms, they then received their holdings from the Mughal Empire, and committed support with their troops to future Mughal campaigns.[38] In this political system, many players— from the defeated sultan on down to local militarized families holding a few dozen villages—had to choose whether to back the new regime.

In Malwa by the end of the 1560s, virtually all of the militarized families accepted the new Mughal sovereignty.

Extant documents allow an even more detailed picture of the Maratha conquest of the Mughal province of Malwa in the 1730s.[39] From about 1725 to 1735, yearly Maratha raids on Mughal towns and forts were followed by negotiations with militarized families. These negotiations generally followed a Maratha raid that showed both that Maratha main-force troops were decisively stronger than these local forces and that Mughal local forces could not protect the area. A large single battle in 1738 demonstrated that the Mughals could no longer protect the whole province. Exactly like their Mughal predecessors, the Marathas brought dozens of local militarized families to the battlefield camp, honored them, and received their oath of loyalty. Who, then,were these local militarized families so crucial to converting battlefield victory in to a functioning conquered province?

Local Militarized Families

A family became the dominant militarized holder of villages as a result of an entrepreneurial activity that involved war, colonization, conquest, and bestowal. The extant records of Mughal times do not allow an exact count, but scattered Maratha records of the eighteenth century suggest as many as five hundred such extended families on the plateau, many split into factions. Some had recruited cultivators, opened vacant land and built a local fort even before the Mughal conquest of 1560 CE. Others were the military elite of the Muslim kingdom of Malwa from which the Mughals conquered the plateau. Still others were migrants from Rajasthan (to the northwest of Malwa) who conquered local kingdoms of "tribals" on the margins of the plateau. Some took military service in the Mughal armies in the early seventeenth century and received lands for the maintenance of their troops. A large number, however, did so only in the late seventeenth and early eighteenth centuries.[40] They had, thus, taken up dominant local positions only a generation before the Maratha conquest. All of these local militarized families played a crucial role in Mughal tax collection. One and all, these local militarized families signed off as responsible for the Mughal taxes each year.

The most recent entrants to this process had, however, few local ties. They were simply generals to whom the Mughal Empire had recently granted the taxes of a village or a group of villages for the maintenance of their troops. When they were not on campaign, this village was home to these troops and their leader. In similar fashion, local Mughal tax-collecting officials, with troops, were resident in towns and cities.[41]

In both the Mughal and Maratha conquests, the level of violence in the countryside actually went up after the losing side conceded the province by the act of turning over tax and revenue documents to the winning side. Both the Mughals (in the 1560s) and the Marathas (in the 1730s) had to displace or deal with all the local militarized families and resident generals, generally by force, before they could take control of the province. These battles generally involved hundreds of troops and devastated a wider area of the countryside than the large encounters. Maratha letters of the 1730s talk of nearly half of the local villages empty as peasants fled.[42] Other letters talk of periods of five years or more without cultivation. As the Marathas slowly defeated or negotiated with these local forces, the government recognized that extended local conflict had produced significant degradation of the agricultural fields. Where forest surrounded villages, the fields could simply disappear in five fallow, untended years. Early Maratha collectors wrote of villages on the Mughal tax rolls that they could no longer find.

Still, in both the 1560 and 1730 conquests, this phase lasted less than a decade. The number of "disappeared" villages rarely exceeded 10 percent. Peasants generally came back from nearby retreats and took up cultivation again. They may have had to clear some fields, perhaps even rebuild some dams and weirs, but there was little long-term alteration to the environment.[43]

"Normal" War and the Environment

For a sense of the "normalcy" of war in the South Asian context, we must turn from relatively infrequent periods of conquest to much longer periods of administration. This was "business as usual" for South Asian empires—collection of taxes, protection of roads, promotion of trade, the integration of men into the courtly elite. War was central to this process in three ways.

First, military service was the principal form of entrepreneurial activity in precolonial South Asia. If we consider the origin of the elite families of Malwa, they had all served in armies and received taxation rights to particular lands for their successful effort. We should note the intimate link between these entrepreneurial military families and "development" both under the Mughals and the Marathas. These militarized families had both the duty and the desire to open new lands and bring in new cultivators. These two successive empires often granted tax-collection rights (termed *madad-i-ma'ash* in Mughal parlance and *istawa makta* in Marathi) in areas barely conquered, or never cultivated, or from which peasants had fled. It was the job of these militarized families to recruit cultivators and make the places paying concerns both for their immediate income and as a demonstration of suitability for higher military rank for their families. In the centuries before British conquest, there was generally plenty of cultivable land in Malwa. People were the scarcest resource, and control of population was the key to turning forest lands into tax-paying sedentary agricultural fields.[44]

Local war was central to this process. The militarized family often had to fight the previous holder—sometimes a tribal chieftain—for control of the land; in addition, they had to protect peasants they recruited from attacks by nearby forest dwellers.[45] In this process, it was essential that a militarized family build a substantial local fort. Malwa, in these centuries, was peppered with such forts.[46]

Second, we should be very clear that the troops of these militarized families were essential to the functioning of the empire. They were expected to join main force troops for battles in their area. More importantly, however, they were the first line of force of the empire in any local disturbance. There were many more local landed troops than there were, for example, royal troops in fortresses in Malwa.

Third, these militarized families were never simply bureaucratic functionaries or tax collectors. Their relation to empire was more complicated. Andre Wink some years ago noticed in Maratha records the Persian term *zamindar* (holder of the land) for these families.[47] An astute Maratha statesman of the late eighteenth century summarized their position thusly.

> *These people are really the sharers of the kingdom. They are not inclined to live on whatever watan [holdings] they possess, or to act loyally towards the king who is the lord of the whole country and to abstain from committing wrong against any one. All the time they want to acquire new possessions bit by bit, and to become strong: and after becoming strong their ambition is to*

> *seize forcibly from some, and to create enmities and*
> *depredations against others. Knowing that royal punishment*
> *will fall on them, they first take refuge with others, fortify their*
> *places with their help, rob the travellers, loot the territories,*
> *and fight desperately, not even caring for their lives. When a*
> *foreign invasion comes they make peace with the invader, with*
> *a desire for gaining or protecting a watan, meet personally*
> *with the enemy, allow the enemy to enter the kingdom by*
> *divulging secrets of both sides, and then becoming harmful to*
> *the kingdom get to be difficult of control. For this reason, the*
> *control of these people has to be very cleverly devised.*

These local militarized families gained strength whenever the empire was weak, for example, at times of succession, civil war, invasion, or a minority government. Factions needed them and their troops.

Even in the empire's best times, these local militarized families often brought war to the local countryside. In one scenario, an ousted faction or an unsuccessful successor retired to the forest and raided nearby lands; this process is so old in India that it is part of mythical kingship in the texts of the first millennium BCE. In our period, this practice, termed *girasia*, appears in both the Maratha and British records. The term comes from neighboring Rajasthan and is Rajasthani. It means "share" or, more descriptively, "mouthful."[48] In militarized families, sons received a "share" or maintenance "mouthful." Squabbling over "mouthfuls" was endless. *Girasia* came to mean a member of the family displaced from his "mouthful" who looted and devastated villages controlled by the family until he was satisfactorily reinstated.

Let us consider a second, equally common scenario. In Marathi records of the eighteenth century, groups of villages were divided into *raiti* (having village headmen only) and *taluki* (headed by a militarized family or families). If a militarized family did not come to terms with the empire's tax-collection official, they revolted. Revolt began with withholding taxes.

> *Each of these chieftains possesses one or more strongholds with*
> *which the province abounds; their subjugation, when*
> *refractory, is attended with considerable difficulty and*
> *expense, and they frequently make it a point of honour to*
> *withhold their revenue until payment is compelled by adequate*
> *force.*[49]

If the dispute was not resolved, a more disruptive phase began. The militarized family attacked nearby *raiti* villages, thus denying revenue to the government. Both of these scenarios brought looting and warfare on an intimate scale to a group of villages.

Let us, then, summarize the argument thus far. We have found the definition of "war" in the precolonial Indian context quite complex. States and empires had the force to initiate large-scale war, but not enough administration to consolidate and repopulate conquests in most areas; for this function, they depended on families in their military service. The empire's intention (both Mughal and Maratha) was to settle these militarized families in unproductive areas and use them for land clearing and development. These families quickly became "co-sharers" in the kingdom and often resisted imperial authority with attacks on nearby villages. Their troop strength was often larger than nearby imperial garrisons. Especially in central and western Malwa and the hills surrounding the plateau, there was adequate jungle and forest to provide refuge and staging areas for their raids.

The records suggest that although invasion by main-force armies was quite destructive, it was relatively rare. Local disruption by disgruntled militarized families was relatively more common, but was generally confined to a single group of villages. Throughout, peasants were not passive victims, but tended to move both to opportunities and away from destructive warfare. The records suggest that most areas recovered quickly from either invasion or local war and little long-term environmental damage resulted from these military actions. Now, let us turn to military action that did produce long-term, serious environmental change.

A "Time of War"

If warfare continued for more than about a decade, its effects were much more serious. The interregnum (1795-1818) between Maratha rule and British conquest was one such period (termed in the documents *gardi ki wakt,* or "time of war"). It began with the death of an older generation of Maratha generals who had large holdings in Malwa. Succession disputes followed because the Maratha central government had become too weak to dictate succession. Strapped for cash to hire troops, all parties in the succession disputes recruited irregular troops, all of whom survived by looting villages.

The most destructive expedients were at this time resorted to, in order to support the court and army ... Several of the principal officers were ... sent with military detachments, which they were directed to subsist, and to remit what they could collect beyond their expenditure to the government. ... These commands were given generally to persons who became answerable for the arrears to the soldiers, and paid a certain sum in advance to the treasury, besides bribes. ... They received in return latitude to plunder.[50]

As the plateau became more and more disrupted, the irregular forces grew to a size that regularly overwhelmed the local militarized families.

They use sword and lance, and pillage without distinction. They move in bodies seldom exceeding two or three thousand men, and hold direct undeviating course until they reach their destination, when they at once divide into smaller parties, that they may with more facility plunder the country, and carry off a larger quantity of booty; destroying, at the same time what they cannot remove.[51]

The first response of villagers was to decrease the areas cultivated to more easily protected fields close to the village. We see this change in the village records of the early years of this disrupted period. The forest, thus, encroached at the margins of all of the villages. Attacks on towns almost certainly meant a decrease in demand for crops and products from surrounding hinterland areas. The smaller cultivated areas probably grew mainly subsistence food for the villagers.

Following several years of raids and disruption, however, villagers began to move, first to safer areas near the forts of local militarized families, next to a nearby area perceived as safer, and finally out of the region entirely. Surely, some peasants and members of militarized families joined the irregular forces. The final phase of Malwa's depopulation saw attacks by the forest dwellers on remaining sedentary agriculturists over large portions of the plateau.[52] This downward spiral in population continued for almost two decades; it stopped only when the British sent a large army onto the plateau and defeated both the remaining Maratha generals and the irregular armies, which had, by that time, given up all pretense of loyalty to the Marathas. By the end of this large-scale military action, much of the previously cultivated area of the plateau was depopulated.[53] In a broad area of northeastern Malwa, for example, initial British surveys found more than one-third of the villages vacant. In a southeastern portion of the plateau, the proportion was slightly less than one-third.[54]

Adversity of this scale and intensity had profound long-term effects. Cities and towns dropped dramatically in population. Dhar in southwestern Malwa, for example, dropped from more than twenty thousand houses in the late eighteenth century to around seven thousand in 1820.[55] Villages, deserted for several years, disappeared. Scrub native grasses and tough bushes and trees subsequently displaced weeds. With the destruction of dams and weirs, drainage so altered in some areas that they became malarial. Even decades after the British conquest, troops could not barrack in these areas during the rainy season. Large mammals returned to the unoccupied villages from nearby forest. There was a resurgence of tigers, wild boar, and nondomesticated grazing animals.

> *Some of this tract of country might almost be said to have been usurped by wild beasts, and these literally fought with the returning inhabitants for their fields. I had detached Captain Ambrose to protect the countries near Oonchode and Baglee. … The following is his statement [of those killed by tigers]:*

At Oonchode	*39*
Baglee	*17*
Bhyre and Gorara	*8*
Argooley	*15*
Chousay	*5*
Total	*84*

> *A subsequent statement, from an intelligent native, swelled the number of men killed, in 1818, to about 150. … In many other parts of this country, the tigers have been as formidable to the returning population as near Baglee.*[56]

In these conditions, the few remaining cultivators refused to settle in a single village and develop it. Rather, they moved from village to village every few years, offering their labor on contract.[57] John Malcolm summarized what he found on the ground in the years after British conquest, as follows:

> *Suffice it to say, that a great proportion of the revenue of that country was reduced below one-half of what it had been in better times: many districts did not produce one-quarter, and others not one-tenth of their former revenues. Nay, in one instance the desolation was so complete, that not only every trace of cultivation, and of the inhabitants of a tract which had one valuable, had disappeared, but the principality to which it belonged had lost all records of the possession.*[58]

After extended military action to defeat plundering bands and raiding forest-dwellers, the new British colonial government had much to do to reverse this serious disruption. First and foremost, the government had to recognize and sign treaties with virtually every local militarized family they found actually in possession of villages and a fort in Malwa.[59] The plateau, therefore, became composed entirely of "princely states," that were not directly ruled by the British colonial government.

The government, thus, followed the time-tested method of settling the plateau, accepting local militarized families as "co-sharers".[60] These families next offered land virtually tax-free to speculators who brought in cultivators from regions less disrupted.[61] Slowly, pioneers cleared the forest and began agriculture. This process took decades and created a new rural elite consisting of families that had successfully speculated in land development.

Even in the middle of the nineteenth century, large areas of the plateau and its surrounding river valleys were still largely forested, with small patches of relatively new cultivation. It was only in the twentieth century that population growth and concomitant pressure on the land reduced the forest to small patches between cultivated fields. Only in the last few decades has there been serious environmental pressure on the larger forested areas at the margins of the plateau. None of this pressure on the environment is the result of war or the military.

Conclusions and Larger Issues

Armies of precolonial India did not, of course, have the direct destructive capacity of modern armies—they had no land mines, aerial bombing, or napalm. War and the military, nevertheless, had both direct and indirect effects on the South Asian environment. Perhaps most fundamentally, unlike modern nation-states, no government particularly cared about areas without sedentary, taxable agriculture. The jungle or forest between villages did not figure in tax collection and, thus, was not treated as an asset or a conquest in war. These areas were, however, quite important to villagers and nearby towns for firewood, medicinal plants, game, grazing, and refuge. In addition, large areas of hills and ravines (on all perimeters of the Malwa plateau, for example) had few roads, saw virtually no government control, and were not colonized for agriculture. These regions remained the realm of hunter-gatherers who only came to the notice of empires when they attacked cultivators on the plains. The military, however, impacted some of these areas through their demands for tribute in elephants.

Conquering empires understood the taxation potential of expanding agriculture and the role of the military in it. They realized that existing vacant villages were the easiest point of development and encouraged local officials to find villages, find their former occupants, and negotiate their return. If, however, a whole group of villages needed resettlement, as we have seen, this was work for a military family in government service. They built a fort, located cultivators, and enticed them to come and start production. Conquering empires understood that this process had to proceed relatively quickly and that the main beneficiaries would, in fact, be the locals—the cultivators and the militarized family. Taxes had to remain low to encourage cultivation. Imperial attempts to renegotiate these light taxes often set off local rebellion by the militarized families. The balance was, however, delicate. If government could not settle or contain these local rebellions, a downward spiral might begin. Within a few years, bands of marauders nominally linked to local families would have devastated the whole region.

We tend to think that a dominant role of the central government in development and in the promotion or destruction of existing environments is a feature of the "modern." The data from precolonial Central India suggest otherwise. It was precisely at points that an empire was unable to dictate succession among the militarized families that serious local war and spreading environmental damage occurred. Similarly, it was vigorous action by an empire that halted the occasional downward spiral of raids and counter-raids by unpaid irregular troops. Just as in the modern period, for an understanding of the environment, we need to consider many actors—villages, militarized families, local imperial representatives, and imperial forces—each with agency in the system.

The system changed all through our period. The importance of elephants, for example, declined over all three centuries with the gradual introduction of artillery and guns. Elephants were literally "towers of strength" for pre-artillery warfare in India. Kings directed battle from a box on an elephant; they could see and be seen by their troops. Elephants effectively advanced in a line against infantry with archers firing from fortified boxes on their backs and were also useful on defense, holding a line and providing cover for infantry. They were routinely used to batter down doors of forts. Apparently, elephants could not stand the noise of artillery and gunfire and tended to run amok, killing their own troops as often as the enemy.

Change was even more swift with the shift to European-style infantry at the end of the eighteenth century. The issue is complex. Some local powers actively embraced the newly introduced system, others tried to graft it on to prior military practice, and others simply ignored it. All of these "native" powers (as the British called them) realized that European-style infantry and artillery were categorically more expensive than the older horse troops garrisoned on specific lands. Of necessity, every ruler in South Asia who adopted the new system had to push his agriculture in the direction of marketable cash crops and away from subsistence agriculture. He also had to both push land development and to accept tax systems (such as tax farming) that yielded cash for his new European-style troops. The debt that ensued was a dangerous game for any ruler, but the environmental effects have only been worked out in a few areas, mainly Bengal and the Ganges valley. We need to look at other areas and compare the environmental effects to areas where rulers did not adopt European-style troops before we can make any wide generalizations.

There were profound human and environmental effects of the relative "peace" established by the British colonial presence in the nineteenth century. This limited peace, in addition to the shift to infantry and artillery, and cash salaries meant the end of military service that led to rights in land and taxation. The families of successful Indian soldiers could no longer become "co-sharers" of the kingdom. Instead, the British colonial state froze the militarized families that they found in the early nineteenth century as the princely states, and saddled them with heavy taxes to pay for colonial troops stationed nearby. In North India, the environmental pressures of cash cropping and the displacement of such rulers who could not pay were large factors in the First War of Indian Independence in 1857.

Notes

1   See *The Rig Veda: An Anthology,* trans. Wendy Doniger O'Flaherty (London: Penguin Books, 1981).

2   See, for example, Ronald Inden's discussion of Kashmiri imperial *puranas* in Ronald Inden, Jonathan Walters, and Daud Ali, *Querying the Medieval: Texts and the History of Practices in South Asia* (Oxford: Oxford University Press, 2000), 80-81.

3   See, for example, the emphasis on the nonviolent tradition in Mahadev Gadgil and Ramachandra Guha, *This Fissured Land: An Ecological History of India* (Berkeley: University of California Press, 1992), 89-91. War and warrior lineages barely appear in David Ludden, *The New Cambridge History of India, Vol.* 4, Part 4, *An Agrarian History of South Asia* (New York: Cambridge University Press, 1999).

4   *National Atlas of India, III* (Delhi: National and Thematic Mapping Organization, 1986), plate 74. Much monsoon rain is lost on the slopes of the plateau. Thus, only 50 miles east of the plateau, the monsoon yields 140-160 cm of rain per year.

5   *Atlas of Forest Resources of India,* ed. S. P. Gupta (New Delhi: National Atlas Organization, 1976), Plates 7 and 17. See also *Madhya Pradesh, District Gazetteers* (Bhopal: Government Central Press, 1965). Particularly useful are various earlier gazetteers produced by princely states such as Gwalior and Dewas.

6   *National Atlas, VII,* Plate 281.

7   An area of the north-central portion of the plateau has a series of ravines of seasonal streams that run down to the Chambal River. This area is known as the Chambal Ravines and has been a hideout for outlaws for centuries. It remains so today. See *River Basin Atlas of India* (New Delhi: Central Board for the Prevention and Control of Water Pollution, 1988), map opposite 114.

8   N. D. Banerjee, *The Iron Age in India* (Delhi: Munshiram Manoharlal, 1965), 5-6.

9   See, for example, the memoir of Xan Sang, the seventh century Buddhist pilgrim. He crossed the plateau on his way to Ajanta, a major Buddhist site in Maharashtra some 150 miles to the south of the plateau.

10 See U. N. Day, *Medieval Malwa: A Political and Cultural History, 1401 - 1562* (Delhi: Mushi Ram Manohar Lal, 1965).

11 Even now, some hilly areas adjacent to the plateau are overwhelmingly "tribal," some areas over 90 percent of the population. See O. S. Shrivastava, *Tribals in Madhya Pradesh* (Bhopal: Diwa Prakashan, 1998), 11-13.

12 Stephen J. Pyne, "Nataraja: India's Cycle of Fire" in *Out of the Woods: Essays in Environmental History,* ed. Char Miller and Hal Rothman (Pittsburgh, PA: University of Pittsburgh Press, 1997), 290-308.

13 *Pune Archive,* Hindustan Bundles # 187, A Raja Mandal paper of 1742 listing villages of Sironj *pargana.* (The manuscript originals of the Hindustan Bundles are in Marathi, Modi script. All translations are mine)

14 A "fine, well-cultivated plain" is how W. Smith, the official chronicler of the first British expedition to cross the plateau in 1778, described the Sironj region. *British Library* Add. 29213. "A journal of the road traveled by Colonel Upton from Kalpi through Narwar to Bhopaul and Boorhaunpore by order of the Governor General and Council kept by W. Smith."

15 *Pune Archive,* Hindustan Bundles # 162, An Account of Sironj, 1741.

16 *Pune Archive,* Hindustan Bundles #162, An Account of Village Jamabandi [Settlement] of Sironj According to Orders, 1742.

17 By the nineteenth century, corn (maize) had been added to this mix. See John Malcolm, *Memoir of Central India,* II (London: Parbury, Allen, & Co., third edition, 1832), 33.
18 I regard Gadgil and Guha's speculation that various castes occupied different ecological niches as interesting, but entirely unproven. For example, if one closely considers Maratha crop records of sedentary agriculturalists in Malwa, one finds no particular correlation between caste and the actual crops they produced. It is, of course, possible, that hunters and gatherers occupied more specialized niches. The Maratha documents take little notice of them. See Gadgil and Guha, *Fissured Land,* 109-110.
19 *Pune Archive,* Hindustan Bundles #123, A Jhadti year-end account of Sironj Pargana, *1143.*
20 See, for example, *Pune Archive,* Hindustan Bundles #162. An Account of the Village of Jagar, *1743.* This account of a single village names the cultivators and how much of each one's land was sown in what crops, both for the monsoon and the winter season.
21 These figures come from a pack of detailed village revenue records from Sironj Pargana, *1743. Pune Archive,* Hindustan Bundles # 162.
22 "Kinship and Pargana in Eighteenth-Century Khandesh," Stewart Gordon and John Richards in Stewart Gordon, *Marathas, Marauders, and State Formation in Eighteenth Century India* (Delhi: Oxford University Press, 1994), 121-50.
23 The Mughal government did not, for example, directly tax forest products, sheep raising, or fisheries. Gadgil and Guha, *Fissured Land,* 108. The Mughal government's preoccupation with revenue-producing sedentary agriculture was so complete that the statistics of what they produced allow a present-day historian to make reasonably accurate estimates of cropped area, crop yields, and expenses. See Shireen Moosvi, *The Economy of the Mughal Empire c. 1595: A Statistical Study* (Delhi: Oxford University Press, 1987).
24 *Ain-I-Akbari,* Abul-Fazl Allami, trans. H. S. Jarrett, corrected and annotated by J. N. Sarkar (Delhi: Low Price Publications, reprinted edition, 1989), 207. Several towns in Mughal Malwa (Chanderi, Ashta, Sehore, Sarungpur, Sironj) exported locally loomed specialty cotton fabrics of Malwa cotton. These towns were the same in the eighteenth century. See Malcolm, *Memoir of Central India* II, 77-78.
25 *Pune Archive,* Hindustan Bundles # 154, An Account of Dewas, 1740.
26 *British Library,* Add. *25587,* "Journal of the march of Colonel Charles Morgan's Detachment from Surat to Etayah, kept by Sgt. Joseph Stoke."
27 See Malcolm, *Memoir of Central India* II, 65-68.
28 Such an army is thoroughly described in the memoirs of Babur. Zahiru'din Muhammad Babur Padshah Ghazi, *Babur-Nama,* trans. A. S. Beveridge (1921, New Delhi: Low Price Publications, reprinted edition, 1989). It is pictured in many Mughal paintings. For example, see G. N. Pant, *Mughal Weapons in the Babur-Nama* (New Delhi, 1989), Plate #1 and Plate #4.
29 See William Irvine, *The Army of the Indian Moghols* (New Delhi: Eurasia Publishing, reprinted edition, 1962), 190-214. Such a camp is pictured in several Mughal paintings. See, for example, P. Pal, *Court Paintings of India* (New York: Navin Kumar, 1983), plate M 11.
30 Allami, trans. H. S. Jarrett, *Ain-I-Akbari,* 49.
31 See Simon Digby, *War-Horse and Elephant in the Delhi Sultanate* (Oxford: Oxford University Press, Orient Mongraphs, 1971).
32 Allami, trans. H. S. Jarrett, *Ain-I-Akbari,* 11, 208-9.

33 My rough calculation goes thusly. The Mughal Emperor kept about five hundred elephants. His top one thousand nobles might keep a couple of elephants each. The independent Rajput states at the time might account for another five hundred or so. Independent kings in the Ganges valley probably kept at least another one thousand, especially in Bengal, where elephants were plentiful. Provincial Mughal forts—as listed in the *Ain-I-Akbari*—account for another two thousand. The Deccan Sultanates might account for at least another one thousand. As Digby points out, the number of war elephants roughly correlates with the strength of an empire. The Mughal Empire, at its height, had in excess of twelve hundred war elephants. This number shrank to less than five hundred when the empire was in decline in the late seventeenth century. The overall number shrank as guns became more effective and central to warfare throughout the seventeenth century. See Digby, *War-Horse and Elephant*, 68-71, 77.

34 Pant, *Mughal Weapons*, 202. In the middle period of Mughal rule, the top nobles alone kept more than one hundred thousand actual cavalry troopers. This number does not include any of the independent states of North India, the militarized families, or the independent sultanates of the southern portion of India. The number of horses in military use in our period is staggering.

35 James Forbes, *Oriental memoirs: selected and abridged from a series of familiar letters written during seventeen years residence in India: including observations on parts of Africa and South America, and a narrative of occurrences in four India voyages* (London: White, Cochrane, and Co., 1813) 1, 53.

36 See the stylized contemporary account of the conquest by one not actually present on the battlefield. Muhammad Arif Qandhari, *Tarikh-I Akbari,* trans. Tasneem Ahmad (Delhi: Pragati Publications, 1993), 96-97.

37 Ibid.

38 Abu al-Fazl ibn Mubarak, *The Akbar Nama of Abu-1-Fazl (History of the reign of Akbar including an account of his predecessors)*, trans. H. Beveridge, II (Delhi, Ess Ess Publications, reprinted edition, 1977), 257-60.

39 I have examined the Maratha conquest of Malwa in some detail in Stewart Gordon, *Marathas, Marauders, and State Formation in Eighteenth-Century India* (Delhi: Oxford University Press, 1994), 23--64.

40 See Malcolm, *Memoir of Central India* II, pp. 9-10. More detail of the activities of these militarily entrepreneurial families is found in Dirk H. A. Kolff, *Naukar, Rajput & Sepoy: The Ethnohistory of the Military Labour Market in Hindustan, 1450-1850* (Cambridge: Cambridge University Press, 1990).

41 Gordon, *Marathas, Marauders,* 24-28.

42 See the seizing of the rights of a local militarized family and their displacement. *Pune Archive,* Hindustan Bundles # 192, A Rajamandal Paper of Mandu, 1739. During full conflict with militarized families, no revenue reached the Maratha central government in Pune. See *Pune Archive,* Hindustan Bundles #185 on Rewa.

43 The right of return after peasants had fled seems to have extended to a decade or more. See Malcolm, *Memoir of Central India* II, 22-23.

44 For the story of one of the early conquests of one of the militarized families, see Malcolm, *Memoir of Central India* II, 127-28.

45 I agree with Sumit Guha that in this period forest dwellers were not passive, archaic throwbacks to an earlier economic form. The eighteenth-century Marathi documents show these forest dwellers forming small kingdoms and playing an active part in the war and politics of the day. At the very least,

they were capable of closing roads through their region and raiding nearby sedentary agriculture when opportunity presented or necessity demanded. See Sumit Guha, *Environment and Ethnicity in India, 1200 - 1991* (Cambridge: Cambridge University Press, 1999), 108-21.

46 There are areas of eastern Malwa where even today the remains of two or even three such forts are visible at the same time. For a similar observation on Khandesh West to the south of Malwa) in the early nineteenth century, see W. H. Tone, *Illustrations of some Institutions of Maratha People* (London: J. Debery, 1818) 9.

47 John Malcolm summarized, as follows, the formal features of such grants as he found them in the 1820s:

> *His station is hereditary; he is supported by a grant of land, which differs in amount according to the size of the district and other circumstances; and he has, besides lesser dues, a percentage upon the collections, which, in Malwa, varies from four to eight percent. He pays no revenue to the government, but usually presents at the Dussera feast an offering to the Collector. ... The Zemindar has a due (generally one or two rupees) from every village in the district. He also has a trifling claim on each caste and trade: as a blanket from the weavers, oil from the oilmen, a pair of shoes from shoemakers, and so forth.*
>
> *The duties of the Zemindar are to preserve order and peace (he is expected to maintain a body of armed adherents: ... he is the person to whom the cultivators look up as their protector against acts or power that are in violation of established usage.* Malcolm, *Memoir of Central India* II, 8-9.

André Wink, *Land and Sovereignty in India: Agrarian Society and Politics under the Eighteenth-Century Maratha Svarajya* (Cambridge: Cambridge University Press, 1986), 183-92.

48 Ramchandrapant Amatya, *Ajnapatra*, trans. S. V. Puntambekar in *Journal of Indian History VII*, part 2 (April, 1929), 214.

49 I wish to thank Richard Saran, University of Michigan, for translation and discussion of this term. His explanation, based on middle-period Rajasthani, makes much more sense than any of the standard dictionaries or reference books that characterize *girasia* as merely an outlaw.

50 Walter Hamilton, *A Geographical, Statistical and Historical Description of Hindustan and Adjacent Countries I* (London: Spink, 1822), 729.

51 Malcolm, *Memoir of Central India* I, 275.

52 (An Officer in the East India company), *Origin of the Pindaris* (London: Murray, 1818), 96.

53 Malcolm, *Memoir of Central India* I, 384-97.

54 We have rather fragmentary British records of the extent of depopulation because subsequent jurisdiction was divided among militarized families and there were no areas of direct British rule. Malcolm, *Memoir of Central India* II, 387-89. John Malcolm commented on some of the areas he saw personally.

> *The Salunkee Rajpoots occupy a tract in Beirseah, extending along the right bank of the Parbutty, which, in 1820, nominally contained 144 villages; but of these, one-half were deserted and in ruins, and only to be discovered by the large trees that marked their former sites. The face of the country is, in general, covered with jungle; the cultivation being confined to the small spots in the neighborhood of the inhabited villages.* Malcolm, *Memoir of Central India* II, 482.

55 Malcolm, *Memoir of Central India* II, 489.

56 Malcolm, *Memoir of Central India* II, 232n.

57 Malcolm, *Memoir of Central India* II, 27.

58 Malcolm, *Memoir of Central India* II, 100-101.
59 Summaries of the actual treaties are found in Malcolm, *Memoir of Central India* II, 390-426. The general attitude that finding a militarized family to protect the local countryside was essential to re-establishing some sort of order is forcefully put in Malcolm, *Memoir of Central India* II, 56-57.
60 The victorious British army managed to disband a number of large irregular armies in the first few years after the conquest of Malwa. Nevertheless, acknowledged troop strength of just the larger of the militarized families in these years was more than seventy-five thousand cavalry and infantry.
61 Malcolm, *Memoir of Central India* II, 378-79.

"African Warfare in All Its Ferocity": Changing Military Landscapes and Precolonial and Colonial Conflict in Southern Africa

Roger S. Levine

> *Many features of precolonial Xhosa warfare were shared with other Nguni peoples, including several usually attributed to Zulu innovation, such as the short stabbing-spear and the conventional battle strategy (Xhosa, centre plus wings, equals Zulu, chest plus horns). The Zulu elaborated these strategies and tactics to a far higher degree than the Xhosa ever did, but the Xhosa had a distinct military genius of their own which should not be underestimated. This consisted not in refining traditional fighting methods but in knowing when to abandon them.* —Jeffrey Peires, *House of Phalo*, 1981[1]

Glistening, half-naked African warriors, heads crowned by feathers and spears glinting, swarming upon and over European soldiers who strike heroic poses as they fire into the mass of bodies that encircle them. This portrait forms the enduring image in the popular imagination of colonial warfare in southern Africa. The derivation of this unfortunate iconography lies primarily in the popular press coverage of the Anglo-Zulu conflict in the late 1870s.[2] Scholars have written long and often about this war and its antecedents as the Zulu nation confronted Dutch and then British forces beginning in the 1830s. Indeed, the preeminent military historian, John Keegan, identifies this "highly coloured confrontation" as "one of the great popular history stories of modern times."[3] But these images only tell a part of the story.

This chapter focuses on ways that insights derived from environmental history can recast and reinvigorate our understanding of the nature of the military encounter between Africans and the British colonial regime in South Africa in the early to mid-nineteenth century. A fresh look at colonial conflict in southern Africa—one that incorporates the insights of environmental history—can revive the study of the Zulu military legacy by suggesting some ways in which environmental factors contributed to the evolution of the Zulu military system and its lack of success in its final confrontations with European armies. Furthermore, if we turn our attention further to the west, towards the frontier of conflict between Europeans and Xhosa-speaking peoples, taking a fresh look can reveal a startling historical lacuna. For as Jeff Peires, the distinguished student of Xhosa history, suggests in his ground-breaking work, *House of Phalo*, the Xhosa-speaking nation in its one-hundred-year-long military engagement with the Dutch and British settlers of southern Africa evinced remarkable cultural and military innovation.

The chapter begins by looking at the precolonial military legacy that both Xhosa- and Zulu-speaking groups[4] inherited and the environmental factors that influenced this legacy. It then examines colonial encounters with both Xhosa- and Zulu-speaking groups during a period of almost constant warfare and skirmishing in the nineteenth century and analyzes how environmental factors can help to explain each group's markedly different military response to colonial campaigns. Lastly, it discusses the impact on the physical environment of the changing military strategies of both African and colonial armies.

Environmental historians who have focused their work on the African continent have produced one of the richest and most varied bodies of work in this burgeoning field. These works tend to follow from a tradition of agrarian studies and anthropology, and they focus on issues such as large-scale climatic shifts, crop production, strategies of resource extraction, management and mismanagement of natural resources by both Africans and colonial authorities, disastrous development schemes, and land-use policies with regard in particular to livestock rearing.[5] The literature of military history in Africa is similarly extensive, with close attention paid to every detail of famous campaigns such as that of the British against the Zulu kingdom in 1879.

There is almost no work, however, that begins to look at ways in which historians might fruitfully combine military and environmental history.[6] For example, the most recent effort to synthesize the secondary literature in the area of African environmental history contains very few references to military matters.[7] Since the majority of African societies in precolonial and colonial times were exposed to warfare, either in expanding or defending their land and herds, or raiding for, or protecting, people in the era of the slave trade, there is a good case to be made for renewed attention to be paid to military concerns and ample opportunity for historians to do so.

The chapter attempts a historical approach in which southern African environmental and military history are brought together and used holistically. It points out the ways in which military preparations, strategic decisions, and actual fighting have impacted the physical environment, but focuses on how both the physical environment and differing perceptions and imaginings of the physical environment as a military landscape shaped the course of warfare in a tactical and strategic sense. This approach allows us to understand more clearly why the Zulu campaigns were fought as they were, to acknowledge the level of innovation exhibited by the Xhosa speakers, and to begin to question these new developments. Differing physical environments and differing perceptions of environmental constraints drove the course of warfare for both Africans and Europeans.

Changing Military Landscapes

In recent years, more and more environmental historians, drawing on an extensive legacy of analyses in the field that incorporate cultural or intellectual approaches, have begun to focus their studies on the role of human perceptions of the environment.[8] Underlying this historical approach is the notion that the same physical environment can be thought of as multiple, differing, landscapes depending on the differing individuals or segments of societies that are viewing and thinking about it. Many factors—such as the importation of new ideas about nature or an awareness of increased technological abilities—can quite literally create new landscapes.

Military history has, in a narrow sense, been aware of this notion of perceived landscapes for a long while. As a military scientist has written, "strategy involves a combination of applied geography and psychology."[9] People developing strategy look at the terrain, the actual physical environment. They formulate their approach based on the environmental constraints of the landscape, their understanding of strategy and tactics, and their ideas about the nature of the technology they can wield while fighting in the physical environment. Surveying a battlefield, or plotting the course of an extended campaign, military strategists combine an appreciation for terrain, their ingrained understandings, and perceptions of technology, to arrive at an understanding of the physical environment based on its ever-changing military possibilities. I would like to call this understanding a military landscape. Thus, the notion of a changing military landscape builds on the concept from environmental history that a given landscape is an entity whose reality depends on the perspective of its viewer, and it attempts to use this concept in the service of military history.

Precolonial Origins, Environments, and Landscapes

Both Xhosa- and Zulu-speaking groups derive from a migration into southeastern Africa of Bantu-speaking Africans from further north in Africa, and their languages and cultures are closely related. It is necessary to develop a quick sketch of the different physical environments in the regions where the two groups settled, and the aspects of their precolonial culture that they held in common. In this way, we might begin to sketch out the different military landscapes that presented themselves to Xhosa and Zulu speakers as they confronted colonial forces.

The ancestors of the Xhosa and Zulu speakers settled the southeastern sections of Africa, from Delagoa Bay (26° south latitude) in the north to Algoa Bay (34° south latitude) in the south, along a zone of mixed ecological niches that extended from the Indian Ocean coast about one hundred and fifty miles to the interior. A line about five hundred miles from the Cape of Good Hope, where the average annual rainfall became twenty inches or less, and rain-fed agriculture was no longer feasible, halted settlement in the west.[10] The coastline was ragged and treacherous; few people ventured much farther than the tidewater edge. Heading inland, a coastal belt of rainforest extended about thirty to fifty miles into the interior, rising up the slopes of the coastal mountain range and wringing any moisture out of clouds streaming into the interior. In the rain shadow behind the mountains, pasturage and rain-fed agriculture became an uncertain proposition. Microclimates dominated the mountain slopes as river valleys tended to be overgrown with vegetation. Large open grasslands completed the scene.[11]

Grasses could be divided into two kinds: sourveld on the upland leas was suitable for grazing only in the spring while the young grass shoots were in their infancy; sweetveld, grazeable year round, was found lower down the mountains and in the river valleys.

The physical environment was fairly uniform across the region of settlement, except towards the west, where the Xhosa speakers had extended their kingdoms. Here, several inland mountain ranges towered over the plains, and the terrain, while following the general geographic pattern that characterized the eastern reaches of the region where Zulu speakers became established, was more densely forested and more frequently scarred by deep ravines. Three hundred miles of open country, inhabited by groups that resembled them in language and custom, separated the Xhosa and Zulu speakers. These groups served as a buffer for many years, absorbing refugees and subject to invasions. After European encroachment began, from the west via Cape Town and the new harbor at Port Elizabeth onto the periphery of land claimed by Xhosa speakers, and from the east via Delagoa Bay in present-day Mozambique, these groups were sheltered from the immediate imposition of colonial rule and among the last to be subjugated in South Africa.[12]

The African settlers of this region of southeastern Africa who later became differentiated into Xhosa speakers and Zulu speakers and those in between faced two critical factors: the need for a transhumant lifestyle to move cattle and other domesticated animals to different pastures throughout the year, and the need to ensure the success of their agriculture, chiefly sorghum but also millet and maize. At different times of the year, cattle needed to be moved to different microclimates within the whole ecological zone. But crops had to be planted and tended in areas with the right combination of soil type, access to water, and sunlight. These needs and the common cultural inheritance on which the African groups drew contributed to societies that shared habits of warfare and cattle raising, along with a political organization centered on chiefly power.

Cattle were the preeminent source of wealth in society, and as such, featured as the chief means by which those in power attached clients to their rule. The importance of cattle cannot be overstated. Chiefs came to be known by the names of their prize bulls. Young men aspired to two or three cows in order to begin a herd by which, ultimately, they might pay bride wealth for a wife and begin their own homestead. Chiefs and older men controlled access to cattle and prescribed the movements of the herds. While these provisions held the young men under their sway, they also ensured that the precious, small, and vulnerable ecological niches on which the cattle depended, especially in times of drought, did not become overexploited. Having chiefs and their counselors in charge of the distribution of land for farming and the movements of the cattle herds meant that the division of labor within society fit the ecology of the region.

Young boys herded the cattle and were capable of moving far from homesteads in search of pasturage. Because the cattle were herded in common, there was less possibility of the cattle belonging to certain individuals overgrazing essential areas. Women tended the gardens near the settled homesteads while the men, gathered together under the chief's rule, served as defenders of the valuable agricultural land. The men supervised the cattle herding and spent a great deal of time hunting, procuring meat and skins, and as a corollary, scouting the surrounding area and maintaining a defensive perimeter.

The chiefs' power lay in the amount of labor they could mobilize and thereby the amount of cattle they controlled. The threat of people leaving their control was ever-present and was the cause of most wars. Wars as they occurred in precolonial times were largely ritualistic affairs. Often, the issue was one of dynastic succession as chiefs attempted to keep breakaway groups within their fold. At other times, men fought over slights or insults, or marriage transactions gone awry. Observers commenting in the nineteenth century, including Xhosa speakers, often compared the political and military situation in precolonial Xhosaland to the system of clans at work in Scotland.[13] One colonial official observed: "This tract of country … is inhabited by clans of a remarkable race called kafirs, each clan having a chief who is assisted in governing by a council, and owning a certain portion of territory within defined limits."[14]

The technology and strategy of warfare emphasized large, open field battles where neither side could launch a "screened attack."[15] Warriors, armed with a large cowhide shield and eight to ten assagais or throwing spears apiece, rushed towards each other, hurling insults and spears, but rarely making contact. In a particularly pitched battle, one side (almost always with the chief and his sons and advisors leading the charge) attempted to engage the enemy at close quarters with a shorter stabbing spear or a club with a heavy, bulbous end—the knobkerrie—keeping the center of the lines engaged while an encirclement was attempted by both flanks. Casualties were low; women and children were spared the blade and instead captured and incorporated into the victors' homesteads. However, warfare did not always hold to this preordained cultural form. The wars of extermination waged by the African settlers on their Khoisan (Bushmen or Hottentot) neighbors, who often survived on subsistence raiding of flocks and supplies, prove the exception to the military strategy described above.[16]

As population pressure increased, most severely in the east of the region, where Zulu speakers settled, the unpredictability of rainfall became a major source of conflict. Chiefs employed rainmakers, hoping to facilitate the continuation of chiefly rule. But when major droughts hit and quality pastureland became scarce, dispersed groups began to consolidate and fight for control of cattle and grazing rights. The weight of climate and resource cycles was most keenly felt in the more marginal and arid zones in the east, where, additionally, demographic growth led to more extreme population pressure on the scarce resources.

The twin factors of climate and environment began to change the precolonial political and military culture, especially in the eastern section of the region, where increasing contact with European ivory and slave-traders, sporadically from the mid-sixteenth century but with increasing importance beginning in the mid-eighteenth century, presented additional pressures.[17] Before I discuss these changes, their environmental components, and the impact they had on military organization and culture, it is crucial to acknowledge one other aspect of precolonial culture that had a critical role in the formation of new modes of fighting.

Hunting of birds, antelope, and large predators such as lions and leopards was an integral part of precolonial society and one that historians have overlooked as the truly critical social and cultural activity that it was. John MacKenzie, in *The Empire of Nature*,[18] was one of the first historians to call attention to African hunting. MacKenzie focused on hunting as a subsistence activity, with elites using the activity to divide up the land under their control and tie up the productive resources of their subjects' labor time. This is a limited view. Historians, in the light of developments in cultural and environmental history, need to give African hunting renewed scholarly attention. Writing in the context of segregation and apartheid, many historians overlooked the copious references to hunting that appear in the colonial archive.

Yet, as the early-twentieth-century Xhosa historian, John Henderson Soga, states in his anthropological study, the "Xosas are essentially a hunting people … hunting was all-important."[19] Soga notes that groups lived "largely by means of the proceeds of the chase," and that they would migrate in search of game. He remarks on the use of hunting dogs, and the rituals involved in killing the prey. Other contemporary observers echoed Soga's attention to hunting as providing all the meat consumed by the Xhosa.[20]

Most importantly, Soga distinguishes between two forms of hunting, an "ordinary hunt," the *i-ngqina*, that took hunters out from their villages for a day, and the *i-pulo*. A *pulo* was convened by a "chief of importance for it [was] a tribal affair." The chief gathered many family groups together at his kraal, where the weapons were individually blessed by the *um-xobisi* or "armer." Then the party set out, accompanied by women and girls with food and camp implements, for the hunt, which would last for weeks or even a month.

The *pulo* took place in a designated forest, bounded by grassland. The region's ecological niches mentioned earlier allowed for the growth of such isolated forests. Here, the "clans" were assigned roles, some as beaters, moving through the forest, others stationed on the edge of the forest. More men with dogs on leash stationed themselves beyond the forest to corral any breakaway game.[21] John Brownlee, a keenly observant British missionary who established the first permanent mission within Xhosa-land, described hunting by Xhosa speakers as an "active and animating amusement":

> *Though not, like the poor Bushmen, impelled to the chase to provide for their subsistence, they are passionately fond of it … They generally go out to hunt in large parties; and when they find game in the open fields, they endeavour to surround the animals, or drive them to some narrow pass, which is previously occupied by long files of hunters, stationed on either side, who, as the herd rushes through between, pierce them with showers of assagais.*[22]

Hunting was so ingrained in Xhosa culture that it figures prominently alongside references to creation, agriculture, and personal salvation in the first recorded literary effort by a Xhosa speaker, Ntsikana's "Great Hymn" of the early nineteenth century. The hymn which begins "*Ulo Tixo omkulu, ngosezulwini,*" or "The Great God, He is in Heaven," and contains the lines "Thy blood, why is it streaming; Thy blood, it was shed for us," also has the following: "The Maker of the stars …The Maker of the blind … The trumpet sounded, it has called us … As for his hunting, he hunteth for souls."[23]

I want to highlight two aspects of precolonial culture that follow from the important cultural position of hunting. Every man was a hunter and thus potentially a warrior. Each maintained a selection of weapons, a set of clothing and shoe coverings capable of dealing with stone, rock, and thorn. Each was trained from an early age to follow spoor, throw assagais with accuracy, and deal deadly blows with the knobkerrie. As they grew up, men graduated from herd-boys to hunters and warriors. But both activities prepared them for a life of hardship, teaching them to rely on the natural world and to discover and remember the many features of the terrain around them. Hunters were ready and trained to mobilize at short notice, and to march long distances with skimpy provisions. Whether hunting trips were intended to serve, in part, as military maneuvers and reconnaissance is hard to establish. Clearly, though, hunting parties resembled military campaigns with differing formations, regiments, and tactics for the situations that parties might encounter.

Any activity so integrated into the marrow of society attracted the attention of young men and, thus, a culture of militarism clothed in hunting garb may well have emerged. Youngsters certainly trained for the chase as well as for war, honing their weapons skills and developing their endurance. A reevaluation may be in order for the numerous colonial and African auxiliary complaints of cattle-raiding parties from Xhosa-land, in particular, affecting the eastern Cape frontier. Overall, renewed attention to precolonial hunting seems to suggest a more martial culture in precolonial society than has previously been surmised.

In moving from an understanding of precolonial culture to an understanding of how Zulu- and Xhosa-speaking societies became differentiated especially with regard to warfare, it is important to remember that colonialism brought with it many new tools, diseases, strategies, and military technologies. The important introduction of corn, or maize, which tolerated drought conditions better than other crops, benefited both groups and allowed for a surge in population.

Epidemic diseases, too, swept through the areas, but without the dramatic casualty figures noted in other frontier zones around the world.

The high degree of contact and cultural transmission along the frontier zone between Xhosa speakers and the Dutch and English, compared to that between the Zulu and the Portuguese, exposed the Xhosa speakers more completely to innovations such as the horse and, of course, the gun, and left them better able to adapt to them. But it is crucial to remember that both were available to Zulu speakers, especially once the thriving port of Durban began to flourish in the 1840s. In both regions, a market in ivory and other animal-derived trade goods such as horns and hides had long existed; guns and gunpowder were a crucial component of the trade.

Zulu Warfare

Starting from a common precolonial culture, Xhosa and Zulu speakers diverged in cultural terms, especially, in the ways in which they came to confront colonial warfare. New historical research points out that, during the process of cultural differentiation, environmental factors such as population pressure resulting from new food crops and differences in the physical environment surrounding each group were key. As a result of the different paths taken by each society, war leaders when confronted by colonial encroachment came to envision starkly different military landscapes. These landscapes were based in part on differences in terrain, but largely they derived from contrary martial cultures.

Much of what the general public and lay historians take to be common and established knowledge about the rise of the Zulu kingdom and King Shaka in the early nineteenth century in particular has recently been called into question by historians working both inside and outside South Africa. Beginning with work by Julian Cobbing[24] that questions the actual existence of the Mfecane—the perceived series of wars and dislocations in southern Africa arising from the military campaigns of the Zulu state and proceeding wavelike into the interior as groups jostled for cattle, captives, and land—scholars have reevaluated most historiography in light of the biases that Cobbing identifies. He suggests that European settlers and slavers invented the notion of the Mfecane and the tyrannical nature of Shaka, and exaggerated his role in state building and warfare, in order to provide themselves with an alibi for their slave-raiding activities in the area. A new consensus has yet to emerge, but when it does, it will probably include the following aspects.[25]

In the early nineteenth century, the Zulu kingdom was the last stage in a long series of political and cultural consolidations in the well-watered, relatively open country from the Thukela River in the west to Delagoa Bay in the east. As a result of overpopulation and shifting climatic conditions, groups consolidated to gain access to grazing and agricultural land that included all of the ecological zones noted earlier, and was thus suited to maintaining food production and healthy cattle during periods of lowered rainfall. These groups were probably also responding to opportunities to control the ivory trade with Delagoa Bay[26] and defending themselves against predatory states sponsored and in some cases aided by Portuguese slavers operating to their east. As a result, consolidation of political control and the ability to mobilize large segments of society as a standing army became critical.

Gump's synthesis of the historical literature on the rise of the Zulu kingdom points to the "dynamics of agricultural production" as an early factor in political consolidation, as groups looked for land that required less time in fallow. Later, cattle and the land they required became all-important because cattle were the currency by which men acquired labor power in the form of wives or potential clients.[27]

Given an unstable environment and the need for defensive security, cattle became even more prominent as a mobile source of wealth and status. Elites gained more incentive to assert control over their subjects. Zulu-speaking polities grew in size and in the degree to which their leaders separated their men, especially younger men, from their allegiance to their individual homesteads, and instead mobilized them by age-group. In Gump's words, the Zulu "modified their traditional circumcision sets into multifunctional age-set regiments."[28] These new regiments were known as *amabutho*.

In the late 1810s, an illegitimate son of one of the group's chiefs arose to take power over his group and then to consolidate neighboring groups under the cultural identity of the Zulu clan. His name was Shaka. Shaka took the developments in his society to their natural extreme. He completely removed the *amabutho* from their homesteads and instead made them vassals of the state. Only after many years of service in the king's regiments could the young men gain access to cattle and thereby to wives. Shaka revolutionized the tactical approach of his army but not to the extent with which history has credited him. He did not introduce the short stabbing spear, but may well have perfected its use. Similarly, he turned the overwhelming number of mobilized soldiers under his control into a strategic juggernaut. Wars changed from the largely symbolic confrontations of precolonial culture into all-encompassing affairs. The enemy was either slaughtered or completely subsumed into Zulu culture. Cattle and land were confiscated.[29] Many groups of people led by clan leaders or prominent warriors fled from the areas now controlled by the Zulu state.

It is my contention that Shaka and the generals who preceded him built an army and a military structure that was particularly adapted to the terrain, or physical environment, in which they fought their campaigns. In order to prosper as a society, they needed to gain access to a wide-ranging territory incorporating varied ecological niches. They mobilized warriors from the breadth of the territory and tied their individual fates into the success of the kingdom as a whole. Thus, they could bring a huge force to bear on any group that mobilized in the old way, by regional affiliation. Because they held such a vastly superior strategic position and numerical advantage vis-à-vis their opposition, their tactics of engagement and encirclement worked to perfection. The groups they encountered fled or surrendered; seldom if ever did they flee to defensible positions, or fight a rearguard action. The use of the horse and even the gun was unnecessary, because of the success the Zulu armies enjoyed with their overwhelming numerical advantage.

The terrain where the Zulu speakers lived was relatively open compared to that of the Xhosa speakers. This geography meant that the large Zulu armies could move quickly, keeping their entire force intact, and bring it to bear in an overwhelming fashion. Their set-piece battles were fought in open country, where large tactical maneuvers became practical, and it was possible to coordinate the movement of large bodies of troops without interference from trees, brush, mountains, or valleys. Their opposition had few natural citadels of dense forest and soaring mountains to which to flee, in which to hide their cattle, and from which to fight a defensive war. They were either conquered or they fled. The Zulu armies thus had little experience in assaulting a well-defended position.

Zulu military culture was built on a brilliant understanding of the military landscape of the region, and it enjoyed every success. With its success, it became dependent upon the notion of overwhelming frontal attacks. These attacks relied on the fact that just about every man of fighting age was mobilized into the army and forced to demonstrate his courage on the battlefield in order to advance into the ranks of married and successful elders. These adaptations gave the army its overwhelming size and its ability to dominate a smaller group by sheer ferocity. But they also led to a military mindset that would prove particularly unsuccessful—with one notable exception—in confronting colonial forces.

The results of the confrontation between the Zulu *impis* (or armies) and groups of Europeans employing guns and defensive firing tactics are nothing less than startling. In the initial confrontations in the 1830s with Dutch Boer trekkers in the interior, frontal assaults cost the Zulu army a dramatic number of casualties. On December 16, 1838, on the banks of the Ncome River, five hundred well-armed male Afrikaners with sixty supply wagons drawn up next to each other in a circle and two cannons defended themselves from this enclosed laager against an estimated ten thousand Zulu warriors. The Zulus conducted repeated waves of a frontal attack, leaving three thousand Zulu dead, but not a single fatal European casualty.[30] Yet the Zulu military ethos remained conservative and, despite a stunning victory at Isandhlwana in 1879,[31] the Zulu kingdom was defeated without much resistance and with scant attempts to make tactical or strategic adjustments to the confrontation with Europeans and their guns.

To sum up, the Zulu state and armies that confronted colonial cannons and guns had changed dramatically from the precolonial organization noted in the first section. Drought and population pressure encouraged a society that could operate over a wider range of ecological niches and exert control over smaller groups that might overexploit sensitive areas. To do this, the state needed the most valuable land and it mobilized its whole society in order to develop a huge military presence capable of conquering and maintaining control over a wide area. The generals used this overwhelming force to great effect with coordinated frontal assaults made possible by the open physical environment in which they confronted their opponents.

The new organization and methods of fighting had significant consequences for the physical environment where the Zulu kingdom held sway. The kingdom actively sought to clear a buffer around its key towns by depopulating the region, allowing grazing and agricultural lands to return to their wild state, and probably encouraging the rise of diseases that flourished in dense bush and among the wild antelope that repopulated the area. Animal populations almost certainly rose in number from earlier years, leading ultimately to the establishment of various game parks in the area. The cattle herds of the region became even more concentrated and certainly wreaked havoc wherever they were pastured. Agriculture in the kingdom's center intensified, and quite likely began the processes of soil degradation that continue through the present day. And diseases associated with clustered human settlement, such as cholera, almost certainly became more prevalent.

Why did the Zulu armies, when they encountered European firepower, persist with frontal assaults that devastated their numbers and gained relatively little success?

My answer is that the Zulu-speaking generals' particular military landscape was skewed towards this result. The terrain on which they confronted the Europeans was open and suited to frontal assaults, with few places to hide and fight defensively. But more importantly, the Zulu-speaking generals were beholden to a martial culture that had evolved along with the success of the Zulu armies. As the military culture adapted to the new realities of warfare with the Europeans, the older military mindset overpowered any conception of the limited defensive possibilities inherent in the terrain, in part because more prudent tactics would have seemed cowardly. Zulu society had, in the process of gaining domination over its hinterland, acquired a fatal flaw that resulted in the death of far too many of its warriors.

Xhosa Warfare

Having tried to explain why the Zulu approach to warfare that evolved over the course of the nineteenth century remained so dramatically unchanged in the face of staggering losses during frontal assaults on European positions in the 1870s, I will now try to account for the equally startling degree of change exhibited by the Xhosa speakers. Unlike the Zulu speakers, who chose to confront the British by using the military landscape they had developed during their years of effective campaigning against African foes, Xhosa speakers showed remarkable innovation in developing a new military landscape. Their new vision quickly rejected the tactics of frontal assault inherited from their precolonial military culture in favor of an understanding that combined their knowledge of the unique terrain of their region, with its many thick forests, high mountains, and deep ravines, its cycles of drought and rain; an appreciation of new technology in the form of the gun and the horse; and a startling strategic and tactical innovation that I think was based on the central role of hunting in their precolonial culture. The British came to call this approach "Caffre warfare" or "bush-fighting."

It is even more stunning to reflect that this change occurred in the years between the defeat of a large Xhosa army in a frontal assault on Graham's Town in 1819 and the renewed declaration of hostilities in 1834. Our explanation must begin with the Xhosa precolonial military landscape and the ways it differed from that of the Zulu. Both military landscapes derived from the common culture described above, and their divergence can be partly explained by looking at environmental factors.

Abundant pastureland, and a lack of the demographic pressure on grazing land that drove developments to their east, allowed Xhosa speakers to accommodate to drought cycles by moving their herds to fairly accessible pasturage. The stress of drought does seem to have occasioned conflict, as the strong defended their supplies, but once the rains returned cultural organization reverted back to its usual model.[32] As a result, political centralization did not occur as it did among the Zulu speakers; in fact, decentralization of political power was the norm, as is demonstrated by the incorporation into the Xhosa polity of various Khoisan herding groups living to the west of the Xhosa speakers. The physical environment, with its dense vegetation, hilly terrain, and impenetrable ravines, limited communication among groups to a great degree, rendering any attempts at political centralization considerably more difficult. The need to centralize from a defensive point of view was small, as Xhosa speakers did not face pressure from slavers as did Zulu speakers, and first met encroaching Europeans in the late 1700s. The struggles over land that resulted were initially fought on a fairly equal footing.

Unlike the east, where in the seventeenth, eighteenth, and especially early nineteenth centuries, a powerful state began to mobilize warriors from a broad region in order to control a vast array of resources and defend itself effectively, those military conflicts that did occur among the Xhosa speakers remained local in scale. Conflicts arose over insults traded between clans, or in one case the seduction of a wife of one chief by another. The last battle of this kind fought exclusively between Xhosa speakers was on the pitted plain of Amalinde, and while it featured more brutality than was usually the case, it can serve as an example of such a conflict.

An army led by the young Chief Maqoma, sent by his father, Ngqika, to take revenge on his great-uncle Ndlambe, found a small force of Ndlambe's army in open country next to the Amatola mountains. Maqoma led a massed charge, fighting in the conventional manner with assagais and knobkerries. The Ndlambe warriors broke ranks and retreated. But the army in pursuit ran straight into the main body of the Ndlambe troops, who had been hidden in the forest and who now enveloped their attackers and engaged them in hand-to-hand fighting.[33]

The victors at Amalinde, inspired by the charismatic war leader and magician, Makana or Nxele, and building on their success against Maqoma, sought to revenge British commando raids and annexation of territory, with a large-scale invasion of the colony in 1819. This invasion ended when a heavily armed but numerically insignificant force of British soldiers and Khoisan irregulars, aided by muskets and cannons, defended the small village of Graham's Town. Hundreds of Africans soon lay dead on the field of battle. Never again in their continued resistance would Xhosa speakers launch a sustained and suicidal assault against a heavily defended European installation.

The Xhosa speakers instead withdrew and in 1835 fought an entirely different type of war, one that featured the adoption of horses for ease of movement and withdrawal,[34] the gun as a means of attack, and tactics that, in part, can be seen to have drawn on the approaches of hunting parties in preparing ambushes. John Brownlee, quoted earlier in this chapter, noted that Xhosa-speaking hunters would "go out to hunt in large parties; and when they f[ou]nd game in the open fields, they endeav[oured] to surround the animals, or drive them to some narrow pass, which [wa]s previously occupied by long files of hunters, stationed on either side, who...pierce[d] them with showers of assagais."

Reporting to his superiors on the progress of the war of 1835 between the British colonial authorities, their allies, and many, though not all, members of the Xhosa-speaking group, the governor of the Cape Colony, Sir Benjamin D'Urban, a distinguished veteran of the Peninsular Campaign against Napoleon, described many of the features of a new kind of colonial warfare, one that a later governor would characterize as "warfare of the most completely guerilla and desultory nature"[35]:

It is asserted that only 18 men have fallen ... in the paltry skirmishes with such an enemy, most formidable in ambush, a want of activity alone would have caused loss ... The enemy had by some means received a considerable supply of ammunition ... [I] had five thousand men, many "no better than the Caffres themselves, if so good" responsible for 30,000 square miles of country at least ... from Algoa Bay to Bashee, an extent of country full of ravines and fastnesses, in the possession of 20,000 warriors, expert, vigilant, and active; the troops occupied the ground alone they stood on. An ordinary letter could not be conveyed from one post to another without a detachment of 10 or 20 men, according as the country was open or wooded. The waggons required strong detachments as escorts. The difficulties of a Caffre warfare ... are known only to those who have witnessed them; and if the conflict (although the Caffres would make no stand in the field) was unequal, I maintain, the Caffres, in their warfare, had the advantage, their object being plunder, and to cut off every straggler. Sic magnum comparare parvis. The British force in Caffreland was situated precisely amongst Guerillas, like the French army in Spain.[36]

And as if to force home the point that the Colonial Office in London had little idea of the threat posed by the resurgent Xhosa speakers, D'Urban mentioned a meeting where he made overtures of peace:

They assembled 4,000 warriors, many armed with guns, and a numerous cavalry; they rose in their pretences, and talked of rights and grievances. The chiefs pointed to their warriors, who, in discordant and terrific yells, responded to the appeal. They did not appear to regard the conflict as unequal.[37]

This extraordinary transformation in warfare took place after the failure of the frontal assault at Graham's Town. Certainly, it had precedents in the frontier warfare that commenced on the eastern frontier roughly in the 1770s. But 1819 marked the first extended invasion of the colony by the Xhosa speakers, and the most brutal and extended campaign of retribution from the British. After 1819 the frontier wars of 1834-35, 1846-47, and 1850-53 became notable for the ever-increasing cruelty of campaigning on both sides. In between each declared war were periods of détente, with various degrees of violence and stock theft by both sides. The wars came to follow a pattern of Xhosa speakers invading the colony in small parties, taking cattle and burning farms, followed by swift retreat into inaccessible areas of their territory. Then the colony would mount a campaign, and invade Xhosa speakers' land looking for cattle to confiscate, homesteads to burn, and crops to destroy. Since most Xhosa speakers fled with their cattle and food supplies into defensible mountainous areas, the British troops conducted search-and-destroy missions. All the while, Xhosa warriors harassed the British supply lines, lured the soldiers into ambushes, and led them on extended marches through rough terrain.

Throughout the war years, Xhosa speakers came to rely increasingly on the gun, the horse, and a new tactical approach. On February 6th, 1835, the Graham's Town *Journal* reported an attack on nearby Fort Willshire:

> *On Saturday last a daring and successful attack was made by the Kafirs on the cattle guard and herds stationed at Fort Willshire. A corporal and three privates of the 72nd Regiment, together with two armed Hottentots, had been sent out on duty, as usual, and were about a thousand yards from the fort when a body of Kafirs about 300 strong, and partly mounted and armed with guns, rushed down from a neighbouring hill. The guard fired eight or ten shots, but were soon overpowered by numbers and killed. The affair was witnessed by the troops in the Fort, and immediate assistance was afforded, but the enemy succeeded, notwithstanding, in escaping with the sheep which had been in charge of these unfortunate men. Immediately on completing the massacre, the Kafirs assembled on the side of a hill in view of the Fort, but were quickly driven from this position by a few shots from a nine-pounder. The Fort was extremely weak, from the number of men absent on commando, and an effective pursuit was thereby rendered utterly impracticable.*[38]

This skirmish is notable for the hit-and-run tactical approach adopted by the Xhosa speakers along with their use of guns and horses. By 1851, the commanding general on the frontier asked for money from London to buy "light Grey Jackets" for the men of the 73rd Regiment whom he intended to employ in "very active service in the Bush." Besides being too warm, he pointed out, the "red jacket from its Color, as well as texture, is peculiarly unfitted for South African Warfare, serving in the Bush as a direct object of the Kaffir, whose skill as a Marksman is now by no means to be despised."[39]

Along with embracing the new military technology, Xhosa speakers used the terrain and climatic features of their surroundings to conduct their warfare. During the war of 1834-35, one British officer noted they chose the "intricate defiles which skirt the Fish River as a place of rendevous ... No situation could have been chosen better suited to this purpose than that selected. It is thickly wooded; it abounds with terrific precipices, and rugged defiles; and is thereby effectually defended, without immense labour, from the approach of horsemen or wheel carriages."[40]

One notable environmental feature that distinguished all of the war years was devastating drought. Right before the battle of Graham's Town, missionary George Barker wrote of Xhosa-land that "all the verdure is completely burned up."[41] And a despairing James Read bemoaned the continuing conflict in 1847: "We seem as far from peace as we were at beginning ... [there is] no forage to be had for Dragoons or boor's horses ... [this is] one of the severest droughts we have ever had there is no grass—where there was any the Caffres have set fire to it so that the oxen that have to drag the waggons have been dying by the hundreds."[42]

With terrain and drought restricting the movement of British troops and supplies, the Xhosa speakers turned to ambush tactics. The following incident from the war of 1834-35 is instructive:

> [A Colonel Rademeyer, following the spoor of horses and cattle, saw fire in the bush and taking a party of 40 men] descended into kloofs [ravines] in a track which he followed down, until the rocks on the opposite side approached near each other, and the bush presented an almost impassible barrier to further progress. On reaching this point, he was suddenly attacked by a numerous party of the enemy, in fact he was completely surrounded before he had any intimation of the presence of an enemy. A fire of musketry was poured from the rocks around

them, and the enemy rushed boldly on and among them,
assegai in hand, from the bush stabbing and bearing down
every one before them.[43]

These tactics reached their apogee in the war of 1846-47 when a force led by Maqoma intercepted a supply train with 125 wagons. Ascending into the mountains, the officers saw Xhosa-speaking warriors massing on the hillsides, but the warriors did not attack. The road then passed through a narrow defile. As the train was halfway through, the warriors "came leaping out of the bush, and as the drivers fled, cut the oxen [of the leading wagons] from their traces, immobilizing the train."[44]

On a strategic level, the tactics and approach perfected in earlier wars came to full fruition in the war of 1850-53. Early on in the war, the *Eastern Province News* could declare that "Maqoma remains proud master of the field. He has outgeneralled the First Division. He has cut down its men and for the remainder he must entertain something very nearly approaching to supreme contempt."[45]

The time has arrived for historians of southern Africa to begin to acknowledge and analyze the extraordinary nature of the military innovation as shown above which, for varied historical reasons, has not drawn the attention of scholars. In every popular or academic account of the period, the change is remarked upon, but taken for granted. In one of the few instances where a historian has asked why and how tactics and strategy changed to such a remarkable extent, the biographer of Maqoma lays the change entirely at his feet. Stapleton asserts that "Maqoma realized that the only way to defend his chiefdom from both the Europeans and Ngqika was the acquisition of horses and firearms and the development of new tactics. Beginning in late 1825, Jongumsobomvu [Maqoma's praise name] instructed his warriors to steal horses from settler farms and acquire muskets covertly from white traders. Drawing on his experience at Amalinde, the young chief formulated rudimentary ambush tactics."[46] But the issue remains far too complex to be laid at the feet of one man and his strategic brilliance.

In comparing the Xhosa speakers' decisions to change their approach to colonial warfare with other guerrilla campaigns worldwide, scholars have concluded that guerrilla warfare in particular is determined by geographical setting and demands an "intense exploitation of the character of the landscape."[47] Xhosa speakers in concert and individually assessed the physical environment that surrounded them and saw that their best chance in confronting the colonialists lay not in frontal assaults or their old military culture, but in moving themselves and their own property, chiefly cattle, into defensible positions, namely the interior mountain ranges or deeply forested river valleys, and then marrying the martial aspects of their culture that derived from the hunting sphere with the new technology of horse and gun to produce a hit-and-run system of warfare, where raids, dispersal of booty, and inaccessible terrain kept pursuers at bay. When the pursuit arrived, it was often broken down into parties small enough to be lured into ambush. Clearly, the mobility gained by the use of the horse helped in this style of warfare. So too did the gun, which was far more effective than thrown spears at a distance, and kept pursuers pinned down until a short distance charge with the stabbing spear became practicable. Undertaking warfare during times of drought aided the Xhosa speakers by slowing down and concentrating their pursuers, whose oxen-drawn supply wagons relied far more upon fresh supplies of grass and water than the Xhosa speakers' horses did.

In countering the new challenges facing them, the British turned to their own understanding of the military landscape. They realized, first, that they would have to pursue the Xhosa speakers into the hostile terrain with their superior military technology, and second, that they could destroy the resistance by removing food sources in the form of cattle and by chasing war parties around until fatigue became absolute. Thus, they increasingly conducted their campaigns as total wars, engaging and destroying the Xhosa speakers' material base until war became an exhausting and futile stalemate. Then, more often than not, the Xhosa speakers surrendered.

As early as the war of 1834-35, the British conducted just such a search-and-destroy mission, described in the *Graham's Town Journal* of February 13th, 1835:

> *The thick bushy kloofs were studded with the enemy's kraals; on seeing us they raised their cry of alarm, and turned out their cattle, which were soon in the bush and out of view. We cannonaded them where most Kafirs seemed assembled [presumably women and children included], and immediately penetrated the extraordinary thick bush at 3 points; the enemy*

*pertinaciously defended himself, and disputed every inch of
ground, but the gallantry and perseverance of our troops
overcame all obstacles, which were of no ordinary nature.*[48]

After so many wars, however, the British, from military as well as
other concerns, confiscated much of the territory of the Xhosa speakers,
including its defensible positions such as the Amatola mountains, and
incorporated these sections into the colony. Governor Cathcart, writing
in 1852, defended his actions to his superiors in London with the
following strong words. "The Amatola mountains ... proved a citadel
which effectually commands all the surrounding districts of country
which lie at their base ... The forcible ejectment of a powerful and
warlike people from a country to which they are attached, of which
they well know the great value in respect to its own natural resources,
and the great influence it gives to the possessors over all surrounding
districts, can only be rendered permanent by the occupation of it by
some superior power."[49]

It is in this British response that we can note the effects of the style
of warfare adopted by the Xhosa speakers on the environment. Their
refusal to be engaged directly on the field of battle meant that the
British took to destroying the means that enabled the Africans to avoid
capture. Burning of crops and confiscation of cattle led to the
regeneration of forest and savannah, and, with a reduction in hunting,
likely increased the population of wild animals. Increasingly, after each
frontier war, the British realized that their one means of security was
to physically confiscate land and the natural citadels that the land
contained. They, therefore, pushed the remaining Xhosa speakers onto
smaller and smaller plots of land, which quickly became degraded and
over exploited.

With the notion of a changing military landscape, we have seen
how the Xhosa speakers drew on new technology and old methods to
re-envision the possibilities inherent in the physical landscape in which
they fought. Environmental factors proved critical to the ability of the
Xhosa speakers to turn to guerrilla warfare. Without natural fortresses,
their wars would have been short and disastrous. These geographical
features were much more abundant in the west than in the east, as
were wooded and fractured areas of country. But having these natural
features was no guarantee that the choices that were made would turn
out as they did. Unlike their Zulu counterparts, Xhosa warriors did

have improved access to guns and horses. More importantly, their society was inherently flexible and their government decentralized. Each man was a warrior and a hunter, as well as a member of a homestead. This hunting tradition flowed seamlessly into a martial tradition that emphasized flexibility and personal competence. Unlike in Zululand, martial respect could be gained in many different forms, not just from bravery in frontal assaults.

While the brilliance of individual generals like Maqoma should not be underestimated, the transition to guerrilla warfare had far deeper societal roots. The leaders relied on a new military landscape, one that incorporated the societal martial/hunting culture and its tactics. The terrain and the culture enabled the guerrilla approach.

Conclusion

The campaigns and battles of the colonial conflicts had little direct impact on the environment. The numbers of combatants on each side and the limited technology employed meant that few scars were left on the land. But, the ways of fighting, so dependent on environmental factors, did have long-term environmental implications. In the case of Zulu speakers, the development of their kingdom had centralized and intensified grazing and agricultural pressures on key areas, leaving large, unpopulated zones as buffers. Once their frontal assaults failed and they fell under British dominion, the land was apportioned as it was found, leaving the Zulu speakers on degraded land and leading to continually increasing demographic pressure on these areas of settlement.

The colonial government in its pursuit of the Xhosa speakers learned valuable lessons in hunting a hit-and-run foe. It went after and destroyed the army's resources, not the army itself. This strategy would be used to great effect in subsequent wars such as the conflict known as the South African War, or Boer War, and its legacy can be found as well in the United States' use of Agent Orange in Vietnam. As an army's technological ability to destroy natural resources increased through the centuries, the environmental impact of the strategy grew exponentially. The British also discovered that the most effective way to defeat the guerrilla tactics of the Xhosa speakers was to force them onto smaller and smaller parcels of land, where they were more easily kept under surveillance, and where they could be denied easy access to their strongholds in the case of war. These small plots of land became environmentally degraded and are now unsustainable. Ironically, many of the strongholds that saw the bloodiest fighting have become prized national parks and wilderness areas with high plant and animal diversity resulting from their isolation.

A key aspect to the continued vibrancy of environmental history as a field will be its ability to demonstrate that environmental approaches can yield valuable insights into fields of history that might not concede any potential connections at first glance. The starkly different ways in which Zulu- and Xhosa-speaking peoples engaged with colonial forces has been seen to be a product of the physical environment in which they lived, the environment's influence on a shared culture resulting in the development of two distinct precolonial cultures, the varied adaptation of new technology, and access to different understandings of the military possibilities inherent in the terrain and climate. These factors together produced a martial state favoring overwhelming frontal assaults in the case of the Zulu and facilitated the frontier, guerrilla, style of warfare adopted by the Xhosa. Each society, when confronted by the British, looked over the terrain on which the battles were to be fought and saw different military possibilities, different military landscapes.

Using the notion of a changing military landscape allows for a historical analysis that incorporates both the physical environment and changing human perceptions of it. While Zulu-speakers would have had a far more difficult time fighting a guerrilla-style war on their home turf (because of its flat, open appearance and lack of natural, forested redoubts) than Xhosa speakers did on theirs, they failed to do so not because of the terrain, but because the previous, overwhelming success of their military approach had created a military culture in which guerrilla tactics lay beyond their ken. They may very well have conceived of these tactics, but implementing them would have violated the principle that honor and respect derived from bravery in frontal assaults. Xhosa speakers, on the other hand, when confronted with a new challenge in the form of British forces, quickly learned that their hunting techniques could serve as a resource for military tactics. These cases suggest that environmental historians may find fertile ground for future inquiry in examining whether societies and individuals have drawn upon the skills and ideas formed in the process of relating to the physical environment for use in other aspects of their existence.

Moreover, to reverse the formulation offered above, actions taken to influence a skill, idea, or relationship between people and the physical environment might have consequences that reverberate far beyond the initial, environmental, association. Along these lines, it is interesting to note how European settlers in southeastern Africa—once the open warfare of the colonial had been settled in their favor—attempted to thoroughly remove any trace of the African hunting traditions that were so central to precolonial life.[50] Many reasons lie behind this desire to keep the hunting of game an exclusively white occupation and sport. Cutting off hunting denied the Africans a central, and age-old, connection to their own land and transferred this connection to the settlers. This usurpation was yet one more way of demonstrating that the land had been conquered and commandeered. The settlers succeeded to the extent that many contemporary Xhosa speakers are unaware that their forebears were hunters.[51] But I would contend that in addition to trying to divorce Africans from the natural world and thereby reinforce their status as landless laborers in the colonial system, the settlers, consciously or unconsciously, understood the powerful associations between hunting and its military legacy and thought that by destroying one they would be killing off the other.

Notes

1   Jeff Peires, *The House of Phalo: A History of the Xhosa People in the Days of Their Independence* (Berkeley: University of California Press, 1981), 139.
2   James O. Gump, *The Dust Rose Like Smoke : The Subjugation of the Zulu and the Sioux* (Lincoln: University of Nebraska Press, 1994).
3   John Keegan, *A History of Warfare* (London: Hutchinson, 1993), 28.
4   Terminology in the southern African literature is notoriously difficult. I am using Xhosa speaking to refer to groups sometimes known as the southern Nguni and Zulu speaking for the northern Nguni, or collectively, as Nguni. As with French and Italian, isiZulu and isiXhosa are the evolving end-result of an amalgamation of regional dialects. The Nguni languages are especially noted for their incorporation of three Khoisan "clicks." By referring to the groups as Xhosa speakers, I am stressing the fluidity of ethnicity in the period. A person was not born a "Xhosa" but would have been identified in large part by their primary language.
5   See for outstanding examples: James Fairhead and Melissa Leach, *Misreading the African Landscape : Society and Ecology in a Forest-Savanna Mosaic, African Studies Series 90* (Cambridge, U.K.and New York: Cambridge University Press, 1996); James Ferguson, *The Anti-Politics Machine: "Development," Depoliticization, and Bureaucratic Power in Lesotho* (Cambridge, U.K. and New York: Cambridge University Press, 1990); Robert Harms, *Games against Nature: An Eco-Cultural History of the Nunu of Equatorial Africa, Studies in Environment and History* (Cambridge, U.K. and New York: Cambridge University Press, 1987);

Thomas T. Spear, *Mountain Farmers: Moral Economies of Land & Agricultural Development in Arusha & Meru* (Oxford: James Currey and Berkeley, CA: University of California Press, 1997); James L. A. Webb, *Desert Frontier: Ecological and Economic Change Along the Western Sahel, 1600-1850* (Madison: University of Wisconsin Press, 1995).

6   An example of such a work which, however, does not set out to be environmental history is David Lan, *Guns & Rain: Guerrillas & Spirit Mediums in Zimbabwe, Perspectives on Southern Africa,* (Berkeley: University of California Press, 1985).

7   James McCann, *Green Land, Brown Land, Black Land: An Environmental History of Africa, 1800-1990* (Portsmouth, NH, and Oxford: Heinemann; James Currey, 1999).

8   See, for example, Steven Stoll, *The Fruits of Natural Advantage: Making the Industrial Countryside in California* (Berkeley and London: University of California Press, 1998).

9   Patrick Edmund O'Sullivan and Jesse W. Miller, *The Geography of Warfare* (London: Croom Helm, 1983), 81.

10 Leonard Monteath Thompson, *A History of South Africa*, rev. ed. (New Haven, CT: Yale University Press, 1995), 4-5.

11 There is a large likelihood that, as in other semi-arid grassland regions around the world, people helped to maintain grassland through burning regimens.

12 See for example William Beinart, *The Political Economy of Pondoland, 1860-1930* (Cambridge and New York: Cambridge University Press, 1982).

13 See for example John Henderson Soga, *The Ama-Xosa: Life and Customs* (Lovedale, South Africa: Lovedale Press, 1932), 376.

14 Cape Archives, Imperial Blue Books of South Africa, 1/13 2, Cathcart to Pakington, Fort Beaufort, 20 May 1852, 107.

15 Ludwig Alberti, *Account of the Tribal Life and Customs of the Xhosa in 1807* (Cape Town: Balkema, 1968).

16 Peires, *House of Phalo*, 135-60.

17 John Wright and Carolyn Hamilton, "Traditions and Transformations: The Phongolo-Mzimkhulu Region in the Late Eighteenth and Early Nineteenth Centuries," in Andrew Duminy and Bill Guest, eds., *Natal and Zululand from Earliest Times to 1910: A New History* (Pietermaritzburg: University of Natal Press, 1989), 61.

18 John M. MacKenzie, *The Empire of Nature: Hunting, Conservation, and British Imperialism* (New York: St. Martin's Press, 1968).

19 Soga, *Ama-Xosa: Life and Customs.*

20 Alberti, *Account of the Tribal Life and Customs of the Xhosa in 1807*, 23.

21 Soga, *Ama-Xosa: Life and Customs*, 376-77.

22 Brownlee, quoted in Monica Wilson, "The Nguni People," in Monica Wilson and Leonard Thompson, eds., *The Oxford History of South Africa*, I, (New York: Oxford University Press, 1969), 110.

23 South African Library, MSB 294, Bleek collection, 1 (22).

24 Julian Cobbing, "The Mfecane as Alibi: Thoughts on the Battles of Dithakong and Mbolompo," *Journal of African History*, 29 (1988), 487-519.

25 My synthesis is taken largely from Gump, *The Dust Rose Like Smoke*, and, especially, Carolyn Hamilton, *The Mfecane Aftermath: Reconstructive Debates in Southern African History* (Johannesburg: Witwatersrand University Press; Pietermaritzburg: University of Natal Press, 1995).

26 Wright and Hamilton largely dismiss the demographic explanations for consolidation in favor of those offered by the opportunities inherent in the

ivory trade. Interestingly, they claim the regiment system evolved to support hunting expeditions. Wright and Hamilton, "Traditions and Transformations," 61-65.

27 Gump, *The Dust Rose Like Smoke,* 33-34.

28 Ibid., 27.

29 Leading revisionists of the Mfecane, led by Julian Cobbing, argue that the changes in the Zulu state were of a defensive nature in response to settler raiding activity. The expansionary actions noted here seem to contradict this line of thinking.

30 Gump, *The Dust Rose Like Smoke,* 63.

31 Here, the Zulu army handed the British their greatest numerical loss to date in colonial wars, over one thousand men killed. But this battle is the quintessential exception that proves the rule, and is perhaps better relegated to a footnote in history. For once, the British did not man a defensible position and had severe problems in getting ammunition to their soldiers—Zulu frontal tactics worked to perfection. Subsequent battles in the campaign fit the pattern of huge Zulu losses with very few European casualties. After Isandlwana, the final battle at Kambula saw twenty thousand warriors charge a well-defended position, losing two thousand men compared with eighteen British dead. Ibid., 98.

32 Monica Wilson makes this point in her extended essay, *The Interpreters;* she notes that violence erupted during droughts when competition for grazing became most acute. Monica Wilson, *The Interpreters* (Grahamstown, South Africa: 1820 Settlers' National Monument Foundation, 1972).

33 John Milton, *The Edges of War: A History of Frontier Wars (1702-1878)* (Cape Town: Juta, 1983);Timothy Joseph Stapleton, *Maqoma: Xhosa Resistance to Colonial Advance, 1798-1873* (Johannesburg: J. Ball, 1994), 29-30.

34 Unlike their counterparts among the Indian nations of the American West, the Xhosa adopted the use of the horse over one or two, not tens, of decades. This development has not been given the historical attention it deserves, and, unfortunately, it only warrants a footnote in this chapter. The topic in and of itself would make for a fascinating article. One reason for the lack of attention may be that the use of horses was restricted to Xhosa royalty, important warriors, and the well-off, and, hence, it did not penetrate the entire society from top to bottom as it did in other frontier cultures. Also, evidence for increased use of horses in the archival record, though widespread, is fragmented and simplistic, usually consisting of just a passing reference to the fact that Europeans had suddenly encountered Africans mounted on horses. I have not seen evidence of Xhosa people themselves talking about the reasons for, or the means of, the acquisition of horses. Nonetheless, even though the use of horses did not radically change the entire breadth of Xhosa society as it did, for example, among the Plains Indians, it did change the conduct of their warfare in ways that I have tried to indicate—making them more flexible tactically and aiding considerably in their adoption of guerrilla-style warfare—and it was an important dimension in the new military landscape in Xhosa-land, one in which increased mobility led to a compression of geography.

35 Cape Archives, OPB 1/13 2 Smith to Earl Grey, King Williams Town, 5 February 1852.

36 Cape Archives, OPB 1/9 1, D'Urban to Earl of Aberdeen, Graham's Town, 19 September, 1836, 17.

37 Ibid., 33.

38 Cape Archives, A519 *Graham's Town Journal,* 6 February, 1835.

39 Cape Archives, GH 23/20 Smith to Earl Grey, King William's Town, 3 February, 1851.
40 *Graham's Town Journal,* 13 February, 1835.
41 Council for World Missions microfiche, London Missionary Society, SA Incoming, Box 7, Folder 5 A, Barker to Theopolis Burder, 15 September 1818.
42 LMS, South Africa, Incoming, H-2130, Box 22, Folder 2, Fiche # 315, A, Read Senior to Tidman, Kat River, 31 August 1846.
43 *Graham's Town Journal,* 20 March 1835.
44 Milton, *The Edges of War,* 156-60.
45 Ibid., 213.
46 Stapleton, *Maqoma 1873,* 47-48.
47 O'Sullivan and Miller, *The Geography of Warfare,* 110-26.
48 *Graham's Town Journal,* 13 February 1835.
49 OPB 1/13 2, Cathcart to Pakington, Fort Beaufort, 20 May 1852, 108-9.
50 This was accomplished by forcing Africans off their land and onto crowded, game-free, reserves, enforcing poaching laws on public lands, and passing laws that restricted Africans' use and ownership of hunting dogs.
51 Personal communication courtesy of Patricia Hayes, University of the Western Cape, South Africa.

Gettysburg and the Organic Nature of the American Civil War

Mark Fiege

In spring 1863, in the midst of the American Civil War, General Robert E. Lee voiced his greatest concern as commander of the Confederate Army of Northern Virginia. "The question of food for this army," he said, "gives me more trouble than anything else combined."[1] Lee's statement hinted at a crucial feature of the American Civil War: the fundamental connections between fighting forces and the natural world. Nineteenth-century armies like Lee's needed not only food, but weaponry, materials, and animals, all of which, in one way or another, came from the Earth. Moreover, to engage and defeat its enemy, such an army had to mobilize against that enemy and also against weather, terrain, disease, and other natural conditions. That sustenance for his army would so preoccupy Lee in early 1863 suggests the importance of environmental factors in the conduct of the Civil War. As much as it was a political, economic, social, or cultural conflict, the war was an organic struggle in which two societies fought to use and overcome nature in the service of competing national objectives.[2]

Gettysburg, the most famous and perhaps most important battle in the Civil War, exemplified the environmental conditions that motivated and influenced the larger conflict. Lee's comment about food came but a short time before he led his army of some seventy thousand men north into Pennsylvania, where the Federal Army of the Potomac, a force of about ninety thousand, defeated them in a bloody fight that went on for three days. Lee and his soldiers made their bold foray north in late spring-early summer 1863 for several reasons, each of which had some connection to the natural environment. One reason, not to be minimized, was that Virginia no longer could supply Confederate forces with the food, materials, and animal power that they needed to continue the war. With its rich farms untouched by combat, Pennsylvania was the answer to Lee's question of where he might find sustenance for his army. The resulting campaign and battle had additional ties to the biophysical world, as each side tried to use terrain and resources to its advantage.[3]

Gettysburg showed that the Civil War was a duel in which two social and biological entities battled one another in the medium of nature. This was a struggle not simply between economies—between the stereotyped industrial North and agrarian South, for example—but between ecologies. To procure the food and materials necessary for the struggle, each side remade its relationship with nature. Each attempted to fashion a system of extraction, production, and supply, a military ecology, so to speak, the goal of which was to defeat the enemy. In the end, the North proved more proficient than the South in turning grain, flesh, and ore into the tools of victory. The land that sustained the Union armies, and the systems of production and exchange embedded in that land, overwhelmed the Confederacy's war-fighting capacities. Ultimately, the Union's ecological supremacy had important military implications that transcended the Civil War and that became clear only with the passage of time and the advent of other, more global, conflicts.[4]

∞

The origins of Gettysburg were rooted in the environmental causes of the Civil War itself. North and South fundamentally disagreed over the fate of the American West. The two regions had opposing visions of western social development, of the kind of society that western soil, areas such as Kansas, should foster. These competing land ideologies, as they might be called, impelled the two sections into war. Southerners wanted the West—needed it, in their view—for cotton and slavery. Cotton and other staple crops had exhausted southern soil. Meanwhile, expanding markets beckoned. Planters believed that their economic prosperity, indeed their very survival, depended on the westward expansion of their slave agriculture. Many northerners, however, especially "free soil" advocates, had their own dream for the West. Here should be a society of small white farmers and white free laborers. If plantations and unfree labor should take root, small farmers and wage workers could not compete. With western opportunity cut off, the North would wither and die. Neither side could see its way around the stalemate, and war was the consequence.[5]

Conflict over the West illustrated an important feature of the Civil War and of paradigmatic battles like Gettysburg: much of the struggle between North and South was over geographic space. Space is an important product of the nature-human dialectic and a crucial factor in history. Things are arrayed in space, across the Earth, and they have objective distance from one another. Yet space is not simply a neutral physical condition; it is also a product of culture, society, economics, and politics. People define space—"the West." And often, as with the North and South during the Civil War, they fight over the definition of space and its potential uses. North and South competed for space and also used space as an instrument of power. The side that dominated and defined space, either in the West or in actual theaters of combat, was the side that would prevail.[6]

Union armies sought to control space in order to deprive the Confederacy of the food and materials that it needed to continue fighting. Here is one important reason why Lee worried about food in the spring of 1863, and why he would lead his men north to acquire it. By early 1863, Union forces had captured much of the Mississippi and besieged Vicksburg, the last major Confederate stronghold on the river and a key to the economic security of the Confederacy. They had also blockaded southern seaports and captured a good deal of southern farm land. Each acre behind northern lines deprived Rebel stomachs of so much corn or pork. A society that could not procure enough food would lose its ability to fight.[7]

But the geographic noose that Union forces placed on the South was not the only source of its deprivation and hunger. By 1863, much of the region was in environmental collapse, from battle destruction and the exigencies of war, and from drought, flood, cold, and disease. Ultimately a range of environmental factors hurt the Confederacy— and especially such states as Virginia—and played a strong role in motivating Lee and his army to head north.[8]

Across the South, armies from both sides stripped and ruined agricultural landscapes. Union forces took food and horses for their own use, and to deprive the enemy they destroyed crops and livestock along with farm machinery, barns, granaries, and other agricultural facilities. Confederate foragers, too, took what they needed from southern farms. This vast consumption and destruction of resources had side effects that further weakened the South's ability to provide for itself. The enormous Union and Confederate armies that crisscrossed the region regularly knocked down wood fences to allow for the passage of men and animals, and soldiers used the rails for campfires and shelter. Destruction of fences was a serious problem because it left corn and other crops vulnerable to wandering livestock.[9]

The Civil War's voracious appetite for men, animals, and labor perhaps did the most to hurt southern agriculture. The movement of men and horses from farm to army, the impressment of slave labor for military purposes, and the escape of slaves to the Union side made it difficult to keep land in production, even as women, girls, boys, and older men attempted to compensate. But the problem went even deeper, for the removal of labor had serious environmental consequences: on poorly tended or fallow land, weeds moved in, making it even harder for the remaining people on farms and plantations to produce food.[10]

Along with these problems came a series of environmental disasters that by the end of 1862 seriously hurt the South. Drought in Virginia and other southern states drastically reduced grain and hay harvests and caused livestock to starve. A massive flood devastated the Delta, a vast section of rich farmland along the lower Mississippi River. Bacterial afflictions, including glanders, anthrax, and hoof-and-mouth disease, killed or weakened thousands of horses and mules. Disease visited even greater ruin on the South's hog population. At the start of the war, the southern landscape was rich in swine. Although these animals were not as plump as their northern cousins, they were relatively great in number: the ratio of hogs to humans in the South was double that in the North. But much of this great resource disappeared in a viral epidemic, hog cholera, that swept the region. In Mississippi during 1862, disasters compounded, as drought killed corn and cholera killed hogs.[11]

A serious shortage of salt made the Confederacy's livestock problems even worse. The South could not produce enough of the precious mineral to compensate for the imports that it lost because of the war. It tried to boost its output, but Union forces only redoubled their efforts to destroy Confederate saltworks. The resulting "salt famine" had serious environmental consequences. Without salt, horses and mules were less robust and more prone to hoof-and-mouth disease and other maladies. Without salt, the South could not preserve pork, beef, and butter from the ravages of bacteria. Without salt, the South could not properly tan leather.[12]

As the conflict wore on, agriculture deteriorated across the Confederacy and people grew hungry, malnourished, and increasingly desperate. At the start of the war, Southerners tried to boost the food supply by growing less cotton and more corn, but environmental degradation and the disruption of war undercut this effort. Not only did the total acreage in food production fall, but so did yields per acre: land already exhausted by cotton could not sustain the intensive cropping of corn. Civil disorder resulted, as in the spring of 1863 when hungry women from Richmond to Mobile staged "bread riots" in which they marched to granaries and stores and robbed them of food. Rebel soldiers also suffered, and their bodies grew thin as they complained of short or spoiled rations. With so many animals dying and leather in short supply, many men went into battle with no shoes. Desertion increased as conditions degenerated. For some soldiers, especially the poorest, the need to return home to care for land and families became irresistible.[13]

Conditions for Lee's Army of Northern Virginia continued to decline through the winter of 1862-63 and into the following spring. Freezing temperatures, snow, rain, and muddy roads paralyzed the army, which settled into winter camp along the south bank of the Rappahannock River. Lingering around their campfires, huddled in tents or in crude log, rail, and canvas huts, the shivering soldiers waited for the weather to change and for orders to begin moving again. The ravaged, depleted landscape supplied them with almost no food, and other parts of the Confederacy contributed little of the flour, corn, rice, peas, dried fruit, sugar, or bacon on which the soldiers subsisted. Lee wondered if hunger itself might not be a more formidable foe than the Army of the Potomac, bivouacked on the opposite bank.[14]

In early spring, disease appeared among the famished troops. First came scurvy, a vitamin deficiency caused by a lack of fresh fruits and vegetables. In a sensible but ultimately inadequate response, soldiers fanned out across the countryside to gather sassafras buds, wild onions and garlic, lamb's quarter, and poke sprouts. Then came typhoid, one among many diseases of the gut that afflict people living close together under unsanitary conditions. A Civil War army was a "city without sewerage," the Massachusetts cavalry veteran Charles Francis Adams, Jr., later wrote, and it takes little effort to envision the passage of microbes from oozing bowels into water sources, onto hands and food, and into human mouths. Typhoid did not overwhelm the Army of

Northern Virginia, nor was the Army of the Potomac immune to such diseases. But the outbreak was one more indication of the deteriorating conditions that Rebel soldiers suffered in 1862-63.[15]

Another sign of trouble was the degradation of the army's horses and mules, the animals upon which all fighting forces utterly depended. Under the best of circumstances, the life of a Civil War cavalry horse or draft animal was hard, but during the winter of 1862-63 it was especially bad for those creatures in the Army of Northern Virginia. The surrounding disturbed and exhausted farms furnished little fodder. Hungry, malnourished, emaciated, the horses and mules were more vulnerable to harsh weather and diseases. Troops had a difficult time finding replacements when the animals died, so depleted was the landscape. When spring came, Lee worried that the survivors might be so weak that his army would be unable to move. Without healthy mounts, cavalrymen could not ride; without fit horses and mules, supply wagons and artillery would stand idle.[16]

Loss of geographic space and resources, a deteriorating landscape, environmental disasters, and impoverishment at last set into motion a series of events that culminated in the Gettysburg campaign. The Army of Northern Virginia sent out detachments on forage sweeps for food and animals. One force went into West Virginia; another advanced as far as North Carolina. Lee and his staff even contemplated a raid into Kentucky. But these efforts yielded little, for the rest of the South was in much the same condition as Virginia. Lee's thoughts then turned to a more drastic plan of action.[17]

Perhaps the solution to his army's plight, and to the plight of the Confederacy as a whole, lay in the North. A daring Rebel foray into northern space might break the Union's geographic stranglehold and reverse the South's geopolitical fortunes. Such a bold maneuver might pull Federal forces away from the besieged and strategically important Mississippi River town of Vicksburg. By invading Pennsylvania and there defeating the Army of the Potomac, the Confederates might win the recognition of foreign governments and deliver a knockout blow to northern morale. No less important, moving the conflict north would give Virginia farms a rest and allow Confederate forces to feed on Pennsylvania's rich landscape. In sum, a radical movement across the Earth's face—a sudden inversion of the war's spatial relationships— might restore the environmental basis of southern power and turn the war in the Confederacy's favor.[18]

A stunning victory over the Army of the Potomac in early May 1863 at Chancellorsville, a tiny Virginia crossroads, filled Lee and his army with confidence and provided them the opportunity to head north. Union General Joseph Hooker, certain that he could destroy the Rebels and open the way south to Richmond, initiated the fighting. He ordered his army across the Rappahannock River and then east and south in anticipation of smashing into the Rebels from behind. The odds against the Army of Northern Virginia were overwhelming. Not only did it suffer from a dearth of food, equipment, and horsepower, but it was vastly outnumbered. With a substantial portion of his army foraging for supplies, Lee could muster only about sixty thousand men to face the Yankee onslaught of some one hundred ten thousand. But what the "gray fox" lacked in manpower he made up for in nimble maneuvering. In direct violation of the military doctrine that a massed force was strongest, Lee and his commanders twice divided their army and so deftly flanked and routed the Union attack. After first clashing with the enemy in a thicket of trees and brush called the Wilderness, the Rebels pushed the Yankees back across the Rappahannock River. The way was now clear; the momentum would shift north as Lee wanted, not south as Hooker had planned.[19]

Chancellorsville, and the Gettysburg campaign that followed, showed the importance of terrain to Civil War combat. Engaging the enemy was nothing if not the art and science of moving thousands of men and animals across the land in such a way as to maximize one's power at the expense of the enemy. At Chancellorsville, roads, river, bluffs, hills, forests, fields, and fences served as tactical objectives and as instruments of war. In the weeks to come, more features would be added to this list: mountains, valleys, orchards, railroad cuts, towns, buildings. Indeed, the Gettysburg campaign might be characterized as a massive duel in which each army struggled to use the land to its advantage. As weapon, shield, and prize, the terrain was never neutral.[20]

Lee and his generals formulated a plan for the northern push in which the Confederates would make extensive use of landforms and waterways. Shielded from the Yankees by the Rappahannock, the Army of Northern Virginia first would march northeast, through the Blue Ridge Mountains. Hidden by that range, the Rebels would then head north, down the Shenandoah Valley toward the Potomac River. After crossing the Potomac, they would continue north through the Cumberland Valley of Maryland and Pennsylvania, all the while using another north-south range, South Mountain, to obscure their whereabouts. Somewhere, perhaps around Chambersburg, York, or Gettysburg, they would turn and face the Army of the Potomac, which Lee knew would be searching for him and his men.[21]

Although Lee was personally familiar with the geography of his native Virginia as well as Maryland and Pennsylvania, his precise knowledge of the terrain owed much to a detailed map prepared by Jed Hotchkiss, a talented civilian topographer and mapmaker working in the service of the Confederacy. Hotchkiss and his map reveal much about the close connections between science, nature, and war in the Gettysburg campaign. In his youth and early adulthood, Hotchkiss studied nature because it fascinated him and because he loved it. His obsession resembled that of a contemporary, John Muir, the famous scientist, nature preservationist, and founder of the Sierra Club. But unlike Muir, who avoided the Civil War, Hotchkiss turned his knowledge of the Earth to military ends. Figuring distances, calculating grades, and plotting landscape features on maps were standard cartographic and engineering tasks and were crucial to military movement. An army could best outfox its enemy if it knew how far it must travel, the location of forests or river crossings, or how hard its horses would have to work pulling their loads uphill against gravity. The army that best knew nature, in other words, had the best chance of defeating the other side. Lee himself was an engineer, trained like so many officers at the United States Military Academy, and he appreciated the value of Hotchkiss's map. It was a model of the cartographer's craft, depicting in fine detail a broad swath of land from Virginia to Pennsylvania. It showed not only watercourses and major landforms but also cities, villages, roads, even individual farmhouses. It would guide Lee and his army to Gettysburg.[22]

In early June, the Army of Northern Virginia escaped the Army of the Potomac and headed north. Along the way, Lee masterfully deployed his army across the terrain. Prior to Gettysburg, he had divided his infantry force into two large corps, each numbering about thirty thousand soldiers. But Lee decided that a corps of this size was too large for the general in charge of it. Spread out through fields, forests, hills, or mountains, it was "always beyond the range of his vision, and frequently beyond his reach." So Lee divided the two large corps into three smaller, more manageable groups. To prevent them from getting in each other's way, he sent them north on separate roads at different times. To hasten their progress still more, he ordered them to wade across the Potomac at two fords rather than one. Such adroit manipulation of men, horses, and wagons in relation to land helped the Confederates enormously. They clashed with Union troops in skirmishes and minor battles at several places on the route north, but they eluded and outpaced the Army of the Potomac's main body. By the time they arrived in Maryland, they had gained two days, two revolutions of the Earth, on their opponent.[23]

Once in Pennsylvania, the Army of Northern Virginia systematically stripped the terrain. Rebel soldiers diligently rounded up horses, mules, cattle, and sheep, even searching out animals that farmers had hidden in remote corners of their properties or in nearby mountains. Exactly how many head the Confederates took is impossible to know, but the total was surely in the tens of thousands. The Army of Northern Virginia also requisitioned enormous quantities of food and other supplies. When marching through the countryside, the voracious men and animals emptied barns and granaries, ransacked larders and stores, devoured crops, and literally drank wells dry. In each town, officers summoned the citizenry and demanded food, clothing, saddles, harness, horseshoes, and other resources that the South's impoverished environment could no longer furnish in sufficient quantities. General Lee, always the proponent of civilized warfare, ordered his men to pay for what they took. Confederate money and promissory notes, however, had little if any value in the North. And often the troops paid nothing at all. In their view, plundering Pennyslvania's terrain, consuming its vast riches, was just retribution for the ruin that the Yankees had visited upon the South.[24]

By the end of June those Yankees were drawing near. They had started slowly. General Hooker was much less adept than Lee in negotiating terrain. When Hooker learned that the Confederates had departed for the North, he had tarried, thinking that he should strike south toward Richmond, now vulnerable to attack. Lincoln thought otherwise, and ordered him to find the Army of Northern Virginia. But Hooker had lost the initiative, and geographical obstacles on the way north compounded his army's disadvantage. Crossing the Potomac at a bottleneck of roads and bridges, infantry and supply trains became snarled. Rainfall then turned the roads into morasses of mud. Once in Maryland, however, the Union soldiers gained speed. After pausing briefly at the town of Frederick, they headed for the Pennsylvania line.[25]

On July 1, the two armies at last met just northwest of Gettysburg. The great duel for terrain had reached its climax. The initial clash drove the Army of the Potomac—now under the command of General George Gordon Meade—into a defensive position along a series of hills and gentle ridges just south of the settlement. From this high ground, the Union soldiers looked down on the Confederates, who advanced from the north and the west. Lee and his commanders faced a dilemma. Should they assault this formidable Union line? A trusted subordinate, General James Longstreet, thought that their opponent's position was too strong. He proposed that the Army of Northern Virginia instead shift to its right, to the south, and there take up a defensible position that would force the Union side to attack it. But Lee decided to challenge the Army of the Potomac directly. "The enemy is there," he said to Longstreet, pointing to the Army of the Potomac, "and I am going to attack him there."[26]

Historians have tried to understand what impelled Lee to go forward under such unfavorable circumstances. Their explanations are plausible, but overlook the geographical and environmental contraints on the Army of Northern Virginia. A turning movement of the sort that Longstreet advocated would have been difficult and might have allowed the enemy to cut off Lee's safe route back through Cashtown Gap, a mountain pass that led to the Cumberland Valley and Chambersburg, the Confederate base of operations. And to delay the battle further might not have been possible in light of the army's need to live off the countryside. The Confederates could not afford to sit and wait while Union forces threatened their food-gathering activities. As Lee himself explained, "We were unable to await an attack, as the country was unfavorable for collecting supplies in the presence of the enemy, who could restrain our foraging parties by holding the mountain passes with local and other troops. A battle had, therefore, become in a measure unavoidable." Lee's decision to attack makes more sense when viewed in the context of the environmental problems and scarcity that drove him north in the first place, and that ultimately deprived his army of the supplies necessary to fight independently of local resources.[27]

For two days, Lee's men went forward bravely, their eerie, distinctive battle cry, the Rebel yell, rising from their ranks. First hitting the Union right, then left, and finally center, the Confederate forces tried to flank, divide, encircle, and disperse the enemy. But ultimately the Army of the Potomac's superior numbers, grim tenacity, and control of the high ground stopped the Rebel assault. Confederate Captain George Hillyer's assessment of one piece of contested terrain, Little Round Top, applied just as well to the entire Union line. "It was," he said, "the strongest natural position I ever saw." The failure on July 3 of one last all-out frontal attack, Pickett's Charge, finally exhausted the southern forces. On July 4, as a heavy rain fell, Lee ordered his diminished but still intact army on a long retreat back to Virginia.[28]

The war that Lee and other Confederate leaders had hoped to bring to a rapid and favorable close would go on for nearly two more years. Never again would a Rebel army enter northern space. All land in a sense now tilted against the South, all power now flowed downhill with the advancing Union armies.

❧

Gettysburg demonstrated just how much the Civil War was an organic struggle. The distinctive interactions of two societies with the natural world powerfully motivated the conflict. The failure of one society, the South, to procure the things that it needed to thrive ultimately compelled Lee's decision to go north. To defeat the enemy, men and animals had to be mobilized, not just against each other but also against the vagaries of weather, bacteria, and terrain. The "symbolic center of all American history," Gettysburg and the Civil War were all about biology, all about organisms in relation to their environment.[29]

Understanding the organic nature of Gettysburg allows us to see some of the ways that the Civil War combined ancient and modern military ecologies. The conflict had much in common with past wars because its armies lived so intimately with disease organisms, and because those armies relied on human and animal power for much of their movement. In addition, the Civil War was one of the last in which soldiers (mostly Confederate) drew much of their sustenance— food, water, energy, clothing—from household production and from the very landscapes on which they fought. But in certain respects the war had a decidedly modern cast. Most important, it was one of the first in which soldiers (mostly Union) drew much of their livelihood from agricultural and industrial production systems located in distant landscapes. In these ways and more, the Civil War—in environmental terms—was the last of the old and the first of the new.

The experience of the Union and Confederate armies with microorganisms was consistent with the past. Spoiled food, sick animals, loose bowels, and wounds that refused to heal showed the influence of bacteria, viruses, and amoebas, some of humanity's eternal foes— or partners—in life's travails. Like enormous fighting forces in previous centuries, Civil War armies were easy prey for an astonishing array of microbes. However effectively the Army of Northern Virginia and the Army of the Potomac maneuvered against each other, neither could evade their most persistent and debilitating antagonists.[30]

If the microorganisms that afflicted the ranks of Civil War armies harked back to an older military ecology, so too did the basic means by which Union and Confederate forces moved across the landscape. Historians have made much of the use of railroads in the Civil War, but what is so striking about Gettysburg is how little this modern technology mattered and how much both armies still travelled by their legs and feet. This was a conflict in which men marched much as armies had done for centuries. Indeed, a Civil War army's power often flowed from the ability of its soldiers to walk under conditions of extreme heat, cold, damp, exhaustion, or hunger. After the battle at Gettysburg, President Lincoln criticized General Meade for not pursuing the retreating Army of Northern Virginia with greater speed and vigor. Lincoln had no appreciation for the reality of the situation—that after a hard march from Virginia and then three days of hot, bitter fighting followed by a drenching rain, his soldiers were simply worn out and physically unable to move more quickly. Lincoln had the modern machine-age mentality, but his army was not a machine—it was a collection of organisms, of biological bodies, that quite simply got tired.

Not only did men have to walk and continually confront their physical limits, but the armies in the Gettysburg campaign relied heavily on the legs and feet of their animals. This was especially so for the Army of Northern Virginia. Read Lee's letters and dispatches from the winter of 1862-63 and one comes away with an image of a man deeply obsessed not just with the condition of his troops but with the quantity and quality of his army's livestock. To have ample horses and mules was to be able to move artillery, carry supplies, and send the cavalry out to find the enemy. To have too few animals meant potential paralysis and defeat. In stripping so many horses and mules from the Pennsylvania countryside, the Army of Northern Virginia showed just how much more in common it had with ancient armies than with modern ones.

Lee's army was also ancient in the simplicity and directness of its ecological connections to the land. The virtual hand-to-mouth existence of the Army of Northern Virginia is startling in retrospect. As Lee himself acknowledged, nothing was so important as the simple act of getting food. And nowhere in this war was the physical condition of an army so dependent on, so tied to, the physical condition of the land around it. The fat on Rebel soldiers literally waxed and waned in relation to the richness or poverty of the surrounding farms. Bodies, food, and environment were linked in an immediate and compelling way.[31]

In contrast to the Army of Northern Virginia, the Army of the Potomac exhibited more of the characteristics of a modern fighting force. Unlike the Rebels' simple, direct ecological ties to the land, the Union soldiers' links more often were long and complex, and connected them to distant and enormously powerful systems of mass production. Consider just the clothing that soldiers wore. Unlike the Rebels, who often went into battle wearing homemade clothing dyed a gray color that faded to butternut, the Union men's blue pants, coats, and hats came in standardized industrial lots. But even more important, perhaps, was the Army of the Potomac's access to food. Unlike their adversaries, Union soldiers did not have to scrounge their sustenance from the land around them. Unlike Lee, Meade did not have to worry about executing a tactical maneuver for fear that his army did not have enough food on hand to sustain it. The productivity of thousands of distant northern farms from New England to the Great Plains yielded barrels of preserved meat, hard dry crackers ("hardtack"), and other foods in such volumes that Union soldiers always would have the calories necessary to do whatever their commanders ordered. Sometimes the fare was of dubious quality, but the quantity was never in doubt.[32]

The Army of the Potomac's wastefulness perhaps provided the surest sign of its power and its modernity, its newness. The Army of Northern Virginia traveled light, each man carrying only the bare essentials. Soldiers in the Army of the Potomac, in contrast, often carried an enormous burden of clothing, blankets, and other equipment. If on campaign the weather became too warm and the load too heavy, the men simply discarded it by the side of the road. When the Union army marched in Virginia, poor civilians—whom the soldiers called "ready-finders"—followed behind, eager to scavenge the droppings. This juxtaposition of wealth and poverty, of well-endowed Yankees and destitute Virginians, provides a stark and telling picture of the North's fabulous command of resources and the South's relative environmental collapse. The South was ill, hungry, and dying; the North had become an awesome superorganism with the capacity to produce—and consume—virtually unlimited quantities of wool, meat, leather, flour, lead, iron, horses, and ultimately human life.[33]

The Army of the Potomac anticipated future American military forces that by the twentieth century projected their power around the world without the need to rely on local ecologies, even for water. The same material abundance that sustained the Army of the Potomac later supported American armed forces in Europe and the Pacific during the world wars, and in Vietnam, the Persian Gulf, Afghanistan, and many other places. Ultimately, the global reach of the United States arose from its ability to harness an abundant nature in the service of its military objectives. The Army of the Potomac, of course, did not travel as freely as its descendants. But to the extent that it moved independently of local resources, to the extent that it drew on reserves from far, far away, it had much more in common with the future than with the past.

The last of the old and the first of the new: in this simple summation is contained the powerful truths of America's organic Civil War. Examining the nation's great internecine struggle through the lens of environment thus yields a deeper understanding of the many ways that past and present, people and planet, are bound together. Such an approach points the way toward both a different military history and a revised sense of how virtually all realms of human experience are deeply embedded in nature.

Notes

1   Lee quoted in Glenn Tucker, *High Tide at Gettysburg: The Campaign in Pennsylvania* (Indianapolis, IN: Bobbs-Merrill, 1958; rpt. Dayton, OH: Press of Morningside Bookshop, 1973), 18.

2   Numerous works on the Civil War touch on environmental themes and so lend themselves to an environmental history interpretation. See, for example, Paul Wallace Gates, *Agriculture and the Civil War* (New York: Alfred E. Knopf, 1965), and Earl McElfresh, *Maps and Mapmakers of the Civil War* (New York: Henry N. Abrams, 1999). A handful of environmental historians have begun to write about the Civil War. Ted Steinberg, *Down to Earth: Nature's Role in American History* (New York: Oxford University Press, 2002), 89-98, offers a pathbreaking

interpretation. Timothy Silver assesses the environmental history of the Civil War in "An Environmental Historian's Civil War: A View from the Mountaintop," in the proceedings of the Porter L. Fortune Symposium on Southern History, forthcoming from the University of Mississippi Press. The only fully developed environmental history of the conflict is Lisa M. Brady, "War Upon the Land: Nature and Warfare in the American Civil War" (Ph.D. dissertation, University of Kansas, 2003).

3   The literature on the Gettysburg campaign and battle is enormous. A standard text that contains much information useful to the environmental historian is Edwin B. Coddington, *The Gettysburg Campaign: A Study in Command* (New York: Charles Scribner's Sons, 1968). For a recent account, see Noah Andre Trudeau, *Gettysburg: A Test of Courage* (New York: HarperCollins, 2002).

4   Donald Worster, "Transformations of the Earth: Towards an Agroecological Perspective in History," *Journal of American History* 76 (March 1990), 1087-1106, discusses subsistence and capitalist agroecological modes of production as a method of analyzing the ways that people have lived on the Earth. Although both Union and Confederate sides in the Civil War relied on capitalist modes, each side's mode had distinctive ecological and economic features. Each side, furthermore, oriented its mode to military ends. Perhaps it would be more precise to interpret the Civil War not simply as a contest of capitalist agroecological systems but as a conflict between two opposing military modes of production.

5   Environmental and geographic causes of the war can be gleaned from some of the leading overviews of the conflict. See, for example, James M. McPherson, *Battle Cry of Freedom: The Civil War Era* (New York: Oxford University Press, 1988), 6-307.

6   A recent useful text on spatial and geographic theory is Don Mitchell, *Cultural Geography: A Critical Introduction* (Oxford: Blackwell Publishers, 2000).

7   For figures on the reduction of land in production and for a map that depicts the Confederacy's radical loss of space to Union military forces, see Gates, *Agriculture and the Civil War*, 118, 126. Lincoln himself was acutely aware of Vicksburg's importance to the movement of resources through the Confederacy. See Geoffrey C. Ward, *The Civil War: An Illustrated History* (New York: Alfred A. Knopf, 1991), 212.

8   The problems of southern subsistence are covered in Gates, *Agriculture and the Civil War*, 3-126; Emory M. Thomas, *The Confederate Nation, 1861-1865* (New York: Harper and Row, 1979), 1-16, 120-44, 190-214; McPherson, *Battle Cry of Freedom*, 611-25; G. Terry Sharrer, "The Great Glanders Epizootic: A Civil War Legacy," *Agricultural History* 69 (Winter 1995), 79-97; William Blair, *Virginia's Private War: Feeding Body and Soul in the Confederacy, 1861-1865* (New York: Oxford University Press, 1998), 3-107, 202-6; Ella Lonn, *Salt as a Factor in the Confederacy* (New York: Walter Neale, 1933), 13-34, 188-203, 221-30; Mary Elizabeth Massey, *Ersatz in the Confederacy: Shortages and Substitutes on the Southern Home Front* (Columbia: University of South Carolina Press, 1952; rpt. Columbia: University of South Carolina Press, 1993).

9   Gates, *Agriculture and the Civil War*, 57-59, 73-83, 91-95, 111-15, 118-25.

10   Ibid.

11   Gates, *Agriculture and the Civil War*, 29, 56, 61, 67-68, 86-87, 90-92; Sharer, "The Great Glanders Epizootic."

12 Gates, *Agriculture in the Civil War*, 67-68, 80-81; Lonn, *Salt as a Factor in the Confederacy*, 13-34, 188-203, 221-30.

13 Gates, *Agriculture and the Civil War*, 116; Blair, *Virginia's Private War*, 73-76, 89; Bruce Catton, *Glory Road: The Bloody Route from Fredericksburg to Gettysburg* (Garden City, NY: Doubleday and Company, 1955), 273; Massey, *Ersatz in the Confederacy*, 80-83; McPherson, *Battle Cry of Freedom*, 611-25; Thomas, *The Confederate Nation*, 202-6; Russell Weigley, *A Great Civil War: A Military and Political History, 1861-1865* (Bloomington: Indiana University Press, 2000), 218.

14 On the subsistence, animal power, and health problems of the Army of Northern Virginia, see War of the Rebellion: A Compilation of the Official Records of the Union and Confederate Armies, Series I, Vol. XXV, Part II (Washington, D.C.: Government Printing Office, 1889), 598, 605-6, 627, 658, 666, 680-82, 686-88, 689-90, 695, 701-2, 703, 709, 730, 735-36, 747-49, 765, 793 (hereafter cited as O.R.); Clifford Dowdey, *The Wartime Papers of R. E. Lee* (New York: Bramhall House, 1961), 328, 400-410, 417-19, 434-35, 450-51, 551; Douglas Southall Freeman, *R. E. Lee: A Biography*, 3 vols. (New York: Charles Scribner's Sons, 1946), II: 415-17, 475-507, III: 245-53; Charles W. Ramsdell, "General Robert E. Lee's Horse Supply, 1862-1865," *American Historical Review* 35 (1930): 758-64.

15 O.R., Series I, Vol. XXV, Part II, 730; Dowdey, *Wartime Papers of R. E. Lee*, 418-19; Freeman, *R. E. Lee*, II: 494; Catton, *Glory Road*, 93-94, 122-23, 158-61; Adams quoted in Paul E. Steiner, *Disease in the Civil War: Natural Biological Warfare in 1861-1865* (Springfield, IL: Charles C. Thomas, 1968), 17.

16 O.R., Series I. Vol. XXV, Part II, 605-6, 627, 680-82, 689-90, 695, 701-2, 709, 747-49, 765, 793; Dowdey, *Wartime Papers of R. E. Lee*, 400-410, 551; Freeman, *R. E. Lee*, II: 417, 484, 491-92, III: 251-53; Ramsdell, "General Robert E. Lee's Horse Supply," 758-64; McPherson, *Battle Cry of Freedom*, 638-39; Coddington, *Gettysburg Campaign*, 16.

17 O.R. Series I, Vol. XXV, Part II, 684-85, 700-701, 710-12, 724-26; McPherson, *Battle Cry of Freedom*, 638-48; Gates, *Agriculture and the Civil War*, 95-96; Freeman, *R. E. Lee*, II: 492.

18 Blair, *Virginia's Private War*, 86-87; Coddington, *Gettysburg Campaign*, 3-25; Tucker, *High Tide at Gettysburg*, 17-20; Ward, *The Civil War*, 214; Weigley, *A Great Civil War*, 229-30; George Wheeler, *Witness to Gettysburg* (New York: Harper and Row, 1987), 1-18. In late summer 1862, Lee had attempted a similar strategy by leading his army into Maryland and ultimately to the battle of Antietam. See Henry Steele Commager, ed., *The Blue and the Gray: The Story of the Civil War as Told by Participants*, 2 vols. (Indianapolis, IN: Bobbs-Merrill, 1950), I: 171.

19 Bruce Catton, *The American Heritage Picture History of the Civil War* (New York: American Heritage, 1960), 291-92, 297-306; McPherson, *Battle Cry of Freedom*, 639-47; Ward, *The Civil War*, 201-11; Weigley, *A Great Civil War*, 223-39.

20 "Terrain is not neutral—it either helps or hinders each of the opposed forces." U.S. Army, Field Manual 100-5 (Washington, D.C.: Department of the Army, 1993), quoted in Harold A. Winters, Gerald E. Galloway, Jr., William J. Reynolds, and David W. Rhyne, *Battling the Elements: Weather and Terrain in the Conduct of War* (Baltimore, MD: Johns Hopkins University Press, 1998), 113.

21 The planning and execution of the Gettysburg campaign are covered in Coddington, *Gettysburg Campaign*, 3-25, 47-102, 105-107, 125.

22 William J. Miller, *Mapping for Stonewall: The Civil War Service of Jed Hotchkiss* (Washington, D.C.: Elliott and Clark, 1993), is the single best source. McElfresh, *Maps and Mapmakers of the Civil War*, superbly covers the work of engineers and mapmakers in relation to topography and other environnmmental conditions; Hotchkiss's map is reproduced on 128-29. For engineers' attitudes toward nature, see, for example, Raymond H. Merritt, *Engineering in American Society, 1850-1875* (Lexington: University Press of Kentucky, 1969), especially chapter 5, "The Manipulators of Nature."

23 O.R., Series I, Vol. XXV, Part II, 810-11 (quotation); Coddington, *Gettysburg Campaign*, 11, 22, 125.

24 On the plundering of Pennsylvania, see Coddington, *Gettysburg Campaign*, 23, 153-79; Commager, *The Blue and the Gray*, II: 594-96; William A. Frassanito, *Early Photography at Gettysburg* (Gettysburg, PA: Thomas Publications, 1995), 150-52; McPherson, *Battle Cry of Freedom*, 649-50; Tucker, *High Tide at Gettysburg*, 27-30.

25 Coddington, *Gettysburg Campaign*, 26-133.

26 Lee quoted in McPherson, *Battle Cry of Freedom*, 656. Historians have described, analyzed, and debated the battle of Gettysburg in excruciating detail. Among many excellent sources, the following are especially useful to the environmental historian: Coddington, *Gettysburg Campaign*; Frassanito, *Early Photography at Gettysburg*; Jay Luvaas and Harold W. Nelson, eds., *Guide to the Battle of Gettysburg* (Lawrence: University Press of Kansas, 1986); McPherson, *Battle Cry of Freedom*, 646-55; George A. Stewart, *Pickett's Charge: A Microhistory of the Final Attack at Gettysburg, July 3, 1863* (Boston, MA: Houghton Mifflin, 1959; rpt. Dayton, OH: Press of Morningside Bookshop, 1983); Weigley, *A Great Civil War*, 236-56. See also the many documents in O.R., Series I, Vol. XXVII, Part I, and O.R., Series I, Vol. XXVII, Part II.

27 See Lee's comments in O.R., Series I, Vol. XXVII, Part II, 299, 307-8, 309, 318.

28 O.R., Series I, Vol. XXVII, Part II, 399-400. Scattered throughout the O.R. and other sources are numerous comments like this about the "nature" of the terrain and the strength of the Union position.

29 Edward T. Linenthal, *Sacred Ground: Americans and Their Battlefields* (Urbana: University of Illinois Press, 1991), 89.

30 Steiner, *Disease in the Civil War*, 13, 33-34; George Worthington Adams, *Doctors in Blue: The Medical History of the Union Army in the Civil War* (Baton Rouge: Louisiana State University Press, 1952; rpt. Baton Rouge: Louisiana State University Press, 1996), 223; H. H. Cunningham, *Doctors in Gray: The Confederate Medical Service* (Gloucester, MA: Peter Smith, 1970), 165-66; Catton, *Glory Road*, 122-23.

31 On bodies as subjects of environmental history, see Christopher Sellers, "Thoreau's Body: Towards an Embodied Environmental History," *Environmental History* 4 (October 1999): 486-514.

32 Catton, *Glory Road*, 40, 42-43, 123-24, 179-80, 254-62.

33 Catton, *Glory Road*, 180; Blair, *Virginia's Private War*, 86. On the Confederacy's demise, see Thomas, *The Confederate Nation*, chapter 7, "The Death of the Nation."

The World Wars and the Globalization of Timber Cutting

Richard P. Tucker

> *Whether a state at war will experience victory or defeat is*
> *inextricably bound, often decisively, to the way it prepares*
> *for the awesome tasks before it, not just in defining a*
> *winning strategy but in locating and producing the huge*
> *resources necessary to implement whatever plans it*
> *has...*[1] —Gabriel Kolko, 1994

Introduction

From 1915 to 1918 the protracted stalemate of the Great War left the battle region of northern France utterly devastated. The unprecedented power of bombs and shells leveled cities and towns, gouged craters in farmlands, and reduced forests to battered crags and stumps. Yet two generations later, when Europe's forest historians met in 1979 at the French forest research headquarters in Nancy, they were treated to a field trip to see maturing tree plantations where battlefields and miles of trenches had been in 1918. Many thousands of acres had been reforested, suggesting that short-term damage to forests from warfare was not necessarily the same as long-term ecological degradation. Exploring the complexity of such issues, this paper traces major patterns of forest products extraction for the Great War and its even greater successor from 1939 to 1945. Both are called world wars, and indeed they demonstrated the combined capacity of industrial civilization, capitalist economic organization, and the nation-state to command strategic resources from virtually the entire biosphere in the crises of war among the major powers. But, as we shall see, the first of these wars, despite its horrendous toll in Europe, represents only a transition toward true globalization of use of strategic resources. Focusing on global forest resources, this paper surveys the extent to which the industrial powers had developed the international infrastructure of timber extraction and transport before war broke out, the intensification of those systems during the fighting, and some of the impacts of the two wars for postwar forest extraction and conservation.

The battle zones of the two world wars were only the core of the wars' unprecedented impacts on forests and forest resources, for the environmental impacts of warfare are not limited to territories where military campaigning goes on, or even the supply zones immediately behind the front lines. In modern times a far greater geographical reach reflects sources of timber supplies far from the battlefield. As industrial technology, including transport, advanced in power, scale, and reach, wars' demands provided acceleration in all operations of natural resource extraction, specifically timber cutting.

World Wars I and II illustrate the globalization of war's appetite for forest resources, and the extremely complex impacts of those wars on postwar consumption patterns. The contrast between the two wars also reveals the long strides that major powers made between the wars in their capacity to commandeer forest products during wartime crisis and to manage those resources for the longer run in peacetime.

The key role of military needs in accelerating logging, milling, and transport, as well as diversifying timber products and processing, showed the power of modern war to shape this entire segment of peacetime society's relations to the natural world.

Systemic effects reached ever farther from theaters of war, enabled by the new global web of railways, steamships, and port facilities. These factors were closely linked, as military operations always are, to the civilian economy: governmental forestry services, private timber contractors, capital flows, marketing systems, and so forth. In turn the wars created feedbacks into civilian economies and resource-extraction and management systems. They expanded patterns of exploiting nature, by expanding under the state of urgency the industrial, organizational, and financial capacity to penetrate farther and more efficiently into forest zones that had previously been largely untouched by modern society, and diversification of species used and products marketed. Finally, timber fellings during the world wars catalyzed large-scale postwar reforestation programs which transformed mixed-species forests into timber plantations.[2]

Precursors: Wars of Colonial Conquest

European navies had searched the world for strategically vital timbers since the sixteenth century, beginning the process of the modern state's long-range stockpiling of strategic materials for naval warfare. In the 1500s Spain began to exploit the mahogany forests of Cuba in its shipyard at Havana, while Portugal commandeered the timbers of coastal Brazil.[3] France imported masts from Scandinavia and the Baltic region as far as Riga and St. Petersburg in the 1600s, adding additional source areas in the Maritime Provinces of New France soon after.[4] Still more momentous, as Britain built the navy that would ultimately command the world's oceans, its Admiralty searched first the Canadian Maritime Provinces and New England, and ultimately the Malabar coast of southwestern India, for ships' timbers.[5] The distinctive military dimension of Europe's ecological imperialism had begun to reach the forests of the tropical world.

By the late 1800s the Dutch empire in the East Indies and Great Britain's far greater empire in India were fully capable of supplying tropical hardwoods to Europe for either peacetime or military use. Germany and France, on the other hand, had hardly begun to develop colonial administrations and timber exploitation in equatorial Africa, and were in a less strong position to utilize African timbers in the Great War.[6] In contrast to the European powers, the United States held no direct control of colonial forest resources until 1898, when its victory in the Spanish-American War added the forest resources of Cuba and the Philippines to its arsenal.[7] Its government foresters and private logging firms were beginning to function there by 1914, especially in the Philippines.

By 1914 the North Atlantic imperial powers' sources of forest products to meet their strategic needs were wider than ever before, beginning to stretch virtually around the world. But rapid access to militarily valuable timber was still constrained by existing technological and organizational limits of the intercontinental forest-products trade.

World War I

This "world" war was not a truly global battlefield, since the Great Powers were only in the process of developing the technological and administrative systems that would enable them to commandeer natural resources throughout the biosphere for their strategic needs. This war was a transition, in other words, toward the powers' nearly global reach by the next war. The urgent wartime struggle to exploit existing production forests to the maximum and open additional stands of virgin timber permanently opened new forests to production, in the tropical colonies and especially in North America. Newly developed timber extraction, processing, and transport technologies had long-term results for the world's forests; the innovation with the greatest long-term impact was motorized vehicles, which invited the construction of many new logging roads.

• *Europe*

The zone most directly devastated by the war lay primarily in northern France. On both sides of the long stalemate a system of trenches 350 miles long used endless trainloads of wood for the trenches themselves and for shelter, warmth, and transport networks. This zone underwent almost total devastation: after the war's end the French Forestry Service estimated that 350,000 hectares of forest—enough trees, it was estimated, to have been harvested for sixty years—had been totally destroyed.[8]

But 90 percent of France's forests lay outside the battle zone; in the rest of the country there was of course far less destruction. Professional forest management in France had emerged out of the French Revolution and Napoleon's empire. In the sandy soils of the Landes in the southwest, over two million acres had been planted in maritime pine in the nineteenth century, constituting the world's largest commercial tree plantation. During World War I these highly managed public forests underwent intensified rotational harvests, but the long-term effects on the tree crop were minimal. In 1914-15 logging rates were in fact reduced below peacetime standards, because manpower had been moved into military service, and severe bottlenecks arose in the national railway system. Only in 1917-18 was there unprecedentedly heavy cutting, with the help of American and Canadian forest battalions, which numbered over thirty thousand men. In that work, long-experienced French foresters complained that the American workers were often inefficient and wasteful, reflecting their extensive forest resources and inexpensive lumber in the United States. William Greeley, soon to become the chief of the American Forest Service, responded, "In issues between their established regime of timber culture and exigencies of Allied manpower or speed in getting wood to the front, the forest always won out. ... A grizzled conservateur said with a fatherly smile, to a bunch of impatient Americans: 'Our forests have fought several wars before this one.' "[9]

French spruce and fir forests, which grew mostly in hilly eastern France, were damaged more severely than the professionally managed pine plantations in the flat terrain of the southwest. On the steep slopes of the Vosges and western Alps, severe soil erosion resulted from wartime cutting. Throughout France, communal and private forests were less carefully managed, but indications were that they were more severely damaged by owners eager (as in many countries) to sell timber for high wartime market prices. In many parts of France, poplar avenues along roads were almost totally eliminated; but poplar regrows within less than ten years, so long-term damage was minimal.

Germany's extensive forests had been systematically managed for timber production for several centuries. German forestry was the model for other European countries and their emerging colonial possessions, as well as North America.[10] German foresters in World War I intensified their timber fellings well beyond their prescribed annual norms, but outside the war zone and its periphery, they emerged from the war with their forest cover basically undamaged for the longer run. This in part reflected the fact that German forests had gradually been pruned to a very narrow range of tree species. The reduction of biodiversity which old-growth forests elsewhere—especially in the tropical world— would begin to suffer by 1945 was no longer an issue in Germany.

Germany also relied on forest resources from its eastern hinterland during the war. For some years before 1914, Germans had worried about an impending timber famine, and envisioned the ancient forests of eastern Poland and southern Lithuania as a necessary segment of their future resource realm. Within a month of the outbreak of war in August 1914, German armies conquered that entire region, East Prussia and beyond, destroying an entire Russian army. As Simon Schama writes, "Heavy artillery turned the hills and meadows into smoking craters, the late summer woodlands into walls of fire. And when the smoke cleared, to reveal a charred landscape of black stumps and gray ashes, the German divisions had passed through the whole of Poland and Lithuania."[11] By the end of the war what had once been the primeval Bialowieza Forest, protected by the tsars as their private hunting reserve, was even further battered. The brutally cold winter of 1918 saw the German army, by now on the defensive, struggling to avoid freezing and starvation in the forest. They shot and ate the last of Europe's wild bison, cooking it with firewood hacked from trees near their camps. The ravaging of a great forest would continue in another war some years later.

In Great Britain there was no actual fighting on home territory, but the war necessitated total mobilization of both human and natural resources for war across the Channel.[12] For timber supplies to support the war, the British were less well prepared than the Germans and French. Britain had only recently established a Forest Service, based largely on men with colonial service in India. Public forests were very limited, hardly 5 percent of total forest cover, since (unlike the situation in Britain's Indian Empire) no formal forest policy existed. For centuries Britain had imported a wide variety of timbers for industrial and naval use (including large amounts from Scandinavia and eastern Canada) through the world's largest complex of timber importers in the London docks. But during the war imports were severely reduced by the high cost and higher risk of oceanic shipping.[13] In 1917 they were forced to log game preserves and great estates.[14] By the end of the war, the British had cut down 450,000 acres of domestic woodlands, half of their productive forest base. Faced with this massive devastation of the country's woodlands, Parliament in 1919 passed a Forestry Act that gave the Forestry Commission greatly expanded leverage over all forests, public and private, and resulted in massive reforestation programs in the years that followed.

In Russia, timber production under the tsars had centered in the hinterland of St. Petersburg, south of the city into northwestern Ukraine. A basic railway system was in place in European Russia by 1914, but feeder lines were few. The preparation of Russian industrial timber production for war was woefully inadequate. Wartime damage to forests was thus minimal, but it is difficult to distinguish between wartime demands and the chaos that followed the October Revolution in 1917.[15] The country took until the late 1920s to reach prewar levels of commercial timber production and export. As yet virtually no timber was exported, even to western Russia, from the planet's most extensive forest, the taiga that stretched across Siberia from the Urals to the Pacific.[16]

• *Europe's Tropical Empires*

Facing these severe limitations on forest resources at home, Europe's imperial powers turned for the first time to their tropical possessions for supplies. In the emergency they mobilized to the maximum possible extent the administrative, financial, labor, and transportation facilities of each empire. Thus World War I began the process of integrating the entire world's forests into a global economy of war. But the reach of the empires in 1914-18 allowed only limited exploitation of the tropics; the second great war would see a far greater scale of damage.

The British Empire, by far the most extensive and institutionally advanced, led the way. The British conquest of India, which was effectively complete by 1853, led to the establishment of a forestry law and its administration in the form of a Forest Department that set standards that later spread to the rest of the British Empire. The crucial feature was a system of working plans for each Reserved Forest, which were intended to achieve sustained-yield timber cutting in response to the public sector's needs and market demand. Before 1914 most timber was used within India; very little was exported, except where hardwoods were available near coastal ports: teak from Malabar on the southwest coast and other hardwoods from the Andaman Islands. Yet this system enabled British India to respond aggressively to the sudden demands of major war in Europe.

During the war, greatly intensified rotational logging absorbed all available British foresters and their Indian subordinates. Their production went largely into strengthening the infrastructure of British military needs and strategic interests in the Middle East and the northern Mediterranean; most of it remained in place after the war. Teak harvested from the great plantations in Malabar and Burma, as well as cedar, pine, and fir from the natural forests of the Himalayas, built new timber depots in Bombay, Karachi, and Rangoon to handle the sudden increase in exports. Indian timbers also went for structural work—bridges, piers, and buildings—in Egypt, Mesopotamia, and Greece, and provided hardwood sleepers (crossties) for 1,855 miles of new railway track in Mesopotamia, Egypt, East Africa, and Aden, at approximately fifteen hundred sleepers per mile. In addition, and very important for the war's contribution to accelerating the global timber economy, timber products research at the Forest Department's headquarters at Dehra Dun identified many new uses for previously ignored tree species, thereby permanently broadening the range of timber harvesting in the Indian subcontinent.[17]

In Africa, British colonies in the equatorial rain forests of the Gold Coast (now Ghana) and southern Nigeria were at an earlier stage of timber operations. Forest Departments and their legislative basis on the model derived from British India had been set up only after 1900. In West Africa, moreover, under systems of Indirect Rule, the British were preoccupied with relations to local chiefs in forest regions, and had to move slowly. The Gold Coast Forest Department was launched in 1908, but an effective forest law was not passed until 1927. Moreover, basic silvicultural knowledge of African rain-forest tree species and their commercial uses was only embryonic in 1914. The first timber plantations, in the Ashanti region of the Gold Coast, were begun in 1913, using teak and sissoo imported from India and Burma. Against this background the war actually resulted in reduced timber cutting in British Africa, the more so because of a severe drain of manpower from the African colonies during the war. The colonies' Forest Departments were closed from 1916 to 1919. During the war, timber exports fell from 3 million cubic feet in 1913 to one fifth of that in 1917.[18] But the determination to extract those resources more intensively became clear to forest managers and loggers alike, and the infrastructure was in place for major postwar expansion.

France and Germany had also established colonies in equatorial Africa after the Berlin Conference in 1885. But by 1914 colonial administration and trade were still rudimentary. Administrators in the French West African colony of Ivory Coast had developed a system of forced labor for timber extraction, but most African laborers were impressed into military service during the war. By 1919 there was little impact on the forest cover of either the coastal rain-forest belt or the drier forest to the north. But just as in British Africa, the war left a legacy of expanded logging infrastructure, as well as a taste for the market potential for tropical woods in metropolitan France.[19]

• *Southeastern United States*

North America was far more deeply involved in providing timber for the insatiable war in Europe; the United States did not enter the war until 1917, but its forests came into wartime production much earlier. The ways this occurred produced complex long-term changes in American forests and their management by 1918. As historian David

Clary observes, "The war was a turning point for the forests of America and the industries and professions dependent upon them. Mobilization converted the timber industry from a migratory consumer of virgin forests to a network of stable regional enterprises engaged in long-term production."[20]

The United States Forest Service had emerged in the 1890s, along the lines of the German model. But most forests around the country were still privately owned by 1914. After the outbreak of war in Europe, both the federal Forest Service and private-sector loggers worked under pressure toward greater public control and management of forests, for more efficient production of forest products, and more methodical sustained-yield management. Another trend accentuated by the war was that both high wartime prices and massive government funding for the war brought in new or accelerated technologies, such as trucks and tracked motor vehicles and new logging roads. Moreover, the war accelerated the diversification of timber species harvested and the range of forest products and markets into the postwar economy, as the U.S. Forest Service Timber Products Laboratory in Madison, Wisconsin, worked overtime.[21]

The most dramatic environmental damage caused by the war occurred in the southeastern pine belt. Large corporate timber operators had moved into the Southeast in the 1880s, having stripped the coniferous forests of the Northeast and Great Lakes region by then.[22] They purchased large tracts of land impoverished by the legacy of slavery, the Civil War, and the prolonged regional depression that followed. These tracts provided construction lumber for rapidly urbanizing eastern states, and after 1900 major markets in Britain and continental Europe as well. By 1914 millions of acres of sandy soils were clear-cut and devastated. But the companies had in place the roads, railroads, sawmills, port facilities (including every major port from Baltimore around to Houston), and skilled labor force to respond aggressively to the huge demand after war broke out in Europe.[23] During the war German purchasers were quickly replaced by British and French buyers, frantic to build wooden supply ships. German submarines sank many ships transporting southern lumber across the north Atlantic.

When the U.S. entered the war in 1917, Southern lumbermen faced further skyrocketing demand for construction timber for new factories, office buildings, warehouses, shipyards, and military camps. It took an estimated 600 million board feet of lumber just to house the new million-man army. The Southern lumber industry lobbied the U.S. government Emergency Fleet Corporation, which chose, in June 1917, to build many wooden supply ships. By January 1918 the EFC issued $400 million in contracts for light wooden ships. Supplies of old-growth maritime pine rapidly shrank, making the end of a logging era near and visible. Dozens of ships were built in southern ports using billions of board feet of top-grade lumber. But most of those ships never crossed the Atlantic, because the war ended in November. As one observer dolefully noted, "For years thereafter Atlantic and gulf coastal inlets and bays were anchorages for the graceful wooden ghosts that never put to sea."[24] New machinery—logging locomotives, steam skidders, etc.—was inefficient and produced mountains of sawdust and many slabs, most of which were burned. "Few of the operators of the larger mills seem to have made plans to continue the operation of their businesses by protecting their timber stands. They made little if any investment in forest research, gave no material support to reforestation, preserved few or no mother trees, practiced no selective cutting, and made no attempts to preserve vital ground mold."[25] They were followed by "peckerwood" sawmill operators, who cut smaller trees to produce second-grade construction lumber for local use. The war also accelerated the demand for packing materials and brown kraft paper, which relied on pulpwood from conifer forests. One of the biggest firms, the Great Southern Lumber Company in Bogalusa, Louisiana, constructed a plant that produced fifty tons of packing paper daily by 1915. Others followed suit, putting a major new demand on softwood forests, and setting in place a major new industry for the postwar period.

The war's overall damage to the southern pine belt was a culmination of a forty-year era that reduced millions of acres of pine forests to smoking slash and denuded, gullied soil. This deforestation was the most momentous ecological dimension of the national timber harvest of six billion board feet during the war.[26] In effect it became a grim model for the clear-cutting of the tropical world's rain forests later in the century.

• *Western Canada*

As the forests of the southeastern United States declined, major interest turned to the great coniferous forests of the Pacific Northwest, both the maturing lumber industry of Oregon and Washington and the infant industry across the Canadian border. In British Columbia the logging industry was on the brink of massive expansion into the great virgin conifer forest belt, but until the war it lacked major capital investment. Eastern Canada's prime forests by then were greatly reduced, and the timber industry was in long-term decline. The inauguration of the Panama Canal in 1914 made possible efficient, inexpensive transport of Northwest timbers to East Coast and European markets. British Columbia boasted "a coastal climate which permitted all-the-year-round logging, trees of an unbelievable size and uniformity of quality, and an abundance of forest right at salt water."[27] Through rapid, government-subsidized wartime expansion of Vancouver's timber industry, British Columbia surpassed both Quebec and Ontario, becoming Canada's timber heartland from then onward. Responding to urgent requests from London for shipments of Douglas fir and other conifers, the Ottowa government transferred the young forester H. R. Macmillan from Ontario to British Columbia. There he set up the western province's forestry administration, then moved into the private sector to mobilize commercial loggers, not just for emergency wartime work but also to build a base for a powerful industry thereafter. His company, Macmillan-Bloedel, would emerge as the largest and most controversial timber corporation in western Canada, and the infrastructure was in place for far more massive timber operations in World War II.[28]

• *The United States' Tropical Possessions*

Finally, the young empire of the United States, like its European competitors, made its initial efforts to provide wartime timber products from the tropics. Before 1898 American knowledge of the entirely different composition of tropical forests and the imports and uses of those forests' timbers had been largely confined to mahogany imports from Mexico, Central America, and the Caribbean.[29] After the conquest of Puerto Rico and the Philippines, the U.S. Forest Service set up management systems and research laboratories there.[30] But by 1914 these facilities were still in their infancy. Their work in the Philippines before 1917 produced shipments to Europe on a small scale. During the war they made accelerated efforts to log Philippine mahogany, but those islands were too far from theaters of war to make much difference, especially because of the United States' briefer term in direct fighting. Yet there too the impetus of the war led directly to the greatly expanded logging operations in the 1920s.

• *The Global Situation by the End of the War*

In the industrialized and bureaucratically mature economies where timber technology and management systems were well developed, there was severe overcutting of forests during the war. But the work was done selectively, depending on the species required for specific military purposes. Moreover, the strategic importance of readily harvested forest resources had become more vividly clear to planners than ever before. Internationally in the 1920s there was intense concern about future shortages of timber products, which led to intensified efforts at reforestation and sustained-yield management. Reforestation programs, however, largely took the form of softwood plantations using fast-growing, commercially valuable species. The old-growth forests, both deciduous and coniferous, that had been damaged or destroyed could not be returned to their prewar species diversity. In most wet or monsoon tropical-forest regions, there was little forest depletion as yet, but greater momentum toward integrating these forests into the global economy for both peacetime and future wars.

World War II

After the global economic expansion of the 1920s and the severe contraction of the 1930s, a second conflagration among the industrial powers produced far greater damage to forests—boreal, temperate and tropical—this time on a nearly global scale.

• *Europe*

Throughout World War II, northern France once again suffered some of the worst fighting on the ground. At war's end, Jean Collardet, one of France's leading experts, summarized the results. Damage from military movements and battles was staggering: over a million acres were devastated or badly damaged, he wrote. "Forest land was cleared for airdromes, rifle ranges and camps. Bombings, explosions and combat destroyed more. Much standing timber is so full of shrapnel as to be rendered useless; other areas are still mined."[31]

Away from combat areas, under German occupation, logging intensified once again: the number of sawlogs rose from 2.5 billion board feet per year before 1939 to 4 billion during the war, and fuelwood harvesting rose from 4 million cords annually to 8.5 million. The German occupiers clear-cut as much as they could in four years in the pine forests of the southwest, using North African and Senegalese prisoners as workers. At the same time, 12 percent of the plantation area burned, as Spanish refugees from their own civil war settled in the forest, and then French Resistance units were based there. Both refugees and guerrilla fighters set forest fires to disrupt German operations. But all this caused little long-term damage, for little soil erosion resulted, and the forest was readily replanted after the war. Wartime overcutting was more piecemeal in the hills and farmlands of the Vosges, Jura, Normandy, and Brittany, where trees of all species and sizes were cut for fuelwood and construction lumber from coppices, hedges, and roadsides. The montane forests of the Alps and Pyrenees were less badly damaged, since transport by road or rail was reduced during the war. In the last stages of the struggle, Collardet reported that as the Germans retreated, they destroyed few of France's fifteen thousand sawmills, so these were ready for intensive reconstruction harvesting. But by 1945-46 long-distance transport was severely curtailed; even traditional imports from Baltic countries, cut off during the war, would be slow to revive for the massive task of postwar reconstruction.

Another assessment in late 1945, conducted by a team of American foresters, concluded that French production forests had come through the war relatively intact; they had been cut at a rate roughly 50 percent faster than in peacetime. Surprisingly, Germany's managed forests seemed to the Americans to be in even better condition, reflecting Germany's longer tradition of silviculture. "American officers ... were full of admiration for the well-stocked, orderly appearing managed stands which are so common throughout Germany."[32] The Americans estimated that the forests had been felled during the war at rates approximately 50 percent beyond those stipulated by German techniques of sustained-yield harvesting in peacetime; this was similar to the rate in France.

Germany had learned an essential strategic lesson from the timber shortages that contributed to its defeat in the previous war. In the 1930s the Nazi regime had made strategic plans to control, and then to conquer, Eastern Europe's forests, so as to preclude the danger of another timber famine from their enemies' naval blockade. Reichsforstmeister Goering was determined to break the "Anglo-American grip" on her timber resources.[33] As a consequence, in the course of the war the conquered forests of Poland, Czechoslovakia, Yugoslavia, Rumania, and the Baltic states suffered severe depletion. In addition the Third Reich undertook intensive work to develop a wide range of wood products with the help of their sophisticated chemical industry, turning tree fibers into alcohol fuel, lubricants, cattle fodder, sugar, textile fibers, plastics, and plywood, as well as mining and structural timber, all of which further reduced forest biomass.[34]

At the end of the war, in setting up their Occupation administration in 1945, Allied foresters found that the German forest industry, widely dispersed, had suffered far less damage than most of the country's industry.[35] The Allies quickly established effective cooperation with German foresters, to meet the enormous need for reconstruction materials of all sorts: firewood, pitprops, pulpwood, and construction timber. The chaotic conditions prevailing in Germany following the collapse of Hitler's army necessitated the emergency provision of wood for daily household use as well as reconstructing the one hundred thirty cities that had been bombed by British and American planes. Many cars and trucks were powered by firewood. Dwarfing all other demands was firewood. In the bitter winter of 1945-46 virtually no coal was available. Normally firewood was 15-20 percent of German wood use; in the first postwar year it was well over half. To rebuild the bombed-out coal mines of the Ruhr basin required enormous numbers of pitprops, which were normally imported from other parts of Europe, but that had become impossible. So all sustained-yield harvesting standards were set aside for several years of clear-felling young stands of trees. The Occupation armies also required saw timber to rebuild bridges and for the "internal reconstruction of cities which have taken centuries to build and now lie in ruins."[36] But as one administrator concluded, "for the next decade or two, the smooth working of this system, which has taken well over a century to establish, will be radically interfered with," partly because German forest resources would also be demanded as reparations for rebuilding countries damaged by German forces.[37]

Eastward into Poland, where German armies had overrun the forest region east of Warsaw in 1914, they repeated the feat within weeks of the outbreak of war in September 1939, leveling Polish cities along the way. Goering, fantasizing himself a latter-day tsar, occupied the old Russian hunting lodges at Bialowieza, and annihilated the forest's Jewish population and parts of its Polish peasantry, forcing other Poles into towns in a futile effort to prevent them from joining partisan warfare in the forest. Only Goering's passion for gunning down wildlife saved the forest from massive logging to provide materiel for the German forces and eliminate cover for the guerrilla units.[38]

Northward into the transition zone from mixed hardwood to boreal softwood forest, Finland was caught in the turmoil of war from the winter of 1939-40 until the war's end. One hundred thousand Finnish men died, and another sixty thousand were seriously wounded, yet 80 percent of the Finnish people remained civilians, and the civilian economy continued to consume resources, though on a greatly restricted scale.[39] Timber cutting intensified for campaigns that involved 1.5 million Finnish, German, and Russian soldiers along a 1,000-kilometer Finland-USSR border. At the end of the war the southeastern region of Karelia, northeast of Leningrad, was permanently taken by the USSR. By then Karelia's ancient forest had been largely leveled for military uses; whatever remained had been opened up for postwar logging and draining of wetlands that completed the destruction of the primeval forest. Indeed, the intense forest cutting in the wartime emergency prepared the Finnish Forest Service and public for the totally unrestrained capitalist exploitation of forest resources that followed in peacetime.

Ironically, the portion of the forest that fell to the USSR and its command economy underwent considerably less-intensive exploitation in the decades following World War II. In the chaos of the early revolutionary years in Russia after 1917 there had been little change in the system of forest exploitation from tsarist times. But after 1928, when central planning and industrial development began, the railway system expanded rapidly, enabling more efficient timber transport from riverside hubs to the Moscow area and eastern Ukraine. Timber was mostly used for fuelwood and construction timber, until the cutbacks of commercial wood harvesting during the Depression. With a chronic shortage of skilled workers and sawmills outside central areas, the vast forests of northern European Russia and east of the Urals remained largely untapped. The war changed that, causing widespread devastation of forests from battles in the Baltic countries and northwestern and central Russia and the Ukraine. One estimate suggests that twenty million hectares of forest were destroyed.[40]

During the war the British attempted to purchase timber at White Sea ports and ship it to Britain during the warm months. But poor coordination with the Soviets, danger from the German navy, the short season, and difficult northeast Atlantic seas prevented much timber from being exported.[41] The bulk of Great Britain's softwood supplies, which had traditionally been imported from the boreal forests of Scandinavia (before the war 60 percent of Britain's raw wood imports and 80 percent of her plywood imports had come from Scandinavia, Russia, and the Baltic countries), were cut off by the German conquest of Norway early in the war. In thousand-year-old Crown forests, the Forest of Dean and the New Forest, ancient beech and oak were felled.

By 1940 the British were thrown back on their own forest resources to an unprecedented degree. At first the government had little power to impose emergency administration, since 97 percent of British forests were privately owned. But London's wartime Timber Commission quickly organized all timber fellings, and soon they achieved eight times as much production as in the immediate prewar years. Starting in the summer of 1942 American logging units joined the work, but not to British satisfaction. As the head of Timber Control later recounted, musing on the Americans' wasteful habits, "The American attitude towards timber was such that much tact was necessary in explaining that timber was in short supply here and was not the unlimited raw material to which they had been used. The equipment brought over by the Americans for their own use was prodigious, and some of it ... was the envy of every timber merchant who saw it."[42]

In a 1943 survey report the Timber Commission stated that in both government and private forests, "enormous devastation is being caused, and the Commissioners have produced proposals for a post-war forest policy to restore the depleted woodlands."[43] Future policy should greatly increase public control over forest management, and its goal should be to triple effective forest cover, since private owners would not be able to afford the costs of increasing this strategic reserve. Another assessment at the end of the war concluded that almost all merchantable stands were exhausted; even plantations sown after the previous war had been clear-cut or severely thinned for thousands of pit props and many other uses. It concluded that "Britain has come to realize how critically important her forests are in time of war and how unsafe it is to depend too largely upon outside sources of supply."[44] Moreover, in Great Britain as elsewhere the drain of forest resources during the war was to be sustained for half a decade into peacetime by the international effort of reconstruction, for "the rehabilitation needs of the United Kingdom are extremely large and of great urgency, hundreds of thousands of houses having been completely destroyed or severely damaged by the blitz and the V-bombings."[45]

• *Northwestern North America*

William Greeley, by then one of the foremost foresters in the United States, put it succinctly: "World War II was a lumberman's carnival. There was a strong market for every species and grade of wood in our forests."[46] Nowhere was this more transformingly true than in the Pacific Northwest. From 1940 onward the forests of that region, both American and Canadian, were mobilized to fill the strategic gap in Britain's timber resources. In British Columbia Sitka spruce and then Douglas fir were felled for building the Royal Air Force's fighter-bomber, the Mosquito, the world's fastest plane at the time, designed by De Havilland. Its fuselage was a balsa-plywood sandwich, and its wings were of Sitka spruce and Douglas fir, with a stressed skin of birch plywood. The British government had accumulated a strategic reserve of spruce during the 1920s, but had sold most of it by the late 1930s. By early 1940 Britain demanded twelve thousand mature trees, and sent a specialist from Timber Control to Vancouver to accelerate spruce harvesting along the Pacific coast.[47] At the time there was only one firm in Vancouver, plus six in Washington State, prepared for this work. Within a year, this increased to sixteen. The team reorganized plant and equipment, increased logging capacity, and surveyed old-growth forests along the coast as far as southern Alaska, especially the splendid virgin stands of the Queen Charlotte Islands.

In early 1942 the threat of a Japanese advance down the Alaska and British Columbia coasts led Canadian and American foresters to experiment with Douglas fir and western hemlock for airplane construction. But "there was no existing organization on which to work, nor was there the remotest description of the material required other than that it was to be suitable for aircraft and as light in weight as possible." The extent of the resulting logging in Oregon and

Washington can be sensed from the figure of thirteen thousand prime trees felled in 1944-45, and in the October 1944 American government order for three hundred fifty tall spruce of aero grade per month for building gliders alone.[48] There was much friction between the British and the Americans, the British claiming that American methods of harvesting and milling were very inefficient, and that Americans put their domestic needs first and charged outrageously high prices for inferior woods.

Americans had been interested since the 1930s in light, flexible woods for airplane construction, focusing their attention on Sitka spruce and Douglas fir. Wartime urgency quickly led to production controls imposed and supervised by the Lumber Division of the War Production Board. Its chairman, J. A. Krug, described the wide range of modern war's uses of forest products:

> *Forest products were commonly regarded as a great reservoir which could be drawn upon almost at will and in any quantity to meet expanding requirements. When critical shortages developed in other materials—notably the metals— wood, in one form or another, was seized as a substitute. Wood boxes and paper were enlisted for agricultural packaging when the burlap supply from India was cut off; tight cooperage took the place of metal drums in many special uses; timber replaced steel in small, fast marine craft such as subchasers and torpedo boats; construction designs were changed to specify timbers rather than steel for the long beams and arches over plant floors, for bridge members, and for river barges and radio towers; experiments were made looking to the use of veneer and plywood in large quantities in place of the then-scarcer light metals in gliders and in trainers and transport planes.*[49]

Despite considerable inventories at the end of 1941, and strict limitations on civilian use of forest products for the following four years, lumber shortages intensified. Shipping material, which had consumed 5.5 billion board feet in 1941, rose to 16.5 billion in 1943. Construction lumber, which had consumed 27 billion board feet in 1941, rose sharply to 35 billion annually during the war, partly because of a huge program of military camp construction in the early months of the war. Reduced to an individual level, the enormous extent of the demand was illustrated by the fact that it took 500 board feet to ship each soldier and his equipment to a European war zone, and 50 board feet per month thereafter to keep him fighting.[50]

Much of the crucial timber came from the conifer forests of the Northwest: softwood plywood used mostly for military housing, pontoon bridges, ship interiors, packaging, lifeboats, training planes, gliders, and cargo transport planes. By 1944 the pace increased still further. Douglas fir was needed for the Normandy invasion that June, for pilings to rebuild virtually every European port. These had to be 60-120 feet long, lengths that could come only from old-growth trees. Such great lengths had to be shipped by rail across North America, then formed into huge Davis rafts, twenty-five pieces wide, with one hundred sixty more atop, towed by tugs, to the Normandy coast.[51] The scale of this effort could be produced only in the North American industry; it prepared the way for a permanent escalation of timber production from the forests of the Northwest.[52]

By 1945 the forest administration and private timber companies together moved into an urgent program for replanting Northwestern forests, thus accelerating the transition from natural forest to industrial tree plantations. William Greeley, former head of the Forest Service and now head of the West Coast Lumbermen's Association in Seattle, concluded, "The war has ... made West Coast timber more valuable and has convinced many hard-headed lumbermen that it pays good money to grow trees. The war has given timber growing an economic footing that it lacked before. It has extended the area of industrial tree farms and other holdings managed for growing timber to nearly three million acres. It has established industrial tree planting as an accepted practice for the far-sighted landowner. It has brought to fruition long-range federal policies in the management of public timber, to encourage sustained-yield forestry operations by private owners. ... The temporary forest economy of a pioneer country is gradually being replaced by a permanent forest economy like that of Finland and Sweden."[53] Greeley pointed out that the war had sped up the modernization of the timber industry: 102 old mills had closed during the war, and 139 new ones, more up-to-date, efficient, and versatile, had opened. Their total annual capacity was a remarkable 350 million board feet greater than total prewar capacity. Without the stimulus of the war and government support, neither the Forest Service nor industry could have achieved this expansion of production. Whether this increased power would be managed sustainably in the postwar era of heightened consumerism remained to be seen.

• *The Colonial and Tropical World*

Far more than in the previous war between the Great Powers, this war devoured the forest resources of the colonial and tropical world, for the fifteen years between 1914 and the onset of the Great Depression had produced a great expansion of tropical timber extraction. India, the most highly developed possession in the British Empire, had the professional and technological infrastructure in place for intensive operations during World War II, more than any other country in the colonial or tropical world. Early in the war felling schedules were greatly accelerated in its highly managed monsoon forests, although most of the young foresters and loggers were drafted into military service, leaving the work in the forests largely to their elders.

But by the end of the war, just two years before India gained independence, the Forest Service concluded that this had not been beyond the capacity of the government forests to sustain.[54] In contrast, private forests had been badly damaged, as owners had responded to very high prices in civilian markets. As one senior forester wrote, "Under the pressure of war needs and high prices private forests have in some instances been so over-felled as virtually to have disappeared."[55] The Forest Department worried about increased erosion on hilly lands under both governmental and private control. Timber engineers at the Forest Research Institute in Dehra Dun intensified research on bamboo, aircraft timbers (sissoo, walnut, and Andamans padauk for propellers), treating railway sleepers with creosote, and a wide variety of other uses which would be built into the civilian timber economy thereafter.[56]

India's major forest zone closest to actual war was in Assam in the northeast. There timber cutting doubled between 1939 and 1945, and fuelwood gathering tripled. This occurred primarily after 1942, when many troops moved up the Brahmaputra valley to counter the Japanese army in Burma. Massive profits lay in this work for private contractors, who also built many new roads for military motor lorries and jeeps. All of that infrastructure remained in place after the war, opening Assam's hill forests to exploitation far more than before.

In Britain's less-developed colonies in Equatorial Africa, farther from the war front, African mahogany was logged at unprecedented rates for use as bottom and deck planking and framing in hundreds of new small craft.[57] In Nigeria and the Gold Coast, both Forest Departments and commercial logging operations and their markets were more developed than they had been during World War I, making the trees more susceptible to both logging and sustained-yield management. But in September 1939 the Gold Coast Forest Department was suddenly reduced to "a maintenance basis," because most forest officers went into military service. However, their African staff were trained by then, and kept all stations operating throughout the war. The department undertook many operations previously outside its scope. "In effect, it became a huge buying organization, purchasing and supplying great quantities of timber, furniture, firewood, charcoal, shingles and a host of what had previously been regarded as minor forest products, from rubber down to gums, honey and beeswax."[58] W. E. M. Logan, a senior forester, observed, "The logging industry has enjoyed a boom during this second World War; again, a marked contrast to the first, when it slumped so badly. Exports have been almost entirely Mahogany and in 1944 over 2,500,000 cubic feet were shipped. Most of the more accessible areas have now been worked over, some of them several times, and there has latterly been a decline in the quality of logs. This has been aggravated by the entry into the business of numerous inexperienced contractors who have been attracted by the prospect of making their fortunes but whose knowledge is for the most part of the sketchiest."[59] The wartime experience opened many marketing possibilities through experiments with many new hardwood species. Logan continued, "Not only has further knowledge been gained concerning the growing stock, the characteristics and possible uses of numerous timbers previously looked upon as more or less useless, and problems of conversion, but opportunity has also offered [sic] for scientific management of certain forest areas."[60] The industry was expanding, but in ways that would prove difficult to manage sustainably.

Like sub-Saharan Africa, the Caribbean and Latin America were far from the war zones, and the timber economy and forest management there were both still rudimentary.[61] Reflecting the high risks of ocean transport and severely limited availability of shipping, hardwood-timber extraction was very limited during the war. Prewar Germany had been the largest importer of Latin American hardwoods, but Allied navies cut off that trade. The American agents who replaced the Germans faced all the obstacles of a technically weak industry: Latin American sawmills could supply only logs, not lumber; and at least half of those logs were poor quality.[62] Mahogany, which had traditionally been the main hardwood export of Latin America's forests, was used during the war largely for aircraft and ships.

There was one specialized exception to the region's marginal position in this war. This was balsa, used for British Mosquito fighter-bombers and as flotation material for U.S. rafts supplied to the war in the Pacific. American specialists surveyed the forests of Central America and several tropical South American countries for suitable lightweight wood. Only Ecuador had large, relatively compact, and feasibly accessible stocks in its forests, and only 5 percent of that was light enough for Mosquitos.[63] The U.S. Board of Economic Warfare worked through six private agents in Ecuador. They increased balsa production from 12 million to 37 million board feet during 1942 and 1943, processed in twenty-five sawmills around the port of Guayaquil and in the rain-forest province of Esmeralda. They shipped the timber on a new 205-mile highway connecting the coast to Quito in the uplands. This logging seriously depleted the balsa stocks in natural rain forests, since no plantations existed. Moreover, forest biologists used the opportunity to identify over one hundred commercially valuable tree species in Esmeralda alone.[64]

Much more was happening than statistics of board feet actually cut can indicate. The war was responsible for giving American firms, with their government's administrative and financial backing, a major surge toward exploiting forest wealth from Mexico to Argentina and Chile after the war. In 1942 the Board of Economic Warfare authorized E. J. Stanton and Son of Los Angeles to provide hardwoods for boat building. The Stanton firm was a logical choice for the government: dating back to 1893, it was already a leading importer of Latin American woods, with distribution links to cities around the United States. Its increased wartime penetration of its source locations prompted an industry journalist to observe, "Undoubtedly one of the most far-reaching influences of the war will be the development of new sources of materials, in many cases new sources which are more convenient and more productive than the sources closed by the war. ... Always the needs of a postwar economy are kept in mind. Timber cruisers searching for mahogany keep track of many other finds of rare and beautiful woods."[65]

By the end of that year the U.S. government dispatched senior foresters to survey the timber resources of Mexico, Central America, and South America. The team surveying Central America found previously unknown upland forests, oak and other species, in easy reach of the Pan American Highway, which was being pushed urgently down through Nicaragua and Costa Rica. The team carried samples of fifty previously unknown hardwood species back to forest products laboratories for analysis of their possible commercial and industrial uses. While they were in Costa Rica they planned new logging operations, sawmills, and veneer and woodworking plants for what was to become Latin America's most advanced timber products industry.[66] There, as elsewhere in the tropical world, the war greatly accelerated the infrastructure for later forest exploitation.

• *The War Zone of Southeast Asia and the Pacific*

Two countries of the rain-forest region of Southeast Asia indicate the extent and character of the war's impact there. In Burma, while it was still under British control in 1939 to 1941, crews maximized harvesting of teak for military uses in Europe, and other hardwoods for 125,000 railway ties. The demand was so great that many species not normally marketable were accepted, and the Forest Department could undertake profitable fellings in the teak and hardwood forests where work had never been funded before. Then in early 1942 the Japanese conquered lower Burma, and Burmese dock laborers fled Rangoon, so timber stocks piled up. The British left behind 15,000 tons of sawn teak, 1,200,000 tons of teak logs, 75,000 tons of sawn hardwoods and 250,000 tons of hardwood logs, a great treasure for Japan.[67] That May the Japanese combined four large Japanese firms into Nippon Burma Timber Union, to cut teak wherever facilities existed; they forced Burmese foresters trained under the British to carry out the work. Beginning in the winter of 1943-44 they cut intensively in the teak forests of lower Burma, completely setting aside previous working plans. Many reserves were virtually wiped out.[68] But "extraction was never satisfactory as labour troubles were persistent and floating was prohibited in many streams to avoid damage to the temporary road and rail bridges necessitated by our bombing."[69]

As the tide of war turned, the British-Burmese forest administration was reconstituted, starting in January 1945. On their return the foresters found that forests in the vicinity of moving armies had been badly damaged. Some mills had been destroyed, and most stocks of teak in depots had been used or stolen. Moreover, at least half of a prewar force of six thousand working elephants in Forest Reserves had been lost. Moving toward independence two years later, Burma had already lost considerable teak wealth; expanding market demand would accelerate the process further thereafter.

The Philippines presented an even more dramatic picture. The Philippine forest industry under American colonial control had developed by far the largest operations of any country in Southeast Asia's tropical rain-forest zone. After the Japanese conquest in the first days of 1942, the Japanese military authorities took over all timber harvesting and milling capacity they could. But most Filipino foresters, loyal to their American mentors, either refused to cooperate or actively sabotaged production. As the tide of war turned and Japanese forces withdrew in 1945, they destroyed the bulk of the Philippines forest industry. Postwar reconstruction required vast amounts of hardwood timbers for use throughout the southern Pacific basin. At first even the reconstruction of Manila's docks had to be done with lumber from Washington and Oregon. When local sawmills were reconstituted, much of their timber came from private forests, badly managed and logged in response to high market prices. This process led to devastating deforestation, the worst in the rain-forest region of Southeast Asia.[70]

In each of Europe's moribund colonies in the region—Dutch Indonesia, British Malaya, and French Indochina—the Japanese occupation in 1942-45 took a somewhat separate course. One of the most dramatic developments was in Java, where teak forests had been one of the Dutch empire's great treasures.[71] Indeed, the Dutch system of managing teak plantations in Java had been a model for British teak production in Burma and South India. When the Japanese army overwhelmed Java in early 1942, the retreating Dutch destroyed sawmills and lumber camps and burned piles of giant teak logs in their depots as they left.[72] The Japanese military occupation set up logging operations to provide timber for new railways in the forests, firewood and charcoal for Java's cities, lumber for war-related factories, and most dramatically, new wooden ships. Long timbers from ancient trees were requisitioned to build hundreds of ships by late 1944. The impact on forests and villagers alike was grim. As Nancy Peluso writes, "No matter what form local forest management took, forest villagers who lived through this chaotic three and a half years today recall the rampant, and ubiquitous, cutting of trees. Everyone took part. ... The forest villagers bore the brunt of the Japanese excesses in the forest. Vast armies of forest laborers were put to work cutting and hauling timber under the Japanese forced labor system." [73] Villagers who had at first felt liberated from the restrictions of forest access imposed by the Dutch, and had reclaimed their old rights to forest lands, soon began undermining the heavy-handed Japanese officials. While Japanese industry was learning of the forest wealth they would massively extract for the country's postwar economic rebound, the rural Javanese participated in the political instability that would haunt Indonesia's forests long after the war was over and independence came in 1949.

At least in Java there was little actual fighting between the Japanese and the Allies. The story was worse in the island groups of the Pacific, from Hawaii southward, many of which were badly battered by the tides of war. This is particularly significant because island ecosystems are inherently limited in size and species diversity, and are thus vulnerable to permanent degradation. Unfortunately, no full survey of the impact of the Pacific war on either the forests of the high volcanic islands or the coral ecosystems of the atolls has yet been completed, though the issue is widely recognized. A model for the required research is Judith Bennett's work on Fiji during the war. Construction of new airfields, roads, and harbor facilities was underway even before Pearl Harbor, for all governments in the Pacific had seen war clouds brewing since the late 1930s. There was heavy logging along coasts and rivers before the government set up a Forestry Department in 1938, barely in time to manage accelerated timber extraction in the event of war. As Japanese forces swept southward across the Pacific in early 1942, Fiji faced the end of timber imports for its civilian economy, just when both the Forestry Department's budget and the logging labor force were collapsing. Nonetheless, some 5 to 10 million board feet of poles were harvested for military construction purposes in 1942 alone, mainly from coastal mangrove forests. Also increased firewood was cut, mostly from mangrove forests, as well as wood from secondary tree species and bamboos. By war's end no fighting had reached Fiji, but both coastal woodlands and hill forests had been damaged, and soil erosion increased. As in many countries, the war enabled the Forestry Department to gain command of increased lands from Fijian owners and Indian tenant farmers, lands that subsequently were turned into managed production forests.[74]

In sum, the war's impact on tropical forests was again limited. In the last analysis, tropical woods from Africa or Latin America were not used extensively; they were still only beginning to enter the mainstream of the global timber economy. In Southeast Asia the Japanese occupation was brief enough that it did not provide much timber to Japan. The devastation to the timber industry made postwar expansion of tropical logging less well managed than it otherwise would have been. But the war intensified research into the uses of tropical woods, enabling loggers to penetrate the mixed-species tropical-hardwood forests more fully after 1945. Wartime governments, by providing larger budgets and emergency administrative support for research and technical development as well as actual timber production, paved the way for massive postwar expansion of tropical logging.

• *The Aftermath*

In *Deforesting the Earth: From Prehistory to Global Crisis*, geographer and forest historian Michael Williams writes, "The cataclysmic events of World War II altered the world's forests more surely than any [previous stresses] could have ever brought about. But it was not the five years of conflict, devastating as they were, that caused deforestation; rather, it was the aftermath of political, economic, technological, and demographic changes that they unleashed during subsequent decades."[75] He goes on to show that even in the interwar years 70 percent of the clearing of global forests had occurred in the tropics; after 1945 the rapidly accelerating reduction of global forest cover happened entirely in the tropics.

This ominous trend was accelerated in important ways by the nature of modern warfare. World War II greatly intensified both the forestry profession and the private-sector timber industry, for vastly increased global use of forest products.[76] Timber-products laboratories throughout Europe, the U.S., and Canada, and in several tropical and colonial countries, studied and tested new wood species, leading to their broader use in the accelerating postwar civilian economy. Glesinger predicted as early as 1943 that this would "have important repercussions on forest utilization, since they affect all the low-grade woods which used to be practically worthless, and it is conceivable that these new industries might not only reduce the export surplus of pulp and paper of the Scandinavian countries, but revolutionize forest industries by providing a practical solution to the waste problem."[77]

Forestry as a profession around the world emerged much stronger from the war. By 1947 a Forestry Division was set up under the Food and Agriculture Organization of the United Nations, providing a global network of professionals determined to implement sustained-yield practices for the maximum timber production to meet the world's urgent needs. Forestry, with its cachet of rigorous science and its priority of forest production over the biotic values of multiple-species forest ecosystems, quickly spread to many countries emerging from the colonial era. Foresters everywhere pursued reforestation programs, emphasizing single-species timber plantations, including species understood to be vital for military purposes. But for a full understanding of the ecosystemic reverberations of the wars, we would have to look outside the framework of foresters' role and development ideology to studies by wildlife conservationists and ecologists, whose voices were not yet becoming clearly heard.[78]

Conclusions

It is commonly assumed that natural resources issues are largely ignored in the exigencies of wartime. This study has indicated that that is misleading: military and strategic planners have struggled over resource issues with great urgency and complexity, to the extent that the bureaucratic capacity of both government and the private sector have been able, so long as those resources (food, wood, etc.) have been seen as critically important for the war effort, for both military and civilian populations. However, *systemic ecological* impacts have not been seriously considered. During and after the two world wars, for example, military planners and foresters worked feverishly to ensure adequate supplies of forest products to meet both immediate and long-range strategic needs. But this perspective perceived forests as timber, not as entire webs of life. Forest management was designed in terms of sustained yield of forest commodities, and reforestation campaigns almost invariably produced single-species timber stands; they were tree farms, not full-spectrum forests. In this important sense even the forest conservation programs did serious ecological damage, reducing the species diversity of natural forests to the few species required for strategic priorities. And in the aftermath, since governments and private-sector firms were forced to work closely together during wartime, and within the framework of managed market conditions, commercial priorities came to dictate the postwar pattern of forest management.

The impact of the two great wars on the world's forests reflected the state of both administrative capacity and professional knowledge at the time each war commenced. In 1914 the forestry profession emphasized production over maintenance of mature and diverse forests; the science of ecology was in its infancy. Under wartime conditions large logs and long timbers were in heavy demand, and so the loggers worked out many primary forests. Reforestation campaigns in the two decades after 1918 provided materiel for the second great war, but once again from 1939 to 1945 many primary forests were reduced or eliminated. Finally, the technical innovations and new road networks financed by wartime budgets made possible greatly expanded exploitation of forests on every continent in subsequent peacetime, for both the massive, urgent task of postwar reconstruction and the broader patterns of economic and demographic growth that characterized the 1920s and 1950s.

One of the most distinctive effects of warfare on postwar resource exploitation was the state's wartime intervention, in close cooperation with private industry, to provide large amounts of investment capital for the long-term expansion of the timber industry. Consequent to this for postwar conditions was greater public control over forest resources, and the state's greater capacity than that of private forest owners to plan and manage forests. There has been endless controversy over the ecological consequences of this shift, but one thing is clear. By mobilizing resource extraction for the exigencies of mass conflict, the two great wars sharply accelerated humanity's consumption and reduction of forest ecosystems.

A full understanding of these consequences would necessarily distinguish between short-term and long-term ecological change. In many locations that would be very difficult to do in historical retrospect, for lack of longitudinal data on forest composition after the end of these wars. This study has been able to suggest the distinctions between immediate aftermaths and longer-term trends in many locations, but only in broad strokes. This illustrates the deeper challenge of sorting out the specific impacts of warfare, however complex and intensive they have been, from broader processes of the accelerating human impact on the biosphere. When that is done more comprehensively, either for local areas or globally, we will have a more adequate conceptual structure for understanding the unique role that warfare has played in the evolution of both human affairs and the biosphere, and perhaps even more effective ways of influencing strategic planners and public debate as we approach future wars.

Notes

1   Gabriel Kolko, *Century of War: Politics, Conflict, and Society Since 1914* (New York: New Press, 1994), 65.
2   An important limitation of this study is that it does not address what may have been a greater permanent clearance of forest acreage for intensified food production. That closely related subject requires separate treatment. A full study of the impacts of these wars on forest ecosystems would also address the impacts on wildlife and non-timber species.
3   Robert G. Albion, *Forests and Sea Power: The Timber Problem of the Royal Navy, 1652-1862* (Cambridge, MA: Harvard University Press, 1926); Graeme Wynn, *Timber Colony* (Toronto: University of Toronto Press, 1981); E. P. Stebbing, *The Forests of India*, 4 vols. (London: John Lane, 1922-1946).
4   Paul Walden Bamford, *Forests and French Sea Power, 1660-1789* (Toronto: University of Toronto Press, 1956).
5   Shawn William Miller, *Fruitless Trees: Portuguese Conservation and Brazil's Colonial Timber* (Stanford, CA: Stanford University Press, 2000).
6   For the German forest administration in Togo, see Candace L. Goucher, "The Impact of German Colonial Rule on the Forests of Togo," in John F. Richards and Richard P. Tucker, eds., *World Deforestation in the Twentieth Century* (Durham, NC: Duke University Press, 1988), 56-69.
7   Dennis M. Roth, "Philippine Forests and Forestry: 1565-1920," in Richard P. Tucker and J. F. Richards, eds., *Global Deforestation and the Nineteenth-Century World Economy* (Durham, NC: Duke University Press, 1983), 30-49.
8   John R. Jeanneney, "The Impact of World War I on French Timber Resources," *Journal of Forest History* 22:4 (October 1978), 226-27. Much greater detail, especially concerning management of local forests during the war, is in the conference volume of the French Forest History Society, Andrée Corvol, ed., *Guerre et Forêt* (Paris: Harmattan, 1994). The work of the American army loggers in France in 1917-18 is described by several participants, such as Theodore S. Woolsey, *Studies in French Forestry* (London: John Wiley and Sons, 1920).
9   David A. Clary, *Timber and the Forest Service* (Lawrence: University Press of Kansas, 1986), 70. For further perspective, see R. C. Bryant, "The War and the Lumber Industry," *Journal of Forestry* 17:2 (February 1919), 125-34.
10 For background, see Franz Heske, *German Forestry* (New Haven, CT: Yale University Press, 1938).
11 Simon Schama, *Landscape and Memory* (New York: Vintage Books, 1995), 65.
12 For an excellent summary of the war's long-range impact on British forestry policy and management, see A. Joshua West, "Forests and National Security: British and American Forestry Policy in the Wake of World War I, *Environmental History* 8:2 (April 2003), 270-78.
13 Thomas Thomson, "Post-War Forest Policy," *Empire Forestry Journal* 22 (1943), 25-31.
14 Harold K. Steen, *The U.S. Forest Service, A History* (Seattle: University of Washington Press, 1976), 247.

15 Brenton M. Barr and Kathleen E. Braden, *The Disappearing Russian Forest: A Dilemma in Soviet Resource Management* (London: Rowman and Littlefield, 1988), 64.
16 Egon Glesinger, "Canada: The Impact of the War on Forest Industries," *Empire Forestry Journal* 23 (1943), 54.
17 Stebbing, *Forests of India*, vol. III, chap. 19: "The Record of the Forest Department during the Great War, 1914-1919"; "India's Contribution to the Great War," *Indian Forester* 49 (1923), 117, 124-26; Richard P. Tucker, "The British Empire and India's Forest Resources: The Timberlands of Assam and Kumaon, 1914-1950," in Richards and Tucker, *World Deforestation*, 94-97.
18 W. E. M. Logan, "The Gold Coast Forestry Department, 1908-1945," *Empire Forestry Journal* 25 (1946), 52-54.
19 Timothy Weiskel, "Toward an Archeology of Colonialism: Elements in the Ecological Transformation of the Ivory Coast," in Donald Worster, ed., *The Ends of the Earth* (Cambridge: Cambridge University Press, 1988), 145.
20 David A. Clary, *Timber and the Forest Service* (Lawrence: University Press of Kansas, 1986), 68. See also William B. Greeley, *Forests and Men* (Garden City, NY: Doubleday, 1951), chap. 6: "World War Touches Off New Forest Explosions."
21 Earle H. Clapp, "Forest Research and the War," *Journal of Forestry* 17:3 (March 1919), 260-72.
22 Michael Williams, *Americans and Their Forests: A Historical Geography* (Cambridge, U.K.: Cambridge University Press, 1989).
23 Thomas D. Clark, *The Greening of the South: The Recovery of Land and Forest* (Lexington: University of Kentucky Press, 1984), 24-35.
24 Ibid., 29.
25 Ibid., 32.
26 For the consequence of the war's overall experience on American forest policy in the 1920s, especially the changing relations between the U. S. Forest Service and private landowners, see West, "Forests and National Security," 279-87.
27 A. R. M. Lower, *The North American Assault on the Canadian Forest: A History of the Lumber Trade between Canada and the United States* (Toronto: Ryerson Press, 1938), 197.
28 For details see the biography of the founder of the province's corporate timber economy, Ken Drushka, *H. R.: A Biography of H. R. Macmillan* (Madeira Park, B.C.: Harbour Publishing, 1995).
29 Richard Tucker, *Insatiable Appetite: The United States and the Ecological Degradation of the Tropical World* (Berkeley: University of California Press, 2000), chap. 7.
30 Roth, "Philippine Forests," 40-47.
31 Collardet's study is summarized in Henry S. Kernan, "War's Toll of French Forests," *American Forests* 51 (September 1945), 442.
32 A. C. Cline, "A Brief View of Forest Conditions in Europe," *Journal of Forestry* 43 (1945), 628.
33 Egon Glesinger, *Nazis in the Woodpile* (New York: Bobbs-Merrill, 1942).
34 For a summary, see Glesinger, "Canada," 54.
35 A. L. Poole, "The Forests of the British Occupation Zone of Germany," *Empire Forestry Journal* 25 (1946), 25-31; A. B. Cahusac, "Forestry in Germany," *Empire Forestry Journal* 25 (1946), 49-51.
36 Poole, "The Forests of the British Occupation Zone," 30.
37 Cahusac, p. 51. For an overview of reconstruction's demands, see "Timber Shortage in Europe," *Unasylva* 1:2 (September – October 1947), 12-16.

38 For details of the grotesquerie, see Schama, *Landscape and Memory*, 65-72.
39 See Simo Laakkonen, "War – An Ecological Alternative to Peace? Indirect Impacts of the Second World War on the Finnish Environment," in this volume.
40 Barr and Braden, *The Disappearing Russian Forest*, 66-68. For suggestions of still broader consequences, see Y. G. Noskov, "Environmental Devastation in the USSR during the Second World War," *Environmental Management in the USSR* 4 (1985), 87-95, and Douglas Weiner, *A Little Corner of Freedom: Russian Nature Protection from Stalin to Gorbachev* (Berkeley: University of California Press, 1999), 57-59.
41 Frank H. House, *Timber at War: An Account of the Organization and Activities of the Timber Control, 1939-1945* (London: Ernest Benn, 1965), 85.
42 House, *Timber at War*, 73.
43 Thomson, "Post-War Forest Policy," 26.
44 Ibid.
45 Cline, "A Brief View of Forest Conditions," 627.
46 Greeley, *Forests and Men*, 169.
47 House, *Timber at War*, 38-40.
48 Ibid., 40.
49 David Novick, Melvin Anshen, and W. C. Truppner, *Wartime Production Controls* (New York: Columbia University Press, 1949), 205-6.
50 Ibid., 207.
51 House, *Timber at War*, 74-75.
52 The impacts on each lumber port and its hinterland could be paradoxical. Coos Bay, Oregon, an important timber exporter, had severely curtailed production in the late 1930s, when Japan, its largest customer, cancelled all orders. Even during the war, labor and shipping scarcities meant a continuing reduction of lumbering upriver from Coos Bay. Nonetheless, the war brought high profits and government-funded new technology to the town's mill owners, preparing the way for major postwar expansion of the industry there. William G. Robbins, *Hard Times in Paradise: Coos Bay, Oregon, 1850-1986.* (Seattle: University of Washington Press, 1988), 95-106.
53 W. B. Greeley, "Lumber Looks Out of the Foxholes," *Journal of Forestry* 43:9 (September 1945), 799. See also Gerald D. Nash, *World War II and the West: Reshaping the Economy* (Lincoln: University of Nebraska Press, 1990), chaps. 3-4; Richard A. Rajala, *Clearcutting the Pacific Rain Forest: Production, Science, and Regulation* (Vancouver: University of British Columbia Press, 1998).
54 E. P. Stebbing, "The Record of the Forest Departments during the Second World War," in Stebbing, *Forests of India*, vol. IV, 145-63; Reconstruction Committee of Council (Government of India), *Second Report on Reconstruction Planning* (New Delhi: Government Press, 1944); Herbert Howard, *Post-war Forest Policy for India* (New Delhi: Government Press, 1944); R. D. Richmond, "Post-war Forest Policy for India," *Empire Forestry Journal* 23:2 (1944), 103-9, and 24:1 (1945), 52-55; *India's Forests and the War* (New Delhi: Ministry of Agriculture, 1948).
55 Richmond, "Post-war Forest Policy for India," 53.
56 S. H. Howard, "Forest Research and War Problems," *Empire Forestry Journal* 22 (1943), 43-45.
57 House, *Timber at War*, 78.
58 Logan, "The Gold Coast Forestry Department," 58.

59 Ibid.

60 Ibid., 59.

61 For a survey that dramatized the vast commercial potential, contrasted with the embryonic state of the international timber industry in the region, see Tom Gill, *Tropical Forests of the Caribbean* (Washington, DC: Charles Lathrup Pack Foundation, 1931).

62 Novick et al., *Wartime Production Controls*, 209-10.

63 House, *Timber at War*, 48, 87. The search for tropical woods as alternatives to balsa also led to the quipo wood of Panama's largely virgin Darien peninsula. Crews built logging roads and camps, allowing operations in previously untouched forests. In the event, only small amounts of timber from this region were actually used, but the area was opened to postwar commercial logging. House, *Timber at War*, 48-49.

64 William T. Cox, "Some Facts about Balsa," *Journal of Forestry* 42 (1944), 714-15.

65 "Latin American Lumber," *The Timberman* (June 1943), 18, 19, 32.

66 "Timber of Latin America: Prospects for Development," *The Timberman* (December 1943), 12.

67 A. N. Barker, "The Forest Position in Burma – January 1946," *Empire Forestry Journal* 25 (1946), 36-38.

68 "The Forest Estate in Burma during the Japanese Occupation," *Empire Forestry Journal* 24 (1945), 119.

69 Barker, "The Forest Position in Burma," 37.

70 Tucker, *Insatiable Appetite*, chap. 7.

71 Peter Boomgaard, "Forest Management and Exploitation in Colonial Java, 1677-1897," *Forest and Conservation History* 36 (January 1992), 4-14.

72 Nancy Lee Peluso, *Rich Forests, Poor People: Resource Control and Resistance in Java* (Berkeley: University of California Press, 1992), 93-97.

73 Ibid., 97.

74 For a contribution to that broader task, see Judith A. Bennett, "War, Emergency and the Environment: Fiji, 1939-1946," *Environment and History* 7 (2001), 255-87. Other relevant materials for the Pacific region as a whole are in Roy M. MacLeod, ed., *Science and the Pacific War: Science and Survival in the Pacific, 1939-1945* (Dordrecht and Boston: Kluwer, 1999).

75 Michael Williams, *Deforesting the Earth: From Prehistory to Global Crisis* (Chicago: University of Chicago Press, 2003), 420.

76 For what many timber experts considered an authoritative view of the future, see Egon Glesinger, *The Coming Age of Wood* (New York: Simon and Schuster, 1949).

77 Glesinger, "Canada," 56.

78 For the role of the nature conservation movement, which also accelerated in the years immediately after the war, and especially the founding of the International Union for the Protection of Nature in informal association with the United Nations, see Martin Holdgate, *The Green Web: A Union for World Conservation* (London: Earthscan, 1999).

"Speaking of Annihilation": Mobilizing for War Against Human and Insect Enemies, 1914-1945

Edmund Russell

In 1944 and 1945, two periodicals with very different audiences published similar images. Both showed half-human, half-insect creatures, talked of the "annihilation" of these vermin, and touted modern technology as the means to accomplish that end. One piece, a cartoon in the United States Marines' magazine *Leatherneck*, showed a creature labeled "Louseous Japanicas" and said its "breeding grounds around the Tokyo area ... must be completely annihilated".[1] A month after the cartoon appeared, the United States began mass incendiary bombings of Japanese cities, followed by the atomic blasts that leveled Hiroshima and Nagasaki. Although the *Leatherneck* cartoon was surely intended to be humorous and hyperbolic, calls for annihilation of human enemies had, by the end of the war, become realistic.

So too with insect enemies. The second cartoon, an advertisement in a chemical industry journal, promoted perfumes to eliminate insecticide odors (see Figure 1). Tapping the rhetoric that pervaded World War II, the text began, "Speaking of annihilation." The accompanying image showed three creatures with insect bodies, each with stereotypical head representing a national enemy. The Italian creature lay on its back, an allusion to Allied victory over the Italian army. German and Japanese creatures remained standing, as guns blasted all three with chemical clouds. Like human enemies, the advertisement implied, insect enemies could and should be annihilated. That possibility, too, had come within reach by the end of World War II. The Allies killed disease-bearing lice and mosquitoes over wide areas using a powerful new insecticide called DDT (dichlorodiphenyltri-chloroethane), and entomologists called for the extermination of entire species.

142

Two to go!

Speaking of annihilation – the odors created
by our adept perfume-chemists for your insecticides, slay the killing agent, pronto and
quietly depart the battle scene. No trace remains—perfumed or otherwise.

Send us a gallon of
your unperfumed spray
We want to show you
what we consider a per-
fect perfuming job

VAN **AMERINGEN-HAEBLER** INC. · 315 FOURTH AVENUE · NEW YORK 10, N. Y.

Figure 1. This 1944 advertisement, which appeared in a journal that served the National Association of Insecticide and Disinfectant Manufacturers, took it for granted that national and insect enemies required annihilation. Reprinted from Soap and Sanitary Chemicals (April 1944), 92.

Most Americans welcomed technology that brought "total victory" over national and natural enemies. They felt grateful for a bomb that saved the lives of American soldiers, and for a chemical that enabled people to "bomb" insect pests. As time passed, however, many came to wonder whether human beings had struck a Faustian bargain. Did "weapons of mass destruction" threaten, rather than promote, human welfare? Opponents of chemical and nuclear weapons thought so. Had the ability of human beings to conquer nature surpassed some limit, threatening not only human well-being but the planet itself? After Rachel Carson published *Silent Spring* in 1962, many feared that DDT exemplified this threat.[2]

Although war and concerns about the impact of human beings on the environment were two of the most important forces shaping the twentieth century, scholars have tended to analyze these issues separately. Several historical fields illustrate this tendency. Military historians have pushed beyond studies of battles and armies to examine the impact of military institutions on society, politics, and economics—

but rarely on the environment. Environmental historians have emphasized the role of nature in many events of our past—but rarely in war. Historians of technology have analyzed the impact of military technology on society—but rarely on the environment. Cultural historians have emphasized the impact of war on the way people interact with each other—but rarely its impact on people's interactions with the environment.[3]

The tendency to separate war from environmental change (or military from civilian affairs) has deep roots. Isaiah's metaphor, "They shall beat their swords into plowshares," suggests that people have long seen one of the most important ways they change the environment—agriculture—as the opposite of war. In Cartesian philosophy, relations among human beings belong to a separate sphere from relations between human beings and species. Observers have argued that Americans in particular "are inclined to see peace and war as two totally separate quanta. War is abnormal and peace is normal and returns us to the status quo ante."[4]

Historians of insecticides have shown, however, that efforts to control human and natural enemies have not proceeded independently. Between them, Emory Cushing, Vincent Dethier, Thomas Dunlap, and John Perkins have pointed out that manufacturing of explosives in World War I produced a by-product called PDB (paradichlorobenzene), which entomologists then developed into an insecticide; that entomologists often used military metaphors; that World War II stimulated development of DDT; and that some insecticides were related to nerve gases. Historians of chemical weapons, too, have noted this last point.[5]

These events were, I believe, part of a larger pattern. The ability of human beings to kill national and natural enemies on an unprecedented scale, as well as fears about those abilities, developed in the twentieth century partly because of links between war and pest control. This article focuses on three such links: science and technology, institutions, and metaphor.

In the first half of the twentieth century, the science and technology of pest control sometimes became the science and technology of war, and vice versa. Chemists, entomologists, and military researchers knew that chemicals toxic to one species often killed others, so they developed similar chemicals to fight human and insect enemies. They also developed similar methods of dispersing chemicals to poison both.

Ideas and hardware moved between civilian and military spheres partly because of institutional links. The two world wars stimulated nations to mobilize civilian and military institutions to achieve military victory. They also catalyzed the founding of new organizations that coordinated civilian and military efforts. Peace also catalyzed links among institutions. When guns fell silent on battlefields, military and civilian institutions worked together to apply military ideas and technology to farm fields as a way to survive and meet their institutional goals.

Shared metaphors helped military and civilian institutions shape and express the way people experienced both war and nature.[6] Publicists described war as pest control, pest control as war, and the two endeavors as similar. On the one hand, describing war as pest control transformed participation in war from a potentially troubling moral issue to a moral virtue. Comparing chemical weapons to insecticides made it easier to portray poison gas as natural and humane. (Ironically, opponents of poison gas used the same metaphor to argue that chemical warfare was inhumane because it treated human beings like insects.) On the other hand, describing pest control as war helped entomologists portray nature as a battlefield, elevate the status of their profession, and mobilize resources.

The evolution of a word used for both human and insect enemies, *exterminate*, suggests that these metaphors appealed to long-standing values. The Latin root means "to drive beyond the boundaries." People and insects that did not respect boundaries of nations, farms, and homes were enemies, this meaning implied, and could or should be driven out. Often, however, twentieth-century publicists used *exterminate* with a connotation that had emerged in the fourth century: "to destroy utterly," or annihilate. Since people had previously imagined (and sometimes succeeded in) annihilating enemies, what set the twentieth century apart? The scale on which people could plan and carry out killing stands out. Technology, industry, and government grew large enough to enable us to wage "total war"—not just against armies, but against insects and civilians. People could plan, carry out, and (even when it did not come to pass) fear annihilation on a breathtaking scale across geographic and phylar boundaries. Zygmunt Bauman has suggested that modernity aimed to make the world into a garden in which some organisms belonged and from which others, which did not belong, were to be extirpated. The story told here complements his arguments. Warfare resembled gardening, gardening resembled warfare, and both were attempts to shape the world to long-standing human visions.[7]

This article explores only some aspects of the topic. It focuses more on alliances among institutions than on conflicts, more on institutional politics than on economics, more on harms than on benefits, and more on similarities than on differences. Noting similarities does not mean equating. In World War II, for example, Germans, Americans, propagandists, and entomologists all talked of annihilating enemies. However, the actions of the United States and entomologists differed in critical moral ways from those of Germany and of the architects of the horrors of the Holocaust.

This story prompts two reflections about the ways we write history. First, we often talk about the impact of one aspect of life (war, science, politics) on another (the state, culture, the environment). This framework tells us a great deal, but is it complete? Few forces are monolithic, and two-way interactions may be more common than one-way impacts. War changed the natural environment, and the environment changed war. Metaphors shaped human understanding of the material world, and the material world shaped metaphors. Second, we may tend to tell stories of progress *or* decline, but life is a mixture of the two.[8] For some people insecticides and chemical weapons were blessings; for others they were curses; and for some they were both. The world gets both better and worse, and we have yet to exterminate either good or evil.

World War I: Chemistry and War (1914-18)

On April 22, 1915, Germany initiated a new chapter in the evolution of war. That day, Allied troops huddled in trenches near Ypres, France, found themselves enveloped in a greenish-yellow cloud of chlorine gas released by German troops. Allied soldiers futilely tried to outrun the cloud, which reportedly killed five thousand soldiers and injured ten thousand more. German military leaders lost the initial advantage when they failed to mount a large-scale attack, but they succeeded in demonstrating the military power that flowed from knowledge and control of nature.[9]

Knowledge about nature comes in many forms, including scientific understanding of molecules, and Germany's preeminence in chemistry underpinned its initial success with chemical weapons. This preeminence depended both on the brilliance of civilian scientists such as Fritz Haber, the chemist who oversaw development of chemical weapons at the Kaiser Wilhelm Gesellschaft (Institute) in Berlin, and on Germany's huge chemical industry. Haber relied on chlorine for Germany's first gas attack partly because Germany had an ample supply of this dyestuff intermediate.[10]

Other nations followed Germany's lead in turning civilian science and industry to military research and production. Great Britain set thirty-three laboratories to work testing one hundred fifty thousand compounds as chemical weapons. In the United States, the National Research Council (an arm of the National Academy of Sciences) organized academic, industrial, and governmental scientists to work on offensive and defensive aspects of poison gases. In 1918 the United States Army incorporated this mammoth civilian enterprise into its new Chemical Warfare Service. Other nations created similar organizations, and tons of poison gases wafted across Europe. By the end of the war, gas reportedly had killed ninety thousand people and caused 1.3 million casualties. Observers dubbed World War I "the chemists' war."[11]

Chemists relied on their knowledge of laboratory curiosities to find some new chemical weapons. The most heavily used gas in World War I, chloropicrin, followed this route. Russia introduced chloropicrin in battle in 1916, and other nations soon followed suit. Although sometimes lethal to human beings in its own right, chloropicrin found wide use primarily because it penetrated gas masks. The compound induced tearing and vomiting, which led soldiers to rip off their masks and expose themselves to less penetrating, but more lethal, gases mixed with chloropicrin. By January 1, 1919, the United States Chemical Warfare Service's arsenal at Edgewood, Maryland, could produce three million pounds of chloropicrin per month.[12]

Chemical warriors also relied on compounds already known to kill organisms, including insects. French soldiers demonstrated the value of this approach at the battle of the Somme in 1916, when they fired artillery shells containing hydrogen cyanide. Since the nineteenth century, farmers and entomologists had used hydrogen cyanide to fumigate insects in orchards and buildings. Arsenic, too, made its way from farm fields to battlefields. In the United States, the Chemical

Warfare Service turned a third of the country's arsenic supply into the poison gas diphenylchloroarsine, causing shortages of arsenical insecticides used to kill orchard pests.[13]

War prompted scientists not only to convert insecticidal chemicals into chemical weapons, but also to reverse the process. Lice, which sometimes carried deadly typhus, infested American troops in France. Military and civilian researchers alike hoped that war gases might offer a way to conquer this plague of war. In a collaborative experiment, researchers from the Chemical Warfare Service and the Bureau of Entomology of the United States Department of Agriculture tested four chemical weapons on lice. They hoped to find "a gas which can be placed in a chamber and be experienced safely for a short period of time by men wearing gas masks and which in this time will kill all cooties and their nits."[14]

These experiments stimulated tests of other chemical weapons as insecticides. The Chemical Warfare Service, the Bureau of Entomology, and other agencies of the Department of Agriculture researched the efficacy of war gases against dozens of species of insects. Most fell short, but chloropicrin, the compound that chemical warfare had lifted from obscurity, killed insects effectively. Chloropicrin harmed civilian exterminators as readily as enemy soldiers, of course, but entomologists found it less dangerous (as a tear gas, chloropicrin had good "warning properties") or more effective than other fumigants. The battlefields of Europe approximated, albeit unintentionally, laboratory experiments on a massive scale, and entomologists took note. *American Miller* magazine reported that the "scarcity of insect pests around Rheims is attributed to the use of poisonous gases in that region during the World War," and French researchers tested chloropicrin as an insecticide on grain in closed rooms.[15]

While scientists researched ways to use pest-control technology in war, soldiers and publicists in World War I, like their predecessors in previous wars, described military enemies as animals, including insect pests. A British soldier, for example, described German soldiers as running around like "disturbed earwigs under a rotten tree stump." By dehumanizing enemies, animal metaphors reduced the sense of guilt about killing human beings in battle. The "lower" the phylum, the lower the sense of guilt, and few phyla ranked lower than insects. Moreover, Europeans had long regarded nature, defined as everything on earth other than humans and their creations, as something that human beings not only could but should conquer. Describing war as an exercise in control of nature helped define war as not just morally permissible, but morally necessary.[16]

While soldiers found insect metaphors useful for minimizing the significance of killing human beings, entomologists found war metaphors useful in elevating the significance of killing insects. L. O. Howard, chief of the Bureau of Entomology, for example, described his bureau as waging "warfare against insect life." Military rhetoric was not new to science. Francis Bacon described science as an antagonist of nature, and Darwinian rhetoric had portrayed nature as a giant battlefield. But such rhetoric took on added resonance in wartime. It implied that insects threatened the nation much as human armies did, associated scientific activity with patriotic national priorities, imbued the Bureau of Entomology with the prestige of the armed forces, and provided a rallying cry to mobilize resources against nonhuman threats.[17]

"Peaceful War" in the United States (1919-1939)

Links between military and civilian endeavors forged in World War I bent, but did not always break, after the Treaty of Versailles. In the United States, the Bureau of Entomology and the Chemical Warfare Service continued to borrow each other's technology and metaphors, a process facilitated by explicit collaboration. On the other side of the Atlantic Ocean, Germany surged ahead in the search for new chemical weapons by uniting research on poison gases and insecticides. Out of these alliances came technology that shaped campaigns against both human beings and insects in World War II.

For L. O. Howard of the Bureau of Entomology, the cessation of the war in Europe set the stage for escalating "the war against insects." Long worried about public and congressional tendencies to view entomologists as engaged in "trivial" studies, Howard chose his December 1921 address as retiring president of the American Association for the Advancement of Science to promote a new image. Titled "The War Against Insects," the speech sounded like propaganda from the just-completed war in Europe. Ignoring the benefits insects provided—which he had praised earlier in his career—Howard portrayed his enemy in only one dimension. Quoting Maurice Maeterlinck, Howard said that insects seemed to have a quality born of "another planet, more monstrous, more insensate, more atrocious, more infernal than ours." How was the nation to protect itself from this threat? Federal entomologists, "a force of four hundred trained men," would fight a "defensive and offensive campaign" against these hordes.[18]

With this speech, Howard moved military metaphors—which had jostled with public health metaphors in entomological discourse—to the center of his agency's public rhetoric. Other entomologists repeated Howard's warning that insects threatened human survival. After quoting Howard's bellicose rhetoric to a 1935 meeting of exterminators, R. C. Roark, chief of the Insecticide Division of the Department of Agriculture, identified the mix of altruism and self-interest that led entomologists to promote insects as enemies: "People must be taught that insects are enemies of man; and as the public becomes insect conscious the opportunities for service by the entomologist, the insecticide chemist, the chemical manufacturer and the exterminator will increase." Chemical companies, too, called on martial and cultural traditions to promote their products (see Figure 2). As Thomas Dunlap has suggested, it is difficult to resist the idea that the appeal of insecticides arose partly from their promise of victory over, rather than coexistence with, insect enemies.[19]

Howard could not have asked for a better symbol of "the war on insects" than the airplane, the technology that epitomized martial glory in World War I. The text of Howard's "War against Insects" speech appeared in *Chemical Age* with a photograph of an airplane dusting a farm with insecticides. This technique was so new that it went unmentioned in Howard's speech; Howard praised airplanes for their usefulness in scouting for insect infestations. But three days after Howard's talk, entomologist J. S. Houser announced that, in collaboration with Army Air Service researchers, he had converted a military airplane to disperse insecticides.[20]

Chemical warfare may have inspired this development. *McClure's Magazine* reported that a colonel returning from France to his job as an Ohio entomologist "knew that near the close of the war preparations were being made to sprinkle poison gas and liquid fire by airplane on soldiers in the trenches and he thought something like this could probably be used against caterpillars." The *New York Times* suggested a more mundane origin of the idea, saying that birds inspired aerial dispersal. Whatever the inspiration, the availability of military airplanes and the willingness of the Army Air Service to work on this technique

AMBUSHED ARMY

Insects don't stand a chance when an Atlantic Ultrasene-base insecticide goes after them.

Atlantic Ultrasene is refined solely for use as a carrier for insect killers. Unlike a kerosene base, Ultrasene evaporates readily, leaves no unpleasant odor, no oily residue. That's why proprietors of places where food is stored or prepared—men who must constantly guard against dirt-collecting oil films and disagreeable

odors in restaurants, hotels, markets—are demanding Ultrasene-base insecticides. That's why successful insecticide manufacturers are choosing Ultrasene for their spray-base.

Find out more about Atlantic Ultrasene. Our technical department will help you with further information and liberal experimental samples. The Atlantic Refining Company, Specialty Sales Department, 260 South Broad St., Philadelphia, Pa.

ATLANTIC ULTRASENE —A BETTER BASE FOR BETTER INSECTICIDES

Figure 2. Old Testament writers described insects as invading armies, and subsequent generations updated the metaphor. In 1938, an advertisement for a chemical company suggested that rifle-toting insects stood no chance against snipers spraying scentless insecticides. Reprinted from Soap and Sanitary Chemicals 14 (Feb. 1938), 80.

made aerial dispersal of insecticides feasible. J. A. Truesdell, a newspaperman impressed by Houser's experiments, in 1922 told a congressional committee that the Army Air Service wanted to combine experiments on crop dusting with pilot training. Truesdell thought the growth of commercial aviation, including crop dusting, would create an auxiliary to the air service. The hearings led to a policy of cooperation between the Army Air Service and the Bureau of Entomology, which in turn led to the development of aerial dusting of cotton.[21]

Collaboration between military and civilian institutions also transferred airplanes from experimental farms to commercial agriculture. In March 1923, acting Secretary of War Dwight F. Davis declared that the United States Army should do whatever possible to help crop dusting "in a commercial way." The Huff-Daland Corporation, which built experimental planes for the air service, sent representatives to a Bureau of Entomology laboratory in 1923 to work on a special dusting plane. In 1924, Huff-Daland formed Huff-Daland Dusters. Lt. H. R. Harris of the Army Air Service, formerly chief of the flying section at McCook Field, became the company's chief of operations. The air service temporarily released Harris, who selected twelve pilots and about eighteen mechanics from army airfields to join Huff-Daland Dusters, Inc. In 1925, Huff-Daland Dusters began large-scale dusting in Louisiana. In 1926, Harris resigned from the military to work full-time for Huff-Daland. Before long, commercial crop dusters became important symbols of wars on insects, especially against the boll weevil.[22]

Despite Howard's predictions, and unlike airplanes, most chemical weapons did not prove immediately impressive in fighting insects. Howard told the 1924 meeting of the Entomological Society of America that postwar collaboration between the Chemical Warfare Service and the Bureau of Entomology had produced mountains of data of "undoubted value," but the Chemical Warfare Service was keeping almost all of the results secret. But in 1931 Howard laconically reported that the experiments were "not promising, on account of the resultant damage to vegetation," which ended the Bureau of Entomology's public discussion of the war gas experiments. The exception was chloropicrin, which became a popular fumigant for clothing, households, and grain elevators.[23]

The disappointing results did not derive from lack of effort. For its own reasons, the Chemical Warfare Service devoted resources in the 1920s to the search for insecticidal uses of war gases. Because poison gases had symbolized, for many, the brutality and senselessness of modern warfare, post-World War I peace movements focused much of their energy on chemical weapons. International conventions twice almost banned use of chemical weapons in the 1920s, and even within the United States Army powerful individuals wanted to eliminate the Chemical Warfare Service and to transfer its responsibilities to other units.[24]

The Chemical Warfare Service and its allies responded by emphasizing the humanity of poison gas (which killed a smaller proportion of casualties than did bullets and bombs) and civilian uses of war gases, including their use as insecticides. Borrowing a metaphor from Isaiah, the journal *Chemical Warfare* reported in 1922 that chemical warriors had beaten "the sword into the plowshare." By emphasizing agricultural uses of war gases, the service tried to reverse its image from agent of war to agent of peace. According to the *Pittsburgh Gazette Times,* Amos Fries, chief of the Chemical Warfare Service, described his agency as doing "peace work principally." Since conquest of nature had long been seen as a morally uncontroversial endeavor, insecticide projects provided an ideal way to place chemical warfare in a more positive light. An article in *Chemical Warfare,* for example, stated, "Efficient offensive warfare must be developed against animal, bird and insect life." In 1922 the *Boston Transcript* captured the Chemical Warfare Service's dissonant message in an oxymoron: " 'peaceful' war."[25]

One of the most heavily publicized "swords into plowshares" projects involved the search, in collaboration with the Bureau of Entomology and state experiment stations, for insecticides to kill the boll weevil. For seven years, the Chemical Warfare Service held out hope for a solution to "the boll weevil problem, the curse of the cotton states of the South" to the public and Congress. In the end, however, it had little to show. In 1926, H. W. Walker and J. E. Mills of the Chemical Warfare Service reported that toxic gases were "ineffective against the weevil due to its apparent ability to suspend breathing more or less at will."[26]

Although of little use to farmers, the research project did help the Chemical Warfare Service. The advantages grew partly out the service's ability to conduct military research while publicizing civilian applications. Substances toxic to insects stood a good chance of being toxic to human beings, and the Chemical Warfare Service could learn about the physiology of poisoning in human beings by studying the effects of chemicals on insects. The Chemical Warfare Service lauded this side of the boll weevil investigations in its 1927 report, saying that the project had "extended our knowledge of the fundamental facts concerning the toxicity of compounds which will prove beneficial to certain investigations undertaken with a view to the solution of specific Chemical Warfare problems."[27]

Similarly, projects on aerial dispersal of insecticides helped develop aerial dispersal of poison gases, which chemical warriors expected to be a prominent feature of future wars. A 1921 pamphlet issued under the auspices of the National Research Council predicted, "Armed with such [poisonous] liquids and solids the airman of the next war will not need a machine gun or even bombs to attack the enemy underneath. ... All he need do is to attach a sprayer to the tail of his machine and rain down poison on the earth beneath as the farmer kills the bugs on his potato field."[28]

Insecticide projects allowed the Chemical Warfare Service not only to equate chemical weapons and insecticides but also to portray the targets of those chemicals—human beings and insects—as similar. Fries made this comparison explicit in 1922 when he said "that the human pest is the worst of all pests to handle." Others saw parallels between gassing insects and human beings but resisted the implication that such similarities were desirable. A 1921 piece in the *New York Herald* criticized a report of potential use of poison gas against moonshiners, saying, "In the great war the world saw too much of human beings being killed or tortured with poison gas . ... Ordinary killing is bad enough, but that man should treat his fellow as he treats a rat or a cockroach is inherently repugnant to all from whom decent instincts have not fled."[29][28]

The Chemical Warfare Service's projects on insecticides and other civilian applications for war gases faded away in the late 1920s, perhaps because the need for improved public relations declined after the United States rejected the 1925 Geneva Protocol.[30] Although neither the Chemical Warfare Service nor the Bureau of Entomology discovered powerful new chemicals in the 1920s, they made heavy use of each other's metaphors. Portraying insect control as war built up the practical significance of entomology, while portraying war as insect control played down the political and moral issues associated with chemical weapons.

Mobilization in Germany (1935-39)

In Germany, too, researchers in the interwar period saw the value of linking research on insecticides and chemical weapons. But while heavy publicity and meager results marked the American efforts, the opposite held true in Germany. Out of a laboratory in the giant chemical combine I. G. Farben came little publicity and big discoveries, including a new family of chemicals called organophosphates with tremendous lethality to both insects and human beings.

The difference in outcomes arose largely from differences in attitudes toward mobilization. While Americans struggled with the legacy of World War I—Congress went so far as to hold hearings on whether corporations stimulated the war in order to boost profits—and the economic distress of the Great Depression, Germany prepared its civilians and industry for war. In 1936 Adolf Hitler ordered the armed forces to be ready for war within four years. Politicians used poison gas and gas-dispersing airplanes as icons of the threat posed by other nations, and drills with gas masks reinforced the need for discipline and technology to protect the nation.[31]

Similarly, the central government mobilized chemical technology to protect the nation from insect enemies. In 1937, the German government mandated that farmers use insecticides. Unfortunately for this program, Germany imported most of its insecticides. The country's reliance on expensive imports stimulated the German chemical industry to search for cheaper synthetic insecticides.[32]

The giant German chemical combine I. G. Farben developed a working relationship with the Nazi leadership and became involved in the chemical warfare program. In November 1936, I. G. Farben officers urged the military economic staff to produce and stockpile chemical weapons. Poison gas, they argued, could determine the outcome of the next war if it were used against civilian populations, who would be panic-stricken and find "every door-handle, every fence, every paving stone a weapon of the enemy." I. G. Farben officials thought Germans were too disciplined and technically equipped to collapse should an enemy retaliate.[33]

The search for new insecticides and poison gases came together in the laboratory of I. G. Farben's Gerhard Schrader. In fact, all German chemical laboratories became de facto parts of the country's chemical-warfare program in 1935, when the central government mandated the reporting of all toxic substances. The definition of toxicity issued by the War Ministry—substances that killed in low concentration—left little doubt about the reason for the order. When Schrader sprayed chemicals on insects, he was in fact screening chemical weapons. Schrader began with a compound, chloroethyl alcohol, known to be toxic to human beings and dogs, varied the atoms on the molecule, and screened the resulting compounds on insects. A series of substitutions led him to a little-studied family of compounds called organophosphates, which killed insects effectively. Schrader and a colleague patented the generic blueprint of the molecule in 1939.[34]

Few people knew about this patent, for it was declared "top secret." The basic molecule constituted the basis not only for new insecticides but for highly lethal new nerve gases. On December 23, 1936, Schrader had attached cyanide to his basic organophosphate molecule. The compound killed plant lice at a concentration of only 1 part per 200,000. When inhaled in small doses, it also would kill human beings. I. G. Farben patented the substance in February 1937 and sent a sample to the chemical warfare section of the Army Weapons Office in May. Schrader traveled to Berlin to demonstrate its effects. Later named tabun, the compound was the first organophosphate nerve gas.[35]

In 1938, Schrader found a related compound whose potential "as a toxic war substance" he judged to be "astonishingly high." On animals, the substance tested ten times as toxic as tabun. Schrader dubbed it sarin. Other nerve gases followed. Through his superiors at I. G. Farben, Schrader reported between one and two hundred highly toxic compounds to the government in the late 1930s and early 1940s. In 1939, Germany set up a tabun pilot plant at Munster-Lager (Heidkrug) to make gas for the army.[36]

At the same time that Schrader's work demonstrated biochemical similarities between human beings and insects, Nazi propagandists promoted metaphorical links between human and insect enemies. Nineteenth-century German theologians had described Jews as "vermin, spiders, swarms of locusts, leeches, giant parasite growths, poisonous worms." Nazis capitalized on such long-standing metaphors, with Hitler calling Jews a "pestilence," "typical parasites," and "carriers of bacilli worse than Black Death." As the Nazis grew in power, so did their propaganda. Joseph Goebbels said that "since the flea is not a pleasant animal we are not obliged to keep it, protect it and let it prosper so that it may prick and torture us, but our duty is rather to exterminate it. Likewise the Jew." Metaphor and "reality" blurred in Nazi rhetoric: Jews were to be exterminated as deliberately, and literally, as insects.[37]

World War II: War on Human Beings and Insects (1940-45)

World War II, scientific discoveries, and a massive bureaucracy offered Nazi Germany the chance to put the rhetoric of extermination into practice on a massive scale. Early efforts to gas Jews relied on carbon monoxide from the exhaust of vans.[38] Greater efficiency came when the SS began using technology more closely suited to its rhetoric. Auschwitz Kommandant Rudolf Hoess later said that fumigation of insects in the concentration camp inspired the use of an insecticide, Zyklon B, on human beings. Zyklon B was hydrocyanic acid, one of the substances called an "insecticide" in civilian settings and a "chemical weapon" in military settings. (During World War I, the compound had been used for both purposes; Germany had developed hydrocyanic acid to kill lice that transmitted typhus and used it to fumigate submarines, barracks, and prison camps.) In Auschwitz, Soviet prisoners of war appear to have been the first intentional victims of Zyklon B. Jews and other targets of the Nazi regime followed.[39]

The "fit" between insecticide technology and Nazi "extermination" rhetoric did not escape notice. When the manager of the insecticide manufacturer asked the SS procurement officer the purpose of Zyklon B shipments, he learned that the insecticide would be used to "exterminate criminals, incurable patients, and inferior human beings."[40]

Indirectly, I. G. Farben supported the SS campaign. The company manufactured Degesch's Zyklon B at its Leverkusen plant, and owned 42.5 percent of Degesch, as well as one-third of Degussa, which owned another 42.5 percent of Degesch. Several members of Degesch's supervisory board came from I. G. Farben. I. G. Farben was linked to the horrors of the death camps in another way. Tabun and sarin, the nerve gases developed along with insecticides by Schrader, offered Germany new weapons of great but unmeasured power. Guinea pigs and white rats seemed inadequate for testing the effects of nerve gases on human beings, so, after ill-fated experiments with apes, experiments began on Jews in concentration camps.[41]

Some observers believed that metaphorical redefinition of human enemies as animals, including insects, also facilitated bloodletting in the Pacific theater. When describing Japanese soldiers and civilians, American propagandists and soldiers employed vermin metaphors more often than when describing Germans. Ernie Pyle noted this difference in 1945, when he visited the Pacific after seeing some of the worst fighting in Europe: "In Europe we felt our enemies, horrible and deadly as they were, were still people. But out here I gathered that the Japanese were looked upon as something subhuman and repulsive; the way some people feel about cockroaches or mice." Claire Chennault, a retired United States Army officer and adviser to the air force of Chiang

Kai-Shek, later said that in 1940 he had wanted to "burn out the industrial heart of the Empire with fire-bomb attacks on the teeming bamboo ant heaps of Honshu and Kyushu." In *God Is My Co-Pilot*, Robert Scott, Jr., wrote that every time he killed a "Jap" he felt he "had stepped on another black-widow spider or scorpion."[42]

Why did Americans describe the Japanese as insects and other vermin? Historians have noted that Americans had previously feared a "yellow peril" and discriminated against Asians, and that in World War II they found the Japanese approach to war brutal and irrational. Japanese treatment of prisoners of war (symbolized by the Bataan Death March) contributed to the view that the Japanese behaved in subhuman ways.[43]

Whatever the cause, seeing enemies as vermin must have made it seem "natural" to talk of extermination. Admiral William F. Halsey congratulated troops who captured Peleliu in 1944: "The sincere admiration of the entire Third Fleet is yours for the hill[-]blasting, cave[-]smashing extermination of 11,000 slant-eyed gophers." The novelist Herman Wouk, who experienced World War II aboard a destroyer in the South Pacific, later wrote:

> This cold-bloodedness, worthy of a horseman of Genghis Khan, was quite strange in a pleasant little fellow like Ensign Keith. Militarily, of course, it was an asset beyond price. Like most of the naval executioners at Kwajalein, he seemed to regard the enemy as a species of animal pest. From the grim and desperate taciturnity with which the Japanese died, they seemed on their side to believe they were contending with an invasion of large armed ants. This obliviousness on both sides to the fact that the opponents were human beings may perhaps be cited as the key to the many massacres of the Pacific war.[44]

American forces did not rely on poison gas against the Japanese; other weapons (such as artillery and mortar fire) made "methodical extermination" of Japanese soldiers feasible. Some tacticians held out the hope, however, that use of poison gas would raise fears of "extermination" among Japanese civilians. An Army Operations Division report noted, "Mass employment of gas throughout Japan will bring home with great force to the Japanese people the hopelessness of continuing the war and emphasize to them that their only choice is between capitulation and extermination."[45]

Metaphorical comparisons of insects to human enemies and of insecticides to military weapons laced the speech of civilians as well as soldiers. The Rohm & Haas Company, for example, published an advertisement in 1945 that implicitly compared "Japs" to flies, bullets to insecticides, and rifles to spray guns. In other cases, chemical companies urged consumers to see insecticides, not as bullets, but as chemical weapons. Monsanto, for example, advertised that "chemical warfare defeats moths and larvae." In a more lighthearted vein, a chemical perfuming company, van Ameringen-Haebler, published an advertisement showing a woman spraying insecticides on a mask-wearing man in the "war on the home front."[46]

Combatants (except, probably, Japan) did not use gas against human enemies on battlefields in World War II. On the insect front, however, technology made it feasible to annihilate enemies. In 1939, a chemist at the Swiss chemical company Geigy had found that DDT killed insects at low doses, remained toxic to insects long after application, and had low acute toxicity to humans. In 1941, Geigy offered DDT to its subsidiary in the United States, but the subsidiary did not find it of much interest. DDT's only known use was to kill the Colorado potato beetle, which the subsidiary considered well controlled with lead arsenate. Then World War II prompted the (renamed) United States Bureau of Entomology and Plant Quarantine to search for chemicals to protect soldiers from louse-borne typhus. Geigy gave a sample of DDT to the bureau in 1942, and entomologists found DDT powder ideal for killing lice. With help from the War Production Board, Geigy and other companies began making DDT in the United States for the armed forces. After helping to quell a typhus outbreak in war-torn Naples in the winter of 1943-44, DDT became known as the miracle chemical of World War II.[47]

The campaign against another insect-borne disease, malaria, revitalized links between insect control and chemical warfare. Entomologists at the Bureau of Entomology and Plant Quarantine found that DDT killed mosquitoes well, but the standard way to disperse insecticides from the air—as dusts—worked poorly with DDT. The entomologists then tried spraying DDT from the air as a liquid. This method was new to entomology, but not to chemical warfare. The Bureau of Entomology and Plant Quarantine began working with the United States Army Air Forces in 1943 to adapt chemical warfare tanks and nozzles to DDT. By 1945 the armed services could blanket "thousands of acres" with DDT using airplanes, from small combat planes to large transports. Chemical Warfare Service pilots and planes sprayed DDT to control mosquitoes in the malaria-ridden Pacific. As in other campaigns, propagandists unified images of insect and human enemies. One anti-malaria cartoon portrayed Japanese soldiers and mosquitoes as two aspects of a common enemy, with mosquitoes causing eight times as many casualties as did Japanese soldiers.[48]

Military success against insect enemies during World War II inspired entomologists to call for similar wars on insects at home. E. O. Essig used his December 1944 presidential address to the American Association of Economic Entomologists to call for "An All Out Entomological Program." Noting that the world had never been so conscious of insect control as during World War II, Essig urged that entomologists seize "the great opportunities" and create "a new day" for entomology. He thought one of the "most promising prospects" was "the strong emphasis being placed on the complete extermination of not only newly introduced pests but also those of long standing in the country."[49]

Science News Letter summarized Essig's talk as calling for "Total war against man's insect enemies, with the avowed object of total extermination instead of mere 'control.' " Although Essig had not mentioned DDT, *Science News Letter* emphasized that DDT was a "powerful agent in these postwar wars to make crops less costly and personal life safer, more comfortable." *Popular Mechanics* also thought that the home front would become more like a battlefront. In an article titled "Our Next World War—Against Insects," it reported that "Uncle Sam, fighting one World War, is preparing for the next—and this one will be a long and bitter battle to crush the creeping, wriggling, flying, burrowing billions whose numbers and depredations baffle human comprehension."[50]

Publicists for chemical companies showed no doubt that DDT would bring enormous benefits to civilians, but entomologists tempered their hopes with concern. They believed DDT was appropriate on battlefronts, where risks of insect-born diseases ran high, and they hoped that DDT could be used in agriculture. But they found that DDT could create as well as solve problems, by killing off predators and parasites that normally kept pests under control. Results of military tests lent credence to concerns about DDT's effects on other "nontarget" species. A naval medical officer reported that the first use of DDT in the Pacific had led to "complete destruction of plant and animal life."[51]

Worries found expression in metaphors that echoed criticisms of chemical warfare. Col. J. W. Scharff, a British malarialogist who praised the role of DDT in protecting troops from malaria, complained, "DDT is such a crude and powerful weapon that I cannot help regarding the routine use of this material from the air with anything but horror and aversion." The nature writer Edwin Way Teale shared Scharff's distress: "Given sufficient insecticide, airplanes and lackwit officials after the war, and we will be off with yelps of joy on a crusade against all the insects." Teale was sure of the result of this "bug-blitz binge": a "conservation headache of historic magnitude." The Bureau of Entomology and Plant Quarantine's H. H. Stage and C. F. W. Muesebeck fretted, "Biological deserts may be produced by heavy treatments of DDT and these would be, of course, highly undesirable."[52]

Although federal entomologists thought it premature to recommend DDT for unrestricted civilian use, no peacetime government agency had the authority to keep DDT off the market. On August 1, 1945, the War Production Board allowed manufacturers to sell DDT, once military needs were met, without restriction. The United States dropped an atomic bomb on Hiroshima five days later, then another on Nagasaki, and Japan surrendered. (A woman from Milwaukee used an animal metaphor to express her wish that destruction had been more thorough: "When one sets out to destroy vermin, does one try to leave a few alive in the nest? Certainly not!") The War Production Board soon lifted all restrictions on DDT sales. Declaring that "the war against winged pests was under way," *Time* magazine announced DDT's release for civilian use on the same page where it published photographs of the first atomic explosion.[53]

A postwar "insecticide revolution" began, with DDT and its relatives leading the way. Meanwhile, intelligence teams combing through records of the German chemical industry uncovered Schrader's work on organophosphates. They publicized information about insecticides while keeping secret news of the closely related nerve gases. Even as organophosphates opened a new chapter in the history of chemical weaponry, such organophosphates such as parathion joined DDT in revolutionizing pest control in agriculture. Sales of insecticides soared, replacing earlier methods of pest control that relied on preventing insect attacks.[54]

The rhetoric of war pervaded this revolution. On the first anniversary of the bombing of Hiroshima, Rohm & Haas, which earlier had compared "Japs" to flies, used a full-page photograph of a mushroom cloud to publicize DDT. Industrial Management Corporation sold a technology developed during the war for dispersing DDT called "bug bombs" (forerunners of aerosol cans). The name of the DDT bomb, "Insect-O-Blitz," alluded to the German term for fast, mechanized warfare and to bombing of English cities. As *Modern Packaging* noted, "The Bug Bomb derives its name both from its devastating effect on insect life and its appearance." Coupled with DDT, this new weapon promised to play a central role in the "postwar wars" on insects: "One malaria authority has stated that, given sufficient aerosol bombs and unlimited funds, he can wipe malaria off the earth within 20 years after the war." In its advertisement for DDT (Figure 3), S. B. Penick & Company called for women to join a domestic version of World War II, "the continued battle of the home front."[55]

Conclusion

Publicists for S. B. Penick and other advertisers surely saw their cries for a "battle of the home front" as metaphorical. Human beings waged "real" war against each other, after all, not against bugs. But the frequent use of military metaphors in insecticide advertisements, like the use of insect metaphors in warfare, highlighted similarities in ways that human beings dealt with two-legged and six-legged enemies in the first half of the twentieth century.

Wars on human and insect enemies both focused on enemies, and especially enemies that did not respect boundaries. Once erected, international borders, fencerows, and the walls of homes created the rights of citizens, farmers, and homeowners to protect their land and homes against "invading" enemies—including, ironically, some longtime residents. In Europe, Nazis blamed Jews for almost all of the nation's ills, deported them, and killed them. The United States confined American citizens of Japanese ancestry to concentration camps. American farmers referred to insects in fields as "invaders" and "trespassers" even though most insects had arrived long before the farmers.[56] The emphasis on protection against outsiders helps to explain

PENICK INSECTICIDAL BASES...
Super Ammunition for the Continued Battle of the Home Front

For the never-ending battle against pests in and about the home, Penick offers a suitable base proven for its "knock-down" and "knock-out" power.

FOR THE HOUSEFLY AND MOSQUITO:
PYREFUME SUPER 20—A pure pyrethrum extract guaranteed to assay 2 grams pyrethrins per 100 cc. or expressed by percentage it is 2½% pyrethrins. Light in color it reduces possibility of stain.

FOR ROACHES & OTHER HOUSEHOLD PESTS:
PYRETHRUM POWDER—Finely milled and standardized to exact assays. Pyrethrum Powder is available in the following strengths with prices

according to pyrethrum percentages, .8%, .9%, 1.1% and 1.3%. Has great "knock-down" and "knock-out" power.

IMPREGNO—Killing power is immediate as all particles are coated with pyrethrins. Economical —easy to apply.

50% DDT DISPERSIBLE POWDER — Add talc, clay or similar inert material to make a dust containing 1% to 10% DDT. Roach and Flea powders require the higher percentages.

FOR RATS AND MICE — Fortified Red Squill processed to a uniform degree of toxicity which is 500/600 mg/kg. Non-poisonous to domestic animals, it is sure death to mice and rats.

Write For Descriptive Literature

S.B. PENICK & COMPANY

50 CHURCH STREET
NEW YORK 7, N. Y.
Telephone: COrtlandt 7-1970

735 W. DIVISION ST.
CHICAGO 10, ILL.
Telephone: MOHawk 5651

Figure 3. A year after the end of World War II, an insecticide company urged Americans to continue the "battle of the home front" with "super ammunition," including DDT. Unlike battles overseas, this effort would require women to hold the front line. Reprinted from Soap and Sanitary Chemicals *(Aug. 1946), 115.*

the popularity of extermination, or driving beyond boundaries, as a term for dealing with both human and insect enemies.

Like physical structures, mental divisions between human beings and nature created useful boundaries, especially because one could move human beings and animals from one side of the boundary to the other. Describing insects as national enemies elevated them from the category of nuisance to that of national threat. This was not always an exaggeration. In the Pacific, for example, malaria-carrying mosquitoes caused more casualties than did enemy soldiers, making them important dangers for armies. Movement of people into the category of animal had consequences of far more horrifying significance. Wouk emphasized that the ability to redefine a human being as an insect was an "asset beyond price" in a military setting, but an asset that resulted in "massacres." And Nazis surely knew exactly what they were doing when they used "extermination" to describe their campaign against Jews.

Not coincidentally, human beings developed similar technologies to kill human and insect enemies. In many cases, farmers and armies used identical chemicals (chloropicrin and hydrogen cyanide) to kill their enemies; in others, closely related chemicals (arsenicals and organophosphates) served both purposes. For chemical warriors, at least, these similarities came as no surprise. William Porter, chief of the Chemical Warfare Service, noted in 1944, "The fundamental biological principles of poisoning Japanese, insects, rats, bacteria and cancer are essentially the same."[57]

The development of common technologies relied on alliances, usually organized by nation-states, between civilian and military institutions. In the United States, the Bureau of Entomology collaborated intermittently with the Chemical Warfare Service from World War I through World War II. In Germany, I. G. Farben conducted research for the German army. The world wars forged especially close links between military and scientific institutions, and efforts to maintain such links became a hallmark of the post-World War II era.

Although linked metaphorically, technologically, and institutionally, wars on insects and human beings differed in several respects. First, control of poisons rested in different hands. Almost anyone could use insecticides, but chemical weapons remained a monopoly of military institutions. Moreover, in the 1920s many nations signed international agreements designed to limit the use of poison gas in warfare. No international agencies tried to limit the use of insecticides during this period.[58]

Second, insecticides and chemical weapons followed different trajectories in World War II. Insecticides became "miracle chemicals" used widely to halt insect-borne diseases. With the probable exception of Japan, however, combatants did not use poison gas on battlefields.

The primary use of chemicals for extermination of human beings came in the death camps of the Holocaust. After World War II, nuclear weapons eclipsed chemical weapons as the primary target of international arms control efforts.

Third, morality never entered into discussions of killing insects, while it often figured in debates about human warfare. In fact, moral concerns help to explain the popularity of insect metaphors for human enemies. Western thought long regarded conquest of nature as a moral duty, rather than a moral dilemma, and conquest of insects offered an especially useful metaphor for human warfare. The implicit appropriateness of eliminating natural enemies entirely, exemplified in the moral neutrality of the term extermination, suggests that ideas about complete conquest of nature contributed to the ideology of war on human beings.

The rhetoric of exterminating or annihilating enemies—whether insect or human—antedated the twentieth century. The first half of the century, however, saw the development of technology and institutions that enabled nations to kill enemies with chemical compounds more quickly, and over a wider area, than ever before. In practice, insecticides found far wider use than did chemical weapons, but chemicals played a central role in extermination of human beings in the Holocaust. As the United States Army documents about potential use of gas in Japan suggested, chemical weapons could elicit fears of "extermination." Ali Hassan al-Majid, leader of Iraq's chemical attacks on Kurds in the 1980s, declared, "I will kill them all with chemical weapons."[59]

While similar in some ways in their dealings with these chemicals, Germany and the United States were in contrast in other ways. In the 1930s, they differed in their commitment to mobilization, which contributed to Germany's success in finding new chemical weapons. During World War II, Nazi Germany employed chemicals on a horrific scale to exterminate human beings but had little success with new insecticides. The United States, on the other hand, did not use chemical weapons to kill human beings in World War II (with a single, accidental, exception)[60] and did not make genocide a national policy, though it did develop an effective new insecticide (DDT).

By the end of World War II, then, lines between human and insect enemies, military and civilian institutions, and military and civilian technology had all been blurred. Annihilation of national and natural enemies had become realistic on a large scale, a reality both comforting and disturbing to people who lived in the post-World War II era. The twin insecurities raised by military and civilian technology illustrated that war and environmental change were not separate endeavors, but rather related aspects of life in the twentieth century and beyond.

Notes

I am grateful for comments by Brian Balogh, Paul Boyer, Alan Brinkley, Craig Cameron, Bernard Carlson, Pete Daniel, Thomas Dunlap, Paul Forman, Barton Hacker, Pamela Henson, Michael Holt, Linda Lear, Gerald Linderman, Allan Megill, David Nord, Peter Onuf, Katherine Ott, John Perkins, Beverly Rathcke, Terry Sharrer, Merritt Roe Smith, Richard Tucker, Earl Werner, Susan Wright, John Vandermeer, an anonymous reviewer, and scholars who attended presentations at the 1993 meeting of the Society for the History of Technology, Johns Hopkins University, the University of Virginia, and the Smithsonian Institution. Michael Allen kindly identified errors (corrected here) in the journal article's discussion of concentration camps.

I am also grateful for a predoctoral fellowship from the Smithsonian Institution and grants from the University of Michigan and the National Science Foundation (SBR 9511726).

This article draws on Edmund P. Russell, III, "War on Insects: Warfare, Insecticides, and Environmental Change in the United States, 1870-1945" (Ph.D. Dissertation, University of Michigan, 1993).

This chapter previously appeared, in a slightly different form, as Edmund P. Russell III, " 'Speaking of Annihilation': Mobilizing for War against Human and Insect Enemies," *Journal of American History* 82 (March 1996): 1505-29. Some of this material has also been published in Edmund Russell, *War and Nature: Fighting Humans and Insects with Chemicals from World War I to Silent Spring* (New York: Cambridge University Press, 2001). I thank *The Journal of American History* and Cambridge University Press for permission to reprint.

1   Fred Lasswell, "Bugs Every Marine Should Know," *Leatherneck* 28 (March 1945), 37.
2   Rachel Carson, *Silent Spring* (New York: Houghton Mifflin, 1962).
3   Although war and military institutions are different, I follow the practice among British historians and use the former term here to encompass the latter. For a sample of works in military, environmental, technological, and cultural history, see Peter Paret, "The New Military History," *Parameters*, 21 (Autumn 1991), 10-18; William H. McNeill, *The Pursuit of Power: Technology, Armed Force, and Society Since A. D. 1000* (Chicago, IL: University of Chicago Press, 1982); Carolyn Merchant, ed., *Major Problems in American Environmental History* (Lexington, MA: Houghton Mifflin, 1993); Jeffrey K. Stine and Joel A. Tarr, "Technology and the Environment: The Historians' Challenge," *Environmental History Review*, 18 (Spring 1994), 1-7; Merritt Roe Smith, ed., *Military Enterprise and Technological Change: Perspectives on the American Experience* (Cambridge, MA: MIT Press, 1985); Barton C. Hacker, "Military Institutions, Weapons, and Social Change: Toward a New History of Military Technology," *Technology and Culture*, 35:4 (1994), 768-834; Elaine Tyler May, *Homeward Bound: American Families in the Cold War Era* (New York: Basic Books, 1988); and Paul Boyer, *By the Bomb's Early Light: American*

Thought and Culture at the Dawn of the Atomic Age (New York: Pantheon Books, 1985).

On war and the environment, see Susan D. Lanier-Graham, *The Ecology of War: Environmental Impacts of Weapons and Warfare* (New York: Walker, 1993); Seth Shulman, *The Threat at Home: Confronting the Toxic Legacy of the US Military* (Boston, MA: Beacon Press, 1992); J. P. Robinson, *The Effects of Weapons on Ecosystems* (Oxford, U.K.: Pergamon, 1979); Arthur H. Westing and Malvern Lumsden, *Threat of Modern Warfare to Man and His Environment: An Annotated Bibliography Prepared Under the Auspices of the International Peace Research Association* (Paris, France: Unesco, 1979); Avner Offer, *The First World War: An Agrarian Interpretation* (Oxford, U.K.: Clarendon Press, 1989); Alfred W. Crosby, *Ecological Imperialism: The Biological Expansion of Europe, 900-1900* (New York: Cambridge University Press, 1986).

4   Isaiah 2:4; Joseph A. Wildermuth to editor, *Washington Post Book World*, Feb. 20, 1994, 14. See also Keith Thomas, *Man and the Natural World: A History of the Modern Sensibility* (New York: Pantheon Books, 1983). For the suggestion that neoclassical economics (which views the military as an "externality") and "the peculiarly American blindness to the presence of the military" contribute to the view that civilian and military enterprises are separate endeavors, see David F. Noble, "Command Performance: A Perspective on the Social and Economic Consequences of Military Enterprise," in *Military Enterprise and Technological Change*, ed. Merritt Roe Smith, 329-46, esp. 330-31.

5   John H. Perkins, *Insects, Experts, and the Insecticide Crisis: The Quest for New Pest Management Strategies* (New York: Plenum Press, 1982), 4-10; John H. Perkins, "Reshaping Technology in Wartime: The Effect of Military Goals on Entomological Research and Insect-Control Practices," *Technology and Culture*, 19:2 (1978), 169-86; Thomas R. Dunlap, *DDT: Scientists, Citizens, and Public Policy* (Princeton, NJ: Princeton University Press, 1981), 36-37, 59-63; Emory C. Cushing, *History of Entomology in World War II* (Washington, DC: Smithsonian Institution, 1957); V. G. Dethier, *Man's Plague? Insects and Agriculture* (Princeton, NJ: Darwin Press, Inc., 1976), 112; Stockholm International Peace Research Institute, *The Problem of Chemical and Biological Warfare: A Study of the Historical, Technical, Military, Legal, and Political Aspects of CBW, and Possible Disarmament Measures, vol. I: The Rise of CB Weapons* (New York: Humanities Press, 1971), 70-75.

6   Military metaphors have been used to describe a variety of civilian endeavors, so the events described here are part of a larger pattern. I use the term metaphor to include simile, analogy, and imagery. On the role of metaphor in thought and communication, see David E. Leary, "Psyche's Muse: The Role of Metaphor in the History of Psychology," in *Metaphors in the History of Psychology*, ed. David E. Leary (New York: Cambridge University Press, 1990), 1-78; George Lakoff and Mark Johnson, *Metaphors We Live By* (Chicago, IL: University of Chicago Press, 1980); and Mary B. Hesse, *Models and Analogies in Science* (Notre Dame, IN: University of Notre Dame Press, 1966).

7   *Oxford English Dictionary*, 2d ed., s.v. "Exterminate." On imagination, technology, and the expansion of war in the twentieth century, see Zygmunt Bauman, *Modernity and the Holocaust* (Ithaca, NY: Cornell University Press, 1989); Craig M. Cameron, *American Samurai: Myth, Imagination, and the Conduct of Battle in the First Marine Division, 1941-1951* (New York: Cambridge University Press, 1994); and Michael S.

Sherry, *The Rise of American Air Power: The Creation of Armageddon* (New Haven, CT: Yale University Press, 1987).

8   For examples of the weak on the strong, see Eugene D. Genovese, *Roll, Jordan, Roll: The World the Slaves Made* (New York: Pantheon Press, 1974); and James C. Scott, *Weapons of the Weak: Everyday Forms of Peasant Resistance* (New Haven, CT: Yale University Press, 1985). On stories of progress and decline as master narratives, see William Cronon, "A Place for Stories: Nature, History, and Narrative," *Journal of American History*, 78 (March 1992), 1347-76.

9   See Hugh R. Slotten, "Humane Chemistry or Scientific Barbarism? American Responses to World War I Poison Gas, 1915-1930," *Journal of American History*, 77 (Sept. 1990), 476-98; Robert Harris and Jeremy Paxman, *A Higher Form of Killing: The Secret Story of Chemical and Biological Warfare* (New York: Hill and Wang, 1982); L. F. Haber, *The Poisonous Cloud: Chemical Warfare in the First World War* (Oxford, U.K.: Clarendon Press, 1986); and Daniel Patrick Jones, "The Role of Chemists in Research on War Gases in the United States During World War I" (Ph.D. diss., University of Wisconsin, 1969).

10 Harris and Paxman, *Higher Form of Killing*, 9-11.

11 In 1915, combatants released 3,600 tons of gas; in 1916, 15,000 tons. In 1916, the National Academy of Sciences created the National Research Council (NRC) to promote the "national security and welfare" by organizing scientific research in government, industry, and educational institutions for the federal government. In 1917, the council created a Subcommittee on Noxious Gases with members from the army, navy, and the NRC Chemistry Committee. The civilian researchers became part of the Gas Service of the army, which became the Chemical Warfare Service three days later. In 1918, President Woodrow Wilson issued an executive order asking the National Academy of Sciences to perpetuate the NRC. Rexmond C. Cochrane, *The National Academy of Sciences: The First Hundred Years, 1863-1963* (Washington, DC: NetLibrary, Inc., 1978), 209, 231-36; Leo P. Brophy, Wyndham D. Miles, and Rexmond C. Cochrane, *The Chemical Warfare Service: From Laboratory to Field* (Washington, DC: U.S. Department of the Army, Office of Military History, 1959), 1-27; W. A. Noyes, Jr., "Preface," in *Chemistry: A History of the Chemistry Components of the National Defense Research Committee 1940-1946*, ed. W. A. Noyes, Jr., (Boston, MA: Little, Brown, 1948), xv-xvi; and Harris and Paxman, *Higher Form of Killing*, 22-23, 34.

12 Williams Haynes, *American Chemical Industry, vol. III: The World War I Period: 1912-1922* (New York: Van Nostrand, 1945), 111; R. C. Roark, *A Bibliography of Chloropicrin, 1848-1932* (Washington, DC: U.S. Department of Agriculture, 1934), 1-2.

13 Hydrogen cyanide (also called hydrocyanic acid and prussic acid) dispersed in the open air too quickly to kill soldiers effectively, and only the French persisted in using it during World War I. (To kill insect pests in orchards, fumigators enclosed trees in tents before releasing the gas.) Arsenic found use against insects after it was known to be poisonous to humans. Haber, *Poisonous Cloud*, 62-63, 117-118; Brophy, Miles, and Cochrane, *Chemical Warfare Service*, 55-56; Haynes, *American Chemical Industry*, III, 111-12; L. O. Howard, "Entomology and the War," *Scientific Monthly*, 8 (Jan.-June 1919), 109-17; and Dunlap, *DDT*, 20.

14 Surviving records do not indicate whether experimenters in fact tested gases on humans in chambers. W. Dwight Pierce to L.O. Howard, n.d., Correspondence on Body Lice, Vermin, Cooties, in Army, Tests and

Recommendations 1918, Correspondence and Reports Relating to a Study of Body Lice 1918, Records of the Bureau of Entomology and Plant Quarantine, RG 7 (Washington National Records Center, Suitland, Md.); "Report on Experiments Conducted on October 16, 1918, Testing the Effect of Certain Toxic Gases on Body Lice and Their Eggs," ibid.

15 "Killing Weevils with Chloropicirn," abstract, in Roark, *Bibliography of Chloropicrin*, 3. The Bureau of Chemistry, the Bureau of Plant Industry, and the Federal Horticultural Board helped conduct research at Chemical Warfare Service laboratories at American University. "The Chemical Warfare Service in Peace," [n.d.], file 029.0611: Articles and Speeches— Peacetime Activities, Station Series, 1942-1945, Security Classified, Records of the Chemical Warfare Service, U. S. Army, RG 175, (Washington National Records Center); I. E. Neifert and G. L. Garrison, *Experiments on the Toxic Action of Certain Gases on Insects, Seeds, and Fungi* (Washington, DC: Government Printing Office, 1920); Haynes, *American Chemical Industry, III,* 111.

16 For the descripton of soldiers as "earwigs" and other animal metaphors used in World War I, see Paul Fussell, *The Great War and Modern Memory* (New York: Oxford University Press, 1975), 77. On views of enemies, see Sam Keen, *Faces of the Enemy: Reflections of the Hostile Imagination* (San Francisco, CA: Harper and Row, 1986), 60-64; Peter Paret, Beth Irwin Lewis, and Paul Paret, *Persuasive Images: Posters of War and Revolution from the Hoover Institution Archives* (Princeton, NJ: Princeton University Press, 1992); and J. Glenn Gray, *The Warriors: Reflections on Men in Battle* (New York: Harper and Row, 1970). American pioneers talked of wilderness as an "enemy" to be "conquered," "subdued," and "vanquished" by a "pioneer army." See Roderick Nash, *Wilderness and the American Mind* (New Haven, CT: Yale University Press, 1982), 27.

17 Howard, "Entomology and the War," 117. On bellicose traditions in science and entomology, see Carolyn Merchant, *The Death of Nature: Women, Ecology, and the Scientific Revolution* (San Francisco, CA: Harper, 1980); and Dunlap, *DDT*, 36-37. On the use of metaphor to mold public image, see JoAnne Brown, *The Definition of a Profession: The Authority of Metaphor in the History of Intelligence Testing, 1890-1930* (Princeton, NJ: Princeton University Press, 1992).

18 Since insects were already considered lowly, perhaps describing them as creatures from another world was one of the few ways to portray them as unworthy of "fraternity." L. O. Howard, "The War Against Insects: The Insecticide Chemist and Biologist in the Mitigation of Plant Pests," *Chemical Age*, 30:1 (1922), 5-6. On how World War I helped entomologists argue that they were not engaged in "trivial studies," see Howard, "Entomology and the War," 109, 117.

19 Howard identified the 1921 address as a turning point in his representation of insects and hoped that the appreciation for the "insect war" would lead to support for entomology. L. O. Howard, *The Insect Menace* (New York: The Century Company, 1931), ix; Howard, "U.S. Wages Insect War"; R. C. Roark, "Household Insecticides," *Soap and Sanitary Chemicals,* 11 (Nov. 1935), 117; Dunlap, *DDT*, 37. Similarity of rhetoric suggests that Howard may have been influenced by entomologist Stephen Forbes, who in turn was influenced by Charles Darwin and Herbert Spencer, but Howard's practice of rarely citing sources makes it difficult to trace intellectual debts. On Forbes, see Sharon E. Kingsland, *Modeling Nature: Episodes in the History of Population Ecology* (Chicago, IL: University of Chicago Press, 1985), 12-17. On preventive and remedial measures for pest

control, see, for example, C. L. Marlatt, *The Principal Insect Enemies of Growing Wheat* (Washington, DC: U.S. Department of Agriculture, 1908); and W. D. Hunter, *The Boll Weevil Problem, with Special Reference to Means of Reducing Damage* (Washington, DC: U.S. Department of Agriculture, 1909).

20 Eldon W. Downs and George F. Lemmer, "Origins of Aerial Crop Dusting," *Agricultural History,* 39 (July 1965), 123-35, esp. 126.

21 Corley McDarment, "The Use of Airplanes to Destroy the Boll Weevil," *McClure's Magazine,* 57 (Aug. 1924), 90-102, esp. 91-92; Downs and Lemmer, "Origins of Aerial Crop Dusting," 124, 127.

22 Ina L. Hawes and Rose Eisenberg, eds., *Bibliography on Aviation and Economic Entomology* (Washington, DC: U.S. Department of Agriculture, 1947), 8-9; Downs and Lemmer, "Origins of Aerial Crop Dusting," 130-32, esp. 130; and Douglas Helms, "Technological Methods for Boll Weevil Control," *Agricultural History,* 53 (Oct. 1979), 286-99.

23 L. O. Howard, "The Needs of the World as to Entomology," *Smithsonian Institution Annual Report,* 1925 (Washington, 1925), 355-72, esp. 370; Roark, *Bibliography of Chloropicrin;* Howard, *Insect Menace,* 283.

24 Frederic J. Brown, *Chemical Warfare: A Study in Restraints* (Princeton, NJ: Princeton University Press, 1968), 52-96; Daniel P. Jones, "From Military to Civilian Technology: The Introduction of Tear Gas for Civil Riot Control," *Technology and Culture,* 19:2 (1978), 151-68.

25 "Chemical Warfare Making Swords into Plowshares," *Chemical Warfare,* 8:2 (1922), 2-5, esp. 2; "Its Greater Service to Peace: From *Gazette Times,* Pittsburgh, Pa., November 24, 1924," *Chemical Warfare,* 11:2 (1925), 22; "Chemical Warfare: Editorial in 'Army and Navy Register,' January 7, 1922," *Chemical Warfare,* 8:1 (1922), 20-21, esp. 20; "Gassing the Boll-Weevil: Editorial from *Boston Transcript,* September 19, 1922," *Chemical Warfare* 10 (1922), 11; "Chemists Protest Ban on Poison Gas," *Chemical Warfare,* 11:8-9 (1925), 13.

26 Amos A. Fries, "Chemical Warfare Inspires Peace," *Chemical Warfare,* 6:5 (1921), 3-4, esp. 3. See also Amos A. Fries, "Chemical Warfare and its Relation to Art and Industry," *Chemical Warfare,* 7:4 (1921), 2-8, esp. 6-7. H. W. Walker and J. E. Mills, "Progress Report of Work of the Chemical Warfare Service on the Boll Weevil *Anthonomus grandis,*" *Journal of Economic Entomology,* 19 (Aug. 1926), 600-601.

27 H. W. Walker, "A Brief Resume of the Chemical Warfare Service Boll Weevil Investigation," *Chemical Warfare,* 13:12 (1927), 231-37, esp. 233.

28 "Chemistry and War: The Following Was Printed in a Pamphlet Issued Under the Auspices of the National Research Council," *Chemical Warfare,* 6:6 (1921), 13-15, esp. 14. This was not mere rhetoric. As entomologists developed aerial dispersal of insecticides in the 1920s, the Chemical Warfare Service developed aerial dispersal of chemical weapons. Brophy, Miles, and Cochrane, *Chemical Warfare Service,* 32.

29 Amos A. Fries, "Address before Chemical Industries Exposition, New York City," Sept. 12, 1922, file 029.0611: Articles & Speeches—Peacetime Activities, Station Series 1942-1945 Security Classified, Records of the Chemical Warfare Service, U. S. Army. On the piece in the *New York Herald,* see "Not Poison Gas!," *Chemical Warfare,* 9:2 (1921), 22.

30 This hypothesis is the author's. Documents searched for this study, both at the National Archives and in journals, are silent as to why the insecticide projects ended.

31 Rolf-Dieter Müller, "World Power Status Through the Use of Poison Gas? German Preparations for Chemical Warfare, 1919-1945," in *The German*

Military in the Age of Total War, ed. Wilhelm Deist (Dover, NH: Berg Publishers, 1985), 171-209, esp. 183; Peter Fritzsche, "Machine Dreams: Airmindedness and the Reinvention of Germany," *American Historical Review,* 98 (June 1993), 685-709.

32 "Chemicals—Use of Agricultural Insecticides Compulsory in Germany," *Commerce Reports,* May 1, 1937, 354; A. Buxtorf and M. Spindler, *Fifteen Years of Geigy Pest Control* (Basel, Switzerland: Buchdruckerei Karl Werner A.G., 1954), 8.

33 Originally, I. G. Farben emphasized quantitative superiority in traditional chemical weapons, especially mustard gas. For the argument that German chemical companies promoted the use of poison gas because they expected to win large contracts, see Müller, "World Power Status through the Use of Poison Gas?," 184-86, esp. 186. For the argument that I. G. Farben executives held ambivalent views toward Nazi war preparations, see Peter Hayes, *Industry and Ideology: IG Farben in the Nazi Era* (New York: Cambridge University Press, 1987), xvii.

34 The War Ministry defined an inhalation toxicity index: (death time in minutes) x (concentration in milligrams per cubic meter). The War Ministry was interested in compounds with values less than 10,000. Combined Intelligence Objectives Subcommittee, "A New Group of War Gases, No. 23-7," n.d., p. 7, Library Project Files 1946-1951, Records of Assistant Chief of Staff (G-2) Intelligence, Administrative Division, U.S. Army, RG 319 (Washington National Records Center); British Intelligence Objectives Subcommittee, "The Development of New Insecticides, Report No. 714 (Revised)," n.d., 13-14; 21-24, ibid.

35 Harris and Paxman, *Higher Form of Killing,* 57; Stockholm International Peace Research Institute, *The Problem of Chemical and Biological Warfare,* I, 71-72; British Intelligence Objectives Subcommittee, "Development of New Insecticides," 23; Robert L. Metcalf, "The Impact of Organophosphorous Insecticides Upon Basic and Applied Science," *Bulletin of the Entomological Society of America,* 5 (1959), 3-15.

36 Gerard Schrader worked with Eberhard Gross, who did toxicology testing. Gross forwarded results to a Heinrich Hoerlein, director of I. G. Elberfeld, who forwarded them to Berlin. Combined Intelligence Objectives Subcommittee, "A New Group of War Gases, No. 23-7," 3-7; Harris and Paxman, *Higher Form of Killing,* 58-59, esp. 58.

37 In 1884, Theodor Fritsch saw "a clear distinction between the human being and the Jew." Eugen Duhring had urged that "the better peoples" use "the right of war ... against the anti-Aryan, nay anti-human attacks by alien parasites." See C. C. Aronsfeld, *The Text of the Holocaust: A Study of the Nazis' Extermination Propaganda: 1919-1945* (Marblehead, MA: Micah Publishers, 1985), 2, 12.

38 They used the same method at Treblinka, near Warsaw, built in early 1941. Joseph Borkin, *The Crime and Punishment of I. G. Farben* (New York: Free Press, 1978), 121-22. On debates over the origins and dates of Nazi extermination policies, see Gerald Fleming, *Hitler and the Final Solution* (Berkeley: University of California Press, 1984); and Michael R. Marrus, ed., *The Nazi Holocaust: Historical Articles on the Destruction of European Jews, vol. III: The "Final Solution": The Implementation of Mass Murder* (Westport, CT: Meckler, 1989). On the Holocaust, see, among other works, Omer Bartov, *Hitler's Army: Soldiers, Nazis, and War in the Third Reich* (New York: Oxford University Press, 1991); Gerald Reitlinger, *The Final Solution: The Attempt to Exterminate the Jews of Europe 1939-1945* (Northvale, NJ: J. Aronson, 1987); and Yehuda Bauer, *A History of the Holocaust* (New York: F. Watts, 1982).

39 Experiments in the use of hydrocyanic acid on people may have begun as
   early as July 1941. Reitlinger, *Final Solution,* 146. Zyklon B was tested on
   five hundred Russian prisoners of war in August 1941, according to Borkin,
   Crime and Punishment of I. G. Farben, 121-22. According to Hayes,
   Industry and Ideology, 362, Zyklon B was first tested on "about 850 Soviet
   prisoners of war and sick inmates in September 1941."
40 The Degesch manager, Gerhard Peters, is quoted as making the comment
   about extermination. See Josiah E. DuBois Jr., *The Devil's Chemists: 24
   Conspirators of the International Farben Cartel Who Manufacture Wars*
   (Boston, MA: Beacon Press, 1952), 213-16, esp. 214; Borkin, *Crime and
   Punishment of I. G. Farben,* 123; Hayes, *Industry and Ideology,* 361-62.
41 DuBois, *Devil's Chemists,* 213. I. G. Farben had five of eleven seats on
   Degesch's board, according to Borkin, *Crime and Punishment of I. G.
   Farben,* 121, 132. I. G. Farben had three seats on the administrative
   committee (perhaps the supervisory board described by Borkin), according
   to Hayes, *Industry and Ideology,* 361-62. Production of Zyklon B rose from
   242 short tons in 1940 to 321 in 1942 and 411 in 1943; it declined to 231
   in 1944. See Hayes, *Industry and Ideology,* 362.
42 John W. Dower, *War Without Mercy: Race and Power in the Pacific War*
   (New York: Pantheon Books, 1986). For Ernie Pyle's remark, see
   Cameron, *American Samurai,* 1; for Claire Chennnault's and Robert
   Scott's, see Sherry, *Rise of American Air Power,* 101-2, 134.
43 Dower, *War Without Mercy,* 77-180; Cameron, *American Samurai,* 98-
   129. How much weight to attach to various factors in causing American
   contempt for Japanese continues to be debated, for example, in a conflict
   over a scuttled Smithsonian Institution exhibit. *Washington Post,* Sept. 26,
   1994, A1.
44 Cameron, *American Samurai,* 1; Herman Wouk, *The Caine Mutiny*
   (Garden City, NY: Doubleday and Company, 1951), 240. On the
   importance of Wouk's World War II experience for *The Caine Mutiny,* see
   Washington Post, May 16, 1995, C1.
45 The phrase "methodical extermination" is from an official history of the
   Guadalcanal campaign quoted in Cameron, *American Samurai,* 122.
   Operations Division, "U.S. Chemical Warfare Policy," n.d., quoted in John
   Ellis van Courtland Moon, "Project SPHINX: The Question of the Use of
   Gas in the Planned Incasion of Japan," *Journal of Strategic Studies,* 12
   (Sept. 1989), 303-23, esp. 305.
46 Rohm & Haas, "Japs or Flies," advertisement, *Soap and Sanitary Chemicals*
   (May 1945), 110; Monsanto Chemicals, "Chemical Warfare Defeats Moths
   and Larvae," advertisement, *Soap and Sanitary Chemicals* (Sept. 1944), 4;
   van Ameringen-Haebler, "War on the Home Front," advertisement, *Soap
   and Sanitary Chemicals* (Aug. 1944), 79.
47 Scholars trace restraint in the use of gas to deterrence (both sides feared
   retaliation in kind) and dislike of gas by military officers (who found it hard
   to control and use decisively), but reports charged that Japan used poison
   gas in China in the 1930s and 1940s. Brown, *Chemical Warfare,* 288-89;
   Harris and Paxman, *Higher Form of Killing,* 148-49; Jeffrey W. Legro,
   "Cooperation Within Conflict: Submarines, Strategic Bombing, Chemical
   Warfare and Restraint in World War II" (Ph.D. diss, University of
   California, Los Angeles, 1992); Stockholm International Peace Research
   Institute, *Problem of Chemical and Biological Warfare,* I, 147-57. On DDT,
   see Victor Froelicher, "The Story of DDT," *Soap and Sanitary Chemicals*
   (July 1944), p. 115; E. F. Knipling, "Insect Control Investigations of the
   Orlando, Fla., Laboratory During World War II," in Annual Report of the
   Board of Regents of the Smithsonian Institution 1948 (Washington, DC:

Government Printing Office, 1948), 335-48, esp. 335-37; R. C. Roark to
P. N. Annand, Jan. 6, 1945, History of Developments—Bureau of
Entomology and Plant Quarantine—World War 2, 1945, History of
Defense and War Activities 1941-50, Correspondence and Reports,
Records of the Bureau of Entomology and Plant Quarantine;
"Publications," *Soap and Sanitary Chemicals* (May 1944), 107; and
Dunlap, *DDT*, 62.

48 Knipling, "Insect Control Investigations," 338; Brooks E. Kleber and Dale
Birdsell, *The Chemical Warfare Service: Chemicals in Combat* (Washington,
DC: Office of the Chief of Military History, U. S. Army, 1966), 319; P. A.
Harper, E. T. Lisansky, and B. E. Sasse, "Malaria and Other Insect-Borne
Diseases in the South Pacific Campaign," *American Journal of Tropical
Medicine*, Supplement, 27:3 (1947), 1-67, esp. 36. Civilian and military
researchers were linked by the Office of Scientific Research and
Development Committee on Insect and Rodent Control and the National
Academy of Science—National Research Council Coordinating Committee
on Insect Control. See Leo Finkelstein and C. G. Schmitt, *History of
Research and Development of the Chemical Warfare Service in World War II
(1 July 1940-31 December 1945), vol. XIX, pt. 1: Insecticides, Miticides, and
Rodenticides* ([Edgewood?], MD: Army Chemical Center, 1949), 26-27.

49 E. O. Essig, "An All Out Entomological Program," *Journal of Economic
Entomology*, 38 (Feb. 1945), 1-8, esp. 6, 8.

50 "Total Insect War Urged," *Science News Letter*, Jan. 6, 1945, 5; "Our Next
World War—Against Insects," *Popular Mechanics*, 81 (April 1944), 66-70,
esp. 67.

51 Subcommittee on Dispersal, Minutes of the Fourth Meeting, Feb. 18-19,
1946, 18, Miscellaneous Minutes and Conferences, Insect Control,
Committee on Insect Control (OSRD), Minutes (Bulletins) and Reports
(Drawer 7), Committees on Military Medicine, Division of Medical
Sciences, 1940-1045, Records of the National Research Council
(Washington, D.C.: National Academy of Sciences Archives); Frederick S.
Philips, "Medical Division Report No. 13, A Review of the Biological
Properties and Insecticidal Applications of DDT," Nov. 22, 1944, 2, USA
Typhus Commission—DDT—General, USA Typhus Commission, Records
of the Army Surgeon General, RG 112 (Washington National Records
Center).

52 Special Joint Meeting of the Army Committee for Insect and Rodent
Control and the Office of Scientific Research and Development, Insect
Control Committee, Minutes, Jan. 12, 1945, p.7, Report 39, OSRD Insect
Control Committee Reports vol. 1, Minutes (Bulletins) and Reports
(Drawer 7), Committees on Military Medicine, Division of Medical
Sciences 1940-1945, Records of the National Research Council; Edwin
Way Teale, "DDT," *Nature Magazine,* 38 (March 1945), 120; H. H. Stage
and C. F. W. Muesebeck, "Insects Killed by DDT Aerial Spraying in
Panama," July 1, 1945, p. 1, National Research Council Insect Control
Committee Report 108, OSRD Insect Control Committee Reports—
Numbered—vol. 2, Minutes (Bulletins) and Reports (Drawer 7),
Committees on Military Medicine, Division of Medical Sciences, 1940-
1945, Records of the National Research Council.

53 In July 1945, federal entomologists said they wanted to wait for results of
that summer's experiments before making a recommendation about civilian
uses of DDT, but the War Production Board, which controlled distribution,
left it up to manufacturers to decide DDT's fate. They decided to lift
restrictions. "WPB Lifts Restrictions on DDT," *Soap and Sanitary
Chemicals* (Aug. 1945), 125; "DDT Insecticides Rushed on Market," *Soap*

and Sanitary Chemicals (Sept. 1945), p. 124A-C; DDT Producers Industry
Advisory Committee Summary, July 25, 1945, pp. 3-4, file 535.61105,
Policy Documentation File, Records of the War Production Board, RG 179
(National Archives, Washington, D. C.); Leonie M. Cole to editor,
Milwaukee Journal, Aug. 16, 1945, quoted in Boyer, *By the Bomb's Early
Light,* 185; "War on Insects," *Time,* Aug. 27, 1945, 65.
54 Biology-based methods of preventing insect attacks included biological
control (importing insect predators and parasites) and cultural control
(changing crop patterns to disrupt the life cycles of pests). Whether
chemical insecticides "triumphed" over alternative methods of pest control
before 1920 or after World War II is debated. See Thomas R. Dunlap, "The
Triumph of Chemical Pesticides in Insect Control, 1890-1920,"
Environmental Review, 1:5 (1978), 38-47; and Perkins, *Insects, Experts,
and the Insecticide Crisis,* 11-13. On organophosphates, see Metcalf,
"Impact of Organaphosphorous Insecticides." There are two versions of the
official British report on Gerhard Schrader's research, with the nerve gas
information censored from the revised version. British Intelligence
Objectives Subcommittee, "Development of New Insecticides." On
intelligence teams, see John Gimbel, *Science, Technology, and Reparations:
Exploitation and Plunder in Postwar Germany* (Stanford, CA: Stanford
University Press, 1990).
55 Rohm & Haas, "Fastest Action," advertisement, *Soap and Sanitary
Chemicals* (Aug. 1946), 134; Industrial Management Corporation, "Insect-
O-Blitz," advertisement, *Soap and Sanitary Chemicals* (Dec. 1946), 146;
"Bug Bomb," *Modern Packaging,* 18 (Oct. 1944), 98-102, esp. 98.
56 U.S. Entomological Commission, First Annual Report of the United States
Entomological Commission for the Year 1877 Relating to the Rocky
Mountain Locust (Washington, 1878), 115.
57 William N. Porter to Vannevar Bush, Sept. 30, 1944, file 710, Office of
Scientific Development, Miscellaneous Series, 1942-1945, Records of the
Chemical Warfare Service, United States Army.
58 James Whorton, *Before Silent Spring: Pesticides and Public Policy in Pre-
DDT America* (Princeton, NJ: Princeton University Press, 1974), 133-35.
59 Chemical weapons continue to be feared as weapons of mass destruction,
and efforts to eliminate them continue. See *Washington Post,* Jan. 14, 1993,
A24. Ali Hassan al-Majid quoted in Jeffrey Goldberg, "The Great Terror,"
The New Yorker, March 25, 2002; www.newyorker.com, viewed May 25,
2004.
60 In 1943, German airplanes attacked an American ship in the harbor at Bari,
Italy. Mustard gas in the ship's hold escaped and killed about one thousand
Americans and Italians. Institute of Medicine, *Veterans at Risk: The Health
Effects of Mustard Gas and Lewisite* (Washington, DC: National Academy
Press, 1993), 43-44.

War—
An Ecological Alternative to Peace?
Indirect Impacts of World War II
on the Finnish Environment
Simo Laakkonen

∞

In the Snowy Woods

The Winter War fought between Finland and the Soviet Union in the winter of 1939-40 became a legend of a successful battle of David against Goliath. In one of the coldest winters of the twentieth century, the small country of about 3.5 million inhabitants resisted, alone but successfully, the attacks of the socialist superpower of about 175 million people. One of the slogans created to keep up the fighting spirit was "Kollaa kestää," or "Kollaa will hold out." Kollaa was a small creek among many others in eastern Finland over which Russians and Finns fought fiercely. The creek was in the middle of dense and snowy forests. The white-clad Finnish ski troops held out at Kollaa, and the overwhelming Russian forces were never able conquer the Finns at the little creek.

Despite this success, a major Finnish newspaper published an article after the war with a headline claiming, "Kollaa did not hold out." The article with this questionable headline was, however, not about the outcome of the battles, but about the destructive impact of war on the local forests. According to the writer, nothing remained of the majestic pine forests surrounding the creek. The devastated landscape consisted of mutilated logs, burnt stubs, and eroded gullies where hay grew in place of trees. This article was one of the first signs of attention to the negative impact of war on nature in Finland.[1] The writer, like most people, paid attention to the direct and visible damage that the fighting had caused. But what were the indirect consequences of war for nature and the environment?

This essay discusses the indirect impact of World War II on nature, the environment, and their protection in Finland.[2] In this essay, "nature" refers mainly to forests and "environment" to the built environment. Environmental protection here means the control of human-induced flows of energy and materials in the built environment. Successful environmental protection produces conscious and concrete decreases of flows that may damage human beings and/or the environment. The control of hazardous human-made fluxes is important because, in the end, they affect all the processes in the lithosphere, hydrosphere, atmosphere, and biosphere.

The indirect impacts of World War II on the environment and nature have received scant attention in Finland and the other Nordic countries. The aim of this essay is to provide an overview of the indirect ways that the war may have affected societies and environments. The essay presents four case studies in different landscapes (forests, soil, water, air) in Finland and its capital, Helsinki. It makes some tentative comparisons over the Finnish-Soviet border. The themes are discussed from historical but also ahistorical or contemporary points of view.

I maintain that focusing on damage from battles gives a very limited perspective on the ecological impact of wars in general and the Winter War in particular. Warfare constituted a minor part of the activities of Finnish society even during World War II. The fronts covered a minor part of the nations whose soil hosted battles in World War II. The soldiers of the field army made up a small portion of the nation, and they were as dependent on normal basic needs (such as food, water, clothes, shelter, and even entertainment) as the majority of the people. Over 80 percent of the population remained civilians. The economy also remained predominantly civilian. Naturally there was production exclusively for military use, but modern warfare depends mainly on services and products also consumed by civilian society. Therefore, this essay will not focus on battles, but on production and consumption in the civilian society. They are the main life-supporting activities in peace and war alike.

The war introduced both direct and indirect changes in the relationship between people and the environment. The main indirect change was the massive transfer of personnel and resources from production and reproduction to consumption. This fundamental shift

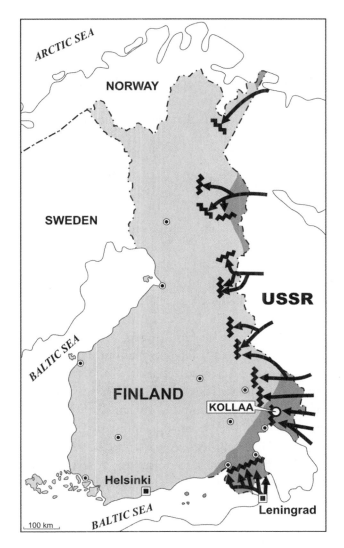

decreased considerably the overall flows of materials and energy in comparison with peacetime. The war-induced recession in material production curtailed the extraction of natural resources, human consumption, and emissions to air, water, soil, and the biosphere. Warfare was a more ecological state of society than peacetime.

World War II in Finland in 1939-45

Finland's history has been tied to that of its western neighbour, Sweden, and its eastern neighbour, Russia. Beginning in the twelfth century, the kingdom of Sweden ruled Finland for about six hundred years.

After the Napoleonic Wars, the country belonged to imperial Russia for a century (1809-1917). The Republic of Finland won its independence in December 1917 after the October Revolution had broken out in Russia. The new socialist government of Lenin did not have the power to maintain the integrity of the tsarist empire, and the Baltic countries, Poland, and Finland finally gained their independence.

Finland is the only state among the Nordic countries that waged total war in the twentieth century. World War II caused minor damage in Norway (except in the northern part of the country) and in Denmark. Sweden escaped the war. But Finland faced three distinct wars. The Winter War started in late 1939, when the Soviet Union attacked, and ended early the next year, mainly due to successful resistance. However, in the peace treaty following the Winter War, Finland had to cede about 10 percent of its territory to the Soviet Union. The second war was the Continuation War fought in 1941-44, when Finland—as an ally of Germany—attacked the Soviet Union to recover these occupied territories. The third was the Lapland War from the autumn of 1944 to the spring of 1945, when the Finns attacked German troops stationed mostly in northern Finland. At most, about 1.5 million Finnish, Russian, and German soldiers participated in the war along the more than one thousand kilometres of the Finnish-Soviet border.

Finland lost about eighty thousand men in World War II, and nearly one hundred thousand were permanently disabled.[3] The country had to cede large areas of its southeastern part, Karelia, to the Soviet Union. About four hundred thousand Karelians lost their homes and livelihoods and had to move to Finnish territory. Otherwise the war ended relatively successfully for Finland. There were few civilian casualties, and the ethical rules of war were in general respected. The state maintained its sovereignty, democratic political system, and capitalist economy over the hard years. Finland was one of only three belligerent countries in Europe that were never completely occupied during World War II. (The other two were the United Kingdom and the Soviet Union.) Postwar austerity lasted until the early 1950s. The country then developed fast, and today Finland is a wealthy Nordic country of five million inhabitants with highly developed environmental protection.

Finland's natural landscape is characterized by about 180,000 lakes, large mixed forests, and bogs. The winters are long and dark; the summers are relatively warm and light but brief. The country is over

1,100 kilometres long, extending from the Baltic Sea nearly to the Arctic Sea. Three quarters of Finland is situated below the Arctic Circle and belongs to the hemiboreal and boreal floral regions that cover Russia, northernmost China, and Canada. Finland is on the western end of the boreal pristine forest (taiga), which extends from Siberia, and is characterized by Scots pine and Norwegian spruce. The taiga zone changes to forest tundra northwards and to a wide zone of mixed forests of coniferous and deciduous trees southwards.

- *The front line and use of forests*

World War II destroyed forests. Battles, artillery fire, and forest fires lit accidentally or on purpose left little standing forest behind. To study the indirect impacts of war, however, one has to understand war outside battle zones. The key is to consider the main characteristic of modern warfare: the front. The front line distinguished industrialized warfare of the twentieth century from preindustrial warfare, which was characterised by small field armies and battlefields, brief battles, nomadic warfare, and notable seasonal changes in military activities.

The front may be seen as a modern form of the classical idea of frontier—the expansion of human settlements to scarcely populated or virgin nature. The war gathered hundreds of thousands of young men, who founded a new type of society, the front, in the forest. The ready-made front comprised men, animals, machines, roads, public transport, services, settlements, administration, communication systems, and so on. In the middle of Finland's taiga, the front formed a new, international, urban or suburban space of over one million inhabitants, with high concentrations of population, high consumption of matter and energy, and rather stable infrastructure. Hence, the front may be conceptualized as a process of founding, maintaining, and dismantling a new type of city, a military city.

During the period of stabilised war, in particular, the front lines changed in material terms from mobile urban zones to wooden towns. These towns used wood in multiple ways: the roads in the bogged areas were laid on logs; the traffic was powered by wood or charcoal; the dugouts, trenches, and barriers were built almost exclusively of logs; firewood was the main source of energy; and soldiers made most everyday objects of wood. In addition, Finnish soldiers and officers bathed regularly in saunas built of logs and heated with wood.[4] Forests and bushes were cleared in order to open space for observation and shooting. Hence, large quantities of wood sustained life in these temporary male cities, and the nearby forests were cut down on both sides to meet the demand. Battles damaged forests occasionally, but warfare, which does not necessarily imply battles, consumed forests continuously.

Nature in the northern Arctic was vulnerable to military operations. The marks of warfare are still visible today in the treeless tundra where nature revives slowly. Fortunately, most of the fighting took place in less fragile, semi-Arctic areas below the Arctic Circle; the heaviest fighting took place in the Karelian Isthmus connecting Finland and the Soviet Union near Leningrad (today St Petersburg). In this area, practically all remnants of old-growth forest (forest with trees over one hundred years old) were wiped out.[5] Elsewhere the damage caused directly by battles or indirectly by warfare was mostly local. The theatre of war was the largest remaining wilderness in northeastern Europe, which was able to recover gradually. The forest saved the trees.

• *Red and white forests*

The political outcome of the war had long-lasting, indirect effects on nature. World War II spread Soviet power over eastern and central Europe. The new spatial division of European nature into different socioeconomic spheres, capitalist and socialist, became visible on the Finnish-Soviet border. Remote-sensing images from the 1980s showed that the forests formed a dense cover on the Soviet side of the border. On the Finnish side, however, the forests formed a sparse cover; there were larger clear-cut areas and the density of trees was lower.[6]

These contrasting conditions resulted from different forest management traditions. In Finland, the sawmill, pulp, and paper industry had an important role in the national economy; it was said that the country rested on wooden legs. Especially during postwar austerity, the income earned by this export industry was badly needed, and forests were utilised efficiently. Forest management was based now on economic and industrial principles. Heavy forest machinery forced horses and lumbermen out. New logging roads were constructed to the remaining primeval forests. Large-scale ditch networks were dug to gather excess water from forest lands, bogs were drained, forests were thinned, deciduous vegetation was removed, toxicants were spread from planes to kill weeds and pests, huge forest areas were cut bare, and sometimes clear-cut areas were burnt. In many places, the soil was ploughed with heavy tractors, and artificial fertilizers were spread on planted stands of saplings. Modern forest-management ideology attempted to make nature more efficient, using the means of industrial society and substituting artificial succession (of repeated clear-cutting combined with plantations) for the natural succession of forests.[7]

The difference between times of war and peace is clear. Nevertheless, in the Finnish landscape the outcomes of war and peacetime were surprisingly similar. According to the nature conservation movement, the cut, burnt, mutilated, and poisoned landscapes created by capitalist forest management in postwar decades resembled the devastated battlefields seen, for example, in Kollaa.[8] Even foresters admitted that clear-cut areas, with endless rows of deep ditches made by caterpillar tractors, were dramatic scenery. After the war, it seemed that the forest industry opened a new front to kill its natural enemies and save useful collaborators in order to maximize production and profits. Hence, the ideology and practices of forest management that became dominant in the 1960s and 1970s resembled literal warfare on nature.[9] The similarity of behaviour in war and peacetime suggests that there was also a deeper connection between the two, that certain modes of behaviour were unconsciously or consciously adopted during the war, and that they were applied during peace. Indeed, it has been argued that the hard-handed treatment of forests during the war made the public more accustomed to, and accepting of, the industrial forest model that became dominant after the war.[10]

These arguments may be looked at from another point of view. War cleared pristine forests, making room for a new forest generation of a certain age and species composition. It removed undesired vegetation and broke the surface of the soil, which made it easier for tree seeds to take root. Clear-cut areas were often burned, creating fertile ground for growth. Organic waste—such as excrement and corpses of men and animals—spread by warfare also fertilised the soil.[11] In addition, explosions and trench building ploughed the soil, bringing up nutrients from lower soil layers for saplings. Trenches also drained excess water. Warfare and battles converted the old-growth forests with trees of mixed age, size, and species to more homogenous forms. Therefore, the front line may be conceptualized as an unintentional yet effective prototype of later industrial forest management and mentality.

Why were forests in better condition on the Soviet side of the border after the war? The forests where major battles took place were ceded after the war to the Soviet Union. All the population in the ceded areas moved to the Finnish side, where the refugees cut forests in order to found new farms in the forest regions.[12] Also, most natural protection areas that Finland had established in the prewar period were situated in the eastern regions of the country that now had to be ceded to the Soviet Union.[13] Uncleared mines and bullets in trees in the ceded areas apparently made industrial logging there difficult. The forest industry in Soviet Karelia was large, leading to clear-cutting of forests near railway lines, in particular. Yet the demand for wood and paper products remained on a relatively low level in the Soviet Union in general. The vast forests remained sparsely populated.[14] In addition, the roughly 100-kilometres-wide border area was a prohibited zone on the Soviet side for military reasons, and the fauna and flora there were efficiently protected for strategic and political reasons.

The outcome of the war saved not only the pristine taiga but also its wildlife on the Soviet side of the border. Wolves, bears, and wolverines continued to enter Finland from Soviet taiga in the postwar decades and prevented the extinction of these species in Finland. This was not an exceptional phenomenon. The state of nature and wildlife was, in general, relatively good in the northwestern part of the Soviet Union, where forced collectivization had emptied the countryside and forests had expanded to abandoned farmsteads. Hence, World War II created, in addition to the Iron Curtain, a Green Curtain that extended from the Barents Sea to the Baltic Sea.

The collapse of the Soviet Union in 1991 signified, however, the end to this red-green era. It opened pristine forests to profit-seeking capitalist forest industries, which resulted in large clear-cuttings and smaller areas to conserve nature.[15] The socialism of the taiga was replaced by the capitalism of the jungle.

• *Cities, energy crises, and air pollution*

War had other indirect impacts on forests—via cities. Finland had no fossil energy sources, and it depended on renewable sources of energy, such as wood, water, peat, and wind, though urbanization and industrialization increased the import of coke, coal, and fuel at the end of the nineteenth century. World War II, which blocked the Baltic Sea from maritime traffic, abruptly brought this development to an end. The import of fossil energy from western Europe to Finland was greatly reduced.

The capital city of Helsinki was, however, relatively well prepared to utilise other sources of energy. It had experienced its first energy crisis during World War I, for the same reason, which had forced the city to rely on firewood as its main energy source. The authorities had set up a special administration that controlled the supply, transport, selling, and delivery of firewood. The city returned to a similar system in World War II, when firewood again became the main source of energy. The annual consumption of firewood increased five times over peacetime consumption (to about 2.5 million cubic metres). If this volume of firewood had been transported at one time, it would have needed a train 10,000 kilometres long. Prisoners of war were sent to help in cutting. Nevertheless, the city and its inhabitants—women, the elderly, and children—had problems obtaining such a large volume of wood.[16]

Firewood remained an important part of the energy supply of the city after the war because the state subsidised its use. The prolonged use of firewood for domestic heating delayed the modernization of the urban energy-supply system, because central and municipal distant-heating systems operated primarily on coke and coal.[17] Delay of the modernization of the energy-supply infrastructure curtailed efforts to limit air pollution. It was more difficult to control air pollution of fragmented energy systems than of central- or distant-heating networks.

Most of the early complaints about air pollution in Helsinki concerned industrial plants or power stations, which used imported fossil-energy sources.[18] However, during the war, as noted previously, industry, power generation, housing blocks, and vehicles increasingly used wood as the main source of energy.[19] This was a positive trend because—in comparison with coke, coal, or diesel oil—firewood was a clean energy source.[20] Even though scientific studies on air pollution were not conducted during the war, the increased use of wood probably diminished emissions of harmful particles and reduced air-pollution problems in Finnish cities.

The war had, however, a controversial impact concerning air pollution. Because of wartime and postwar austerity, institutions or facilities unable to use firewood had to use coke or coal of poor quality, and they relied on worn-out furnaces, and these seem to have increased air-pollution problems in cities. After World War II, the most common complaints about air pollution concerned industries burning cheap coke, coal, or other fuel that heavily polluted the air.[21]

Wood was the main source of energy for cities on the battlefront and on the home front. Cutting focused on easily accessible areas because normal logging was impossible. Increased forest cutting exceeded the natural growth of the forests, first in the vicinity of roads and cities but later elsewhere. For example, Helsinki had to start importing firewood from northern parts of the country.[22] After the war, excessive cutting was found above all in privately owned forests around Finland.[23]

• *Cities, discharges, and the state of watercourses*
Finland was, in the 1940s, a predominantly agricultural country characterised by small private family farms. During World War II, shortage of male labour, horses, and fertilizers, as well as evacuation of the Karelians, reduced agricultural production by a third. Yet there were large new groups of consumers who had to be fed: the Finnish field army, Russian prisoners of war, evacuated people, and wounded soldiers. As agricultural production diminished and consumption increased, food became scarce and the nutrition of the population worsened.[24]

In addition to the agricultural crisis, a number of factors affected the metabolism of cities. Evacuation of the urban population, slowdown of industrial production, more effective use of existing resources, poor nutrition, thrift, and recycling curtailed the volume of waste, wastewater, and gaseous discharges from cities.[25] The discharges of organic matter, nutrients, and other pollutants to the watercourses in cities and in the countryside probably diminished.[26] It is, however, difficult to evaluate the wartime state of watercourses because of the lack of scientific studies. Helsinki had actively supported hydrobiological research on water pollution in the interwar decades, including physical, chemical, and biological studies. This tradition was cut by war. After the war, one chemist alone took care of water-pollution studies for all of Helsinki. The situation improved only in the 1960s.[27] Thus the war had a fatal impact on water-pollution research in Helsinki, and in most other Finnish cities, in the 1940s and 1950s.

In addition to halting water-pollution research, the war affected water protection. In 1928, the city of Helsinki had made a master plan to purify all of its wastewater in the following decades. This plan included construction of eight wastewater-treatment plants. In the 1930s, two large activated sludge plants were completed, and building of the third plant was started. However, these works had to be halted in 1939 when the Soviet Union attacked Finland and the Winter War started. Efforts for water protection were also paralysed in other cities. Finland was unable to build a single municipal wastewater-treatment plant from the beginning of the war until the late 1950s.[28]

In Helsinki, the first municipal wastewater-treatment plant was completed in 1957. Most of the plants were completed in the 1960s, and all the city's wastewater finally went to treatment plants in 1971. Hence, the aims and the schedule of the master plan had to be redesigned almost completely due to the rapid population growth caused by the war. It may be argued that the war caused a delay of about two decades in the realization of the original water-protection plan drawn up by the city of Helsinki in 1928. Due to this delay, the urban sea around the capital became more heavily polluted, and for a longer period of time, than would have been the case without the war.

The war had a deeper impact on Finnish towns occupied by the Soviet Union. The Finnish population of towns in Karelia was completely evacuated during World War II. These "empty towns" became laboratories for a strange experiment: the infrastructure remained but the population was completely changed. After the war, the towns were gradually settled by people transported from various parts of Soviet Union that had been devastated by German troops. For the first generation of Russian newcomers, the empty Finnish towns must have seemed like ghost towns and remained strange for a long time. It is not surprising that the new rulers of these towns paid, and were able to pay, only little attention to environmental protection.[29]

If the cities had stayed in Finnish hands, municipal resources to cope with environmental problems would have been better. On the other hand, the volume of pollutants also would have been larger because the capitalist world economy grew faster than did the Soviet economy. Hence the political outcome of World War II affected not only forests and countryside, but also urban environments on both sides of the current Finnish-Russian border.

• *Paper and pulp industry and water protection*
Economic growth in central Europe demanded growing quantities of wood, cardboard, and paper. The pulp and paper industry was established in Finland in the late nineteenth century due to the availability there of water, wood, and labour. The number of industrial

towns grew, especially near the Lake District and large rivers where these resources existed in abundance.

The Finnish pulp and paper industry expanded rapidly in the interwar period. The environmental consequences of discharges sharpened during this period, especially in the 1930s, becoming visible in the small and middle-sized rivers and shallow lakes that make up the majority of watercourses in Finland. Inhabitants near watercourses complained about nuisances and health hazards induced by water pollution. Forest companies were sued and forced, in some cases, to pay compensation for economic losses, especially to fisheries. Finnish pulp and paper managers were also concerned about the situation in Sweden, where companies were also forced to pay compensation, the local forest industry already had its own pollution committee, and the Swedish Parliament was preparing legislation to limit pollution.[30] The Finnish pulp and paper industry decided that it had to do something.

In 1937, the industry established a special committee to make the first national study of its pollution problems and the technology available to diminish them. Several watercourses near mill towns were studied with limnological methods, including plankton studies designed to measure the degree of pollution. The committee also studied methods to diminish the high volume of wood fibres wasted in the production process. They looked for ways to use raw materials more efficiently and diminish the damage caused to watercourses and consequent nuisances for inhabitants.[31] The work of the committee was, however, abruptly interrupted when the Winter War started in 1939.

The war years proved to be more effective protectors of the environment than the aborted committee. War forced the pulp and paper industry to cut volume drastically—by more than half in 1940 alone.[32] In addition, seventeen mills established sulphite alcohol plants to produce a fuel, motor alcohol, which substituted for about one tenth of the country's gasoline imports.[33] These plants reduced water pollution from sulphite cellulose factories by recapturing the sugar from toxic waste.

All the work that the industry had done for environmental protection before and during the war was, however, neglected until World War II was over. Scientific research on pollution and protection halted. The sulphite alcohol plants gradually closed after the brief boom (1951-52) caused by the Korean War.[34] On the other hand, production and pollution reached their prewar levels in 1950. Yet the general attitude of forest industry companies towards environmental protection was nonchalant or even hostile. The industry made no attempts to revive the committee in postwar years.

Nevertheless, the industry initiated some plans in the 1960s to diminish pollution. Pulp and paper companies planned first, in cooperation with some cities, to construct immense sewers from the interior of the country, where most of the mills were situated, to carry raw, nonpurified wastewater to the Baltic Sea.[35] Extreme pollution, continued protests, and more strict enforcement of the Water Act of 1962 forced the companies gradually to restart water pollution studies and initiate construction of expensive but efficient biological wastewater-treatment plants. Most of the plants were completed in the 1970s and 1980s. It is difficult to estimate the delay that war caused for industrial water protection. Nevertheless, the pulp and paper industry remained by far the worst polluter of watercourses and air in postwar Finland.

War—A More Ecological State of Society?

The dramatic increase of the human population and connected changes in modes of production and consumption are the two basic reasons for human-induced changes in global ecology. The human population has grown in peacetime, in particular in the absence of large-scale violence, connected epidemics, malnutrition, and hunger. The rapid growth of material production during peacetime has been the other main cause of environmental damage, especially over the past few centuries. Together, peacetime changes in reproduction and production have caused most current environmental problems. How did World War II alter the peacetime population and economy and their destructive environmental consequences?

Perhaps surprisingly, war had a rather small impact on the total population. The population growth rate slowed slightly. The impact was more notable in two age groups: the mortality rates of young men increased, and birth rates decreased temporarily.[36] The most far-reaching change was, however, the relocation of young males to the front, which withdrew them from civilian economic production. Hence, warfare transformed young men in their most productive years from producers to consumers that the rest of society on the home front— women, adolescents, and the elderly—had to support. This change cut down economic production, which had a deep impact on society and on the environment.

The economic recession during and after the war meant, in social terms, deprivation, poverty, and even undernourishment.[37] But from an ecological perspective, wartime and postwar austerity may have had more positive effects. During the war, a shift took place from civil industrial production that damaged primarily nature towards military-orientated production that harmed primarily human beings and societies. Problems in importing resources forced Finns to utilise local sources of energy, food, and materials more efficiently. Local alternatives were developed to substitute for imported products. Small-scale cultivation and animal rearing became common in cities. The diet of the people became more local and vegetarian. Energy supply shifted from using foreign fossil energy to domestic, renewable bio-energy. Recycling of paper, cardboard, metals, and glass, in particular, expanded.[38] Despite apparent hygienic problems, the wartime city was, from a contemporary point of view, one model of a sustainable city.

The slowdown in economic production affected not only cities but also the whole nation. War caused shortages of labour, raw materials, and energy, which in turn curtailed agricultural and industrial production and traffic. The production of pulp and paper was cut by half during the war, though it returned to the prewar level in 1950. Agricultural production was cut by a third, and it reached the prewar level only in 1957.[39] On the other hand, production grew in metals, chemicals, the printing industry, and mining.[40] The total volume of traffic decreased slightly during the first war years.[41] Private consumption was cut by about a quarter.[42] Hence, it may be deduced that war curtailed the human-made flows of energy and matter in the environment.[43]

This drop in consumption and production constrained the extraction of raw materials in forestry and agriculture, which in turn limited land use. The collapse of peacetime production constrained the amount of waste, wastewater, and gases discharged to the air, watercourses, soil, and the biosphere. The war decreased the overall volume of human-induced fluxes of materials and energy by perhaps 10-25 percent in comparison with those of peacetime production. Generally speaking, the war caused the largest relative decreases in human-made fluxes in the twentieth century. Therefore it is hypothesised that both world wars and postwar austerity periods considerably delayed or limited, directly or indirectly, the emergence of pollution of air, water, and soil, the greenhouse effect, acid rain, and possibly the ozone hole and climate change.

This hypothesis is made from a contemporary point of view. An ecologically sustainable society was obviously not a conscious aim during World War II. Detailed empirical studies are needed to test the validity of this general hypothesis. In addition, as we have noted, the impact of warfare on the environment was, in most cases, highly complex. First, war increased the use of local and renewable natural resources. This was a positive feature, but the cutting of forest for wartime needs exceeded the natural growth of local forests. Second, wartime caused a drop in reproduction and production, but this positive trend was only temporary. A considerable part of the decrease in the volume of matter and energy used in the war years was made up by an extraordinary increase in production and reproduction after the war. Third, war temporarily decreased discharges, but it paralysed environmental discussion, policy, and protection for long periods of time. The delay that war caused for environmental policy making in cities was about two decades and in industry approximately three.

Conclusions

World War II caused immense human suffering that has not been taken into consideration here. There is an obvious danger of ecofascism if one tries to compare the consequences of war for human beings with its consequences for nature. Hence, a comparative study of war from both ecocentric and anthropocentric perspectives would lead to unsolvable ethical problems.

Studies of the indirect ecological consequences of wars focus not on the most visible phenomena of war, battles, but on the society as a whole, the environment outside battle zones, and processes in over-long periods (including pre- and postwar eras). A holistic perspective is needed to identify and separate the ecological impacts of warfare from those caused by peacetime and/or civilian activities. This essay has been based on the Finnish experience, which may diverge in many ways from the experiences in other countries and on other continents. Hence, comparative qualitative and quantitative empirical studies would be welcome. Due to the lack of empirical studies, arguments in this essay are ideas for future studies rather than formal conclusions. Nevertheless, three different answers are proposed to the question whether World War II was an ecologically positive alternative to peace or not, in terms of wartime material fluxes, long-term socio-ecological changes, and policy making.

The war undoubtedly created new forms of interaction between human beings and nature. However, World War II was predominantly an anthropogenic phenomenon because it decreased interaction between humankind and nature in terms of matter and energy. This was the case especially in countries where battles were fought on native soil. The war transferred personnel and resources from production and reproduction to consumption, which decreased the flow of materials and energy in comparison with peacetime. It may be argued that the two world wars caused the largest relative decreases in human-made fluxes in the twentieth century. From this point of view, warfare curtailed the load on the environment caused by peacetime societies. Hence, in material terms, a society at war was a more ecological alternative than the same society would have been in peacetime.

To sum up, the ecological "bootprint" of the war was considerably smaller than the ecological footprint of peace. Yet, the end of the war brought the rapid revival of peacetime production and reproduction, leading to greater extraction of resources, larger consumption, and massive emissions to air, water, soil, and the biosphere. Crises related to the war also changed mentalities, above all in industry, that led to more effective or even brutal exploitation of natural resources after the war. Massive postwar increases in material flows quickly swamped the advantages gained in the war years. If we look at the postwar decades, the ecological advantages gained in wartime were clearly transitory. Hence, in a long-term assessment, war appears to be a rather contradictory ecological alternative to peace.

World War II had a fatal and long-lasting impact on environmental discussion, policies, and protection. As we have seen, there were numerous initiatives on environmental protection in Finnish cities and industry in the interwar period. World War II put an end to all environmental activism in the public and private sectors for two or three decades. The war caused a long break in environmental policy making that recovered in most countries only gradually in the postwar decades, causing the false impression that environmental protection was a new postwar phenomenon that was born in the 1960s or even later. This essay argues that the world wars, and above all World War II, were socio-ecological interventions that delayed the long-term development of environmental politics and protection perhaps more than any other single factor over the twentieth century. From the point of view of environmental policy making, war was probably the worst possible alternative to peace.

Notes

This study was part of the project "Space, Nature and Culture in the City, 1850-2000" and supported by the Research Council for Culture and Society at the Academy of Finland. I am grateful to Jorma Mattsson, Timo Vuorisalo and Veli-Pekka Tynkkynen, Hugh Clout, and William R. Mead for valuable comments.

1   Kollaa ei kestänyt, *Helsingin Sanomat* [hereafter *HS*], 14 August 1941; see also Heikki Lindroos, *Sotametsän perintö: Ja otteita eräästä metsäpäiväkirjasta* (Teollisuuden metsänhoitajat, Helsinki 1997), 23-29; S.H., "Sota metsien hävittäjänä," *Metsätaloudellinen aikakausikirja,* vihko 12 (1916): 365-69.

2   Some ideas on the indirect impact of war in history have been presented in the following books. I. G. Simmons, *Changing the Face of the Earth: Culture, Environment, History* (Blackwell Publishing, 1996); Charles Southwick, *Global Ecology in Human Perspective* (Oxford University Press, 1996).

3   Markku Honkasalo, *Suomalainen sotainvalidi* (Helsinki: Otava, 2000), 80, 88, 180, 515.

4   Björn Immonen and Toivo Siikarla and Göran Westerlund and Niilo Voipio, *Tammidivisioona: Kertomus jalkaväen ja tykistön yhteistyöstä jatkosodassa* (Porvoo: WSOY, 1999), 109, 118-19, 149, 151; for a pioneering study on war and forests in France see the work of Groupe d´histoire des forêts françaises (GHFF), A. Corvol and J.P. Amat, (eds.), *Forêt et guerre. Textes reunits et présentés par A. Corvol & J.P. Amat* (Paris: L´Harmattan, 1994).

5   Heikki Lindroos, *Puuta mottiin: Puuhuolto sodan varjossa 1939-1947* (Rauma: Teollisuuden metsänhoitajat, 1993), 82; Otso Ovaskainen and Minna Pappila and Jyri Pötry, *The Finnish forest industry in Russia: On the thorny path towards ecological and social responsibility* (Vantaa: The Finnish Nature League, Taiga Rescue Network, 1999); for maps on the old-growth forests in the Karelian Republic and Finland, see: http:// www.taigarescue.org/old_growth/, downloaded in June 2002; Jorma Mattsson who is an expert on remote sensing images and old-growth forests at the University of Turku, Finland, kindly provided additional information on the tundra and the Karelian Isthmus in 4.7.2002.

6   Mikko Punkari, "Maankäyttö ja luonnon tila," in Mikko Punkari (ed.), *Suomi avaruudesta* (Helsinki:Tähtitieteellinen yhdistys URSA, 1984), 74-79.

7   Pekka Ollonqvist, *Metsäpolitiikka ja sen tekijät: Pitkälinja 1928-1997* (Helsinki, Jyväskylä: Metsälehti Kustannus, 1998): 167, 169-73, 188-89; Olavi, Linnamies, *Suomen metsä- ja puutalous* (Helsinki: Kirjayhtymä, 1970), 90-107. The discussion on the Vietnam War in the early 1970s raised attention also in the Nordic countries on the negative impact of herbicides. See Harri Siiskonen, *Myrkyttäkää, ruiskuttakaa, hävittäkää... Ruotsalaisten ja suomalaisten maatalouden ammattilehtien kasvinsuojeluvalistus 1940-1980* (Vammala: Suomalaisen Kirjallisuuden Seura, 2000), 180.

8 See the "forest issue" of the journal of the Finnish Association for Nature Conservation: *Suomen Luonto* 3 (1970).
9 The main difference between war and peacetime forest management was that wars lasted as a rule only for a few years allowing in the end the natural succession to continue. This was not the case with industrial forest management.
10 Lindroos, *Puuta mottiin*, 7.
11 For an early experience of the fertilizing effect of bones and blood see the description of Plutarch from the Roman times cited in Simmons, *Changing the Face of the Earth*, 194.
12 Finland was probably the only country in Europe where the state took care of the resettling of the refugees. The devastation of forest by Karelian refugees in the new farms was of course another indirect ecological impact of war. William R. Mead, "The cold farm in Finland," *Geographical Review* 44 (1951): 529-43.
13 Timo Vuorisalo, "Sota, luonnonsuojelu ja luonnonsuojeluliike." A lecture delivered at the University of Helsinki, 26 January 2004.
14 Veli-Pekka Tynkkynen, *Environmental Health in the Karelian Republic: The popular image of green forests and clean waters is a delusion* (Kuopio: North-Savo Environmental Centre, 1999), 30, 46-47.
15 Ovaskainen, Pappila, Pötry 1999; Ympäristöväki toivoo vihreää vyöhykettä Suomenlahdelta Barentsinmerelle, *HS* 13 June 2002.
16 Timo Mattila, "Halkoskandaalista öljykriisiin: Vuosisata energiahistoriaa" in Simo Laakkonen, Sari Laurila, Pekka Kansanen, and Harry Schulman (eds.), *Näkökulmia Helsingin ympäristöhistoriaan: Kaupungin ja ympäristön muutos 1800- ja 1900-luvuilla* (Helsinki: Helsingin kaupungin tietokeskus, Edita, 2001), 69-71; Heikki, J. Kunnas, *Metsätaloustuotanto Suomessa 1860-1965. Forestry in Finland 1860-1965* (Helsinki: Studies on Finland's economic growth IV. Bank of Finland publications, 1973). Heikki shows that the use of fuelwood in general by industry and other user groups doubled; see tables on page 118-23; Ollonqvist, *Metsäpolitiikka ja sen tekijät*, 70-80; Lindroos, *Puuta mottiin*, 40, 82.
17 Mattila, "Halkoskandaalista öljykriisiin," 66, 69, 72-73.
18 Marja Kruut, *Kivihiilisavua vastaan: Helsingin ilman epäpuhtaudet 1880-luvulta 1920-luvulle.* (MA thesis, University of Helsinki, 1998), 35-37, 57-60.
19 Practically all civilian cars used firewood or charcoal. About 60 percent of all transport by the army was also carried out using these sources of energy. Seppo Leppänen, *Liikenne Suomessa 1900-1965. Transport and communication in Finland* (Bank of Finland Publications. Studies on Finland's economic growth V. Helsinki 1973), 76.
20 The first city physician of Helsinki claimed before the war that the change from firewood to coal had increased air-pollution problems. "Helsinki saanut uusia savun ja noen aiheuttajia", *Sosialidemokraatti*, 5 May 1937; Savupiippujen aiheuttamat valitukset, Terveydenhoitovirasto, Asunnontarkastus, Ea: 6, Archives of the City of Helsinki [hereafter ACH]. Several scientists who studied air-pollution problems in Nordic cities in the interwar period emphasized the negative impact of coal smoke. In Helsinki see Vilho Vaarna, *Helsingin kaupungin puiden ja pensaiden jäkäläkasvisto* (Helsinki: Suomalaisen Eläin- ja Kasvitieteellisen Seuran Vanamon Kasvitieteellisiä Julkaisuja, n:o 6., 1934), 25.
21 Asunnontarkastajan kirje terveydenhoitolautakunnalle 6.9.1951, Terveydenhoitovirasto, Saapuneet kirjeet. Ea 19:9; Havainnot savukiusoista, Asunnontarkastajan kirje terveydenhoitolautakunnalle

2.5.1958, Terveydenhoitovirasto, Saapuneet kirjeet 1958-1959, Ea:23,
ACH. This report briefly described 14 different cases of air pollution.
22 "Kulokorpikaan ei estä!" *HS* 5 August 1941; "Kannaksen metsät paikoin
täydellisesti tuhottu," *HS*, 21 September 1941; "Sahateollisuutemme
varauduttava supistuksiin," *HS* 27 December 1941; "Metsä ja turve," *HS*,
31 March 1943; "Matkalla Lapissa 1945," *HS*, 19 August 1945;
"Pakkohakkaus—pakkoraiskaus?" *HS*, 28 September 1945; Mattila
"Halkoskandaalista öljykriisiin," 70.
23 Lindroos, *Puuta mottiin*, 162-64.
24 The diet consisted predominantly of potatoes, vegetables, and rye. Pentti
Viita, *Maataloustuotanto Suomessa 1860-1960* (Helsinki: Kasvututkimuksia
I. Suomen Pankin taloustieteellinen tutkimuslaitos, 1965), 34-35, Table 1,
Volume of gross production. 1926=100. Volume in 1938 was (141.5), in
1940 (106.7), 1942 (99.5), 1945 (107.1), 1952 (137.2), and 1957
(141.8); Silvo Hietanen, "Perunan ja rukiin maa – ravinto ja asuminen
sotavuosien Suomessa,"in Silvo Hietanen, ed., *Kansakunta sodassa. Osa 2.
Vyö kireällä* (Helsinki: Opetusministeriö, Valtion painatuskeskus, 1990),
301-16. For an excellent description of thrift and recycling on the home
front, see Jouni Kallioniemi, *Kotirintama 1939-1945* (Jyväskylä:
Vähäheikkilän Kustannus, 2000), 67-122.
25 Teemu Veijola, "Jätevedenpuhdistuslaitokset kaasuntuottajina," *Suomen
kemistilehti*, 5-6 (1945); the annuals of the Department of Public Works in
1939-1945 (ACH). See description of operation of wastewater treatment
plants. In the beginning of the war the decrease of the volume of
wastewater was about 10-20 percent but it exceeded its prewar level again
by 1944-45. Timo Herranen, *Vettä ja elämää. Helsingin vesihuollon historia
1876-2001* (Helsingin Vesi, Edita 2001), 81-83, 226.
26 Simo Laakkonen and Sari Laurila, "Vihreä keidas? Töölönlahden
pilaantumisen ja suojelun yhteiskuntahistoriaa 1700-luvun lopulta vuoteen
2000," in Laakkonen et al., *Näkökulmia Helsingin ympäristöhistoriaan*,
268.
27 Harry Cajander, *Ranta- ja merivesitutkimuksia vv. 1947-62* (Helsingin
kaupunki, 1962), see introduction; Terttu Finni and Sari Laurila and Simo
Laakkonen, "The History of Eutrophication in the Sea Area of Helsinki in
the Twentieth Century. Long-term Analysis of Plankton Assemblages," in
Simo Laakkonen and Sari Laurila (eds.), *Ambio, Man and the Baltic Sea*, 4-
5 (August 2001), 265-66; a letter to the chief of the Street Department by
Harry Cajander 19 February 1947, Archives of the Department of Public
Works.
28 Jussi Lehtonen, "Jätevedenpuhdistuksen kehitys Suomessa pitkällä
aikavälillä." (Diplom study, Tampere Technical University, Department of
Building Technology,1994), 83.
29 Tynkkynen, *Environmental Health in the Karelian Republic*, 46-47, 52, 56.
Markus Lehtipuu, *Karjalan tragedia: Kuinka Suomen kauneimmasta
maakunnasta tuli koko Euroopan häpeäpilkku* (Keuruu 2004).
30 Ossi Seppovaara, *Kymijoki: Virran kohtaloita vuosisatojen saatossa*
(Kuusankoski: Kymijoen vesiensuojeluyhdistys, 1988), 365-86; Ossi
Seppovaara, *Vuoksi: Luonto ja ihminen vesistön muovaajina* (Jyväskylä:
Suomalaisen Kirjallisuuden Seura, 1984), 105-25; Mika Pekurinen,
"Jätevesikysymys Suomen metsäteollisuudessa ennen sotia," in Heikki
Roiko-Jokela (ed.), *Moni-ilmeinen metsä: Mielikuvia, asenteita ja arvoja
metsistä ja niiden käytöstä* (Jyväskylä: Historian laitos & Kopijyvä Oy,
2000), 112-15, 122.
31 Pekurinen, "Jätevesikysymys Suomen metsäteollisuudessa ennen sotia,"
116-17; Simo Laakkonen, "Ympäristöpolitiikan kemisti."

Vesitutkimusverkosto 1900-1940," in Simo Laakkonen, Sari Laurila, and Marjatta Rahikainen (eds.), *Harmaat aallot. Ympäristönsuojelun tulo Suomeen* (Vammala: Suomen Historiallinen Seura, 1999), 80-82; "Tehtaiden jätevesien vaikutusta ryhdytään tutkimaan," *HS*, 30 June 1937.

32 Reino Hjerppe, Riitta Hjerppe, Kauko Mannermaa, O.E. Niitamo, and Kaarlo Siltari, *Suomen teollisuus ja teollinen käsityö 1900-1965. Industry and industrial handicraft in Finland, 1900-1965* (Helsinki: Studies on Finland's economic growth VII. Bank of Finland, 1976), 164, 166. See Table 20, Manufacture of paper and paper products. Volume index of production in large and medium scale industry, by branch, 1926=100. Volume index in 1939 (265), in 1940 (114), 1945 (143), and in 1950 (274); The drop of production during World War I was even greater, about 80 percent. Heikki, J. Kunnas, *Metsätaloustuotanto Suomessa 1860-1965. Forestry in Finland 1860-1965* (Helsinki: Studies on Finland's economic growth IV, Bank of Finland, 1973), 66.

33 Antti Kaukoranta, *Sulfiittispriiteollisuus Suomessa vuosina 1918-1978. Sulphite alcohol industry in Finland in 1918-1978* (Paino Polar: Alko, 1981), 7-10.

34 Ibid., 10-11.

35 Sami Louekari, *"Meidän saamaton Ateenamme": Vesiensuojelukysymys Jyväskylässä 1950-1974* (MS thesis, University of Helsinki, 1996), 81, 84-87.

36 Aarno Strömmer, *Väestöllinen muuntuminen Suomessa* (Tornio 1969), liitetaulukko 1.

37 Hietanen, *Kansakunta sodassa*, 301, 315-16.

38 Kallioniemi, *Kotirintama*, 74-100, 110-12; Viita, *Maataloustuotanto Suomessa*, 25-26. The collection of berries and mushrooms almost doubled in the 1940s (annual average 28.3 million kg) compared with the 1930s (16.9 million kg).

39 Viita, *Maataloustuotanto Suomessa*, 33-34.

40 Erkki Pihkala, "Sotaan mobilisoitu talous," in Silvo Hietanen (ed.), *Kansakunta sodassa. Osa 2. Vyö kireällä* (Helsinki: Opetusministeriö, Valtion painatuskeskus, 1990), 267-70, 342, Table 11.

41 Leppänen, *Liikenne Suomessa*, 69, Table 5., Volume indices of transport and communication by type of transport, 1900-1965, 1938=100. The total volume excluding horse transport was in 1939 as follows (107), in 1941 (89), and in 1943 already (114).

42 Pihkala, "Sotaan mobilisoitu talous," 263-64.

Landscapes in the Dark Valley: Toward an Environmental History of Wartime Japan

William M. Tsutsui

Japan's "home front" during World War II has received surprisingly little academic attention over the past half century. Japanese observers have long seen the war years as a "dark valley" (*kuroi tanima*), a time of extreme deprivation and suffering, a memory "too bitter to recall with detachment."[1] Western scholars, with a few notable exceptions, have also tended to slight Japan's domestic experience of war in favor of military history and grander political and diplomatic narratives.[2] Only in recent years have analysts on both sides of the Pacific shown increasing interest in wartime life in Japan, recognizing that mass mobilization had significant long-term consequences for Japanese society. But while studies have suddenly proliferated on topics like wartime industrial and labor policy, the mobilization of Japanese women, and the legacy of statist economic and political structures, some important aspects of Japan's home front have continued to be overlooked.[3]

A striking omission from the scholarly literature is a systematic study of Japan's natural environment during World War II. Wartime mobilization, dislocation, and combat clearly left their marks on the Japanese landscape and on the Japanese people's relationships with the natural world. Structures for managing, utilizing, and perceiving the environment—both formal and informal, economic, political, and cultural—were recast under the pressures of "total war." Many wartime developments—from deforestation to changing patterns of rural land use to the radioactive aftermath at Hiroshima and Nagasaki—would have sweeping implications, even long after the end of the conflict. Gaining a fuller understanding of Japan's complex and compelling wartime experience demands that closer attention be paid to the environmental policies, costs, and consequences of World War II.[4]

This essay represents a preliminary step toward such a reappraisal of wartime Japan from the perspective of environmental history. The central concern here will be a fundamental—and deceptively modest— question: what impact did World War II have on Japan's environment? Few historians have directly addressed this issue. The implicit assumption of most observers has been that war—especially "total war" in the twentieth century—has been recklessly and unambiguously destructive of the natural environment. The atomic bombings in Japan, the use of chemicals like Agent Orange in Indochina, and the burning oil wells of the Persian Gulf are usually taken as evidence aplenty for the notion that modern warfare is, inevitably, ruinous for the environment.[5]

Nevertheless, as this essay argues, the environmental effects of war are much less neat (and often much less obvious) than might at first be assumed. Specifically, while World War II clearly had a deleterious impact on many aspects of Japan's natural environment, there were also significant ways in which the war brought unexpectedly beneficial environmental consequences. War, in other words, need not necessarily be all bad for the environment.[6] At the same time, the case of Japan also suggests that the effects of warfare on the environment (be they favorable or detrimental) are often less lasting and less significant than we might imagine. Nature, happily, has extraordinary powers of regeneration and humankind, regrettably, has an uncanny ability to shatter delicate ecological systems even in times of peace. In short, the environmental legacies of war are complex, contingent, and often surprisingly transitory.

This essay will range widely in attempting to survey the environmental impact of World War II on Japan. The causal factors of wartime environmental change—direct war damage from bombing, indirect damage from economic and military mobilization, the consequences of the wartime scarcity of raw materials, and the repercussions of Japan's disengagement from the world economy— will provide the basic organizational structure. While both natural and human-made environments will be considered, the emphasis will be on the war's impact on the natural, non-human world: Japan's fields and forests, air and water, flora, birds, animals, and fish. To keep this broad summary manageable, the boundaries of both Japan and World

War II will be drawn narrowly. Geographically, this essay will consider only the Japanese home islands (*naichi*). Wartime environmental changes in Okinawa and in the extended Japanese empire (which eventually stretched from Sakhalin and Korea, through much of China and Southeast Asia, to Micronesia and even to the Aleutian Islands) were so varied and complex as to warrant separate treatment. Chronologically, the focus will be on the Pacific War years of 1941-45. During this time of "total war" in Japan, environmental change was rapid and pressure on natural resources was intense. Needless to say, the environmental impact of mobilization was also felt significantly in the 1930s and, during the postwar Allied Occupation (1945-52), the environmental consequences of reconstruction were often directly continuous with wartime patterns. As with consideration of the Japanese empire, however, analysis of the full sweep of Japan's "Fifteen Years' War" and the postwar transition are beyond this scope of this essay.

Direct War Damage

Combat in the Japanese home islands was limited to the incendiary bombing of Japanese cities, the atomic attacks on Hiroshima and Nagasaki, and some very limited shelling of coastal targets by the U.S. Navy. Between mid-1944 and the end of the war, sixty-six Japanese cities were subjected to intense American bombing, most of which made use of incendiary weapons designed to spark widespread fires in Japan's densely populated, largely wood-built urban areas. This strategy proved only too successful and, in the span of just a few months, the centers of most of Japan's large and mid-sized cities were effectively reduced to ashes. In one single mission, the Great Tokyo Air Raid of March 1945, 16.8 square miles of the city were burned to the ground and more than eighty thousand people died. Cumulatively, during 1944 and 1945 almost one-quarter of Japan's housing stock was destroyed by bombs, burned in the subsequent conflagrations, or demolished by the Japanese authorities to form fire breaks; approximately 30 percent of the Japanese population was left homeless. No one can be sure exactly how many died in the bombings, but certainly hundreds of thousands of Japanese were killed or injured as a result of the American attacks.[7]

When one considers the tremendous costs of the incendiary bombings—in human life, in the resulting mass flight from the cities, in sheer physical destruction—it is difficult to imagine that the experience was anything short of an environmental nightmare. Nevertheless, when viewed from the perspective of the non-human environment, and when considered in the broader context of the environmental consequences of the war, the bombings of Japanese cities appear of relatively limited and temporary significance. For example, the raids destroyed approximately 178 square miles of Japan's houses, schools, shops, offices, and factories[8]; this is a considerable area to be sure, yet is but a fraction of the vast tracts of Japanese forest clear-cut and scoured during the war, or the considerable expanses of land and sea tainted by military facilities, mines, and industry. Moreover, most of the areas destroyed were highly environmentally degraded even before the attacks: Japanese cities were (and remain) crowded, polluted, and relatively inhospitable to nature. Parks were few, green space was minimal, and, by 1944, just about the only urban animal life consisted of rats, mice, and crows. As the dyspeptic French journalist Robert Guillain wrote of Tokyo just before the bombings:

> *The capital stirred in its filth. A Japanese house rots in twenty years. So does a city. Tokyo, rebuilt in 1923 after the big earthquake, was rotten. ... You could imagine no way to save this capital from crumbling in rot and ruin except some catastrophe that would again compel rebuilding—a purifying fire, for example, that would destroy it all.[9]*

From the ashes of 1945, Tokyo and the other devastated cities did indeed regenerate and rebuild in good order. Gardens, shacks, and market stalls sprouted from the rubble in a matter of days and reconstruction began in only a matter of weeks. Millions fled Tokyo in the days after the Great Air Raid, but by 1952 the population had returned to its 1944 peak. The housing stock was a little slower to rebound, but by the mid-1950s most of the destroyed cities had erased the scars of the bombings and were growing rapidly.[10]

The experiences of Hiroshima and Nagasaki, at least from the environmental standpoint, were remarkably similar to those of the firebombed cities: the toll in human life and suffering was extreme and the damage to humanmade structures was tremendous. The areas devastated by the atomic bombs were, however, quite small—five square miles in Hiroshima, half that in Nagasaki—and the weapons, certainly compared to the nuclear devices developed during the Cold

War, were relatively very weak. Residual radiation, even at the hypocenters, had declined to unthreatening levels within a matter of days.[11] Perhaps most strikingly, plant and animal life seem to have been relatively unaffected by the bombs. Survivors reported that mosquitos and flies virtually disappeared after the attacks, but that they returned in profusion after several days; fish in shallow ponds perished, while those in deeper ponds tended to survive; the plentiful rats of the two cities, many observers noted, showed few ill effects from radiation. Scientific tests by Japanese researchers confirmed these accounts: earthworms and earwigs collected near the hypocenters showed no structural or genetic abnormalities; aquatic insects, studied over a period of years, lived and reproduced normally; even experimental rabbits and mice, exposed to the bomb in the labs of Hiroshima University of Literature and Science, were found to be in good health physically and genetically. A survey of fauna at the Hiroshima hypocenter in October 1947 found that animal and insect populations had fully recovered.[12]

The flora of Hiroshima and Nagasaki were also remarkably resilient. In the immediate aftermath of the attacks, worries about the biological recovery of the bomb sites abounded: "all Japan wondered then if grass would ever grow again, if a flower would ever bloom in the earth of those two atomized cities."[13] Although bamboo and rice plants were scorched as far as five miles from the hypocenters, even trees at the center of the cities, burned to the ground by the blasts, began to send out new shoots from their roots within two months. Some malformations occurred among plants that sprouted close to the hypocenters, but botanists reported that such abnormalities had ceased to appear within three or four years after the bombings. In general, vegetation erupted in profusion in the cities' ruins, with a wide variety of plants colonizing the disturbed ground: by June of 1946, twenty-five species of weeds grew thickly at the very site of the detonation in Hiroshima and scientists reported luxuriant growth of plants that previously had been rare in the area. Gardens planted in burned-out neighborhoods also prospered: in 1947 it was said that the yields of wheat, eggplants, and soybeans from makeshift fields in Hiroshima surpassed those of neighboring farming villages. To the surprise of many, tomatoes, which city residents had been unable to cultivate for decades because of fungal and insect damage, flourished in the years after the bombing.[14] John Hersey described the scene almost lyrically:

Over everything—up through the wreckage of the city, in gutters, along the riverbanks, tangled among tiles and tin roofing, climbing on charred tree trunks—was a blanket of fresh, vivid, lush, optimistic green; the verdancy rose even from the foundations of ruined houses. Weeds already hid the ashes, and wild flowers were in bloom among the city's bones. … Especially in a circle at the center, sickle senna grew in extraordinary regeneration, not only standing among the charred remnants of the same plant but pushing up in new places, among bricks and through cracks in the asphalt. It actually seemed as if a load of sickle-senna seed had been dropped along with the bomb.[15]

But this postwar vegetative revival was only short lived. As one report by Hiroshima scientists concluded, not without a sense of regret: "In 1948, houses and buildings rapidly increased in number; and urban construction was well underway by the following year. Consequently, vegetation was destroyed; and by the end of 1950, it was difficult for one to retain the early post-atomic bomb images of the city."[16]

In short, the atomic bombs—like the incendiary attacks—were tremendously and tragically destructive for one species, *Homo sapiens*. When viewed from a less anthropocentric viewpoint, however, the environmental implications of direct combat in Japan during World War II are far more ambiguous.

Economic Mobilization

Despite the obvious scars left by American bombing, the more indirect effects of war—and specifically of the economic mobilization for war—seem to have had the more profound consequences for the environment in Japan. Starting in the late 1930s, the exploitation of Japan's natural resources accelerated as the nation prepared for, and subsequently embarked upon, "total war." The examples of this heightened pressure on the environment are seemingly countless. In the years before Pearl Harbor, for example, the Japanese government aggressively promoted a new export drive in the hopes of generating much-needed foreign currency. As a result, deep-sea fishing for tuna and crab was expanded rapidly, with the canned seafood sold almost entirely to the American market. Whaling was also stepped up: in the mid-1930s, for the first time, Japanese fishermen ventured beyond their coastal waters and sent factory ships into the Antarctic, their whale oil destined primarily for the margarine and soap factories of Germany. In 1930, Japan accounted for only 1 percent of the world's whale catch; by 1938, Japan claimed 12 percent of the total and was the largest producer after England and Norway. Japan's forests were also called upon to help the nation's trade balance: imports of lumber and wood pulp were slashed from the early 1930s and domestic cutting was stepped up to meet internal needs and, increasingly over the decade, to be sold on international markets.[17]

The Japanese government also worked assiduously to integrate Japan's economy—and especially the agricultural sector—more fully with the empire. Korean farmers were pressed to grow rice for export to Japan, even though the climate and agricultural infrastructure were not particularly well suited to rice monoculture. In Manchuria, meanwhile, soybeans were promoted as the crop of choice: Japanese farmers were encouraged to move acreage from soybeans into wheat; the wheat was exported to the continent and Manchurian soybeans were imported to satisfy Japanese demand. The problems of these arrangements—which reduced agricultural diversity and self-sufficiency—became apparent during the Pacific War years, when repeated crop failures in Korea and transportation bottlenecks led to serious food shortages in Japan.[18]

Industrial and mining development further contributed to environmental degradation in the mobilization for war. Air and water pollution seem to have worsened during the 1930s, in step with the accelerating industrial preparations for war. Prefectural authorities regularly reported contamination issues related to mines, chemical plants, starch factories, and paper mills through the war years; the Fisheries Agency of the Ministry of Agriculture recorded over a thousand cases of industrial water pollution injurious to commercial fisheries in 1937 alone; smoke, ash, and dust from the humming factories of Kansai choked the air of Osaka and other major cities; and some facilities—such as the Kamioka smelter of Mitsui Mining and the Minamata complex of Nihon Chisso, both later proven to be major sources of heavy-metal wastes—are known to have greatly increased production (and the flow of toxic effluents) during the Pacific War.[19]

Nonetheless, the starkest example of the destruction wrought by mobilization during World War II could be found in Japan's forests. Japan is, of course, a heavily forested country and has historically made extensive use of its timber resources. Even before the war many Japanese forests were heavily utilized and degraded: charcoal was a major source of fuel for homes and small industry (and very large tracts of accessible woodland had long been coppiced for charcoal and firewood production); farmers also made extensive use of the organic materials on the forest floors, gathering leaves, twigs, and nuts for compost and animal feed; and, needless to say, forests were exploited for the needs of industrial society—for telegraph poles, railway ties, and mine supports, for building materials, wood pulp (for paper and rayon), and for countless other uses.

Through the early 1930s, as much as a third of Japan's wood, lumber, and pulp needs were satisfied by imports, largely from the Asian continent and North America. As the state endeavored to reduce import dependence, however, domestic logging increased rapidly, with the pace heightening even further after 1941. This wartime acceleration in timber production—much of it from clear-cut old-growth forests— was driven by the effective end of all wood imports during the Pacific War, the worsening fuel shortage (which led to heavy demand for charcoal), the heightened consumption of industry (especially the mines), and the intense need during the last years of the war for materials to rebuild Japan's bombed cities. Even trees of great age, beauty, and cultural significance—the stately rows of pines along the Tōkaidō highway, the ancient avenue of cryptomeria leading to the Nikkō Shrine—were sacrificed in the war effort. The government also promoted the aggressive reclamation of woodlands for agricultural production and ordered that the nurseries and seedbeds used to grow saplings for reforestation programs be converted to food crops.[20]

The scale of the wartime cutting was staggering and it was clear by the time the Allied Occupation forces arrived that Japan's forest resources were dangerously depleted. Between 1941 and 1945, fourteen thousand square miles (or nine million acres), about 15 percent of Japan's forests, had been logged. Much of that area—over ten thousand square miles (6.5 million acres) or about 10 percent of Japan forests—was clear-cut woodland. In 1945, almost fifty square miles a week were clear-cut. The situation was exacerbated by the fact that artificial reforestation had all but ground to a halt during the war, as the loss of able labor and the dwindling supply of seedlings made replanting impossible.[21] Postwar studies confirmed that the gap between timber harvested and the regeneration of woodland through natural growth and artificial reforestation was sobering. As one American forester wrote in 1951 of Japan's "forest emergency," "Japan is rapidly approaching the point where the wood needs of the nation can no longer be met from its resources":

> *Heavy drain to meet the needs of the population has changed the characteristics of most of the accessible forests so now they show little resemblance to the original stands. Virgin forests in large segments ... are found only on the higher mountains where they are beyond physical or economic accessibility. The accessible forests have been reduced to a depleted condition from poor forest management, prolonged over-utilization, insufficient reforestation, soil erosion and depredation by insects.[22]*

One of the most peculiar—and, for Japan's forests, one of the most destructive—developments of the war years was the pine-root oil project.[23] During 1944 and 1945, as petroleum supplies in Japan dwindled, researchers desperately sought alternative sources of fuel for the war machine. One of these, discovered by Navy chemists, was the distillation of high-octane motor fuel from the resinous roots of pine trees. Such arboreal alchemy required tremendous human energy and tremendous natural destruction: the production of one gallon of pine-root oil required 2.5 days of heavy labor and many tons of freshly dug roots. Japan's imperial subjects, though exhausted from more than a decade of mobilization and scarcity, responded dutifully, establishing thirty-four thousand stills and squeezing seventy thousand barrels of crude a month from the islands' green oil fields. By the end of the war, once dense pine forests lay ravaged: "Monumental piles of roots and stumps lined many of the roadways," one observer reported. "Mountainsides were stripped bare of every tree and sapling."[24] The cruelest irony was that such ecological devastation and communal sacrifice was all for nought: despite the official propaganda, Japanese scientists never perfected the refining of pine-root oil and barely a drop ever made it into the fuel tanks of Japan's bombers and battleships.

The consequences of wartime deforestation were complex and far reaching. The massive loss of forest resources and numerous old-growth stands was just the beginning of the damage. Wartime forestry practices contributed to the proliferation of dangerous pests, most notably pine bark beetles, insects which had little impact before 1939, but which reached epidemic proportions by the end of the war. Hasty clear-cutting and dwindling transportation capacity left many felled trees to rot on forest floors, creating optimum conditions for the beetles' spread. Entomologists reported that more than 1.5 million acres of Japan's coniferous forests had been infested by 1946.[25] Water control was a far greater concern: aggressive logging on hill- and mountainsides created considerable problems of erosion and uncontrollable runoff. Streams and rivers collected silt, choking downstream reservoirs, dams, irrigation systems, and coastal deltas. Flooding, always a problem in Japan, seems to have worsened during the war as deforestation and erosion weakened the land's natural defenses against typhoons and the annual snow-melt.[26] In short, the wartime mobilization of Japan's forests had profound environmental implications that stretched far beyond the woodlands and the coppices.

The Environmental Consequences of Scarcity

While wartime economic and military mobilization would seem to have been uniformly damaging to Japan's air, water, land, and forests, the environmental consequences of scarcity—the endemic wartime shortages of critical natural resources and manufactured goods—were considerably more ambiguous. In some cases, doing without—facing life deprived of agricultural chemicals, gasoline, or the latest industrial technology—brought surprising and significant benefits to the environment. In many other cases, however, scarcity led simply to a frenzied search for substitutes and the heightened exploitation of nature.[27]

Fertilizer is an interesting case. Before the war, Japanese agriculture was one of the world's most intensive users of chemical fertilizers.[28] Supply declined precipitously after 1941 as ammonia production was diverted away from nitrogenous fertilizers and toward the munitions industry, and as imports of phosphate rock and potash, raw materials upon which the Japanese fertilizer industry was dependent, were suspended. Farmers, under tremendous state pressure to produce, desperately sought alternate sources of soil nutrients. Many turned to increased use of compost, an apparently sound, environmentally sensitive, sustainable strategy. Yet much of the material to be composted came from scavenging in upland forests: all woodlands within walking distance of farming villages had their floors swept clean of leaves, needles, undergrowth, windfall, and all other organic matter. The result of this widespread clearing was that forest soils were not replenished, slowing growth and weakening the trees. Moreover, forest litter has an important role in soil conservation: without leaves and other clutter, precipitation was less easily absorbed and runoff from woodlands increased, resulting in accelerated erosion, sedimentation of waterways, and damaging flooding.[29] The lack of chemical amendments also created intense demand for night soil, which had long been an important fertilizer in Japan, especially in the agricultural areas around large cities.[30] Under the acute wartime conditions, night soil was increasingly applied to fields as raw sewage, rather than being composted as had traditionally been the common practice. The result of this unhygienic shortcut was that water supplies were regularly tainted by sewage-polluted runoff, and parasitical and bacterial infections rose both in the countryside and the cities.[31]

Japan's birds and animals, both wild and domesticated, struggled for survival during the years of wartime scarcity. Livestock which competed with humans for food suffered during the war, while those that didn't tended to hold their own and even flourish. The numbers of pigs, chickens, and rabbits on Japanese farms plummeted, as did the number of horses, many of which were drafted into army service in China after 1937. Sheep, whose wool was a valuable wartime commodity, increased modestly in number, while the population of goats (a favorite of impoverished peoples worldwide) grew many times over. Large domestic pets, especially dogs, all but disappeared from Japan during the war and, in a well-known, heartbreaking story, most of the animals in Tokyo's Ueno Zoo had to be sacrificed as safety threats and major consumers of scarce food and forage.[32]

The Japanese tradition of netting and eating migratory songbirds went from being a regional curiosity to being a patriotic duty during World War II. Through gruesomely efficient methods of mist-netting and bird-liming, Japanese hunters delivered huge catches of thrushes, grosbeaks, finches, siskins, and buntings. The "official" wartime harvest was approximately 7.5 million songbirds per year, though even the government estimated that the actual figure was at least twice as many. During the war, the mission of the Game Management Division of the Ministry of Agriculture turned from research and conservation to promoting the rapid exploitation of Japan's wildlife resources. Guides to the most palatable species of song- and shorebirds were published and a program to collect thrush feathers for use in pillows and quilts at veterans' hospitals was introduced. It is not surprising that, when the Allied Occupation forces arrived in Japan in 1945, they were startled to find an almost complete absence of birds—other than crows and the occasional sparrow—everywhere in the country.[33]

The wartime experience of Japan's fisheries is an important counterexample. Japan was the world's greatest fishing nation prior to World War II, with more than twice the annual production of the United States. Japanese fishermen heavily exploited coastal waters and, by the 1930s, Japan boasted an extensive deep-sea fleet as well: crab-canning factory ships worked the Bering Sea, Japanese tuna fleets combed the Central and South Pacific, trawlers swept the East China, South China, and Yellow seas, and Japanese whalers landed rich catches off Antarctica. The ecological pressure of Japan's efficient deep-sea operations was intense and signs of depletion were obvious in many of Japan's offshore fisheries well before the war: crabbers in Hokkaido and the Kuriles overfished their grounds and suffered declining harvests in the 1930s; tuna fishermen, meanwhile, were forced to continually expand the range of their operations, as overfishing depleted traditionally rich areas; in the East China and Yellow seas, at the very heart of Japan's offshore trawling, catches declined steeply after 1931 and certain highly desirable species (including red sea bream and several types of croaker) all but disappeared from the fishermen's nets.[34]

With the start of the Pacific War, however, virtually all deep-sea fishing and whaling came abruptly to an end. The vast majority of Japan's ocean-going fishing vessels—as well as most of its skilled seamen—were drafted into war service by the Navy. All of Japan's large factory ships (numbering some twenty in 1941) were destroyed during the war, as were 95 percent of the nation's otter trawlers. But even had the deep-sea fleets been preserved, there would not have been sufficient supplies to keep them operating during the hostilities. Indeed, even coastal fisheries were severely hampered after 1941 by mounting shortages of cotton yarn, ramie, manila hemp, and, most importantly, petroleum.[35]

Japan's wartime withdrawal from offshore fisheries and the reduced intensity of its coastal operations seem to have had a significant effect on fish stocks in the Western Pacific. Postwar studies of certain fisheries suggested that the respite during 1941-45 allowed for a measurable regeneration in some grounds and some species. Notably, in the once-depleted fisheries of the East China and Yellow seas, Japanese trawlers once again began landing significant catches of bream and croaker in the late 1940s.[36] Although the wartime hiatus in Japanese fishing was short lived—by the 1950s, a rebuilt and much larger Japanese fleet was busily overfishing all of the traditional grounds as well as a number of new ones[37]—the war can thus be said to have had a beneficial environmental impact, at least in the short term, when it came to fisheries resources. Interestingly—and perhaps not surprisingly— researchers have found that a similar temporary recovery of fish stocks took place in the North Atlantic during World War II.[38] It is also worth noting that wars in general may have brought much needed relief to the fish inhabiting the waters around Japan: not only was the Pacific War a welcome break, but in World War I, Japanese offshore fisheries had also closed up shop, as trawler owners found it very profitable to sell their vessels to the European powers for use as patrol boats and mine sweepers.[39]

One additional consequence of scarcity is worth considering. The profound, often crippling wartime shortages of natural resources— especially fossil fuels—had the effect of driving many Japanese, from housewives to corporate engineers to university scientists, to new extremes of desperation, frugality, and creativity. One might even suggest that, impelled by stringency, Japanese individuals and institutions became unconsciously more environmentally responsible in their behavior and their consumption patterns. A similar tendency was apparent in wartime Britain and the United States, although compared at least to America, where the consumer economy actually grew during World War II, the breadth and depth of scarcity was far greater in Japan.[40] Many observers, for example, have noted the ingenuity of wartime Japanese in trying to conduct a modern war and maintain a dignified lifestyle in the absence of many of the essential materials inputs of twentieth-century industry. Few have explored, however, how many Japanese schemes for overcoming wartime shortages were consistent with what are now considered to be environmentally sensitive technologies and the search for renewable sources of energy. The Navy, for instance, conducted extensive experimentation on the production of diesel fuel from coconut oil, birch bark, pine needles, and orange peel. When the battleship *Yamato* made its famous suicide run to Okinawa in April 1945, it was powered entirely by edible refined soybean oil. Sweet potatoes, meanwhile, became a valuable source of aviation fuel: ethanol, mixed in ever greater proportions with precious gasoline, became the standard in Japanese warplanes by 1944.[41] In one of the weirder—and yet most creative—wartime experiments, Japanese oceanographers attempted to utilize ocean currents for the transportation of food and other necessities. Scientists explored the "shipping" of soybeans from the Asian continent after they discovered that the Japan Current would carry 90 percent of bottles set adrift off the east coast of Korea to the northwest coast of Honshū. Plans were laid for floating small wooden vessels and tiny armadas of metal drums (all filled with food or fuel) from as far away as Taiwan to the Japanese home islands.[42] While the surrender made such plans unnecessary, they show how acute scarcity in wartime Japan could give rise to a kind of environmental consciousness and a conservation sensibility born of want.[43]

Autarky and the Environment

"Total war" brought not only the destruction of combat, the pressures of mobilization, and the rigors of deprivation, but also the oblique and often overlooked costs of national isolation. Japan's wartime disengagement from the world economy and the community of nations had complex and unexpected environmental implications. At the start of the twenty-first century, internationalization and globalization are often assumed to be threats to the environment: multinational corporations are viewed with suspicion by environmental activists, multilateral trade agreements are often seen as sacrificing ecological concerns, and many nations (including Japan) are accused, often justifiably, of exporting their environmental ills to developing countries. Such sweeping condemnations of transnational integration are belied, however, by the fact that Japan's withdrawal from the world trading system and from multinational agreements after the start of the Pacific War seem to have had unfavorable environmental consequences. In other words, Japan's environment—indeed, the world's environment— may actually have been better off in many ways if Japan had remained "globalized" in 1941 rather than pursuing a course of diplomatic isolation and economic autarky.

Two examples are particularly revealing. The first is the case of pyrethrum. Little known today outside the ranks of organic gardeners, pyrethrum is a powerful natural insecticide made from the dried flowers of chrysanthemums. Prior to World War II, pyrethrum was considered the international standard in commercial insecticides and was used by homemakers and farmers around the world, though it was utilized in a particularly intensive fashion in the United States. Over 90 percent of the prewar supply of dried chrysanthemum blossoms came from Japan, and the vast majority of this production was exported to the United States, where it was processed into insecticidal powders and sprays. After Pearl Harbor, needless to say, the trans-Pacific trade in pyrethrum ceased. The environmental impact in Japan was minimal: lands formerly used for growing chrysanthemums were simply diverted to more pressing agricultural needs. But in the United States, the implications of this sudden disruption in trade were more striking: American consumers—and especially the military, which had used pyrethrum for delousing front-line troops—howled for the development of a suitable substitute. While chrysanthemum growing in the U.S. might have been considered as a possibility, it was chemists who stepped forward with a solution to the pyrethrum crisis. Apparent salvation came in the form of an obscure synthetic compound, identified as a potent insecticide by Swiss researchers in the late 1930s but not immediately marketed since it was not competitive with cheap and effective pyrethrum products. This compound was, of course, dichloro-diphenyl-trichloroethane, or DDT, which became ubiquitous during World War II and notorious environmentally in later years. To add insult to injury—and make the irony of the situation complete—after World War II, Allied Occupation advisers aggressively promoted the use and production of DDT in Japan, all but assuring that the Japanese pyrethrum industry would not rebound from the wartime rupture in global markets.[44]

Another sobering example is the case of Japanese fur sealing. Japan began intensive sealing operations in the 1890s, first harvesting the migratory fur seals that traveled along the Kuriles and through the Japan Sea, but later expanding the hunt to the rich seal rookeries of the Aleutians and Robben Island off Sakhalin. The rapid decline of the Pacific fur seal population was apparent by the early twentieth century and the major sealing nations (the United States, Canada, Russia, Britain, and Japan) agreed in 1911 to an ambitious treaty that mandated strict kill quotas, with the goal of stabilizing seal populations and guaranteeing a sustainable sealing industry over the long term. The treaty proved remarkably and unexpectedly successful, and for almost three decades was a model of international cooperation in wildlife conservation: the signatories for the most part obeyed the

210 Natural Enemy, Natural Ally

provisions of the agreement and the fur seal populations rebounded strongly. From the moment the treaty was signed, however, critics in Japan called for revisions that would allow for larger seal harvests: owners of sealing ships were especially vocal, but fishermen also complained, asserting (wrongly, as scientists would later prove) that fur seals ate large quantities of valuable fish species, especially salmon. The chorus of discontent grew through the 1930s until, in October 1941, after the Japanese government had already burned most of its international bridges, Tokyo announced the unilateral abrogation of the 1911 Fur Seal Convention. No good statistics exist on how many fur seals Japanese hunters went on to slaughter during the war. During the late 1930s, Japan's quota under the international treaty had been about three thousand seals a year; wartime estimates suggested that at least twice that many were taken annually after 1941 from coastal waters and that many more (perhaps as many as seventy thousand in total) were killed in the Robben Island breeding grounds. Indeed, by the end of the war, the Robben Island colony was devastated and, in just a few years, many of the ecological gains made in three decades of international cooperation were destroyed.[45] The fur seals of the northwest Pacific were thus the unfortunate and largely forgotten victims of Japan's wartime withdrawal from international diplomacy and the global economy.

Conclusions

As this brief survey has suggested, the environmental consequences of World War II in Japan were profound, pervasive, and unpredictable. The war was undeniably extremely damaging to the Japanese environment: human beings suffered terribly, as did songbird populations, old-growth forests, fur seal colonies, and fragile watersheds. Yet casually assuming that World War II was as dismal a "dark valley" for Japan's natural environment as it was for the Japanese people is erroneous. The war was not an unmitigated disaster for Japan's environment: fish stocks swelled, alternate-fuel research flourished, and the soot-belching smokestacks of many Japanese factories were bombed into prolonged inactivity. Although one might hesitate in borrowing John Dower's phrase and christening the Pacific conflict a "useful war" for Japan's environment, one can hardly deny that the war's environmental impact was uneven, contradictory, and often equivocal.[46]

Most of the wartime environmental changes described in this essay, even the most destructive effects of bombing, mobilization, and scarcity, turned out to be remarkably transitory: bombed cities were quickly rebuilt, the Occupation banned the mist-netting of songbirds, mountainsides were reforested, and fishermen rapidly depleted the waters around Japan once again. In this light, it may well have been popular perceptions of the environment, shaped by the traumatic experiences of mobilization and war, that would ultimately have a more lasting and significant impact on Japan's postwar landscape and environmental record. How were individual Japanese, already victimized by bombings, hunger, and incessant sacrifice, affected by a world stripped of trees and birds, a life of scavenging for edible insects and weeds, and the backbreaking labor of unearthing pine roots? How did the profound stringency of the war years shape postwar patterns of consumption, notions of the "good life," and attitudes toward resource conservation, recycling, and waste? How did the wartime relocation of millions of urbanites to the countryside affect perceptions of rural life, agriculture, and the land? How did wartime propaganda use images of nature and shape popular impressions of the environment and Japan's particular relationship with it? Only by addressing such questions—and many more besides—will historians begin to comprehend the environmental impact of World War II in Japan in its full complexity and long-term social, political, and ideological significance.

As Paul Fussell has observed, "The damage the war visited upon bodies and buildings, planes and tanks and ships, is obvious. Less obvious is the damage it did to intellect, discrimination, honesty, individuality, complexity, ambiguity, and irony."[47] Even less obvious, one might add, were the knotty, elusive consequences of World War II for the environment.

Notes

The author wishes to thank Donald Worster, Adam Rome, and audiences at the University of Michigan, the University of Alaska-Anchorage, and Harvard University for their comments on earlier versions of this work. Research on this essay was supported by grants from the General Research Fund of the University of Kansas and the American Council of Learned Societies.

1   Thomas Havens, *Valley of Darkness: The Japanese People and World War II* (New York: Norton, 1978), 6.
2   In addition to Havens' *Valley of Darkness*, Ben-Ami Shillony's *Politics and Culture in Wartime Japan* (Oxford: Clarendon Press, 1981) was another

path-breaking volume. Many of the most valuable sources in English on Japan's wartime experience remain works published in the immediate aftermath of World War II.

3   Important recent works include John Dower, *Japan in War and Peace* (New York: The New Press, 1993); Noguchi Yukio, *1940-nen taisei, saraba "senji keizai"* (Tokyo: Tōyō keizai shimpō sha, 1995); Okazaki Testuji and Okuno Masahiro, eds., *Gendai Nihon keizai shisutemu no genryū* (Tokyo: Nihon keizai shinbunsha, 1993); and Eric Pauer, ed., *Japan's War Economy* (London: Routledge, 1999).

4   Two important recent works which examine war and the environment in East Asia are Julia Thomas, *Reconfiguring Modernity: Concepts of Nature in Japanese Political Ideology* (Berkeley: University of California Press, 2001), Chapter 8; and Ruth Rogaski, "Nature, Annihilation, and Modernity: China's Korean War Germ-Warfare Experience Reconsidered," *Journal of Asian Studies* 61:2 (May 2002), 381-415. Thomas focuses on the meanings and uses of "nature" in Japanese ultranationalist ideology.

5   See, for example, Arthur Westing, *Warfare in a Fragile World: Military Impact on the Human Environment* (London: Taylor and Francis, 1980); Arthur Westing, *Ecological Consequences of the Second Indochina War* (Stockholm: Stockholm International Peace Research Institute, Almqvist and Wiksell, 1976); Barry Weisberg, ed., *Ecocide in Indochina: The Ecology of War* (San Francisco: Canfield Press, 1970).

6   A similar argument is made in Simo Laakkonen's essay on Finland in this volume.

7   Havens, *Valley of Darkness*, 176-82; John Dower, *Embracing Defeat: Japan in the Wake of World War II* (New York: Norton, 1999), 45-48; Shigehara Terusaku, *Tokyo kūshūka no hyakugojū-nichi* (Tokyo: Taihei shuppansha, 1974); Gordon Daniels, "The Great Tokyo Air Raid, 9-10 March 1945" in W. G. Beasley, ed., *Modern Japan: Aspects of History, Literature and Society* (Tokyo: Charles Tuttle, 1976).

8   Kenneth Werrell, *Blankets of Fire: U.S. Bombers over Japan during World War II* (Washington, DC: Smithsonian Institution Press, 1996), 226. For the sake of comparison, in 2000, the approximate area of the city of Albuquerque, New Mexico, was 180 square miles; of the city of Indianapolis, Indiana, 360 square miles.

9   Robert Guillain (William Byron, trans.), *I Saw Tokyo Burning* (Garden City, NY: Doubleday, 1981), 118. Guillain, who was consistently critical of Japan and the Japanese in his wartime writings from Tokyo, may have exaggerated the decrepitude of Japanese cities, even in the straitened circumstances of war. In any case, even the most cynical planners of the U.S. bombing campaign did not rationalize their incendiary attacks as a form of urban renewal for Japan.

10   Tokyo hyakunenshi henshū iinkai, ed., *Tokyo hyakunenshi*, vol. 6 (Tokyo: Tokyo-to, 1972), Chapter 4; *Tokyo-to sensaishi* (Tokyo: Tokyo-to, 1953), Chapter 6; Edward Seidensticker, *Tokyo Rising: The City Since the Great Earthquake* (Tokyo: Charles Tuttle, 1990), 155-64, 165-67. Robert Guillain even adopted a botanical metaphor for the reconstruction of Japanese cities: "Tokyo would sprout like grass, like a forest. On the field of ash and twisted steel into which that capital of unpainted wood had dissolved, three million people were already busy." Guillain, *I Saw Tokyo Burning*, 281.

11   Committee for the Compilation of Materials on Damage Caused by the Atomic Bombs in Hiroshima and Nagasaki (Ishikawa Eisei and David Swain, trans.), *Hiroshima and Nagasaki: The Physical, Medical, and Social Effects of the Atomic Bombings* (New York: Basic Books, 1981), 55, 73-79.

The release of radiation in the 1986 Chernobyl nuclear accident was several hundred times greater than that of either the Hiroshima or Nagasaki atomic bombs. J. R. McNeill, *Something New Under the Sun: An Environmental History of the Twentieth-Century World* (New York: Norton, 2000), 312.

12 Committee for the Compilation of Materials on Damage Caused by the Atomic Bombs, *Hiroshima and Nagasaki*, 80-83; a number of detailed studies are presented in *Genshibakudan saigai chōsa hōkokushū*, vol. 1 (Tokyo: Nihon gakujutsu shinkōkai, 1953), especially 217-25, 247-63, 281-83.

13 Guillain, *I Saw Tokyo Burning*, 240.

14 Committee for the Compilation of Materials on Damage Caused by the Atomic Bombs, *Hiroshima and Nagasaki*, 83-86; *Genshibakudan saigai chōsa hōkokushū*, vol. 1, especially 118-19, 225-41, 263-80.

15 John Hersey, *Hiroshima* (New York: Vintage Books, 1989), 69-70.

16 Committee for the Compilation of Materials on Damage Caused by the Atomic Bombs, *Hiroshima and Nagasaki*, 86.

17 On the offshore fishing industry, see *The Japanese Tuna Fisheries* (Tokyo: Supreme Commander for the Allied Powers, Natural Resources Section Report 104, 1948); *Canned Crab Industry of Japan* (Tokyo: Supreme Commander for the Allied Powers, Natural Resources Section Report 109, 1948). On whaling, *Japanese Whaling Industry Prior to 1946* (Tokyo: Supreme Commander for the Allied Powers, Natural Resources Section Report 126, 1950); Bjorn Basberg, "Convergence or National Styles? The Japanese Challenge to the British-Norwegian Hegemony in the Twentieth-Century Whaling Industry" in David Starkey and Gelina Harlaftis, eds., *Global Markets: The Internationalization of the Sea Transport Industries Since 1850* (St John's, Newfoundland: International Maritime Economic History Association, 1998), 259-83. On lumber and general aspects of economic mobilization in the 1930s, see Jerome Cohen, *Japan's Economy in War and Reconstruction* (Minneapolis: University of Minnesota Press, 1949).

18 B. F. Johnston with Hosoda Mosaburo and Kusumi Yoshio, *Japanese Food Management in World War II* (Stanford, CA: Stanford University Press, 1953), especially Chapter 8.

19 An overview of pollution problems in the 1930s is presented in Kamioka Namiko, *Nihon no kōgaishi* (Tokyo: Sekai shoin, 1987), 75-103. Specific instances of wartime pollution are described in *River Control and Utilization in Japan* (Tokyo: Supreme Commander for the Allied Powers, Natural Resources Section Report 149, 1951), 104-12; O'Neill, *Something New*, 95-6, 138-39; Margaret McKean, *Environmental Protest and Citizen Politics in Japan* (Berkeley: University of California Press, 1981), 45-50; Timothy George, *Minamata: Pollution and the Struggle for Democracy in Postwar Japan* (Cambridge, MA: Harvard University Asia Center, 2001), Chapters 1 and 2.

20 *Reforestation in Japan* (Tokyo: Supreme Commander for the Allied Powers, Natural Resources Section Report 113, 1948), 15-16, 32-34; Kiyosawa Kiyoshi (Eugene Soviak and Kamiyama Tamie, trans.), *A Diary of Darkness* (Princeton, NJ: Princeton University Press, 1999), 11, 63.

21 *Reforestation in Japan*, 19-31. On wartime forestry, see also Nihon ringyŪ hattatsushi hensan iinkai, ed., *Nihon ringyō hattatsushi: nōgyō kyōùkùo, senji tōseiki no katei* (Tokyo: Nihon sanrin kai, 1983).

22 *Forestry in Japan, 1945-51* (Tokyo: Supreme Commander for the Allied Powers, Natural Resources Section Report 153, 1951), 81, 21.

23 For an overview of the pine-root oil project, see Cohen, *Japan's Economy*, 147-48; an excellent summary of the technology of the project is provided

by *Miscellaneous Targets: Japanese Fuels and Lubricants, Article 4, Pine Root Oil Program* (Tokyo: U.S. Naval Technical Mission to Japan Report X-38(N)-4, February 1946).

24 Cohen, *Japan's Economy*, 147.

25 *Bark Beetle Epidemic in Japan* (Tokyo: Supreme Commander for the Allied Powers, Natural Resources Section Report 90, 1947).

26 C. J. Kraebel, *Forestry and Flood Control in Japan* (Tokyo: Supreme Commander for the Allied Powers, Natural Resources Section Preliminary Report 39, July 1950). See also *River Control and Utilization in Japan* (Tokyo: Supreme Commander for the Allied Powers, Natural Resources Section Report 149, 1951), 49ff.

27 Susan Hanley has argued that Tokugawa Japan (1600-1868) was a "resource-efficient culture": "The Tokugawa solutions to limited resources enabled the Japanese to reach a high level of civilization using a minimum of resources, and wherever possible, natural, renewable materials." Susan Hanley, *Everyday Things in Premodern Japan: The Hidden Legacy of Material Culture* (Berkeley: University of California Press, 1997), 75. Hanley does not explore in detail what specific legacies of this economical preindustrial lifestyle may have remained significant in mid-twentieth-century Japan. The anguished response of many Japanese to wartime scarcity suggests that Japanese culture had grown significantly less "resource efficient" during the half-century since the start of industrialization.

28 Cohen, *Japan's Economy*, 365-66.

29 *Fertilizer Practices in Japan: A Preliminary Report* (Tokyo: Supreme Commander for the Allied Powers, Natural Resources Section Report 93, 1947); Walter Lowdermilk, *Water Resources and Related Land Uses in Japan* (Tokyo: Supreme Commander for the Allied Powers, Natural Resources Section Preliminary Report 70, January 1952), 22-23.

30 On Japanese night-soil practices, see Hanley, *Everyday Things*, 110-15; Anne Walthall, "Village Networks: Sᵔodai and the Sale of Edo Nightsoil," *Monumenta Nipponica* 43:3 (Autumn 1988). Japan's wartime preoccupation with night soil was such that the Central Agricultural Experiment Station even collected figures on the relative nutrient value of the night soil of different social groups in Japan. Merchants, government officials, and soldiers, it turned out, were formidable fertilizer resources, although Japanese farmers could claim better productivity of potash, the soil amendment most desperately needed at the time. In what was no doubt a damaging blow to Japanese patriotism, Europeans were found to be first-rate producers of nitrogen and phosphorous.

| Substance | Social Group (Japanese) | | | | | |
	Farmers	Merchants	Middle-class officials	Soldiers	Average Japanese	Average European
Water	95.290	95.310	94.510	94.410	95.000	93.50
Organic matter	3.030	3.180	3.890	4.070	3.400	5.10
Ash	1.680	1.510	1.600	1.520	1.600	1.40
Nitrogen	0.550	0.590	0.570	0.796	0.570	0.70
Potash	0.290	0.280	0.240	0.207	0.270	0.21
Phosphoric Acid	0.116	0.133	0.152	0.297	0.134	0.26

Yoshimura Kiyohisa, *Kōtō hiyrōgaku* (Tokyo: Seibidō shoten, 1943), 109-10; *Fertilizer Practices in Japan*, 54.

31 *Fertilizer Practices in Japan*, 32-34; see also Crawford Sams, *"Medic": The Mission of an American Military Doctor in Occupied Japan and Wartorn Korea* (Armonk, NY: M. E. Sharpe, 1998), 92-96.

32 *Japanese Crop and Livestock Statistics, 1878-1950* (Tokyo: Supreme Commander for the Allied Powers, Natural Resources Section Report 143, 1951), 121-33; Akiyama Masami, *Dōbutsuen no Shōwa shi* (Tokyo: Detahausu, 1995). Kiyosawa Kiyoshi noted matter-of-factly in his diary entry for 24 June 1943 that "This spring in Minami-Azumi in Shinshū, they killed all the dogs and presented the hides to the army." Kiyosawa, *Diary of Darkness*, 42.

33 *Mist Netting for Birds in Japan* (Tokyo: Supreme Commander for the Allied Powers, Natural Resources Section Report 88, 1947); *Wildlife Conservation in Japan* (Tokyo: Supreme Commander for the Allied Powers, Natural Resources Section Report 116, 1948), 22-23; *Japanese Ornithology and Mammology During World War II* (Tokyo: Supreme Commander for the Allied Powers, Natural Resources Section Report 102, 1948), 9.

34 Kuwata Toichi, *Suisan Nihon* (Tokyo: Dai Nihon yūbenkai kōdansha, 1942); Kuwata Toichi, *Gaikan Nihon suisanshi* (Tokyo: Umi to sora sha, 1943); *Canned Crab Industry of Japan*, 16, 19; *The Japanese Tuna Fisheries*, 5, 49; Francois Bourgois, *Japanese Offshore Trawling* (Tokyo: Supreme Commander for the Allied Powers, Natural Resources Section Report 138, 1950), 8. On depletion of whale stocks, see *Japanese Whaling Industry Prior to 1946*, 26ff.

35 *Fisheries Programs in Japan, 1945-51* (Tokyo: Supreme Commander for the Allied Powers, Natural Resources Section Report 152, 1951), 9-13; see also *Japan's Big Fishing Companies* (Tokyo: Supreme Commander for the Allied Powers, Natural Resources Section Preliminary Report 5, March 1947).

36 Bourgois, *Japanese Offshore Trawling*, 52.

37 See Georg Borgstrom, *Japan's World Success in Fishing* (London: Fishing News, 1964), especially Chapter 1; *Fisheries Programs in Japan, 1945-5*, 10-12.

38 Westing, *Warfare in a Fragile World*, 154.

39 Bourgois, *Japanese Offshore Trawling*, 7.

40 Paul Fussell, *Wartime* (New York: Oxford University Press, 1989), 195-207; Susan Strasser, *Waste and Want: A Social History of Trash* (New York: Metropolitan Books, 1999), 229-63.

41 *Japanese Fuels and Lubricants—Article 2, Naval Research on Aviation Gasoline* (Tokyo: U.S. Naval Technical Mission to Japan Report X-38(N)-2, February 1946); *History of Mission* (Tokyo: U.S. Naval Technical Mission to Japan, November 1946), 12-13. Critics have noted that the production of alternative fuels can have negative ecological impacts, especially if previously unexploited land (such as forest or wetlands) is "reclaimed" for the cultivation of biofuel inputs. While an ecological accounting of biofuels is beyond the scope of this essay, it is apparent that wartime Japanese scientists were exploring alternative-fuel technologies that are now considered to be environmentally responsible by many, including the U.S. Department of Energy, for the renewability, sustainability, and reduced emissions that they promise.

42 *History of Mission*, 11.

43 Adam Rome notes, for example, that wartime fuel shortages stimulated interest in solar housing in the United States, but that the postwar return to plenty and a rejuvenated mass-consumption economy stunted the further development of such environmentally sensitive technologies. Adam Rome, *The Bulldozer in the Countryside: Suburban Sprawl and the Rise of American Environmentalism* (Cambridge: Cambridge University Press, 2001), 45-86.

44　On the prewar pyrethrum industry in Japan, see *Pyrethrum in Japan* (Tokyo: Supreme Commander for the Allied Powers, Natural Resources Section Report 78, 1947). On the development of DDT and its wartime adoption in the United States, Edmund Russell, *War and Nature: Fighting Humans and Insects with Chemicals from World War I to Silent Spring* (Cambridge: Cambridge University Press, 2001). On the introduction of DDT into Japan and the postwar pyrethrum industry, Yoshikuni Igarashi, *Bodies of Memory: Narratives of War in Postwar Japanese Culture, 1945-1970* (Princeton, NJ: Princeton University Press, 2000), 65-72; Sams, "Medic," 14, 84-85, 138; Hosono Shigeo, *Yushutsu nōùsanbutsu to shite no jochūgiku* (Tokyo: Nōgyō sō gō kenkyū kankō kai, 1950).

45　*Japanese Fur Sealing* (Tokyo: Supreme Commander for the Allied Powers, Natural Resources Section Report 129, 1950). For an excellent overview of the background to and negotiation of the 1911 Fur Seal Convention, see Kurkpatrick Dorsey, *The Dawn of Conservation Diplomacy: U.S.-Canadian Wildlife Protection Treaties in the Progressive Era* (Seattle: University of Washington Press, 1998), Chapters 4-5.

46　Dower, "The Useful War" in *Japan in War and Peace*, 9-32.

47　Fussell, *Wartime*, ix.

Pests and Disease in the Pacific War: Crossing the Line

Judith A. Bennett

War is about the processes of invasion and colonization. The Pacific Ocean has had its share of both, some more peaceful than others. In ancient times, the distance from homeland Asia meant many nonhuman species could not colonize islands across vast expanses of sea. Consequently, the further east the location of the islands the fewer the number of species. Human colonization initially suffered similar constraints. People moved out of what is now Southeast Asia (called by prehistorians, "Sunda") into the westernmost fringe of the Pacific to colonize the present Australia-New Guinea area ("Sahul") about forty thousand years ago, covering distance by means of land bridges or primitive craft.

Thousands of years later another wave of migrants from east Asia stopped off in the New Guinea archipelago, perhaps for many generations, where they appear to have developed their maritime skills in its predictable winds and currents. Some then pushed off into the unknown waters to the east. These ancestors of the Polynesians, often called the Lapita people after their distinctive pottery, colonized much of the eastern Pacific by about AD 800. They brought with them flora and fauna that invaded the unique ecology of an environment free of humans. These settlers also altered the new lands by preying on easily caught ground-nesting birds and maritime species, hunting many to extinction. They transformed land for cultivation by fire, opening the way for further change from erosion and deposition as well as periodic climatic extremes. Many of these transformations created productive landscapes for their human settlers; others resulted in resource degradation that constricted the population size and lifestyle of their occupants.[1]

The next wave of mainly European settlers began with exploratory surveys in the Pacific in the sixteenth century. By the late nineteenth century, these newcomers had exhausted much of the seas of whales and seals, and participated in the extirpation of bêche-de-mer, sandalwood, pearl shell, and various birds in localized areas for the purposes of global trade.[2] They went on not only to transform large tracts of coastal land into plantations, pastoral lands, and farms, but also to share out the archipelagos among themselves as colonial possessions. Their faunal and floral introductions were myriad. Their cattle, goats, and horses alone brought the end of many soft island grasses and shrubs that had evolved free from browsing herbivores, while their vigorous "weedy" plants found new habitats to cover. And their diseases, incubated in their crowded continental homelands, took a deadly toll among the isolated, small "virgin soil" populations of the scattered Pacific Islands. So massive was the impact of the second wave of settlers and sojourners on this region that it has often been portrayed as "invasion."[3]

Yet in terms of distances covered and the rapid, mass movement of human beings, mainly males, within a short time frame of four years, nothing before or after can compare to the invasion of the military during the Pacific War (1941-45). Vast numbers of Japanese, Americans, Australians, New Zealanders, and a few hundred Indian troops as well as various smaller and mainly civilian groups of Islanders, Koreans, and Chinese were caught in the great centrifuge of conflict that flung them out into the western Pacific Islands. Though the demarcation lines signifying colonial possession crisscrossed wartime maps, they had little meaning to the military unless those lands were colonies of allies and virtually no meaning if they were colonies of enemies. War was fought on a moving front. Its victors would define new boundaries and perhaps claim what had been the front of battle as a new, distant frontier of their own nations.

There were other powerful lines on maps too. These were markers of where certain diseases, parasites, or other pests to humans were prevalent and where they had not invaded. One such line marked the habitat limit of the mosquito genus, *Anopheles*, as carrier of malaria in the west Pacific. Called Buxton's line, it intersected in neat lines of longitude and latitude on the seas around clusters of islands and nipped the tips of Australia.[4] Another of these lines, sketched on Australia itself, marked the domain of the cattle tick, *Boophilus microplus*, as it extended its hold on that great arid land. These parasites cared even less for boundaries than the military. For them as for the human species, the upheavals that war entailed also afforded an opportunity for invasion and possible colonization.

Malaria: Outflanking Buxton?

Mobile people take their diseases with them—in their bodies, on their domesticated species, or via a vector that hitches a ride with them. In the southwest Pacific, malaria has been long a limiting factor on the health of the indigenous population. Although there is a strong likelihood that some in coastal western Melanesia had developed a form of transient partial immunity (premunition) or resistance, the disease was and remains endemic.[5] On several small islands that have *Anopheles* without the malarial parasite, the malaria-free inhabitants often were exposed to the disease in early colonial times when some went to the bigger islands to work or when people from those islands came to work among them.[6] The vector *Anopheles* thus obtained a host with a source of the parasite and quickly passed it on to new human hosts who soon developed malaria. Thus this disease that debilitated and often killed non-immunes could spread and infect others, a process that became clear to Western medicine through the work of Ronald Ross and Giovanni Grassi at the turn of the twentieth century.[7]

To prevent the introduction of a range of human and nonhuman diseases, pests, and parasites, the Fiji-based British Western Pacific High Commission (WPHC) that administered the New Hebrides (with France), Solomon Islands, Gilbert and Ellice Islands, and Tonga, had followed basic quarantine procedures in these islands from the turn of the nineteenth century. These procedures were further tightened in the wake of the Spanish pandemic influenza of 1918-19 that reached several islands via shipping from New Zealand. Although Fiji had introduced thousands of indentured laborers from both western Melanesia and India since the latter part of the nineteenth century, these infected hosts did not spread malaria because the vector, the *Anopheles* mosquito, was not present in Fiji or in islands further to the east.[8] Following closely on the work done by English entomologist Patrick A. Buxton in the 1920s on the mosquitoes that carried filariasis and malaria, and the medical work of the Rockefeller Foundation in the early 1930s, the colonial administrations of the Pacific became more interested in the transmission and control, not only of introduced or continental diseases, but also of endemic ones.[9] It was Buxton who warned in 1927 that *Anopheles* "would easily establish itself in Fiji or Samoa" if visiting shipping had touched malaria-infected ports west of 170 degrees east longitude and north of 20 degrees south latitude (Buxton's line) and picked up infected *Anopheles* mosquitoes or larvae.[10]

• *Mounting fears*

In the late 1930s, as international tensions in Europe and the Far East mounted, naval activity increased in the South Pacific. There were anxieties that these fast ships could spread *Anopheles*. Of even greater concern to the WPHC administration, civilian aircraft operators had plans for a trans-Pacific run. In Fiji, the Chief Medical Officer, V. W. T. McGusty, urged the government in 1938 that, "The vigorous precautions taken to protect Fiji from these dangers [mosquitoes carrying malaria and yellow fever] must never be relaxed, and the threat from aerial navigation should never be forgotten."[11] In June 1939, he reminded the secretary of the WPHC of the 1931 quarantine regulation of the Gilbert and Ellice Islands and asked that these regulations be sent to the New Zealand naval squadron in the Pacific to alert them of precautions necessary to prevent the spread of the malarial vector.[12] Similar regulations prevailed in Tonga, a constitutional kingdom of the house of Tupou, and a British Protectorate. These fears were not unfounded: ships coming from ports such as Rabaul in New Britain were found to have live mosquito larvae in their water tanks at Fiji ports. Had these been an *Anopheles* species, they might, once adult, have found an infected host among travelers and ships' crew from west Melanesia and picked up the parasite from them to transmit to the people of Fiji. The Fiji Medical Department enforced a strict regime of fumigation with the dangerous chemical hydrocyanic acid. By 1940 it was prepared to take similar precautions with visiting aircraft that were scheduled to commence regular runs between the USA and Australia and New Zealand.[13]

But civilian airlines had to postpone their plans. Once the Japanese bombed Pearl Harbor on that "day of infamy," 7 December 1941, and began their thrust into the South Pacific, the aircraft, as well as the ships that plied the Pacific, had more fateful missions, carrying huge cargoes of men and materials around the Pacific rim and basin.

The Japanese advanced with stunning rapidity from Southeast Asia and their mandated territories in Micronesia as far south as the British Solomon Islands Protectorate. Their aircraft, more numerous than those over Pearl Harbor, bombed Darwin in the Northern Territory of Australia in February 1942 and their midget submarines made daring sallies into Sydney Harbor. With the British navy's mantle of protection torn away from them at the fall of Singapore, Australia and New Zealand relied largely on their own slim military resources and the might of the United States of America for defense.[14] All three countries had reason to make their defensive stand in the islands to prevent the Japanese gaining a foothold in their homelands. Forward defense pushed the frontier of battle well beyond the boundaries of the respective national borders, just as offence had for Japan.

Fiji, a British colony, soon became a massive staging depot for the United States forces preparing to counterattack in the Solomons area. At its maximum, the number of introduced military personnel in Fiji reached 20,000 among a local population of about 194,000.[15] The occupation lasted about five years and though numbers fluctuated, was greatest from late 1942 to 1943. It was concentrated on Viti Levu, mainly in the west near Nadi, with some installations near the capital, Suva, in the southeast.[16] The WPHC, with its headquarters in Suva, straddled the malarial and non-malarial zones and its administration was acutely aware of the danger wartime mobility could pose for Fiji and the islands to the east.[17] And just in case it had not been, as early as January 1942, Patrick Buxton at the London School of Hygiene and Tropical Medicine and chairman of a military committee advising on entomological matters, cautioned the British Colonial Office about the dangers of the spread of *Anopheles* by military aircraft in the South Pacific. The Colonial Office conveyed the warning, though it was confident that precautions were already in place within Fiji.[18]

As the war continued, supplies and men flowed from the USA and New Zealand and Pacific Island staging bases via Fiji to the west; the wounded and sick, including men ill with tropical diseases such as malaria, returned in the opposite direction. Later, useful war surplus materials also returned, heading for the U.S.[19] Rotating groups of civilian Fijian laborers and, later in October 1942, the Fijian Labour Corps from all over Fiji worked as stevedores and laborers at Fiji ports.[20] If they contracted malaria, the mosquitoes that could hide in dark corners or breed in water and decaying vegetation in the bottom of boats and canoes could return with them to their home villages and induce an epidemic. The Medical Department redoubled its efforts to protect the colony, paying particular attention to the ports of Suva and Lautoka and the airports of Nadi and Nausori. It had the requisite legislation in place, but the scale of operations was increasingly beyond its capacity.

Elsewhere in the Pacific in 1942, there were fears that malaria was spreading. Parts of Australia, north of 20 degrees south latitude, had foci of endemic malaria, though the scattered nature of the human population had limited its severity. The Australian government quarantined and treated infected refugees from the Dutch East Indies in Queensland and the Northern Territory. Refugees from Australian-controlled east New Guinea, full of the parasites, had created a pool of infection in the northern port of Cairns, Queensland, where a main vector, *Anopheles farauti,* was present. Climatic conditions and concentrations of Australian troops training for war there precipitated an epidemic in June that year. The military removed the troops to the cooler, malaria-free Atherton Tableland for training, instituted control procedures, and concentrated on making the port of Cairns malaria-free for troops embarking for the north. Much was learned from this epidemic. For example, medical authorities as much as possible kept troops stationed in scattered camps in the Northern Territory separate from the Aborigines, some of whom carried malaria parasites. More significantly, infected troops returning from the islands to Australia subsequently were sent to areas south of the *Anopheles* zone.[21]

The Australian forces in New Guinea were hindered in their campaigns in the Owen Stanley mountains (June-September 1942) and Milne Bay (July 1942-April 1943) by heavy malarial infections. The main difficulty was the lack of supplies, including malarial suppressants such as quinine, since the loss of Java and the Dutch East Indies to the Japanese meant that a major source of supply was no longer available. The synthetic anti-malarials—atebrine and plasmoquine—were also hard to obtain at this time and the dosage regime was still uncertain. Mosquito netting was scarce and so too, in these pre-DDT days before 1944, was the insecticide pyrethrum. The commander of the Australian army, General Sir Thomas Blamey, aware of the worsening situation, advised the government to send a military delegation, including malaria specialist Colonel Neil Hamilton Fairley, to Washington and London in September 1942 to outline its problems on the New Guinea front and to find remedies.[22] The cause and course of the Cairns epidemic as well as the situation in New Guinea were of considerable interest to the Americans because malaria was taking a heavy toll of U.S. personnel in the Guadalcanal campaign (August 1942-February 1943) and in bases behind the lines in the New Hebrides.[23]

• *Conflicting priorities: Colonial administrators and the military*
Officials in Washington, by this time, also were hearing more of the potential for malaria to spread on its eastern boundary in the Pacific. Because Fiji had the most effective quarantine and fumigation arrangements in the southwest Pacific Islands, ships going from areas in the malarial zone to places to the east were required to divert there. The military's priorities were not always the same, however, as those of the colonial administration. Military authorities requisitioned civilian transport. The Australia-based Burns Philp and Co., a leading shipper, wholesaler, retailer, and planting company in the South Pacific saw its ships taken off their regular trading rounds to carry troops and supplies, mainly between Australia and the north. Some continued to service the remaining civilian population in places unoccupied by the Japanese, such as the New Hebrides. At the request of the U.S. Naval Command in mid 1942, the Australian government diverted Burns Philp's *Morinda* from its run between Australia and the New Hebrides to Tonga to collect a cargo of bombs for the New Hebrides bases.[24] The matter was considered so urgent that the U.S. navy decided not to direct the ship to Suva for fumigation, although it was coming from Vila in the New Hebrides.[25]

The British Consul in Tonga, A. L. Armstrong, was concerned about the arrival of a ship only four days' direct sailing from a heavily infected malarial island. As Britain was responsible under the Protectorate treaty for the defense of Tonga, the Consul in Nuku'alofa on Tongatapu took an active role during the wartime occupation by the U.S. and New Zealand allies based there. Under Queen Salote, the Kingdom of Tonga was enthusiastic in its support for the allied war effort in Europe, remaining steadfast in its loyalty to Britain even when the Japanese threatened the Pacific. The American task force arrived in May 1942 and Armstrong became the key liaison between the newcomers and the queen, the premier, and the Tongan government.[26]

When the *Morinda* arrived, Armstrong asked the U.S. Naval Commander Charles Olsen to carry out "anti-malarial precautions" under the eye of Tonga's chief medical officer and to see that the ship remained anchored half a mile off land until this had been completed.[27] The navy refused to do this on the advice of one of the navy doctors, and proceeded to load the cargo under conditions favorable for the transmission of any malarial mosquito to the shore.[28] Armstrong protested to the High Commissioner of the Western Pacific and Governor of Fiji, Sir Phillip Mitchell, who was the highest British civilian authority with whom the Americans dealt. Mitchell immediately conveyed his objections to Vice-Admiral Robert Ghormley, Commander of the South Pacific area.[29] Ghormley sought advice from the forces medical officer, who saw the sense in the British stance: "In general the local rules of quarantine and measures laid down at ports of those islands have been evolved by study of experts. These rules of local health officials have been effective for decades in preventing the introduction of malaria."[30] Ghormley was conciliatory and agreed to take regular precautions though he added the proviso, "unless military considerations make such a course impossible."[31]

Mitchell wanted firmer guarantees than this. His ways and means to prevent the spread of malaria were each two-pronged. He realized that "It is no longer safe to rely solely on the keeping out of *Anopheles* mosquitoes. It is now necessary also to eliminate breeding places within the *Anopheles* free zone."[32]

In order to achieve these two goals, Mitchell lobbied internationally though diplomatic channels and also used his considerable standing with the U.S. military to win the support of high officials in the region. He telegraphed the British representative, Field Marshall Sir John Dill of the Combined Chiefs of Staff at Washington DC, who was then engaged in discussions with the Americans and Australians about the problems of malaria and the need for appropriate supplies to win the war against it—in order to win the war against the Japanese. Taking up a criticism of Consul Armstrong about U.S. medical personnel being unfamiliar with malaria, Mitchell urged that malariologists be appointed to all the military bases in the southwest Pacific. He also sought a malaria specialist from the Rockefeller Foundation to further assist the WPHC with an investigation of protective measures, particularly in Fiji. When no expert could be spared from the Rockefeller Foundation, the Colonial Office tried to obtain one from Australia.

Mitchell had cooperation from the U.S. army, but the naval command on the Pacific was less unified and sections of it had been less helpful.[33] The two U.S. military commands in the south Pacific and the southwest Pacific respectively, however, had been poorly prepared for the scope of the malaria problem they faced in Melanesia when bases commenced to be built from March 1942 and landings in unsecured territory began in August.[34]

• *Tightening controls*

Steps were taken to improve the coordination between ships' masters, the U.S. navy and army, and civilian medical officers. Dill obtained the formal agreement of the U.S. navy and army at a conference in Washington in early November 1942.[35] The surgeons-general of both U.S. services, however, regarded the suggestion of malariologists at every malaria-free base as "extravagant" because "[m]en of this type are few in number and are required in areas in which malaria is prevalent," but agreed to train specialist officers in tropical medicine and quarantine procedures with the requisite authority to act against any abuse of procedures.[36] A second medical conference in Washington in late December 1942 also involved the Australians, whose search for supplies for New Guinea was progressing well there and in England. The British Colonial Office canvassed the Australian delegation's Colonel Fairley for a malariologist for Fiji. By late January 1943, the Australian government had found one and suggested that his brief include a survey of the French as well as the British territories. Meanwhile, the U.S. navy continued to avow its willingness to cooperate, but lack of regulations for procedures for "disinsectizing" of ships meant these had to be introduced, with the first posted in December 1942.[37] There were still major problems among the U.S. military with establishing effective anti-malarial operations until mid 1943, but entomologists were being given greater responsibility for malaria control within each combat unit in the malaria zone.[38]

Mitchell also had presented his concerns to Ghormley's successor, Admiral William Halsey, Commander in Chief, South Pacific at Noumea, the capital of French New Caledonia, in February 1943. Convinced of the need to control malaria, Halsey assigned Colonel Kisner, one of the new team of U.S. malariologists to examine the issue. Mitchell then declined the offer of the Australian malariologist because it meant Australian command involvement that he believed would exacerbate tensions between them and the U.S. military in New Caledonia. Kisner advised Mitchell in organizing local British personnel to carry out further prevention and control measures within Fiji.[39] Mitchell used domestic funds initially, but applied to the Colonial Office for additional funding, receiving their full cooperation for a three-year campaign.[40] The measures included quarantine procedures such as fumigation, drainage works, surveys, spraying with oil and chemicals of possible mosquito breeding sites and much public education.[41] A continuing concern was the constant movement of U.S. planes into non-malarial zones. Some planes were being fumigated, but often after the doors had been opened after landing, though the equipment, including freon "bombs" filled with pyrethrum for interior spraying, had been ordered from the States in late 1942 and were in use by 1943. Awareness was rising, however, and throughout 1943-44, the U.S. military continually improved its procedures for fumigating and "disinsectizing" both planes and ships.

The combined efforts of the British administration, the Colonial Office, and the U.S. forces seemed successful, as no significant cases of malaria contracted within non-malarial South Pacific islands ever came to light, though, if the Tonga incident is any example, there must have been several opportunities for the spread of *Anopheles* before 1943.[42] Of course, there may well have been other reasons preventing the invasion of the mosquitoes, inherent in the unfavorable ecological conditions, common in adjacent areas. For example, the French officials on New Caledonia were relatively unconcerned about possible introduction of the malarial vector during the war years, yet their islands were closest of all to a malarial area, the New Hebrides. Though they were supportive of the U.S. control regimes their worry was less with *Anopheles* than with *Aedes aegypti,* the mosquito vector of dengue fever, which had been recorded on the island since the late nineteenth century.[43] The French seemed to rely on experience—after all, malaria-infected Melanesians in their thousands had been entering the colony as laborers since the earliest days of white settlement in the 1860s, as well as indentured Tonkinese labour since the 1870s, usually in less-than-sanitized ships.[44] The New Hebrides was no more than two days' sailing, and less by steamer, from New Caledonia. Yet there is no record of any *Anopheles* species being found in New Caledonia though the opportunities for its introduction in both adult and larval form must have been numerous over the decades. The most likely invader, because it was the only variety in the New Hebrides, was *Anopheles farauti*. This mosquito appears to have been unable to survive and reproduce in New Caledonia, especially on the less-humid west coast. The official port of entry from 1880, the capital Noumea, lay in the west, as did Tontouta and environs, where wartime airfields were.[45] This drought-prone coast has its lowest rainfall in the second half of the year, when the monthly average is for some months below 100 mm, the critical lower level of water needed to provide an extensive habitat of undisturbed pools and puddles for the survival of *A. farauti*,[46] though, of course, it could still breed in long-standing brackish pools and swampy areas along parts of the coast.[47] There may well be other variables influencing the survival of larvae, such as micro-fauna in the waters. Moreover, even if the mosquito lived, only one of the two common Melanesian malarial parasites, *Plasmodium vivax* could survive the below-20 degrees C temperatures that often occur in the southern winter from June to about October.[48]

Scientists like Buxton and Fairley, colonial officials like Mitchell and Armstrong, and some of the U.S. military like Halsey thus may have been misguided in believing in the possible spread of malaria into areas beyond Buxton's line. They exercised the precautionary principle, even so, having the example of the introduction in 1930 of *Anopheles gambiae* from Africa to Brazil and with it malaria as a dangerous precedent.[49] Familiar with the massive research on malaria occasioned by the Pacific War, S. M. Lambert, a medical doctor with extensive experience in the prewar South Pacific,[50] rejected the opinion of those who held that further spread of the malarial mosquito beyond Buxton's line was "somewhat doubtful."[51] He too concluded with those who had formulated malaria control policy in the war that, "… it would seem the highest wisdom to use all known means to prevent the spread of anophelines beyond their present area."[52] Tonga, the catalyst of Mitchell's campaign, had remained safe along with all the other islands outside Buxton's line. Australia, not able to eliminate the vector over its vast areas north of the line, nonetheless successfully contained the potential damage its *Anopheles* could do. In the war against the spread of disease, not all those in power in the islands during these years were to prove so responsible.

• *The cattle tick (*Boophilus microplus*):*
An unnecessary invasion and responsibility denied

Images of mounted horsemen and lines of pack mules traversing palm-fringed beaches, mangrove swamps, and tropical forest do not spring to mind in recollections of the war with Japan in the Pacific Islands. But, as in the Hollywood cowboy movies, the Americans had indeed sent in the cavalry to this other western frontier, though they left their horses at home. The army's 97th Field Artillery Battalion and the 112th Cavalry regiment arrived at New Caledonia in 1942, based themselves at Dumbea, and sought horses and mules to conduct patrols and move supplies and men before the advance north to Guadalcanal planned for May 1943.[53]

The Free French authorities offered local horses as well as horses from the nearby New Hebrides, a condominium governed jointly by Britain and France.[54] These, however, proved unsatisfactory as pack animals. The army obtained a shipment of mules from Panama, but the trip took at least twenty-six days. Suitable horses were closer to hand in Australia, about three to five days away by ship, depending on the port of embarkation. The army imported its first horses from Melbourne, in the southern state of Victoria, in May 1942, its first from Brisbane, capital of the northern state of Queensland, in July, and regular shipments of around two hundred continued until November. In all, 2,048 horses came from Australia, with 1,384 being embarked from the port of Brisbane.

• *French concerns*

By June 1942, the Chief of the Veterinary Service of New Caledonia, Dr. Jean Verges,[55] had learned of the army shipments from places then unspecified and communicated his concerns about the possible importation of livestock disease, citing the colony's quarantine regulation of 1930 to the chief of staff of the American forces, Colonel E. B. Sebree.[56] Verges was determined to see this regulation enforced. New Caledonian regulations dating back to 1891 governed the importation of animals.[57] There were a multitude of diseases that could severely harm the country's livestock. Since the 1910s there had been several scares that *Boophilus microplus*, a cattle tick that could carry pathogens inducing tick fever, known as Texas fever in the USA,[58] had been introduced from the north of Australia into neighboring islands such as the Solomons.[59] Officials there destroyed suspect herds.

None had reached New Caledonia.[60] In 1929, the government veterinary officer in Fiji warned that cattle for Fiji from tick-free Sydney should not be allowed on any vessel taking on horses and dogs at Brisbane, nor should fodder from Brisbane be taken on board for such cattle because it might contain larval cattle ticks.[61] Revising quarantine regulations in 1930, Verges had drawn up more a more specific one for New Caledonia reflecting this same level of concern: all imported animals such as horses and cattle had to be inspected and quarantined before release into the country. So widespread was cattle tick infestation in Queensland that the regulations banned the importation of *all* animals from that state.[62] In the prewar period, the Australian authorities had cooperated with the French to see these regulations observed.[63]

Replying to the concern of the French authorities in what was to be the pivotal document of the French case, Colonel Sebree in June 1942 expressed regret for what he considered "a breach of etiquette" in failing to seek Verges' "collaboration in the examination of these horses." He went on to assure the French liaison officer that "these horses have been carefully examined by competent veterinarians prior to embarkation" and that the Americans would "do as much as we can to work together [with Verges] concerning the future importation of animals into the Colony."[64]

The Americans, however, showed little commitment to these reassuring words. On 6 July 1942, for example, a shipment of mules from the United States arrived in New Caledonia at night without any warning. The United States military claimed to have tried to contact Verges, but he was in the countryside, so they landed them anyway. The Americans seemed to think they had taken sufficient precautions in having had these mules "vaccinated" in the United States, but did not say against what disease.[65] Four days later, Verges boarded one of the ships bringing in horses from Queensland and saw ticks on these animals, as did the U.S. army veterinarian, William Hoffman.[66] Although Verges conveyed the New Caledonian regulations to Hoffman, the animals were unloaded. And in spite of protests by the French governor, the Americans denied Verges access to the military holding areas to inspect the horses and offered the assurance that, "toutes les precautions étaient prises par leurs services compétents pour garantir leur chaptel."[67]

Two men who were probably more familiar with the physical appearance of the tick confirmed its presence on horses embarking from Brisbane. A Queensland civilian horse handler, Russell Michaelhill, hired to assist with the shipping of the animals on all the fourteen voyages, and an Australian military veterinarian, John Barker, assigned to the U.S. Army on the voyages from Brisbane from August to October 1942, both saw cattle ticks on the horses aboard ship and reported this to the American military, who took no action. On one occasion in October, Barker even noted ticks on the horses during loading at Brisbane. From mid August, an American veterinary officer, Captain Snyder, had been responsible for certifying the horses' health when loaded at Brisbane, but did not accompany the horses en route. Neither he nor the American army had made any effort to seek the advice of experienced Queensland quarantine officers or to have the animals inspected and treated for tick eradication prior to embarkation from Australia.[68] The Australian Chief Quarantine Officer, Dr. John Legg, an expert on the tick, attested that even if the horses sent from Brisbane had come from a non-tick area in Australia, as they passed through the yards at Pinkenba, Brisbane, an infected area, "any larval ticks picked up while [the horses were] awaiting embarkation would not be noticed" at the point of shipment. At least half of the horses shipped from Brisbane, however, had originated from tick-infested areas of Queensland.[69]

• *Tick infestation*

Two years later, in April 1944, Jean Verges officially reported cattle in New Caledonia infested with *Boophilus microplus.* Cut off from Pétain-controlled France, he had sent tick specimens for examination to Wellington, New Zealand, where the Department of Agriculture identified them as *Boophilus microplus* in 1943.[70] As an epidemic in a completely susceptible population of cattle, tick fever induced by the blood parasites, *Babesia bovis, Babesia bigemina,* and *Anaplasma marginale* may cause death rates approaching 90 per cent, especially if the "virgin" cattle are one of the *Bos taurus* breeds that evolved in Europe, away from the tropical tick fever parasite. After the parasites settle in to a new environment, disease rates fall as immunity develops in survivors and their progeny and the virulence of the parasites seems to be reduced. Once this has happened, combined mortality and morbidity rates may be of the order of 5 percent. When the breeds are

Bos indicus (originating in Asia and Africa), disease caused by tick fever is much less severe. Fortunately, all animal species other than cattle are strongly resistant to tick fever parasites and never experience disease. *Boophilus* ticks (of which *B. microplus* is one of several species) are reluctant to grow on hosts other than cattle, but occasionally ticks mature and lay eggs after growing on horses, sheep, deer, goats, and dogs. Females engorged with their host's blood fall off and lay thousands of eggs on the grasses, where larval ticks hatch and attach themselves to new and preferred cattle hosts grazing in the pastures.

Even without infection with the blood parasites and resultant fever, tick-infested cattle experience irritation and blood loss ("tick worry"), soon lose condition and milk production, and often die, most commonly when herds have not been exposed to the ticks before and the ticks are not controlled by chemical dipping or spraying. *Bos taurus* breeds are far more susceptible to tick worry than are *Bos indicus*. New Caledonia had not been free of all ticks; for example, *Haemaphysalis bispinosa* (now identified as *H. longicornis*) infested cattle and *Rhipicephalus sanguineus* infested dogs. The former had been present on the island since 1927, but was not a major pest.[71]

Boophilus microplus, on the other hand, was of great concern to the French because of the economic repercussions. New Caledonia's prosperity depended largely on its mines, smallholder growing of cotton and coffee, and cattle raising. Its climate and relatively poor soils were like parts of coastal eastern Australia. On his voyage in 1774, James Cook had noted the similarity between the west coast and Australia's eastern shores.[72] It lay in the same latitude as the area between Rockhampton and Townsville in Queensland where the tick thrived.[73] Though the area is in the tropics, it is, nonetheless, cooler and drier than most of Melanesia and has discernible seasons, with occasional droughts so *la Grande Terre*, the main island, was not a major producer of copra, the export mainstay of most South Pacific islands before the collapse of the market in the Depression days of the 1930s.[74]

Prior to 1935, the cattle industry had been significant to the local economy because many of the French settlers had supplied meat as part of the required rations to the imported Asian indentured labour, but the Depression saw the repatriation of thousands of these people and decline in the meat market. Farmers had eked out a living with herds culled to around one hundred thousand beasts of *Bos taurus* (mainly Limousin, Shorthorn, and Hereford breeds and crosses), until the demand for fresh food for the thousands of Allied personnel brought a wave of prosperity to both the agriculture and pastoral industries. This new market was considerable. In a country where the population was under sixty thousand, numbers increased dramatically with the addition of one hundred thousand Allied military personnel in December 1942, before the main contingents of the Americal Division moved off to fight in Guadalcanal. In 1943-44, military numbers were around twenty thousand, reducing to around half this by early 1945 and dropping to about five thousand in August as the war ended.[75]

• *Control measures frustrated*

The chief veterinary officer had no doubts that the tick had originated with the horses brought in by the Americans.[76] Jean Verges had found that the tick was established in the southern west coast area, in St. Louis, Paita, and Magenta, which were near Dumbea where the horses had been concentrated, with the herds on V. Fayard's property near the remount base said to be the first affected. In the Dumbea valley alone by the end of 1944, Fayard estimated about one thousand cattle had died as a result of the ticks.[77] The French government had acted in May 1944 to establish a cordon marked by the Tontouta River around the infected area. All movement of cattle from the area south of this line to areas to the north was forbidden.[78]

It is hard to imagine a worse time to have tried to limit the movement of cattle. From the second half of 1942, the American occupation resulted in construction of various installations all over the island, especially in the southwest. Troop maneuvers occasioned extensive mobility, sometimes with consequent destruction of property such as fruit trees and, more significant, of fences.[79] The Americans did not lack tinned and preserved meats, but put enormous demands on the local fresh meat supply, especially in Noumea, where shortages had meant rationing for the local people from November 1942.[80] Even in Noumea, the Americans butchered cattle and set up their own outlets for beef, annoying French officials by not paying tax on such establishments.[81] Besides the demands of the legitimate market, cattle were being moved about the country to cater to the black market and these, of course, were being moved as surreptitiously as possible. The American troops not only went into the more remote regions seeking to purchase cattle; they also sometimes helped themselves.[82] From

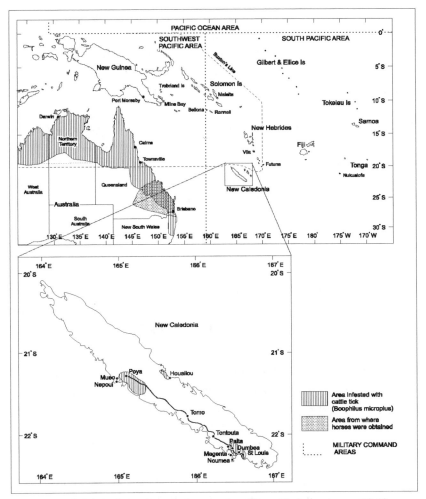

Extent of tick infestation and spread to New Caledonia, c. 1943

May 1942, troop damage to fencing in Muéo and Népoui regions and the loss of cattle were constant irritants to farmers. Moreover, broken fences allowed wandering cattle to spread the tick and quarantining of pastures became impossible. By June 1944 these farmers begged Verges to move against the American forces as the excuse of wartime emergency had long since passed.[83]

In order to control the legitimate trade the government set up abattoirs at points accessible to trucks so cattle could be transported to slaughter and not herded over roads and pastures, spreading the tick. But these measures were of limited value.[84] Prior to the imposition of the ban on cattle movement, the farmers unwittingly had spread the ticks to areas near the road running north from Noumea to Poya. There was another concentration of infestation following the road across the central mountain chain to the east coast, just north of Houailou, where a farmer had taken a cow and bull from Dumbea in 1943. Wild cattle were in the Bouloupari area, north of the Tontouta River in December 1942, over a year before the river was declared the cordon. By 1943 hunters had also reported light infestations of the tick on wild deer (*Rusa unicolor*) near Tomo. There was thus a wild reservoir host for ticks, making eradication very difficult even if the government had been able to fully control the black market and the Americans.[85]

Verges and the French authorities were in a delicate position. The war was still being waged, the Americans were still based in New Caledonia, injecting huge amounts of money into the local economy, and good relations had to be maintained. Yet as late as mid 1944, the Americans continued to violate French quarantine rules, introducing pets, including dogs, one of which was suspected of being rabid.[86] Verges complained,

> *Importation by the United States Army of horses from the Queensland area has been done in violation of our laws and has caused a very serious prejudice to our cattle raising industry in New Caledonia. In spite of the protest of the French Administration, the Americans have continued to introduce animals and, although they no longer import horses, they bring in dogs without checking them at the control office and without warning this department. In consequence we cannot take the necessary steps to examine them and to prohibit the entrance of animals coming from contaminated areas.*[87]

The tick infestation and its alleged source were now common knowledge in the colonial South Pacific.[88] Verges was hopeful of obtaining American supplies to control the infestation to assist in maintaining the fresh meat and milk needed by civilians,[89] but American action might imply American responsibility. He flew to Australia in August 1944 to study control methods, to order equipment needed to combat the pest, and to consult with federal government officials regarding quarantine and trade matters. The French administration made strenuous efforts to cordon infested areas, to construct a series of cattle dips, to spray cattle at three-weekly intervals to kill the ticks with Cooper's arsenic dip, and to encourage systematic rotation of pastures so the larval ticks in the grasses would die out without an obliging host. The administration used French troops and police to assist with this work, which was made more difficult because of the shortage of local laborers as a consequence of intense American demand for workers on wharves and other installations. Verges soon published a handbook on the life cycle of the tick, *Les Tiques du bétail*, advising cattle farmers on ways and means to treat the pest.[90]

• *Claim for compensation*

The Americans for their part were concerned that "a possible claim" might be made "against the [U.S.] government"[91] and remained guarded about admitting any liability.[92] They were aware that the charges laid by the French were serious. Their own elaborate and effective intelligence network reported regularly on all political and economic matters in the French territory, including the spread of the tick into new areas.[93] They began their own investigation in August 1944, yet there is no evidence they let the French know this—or that the French were privy to the findings reported in January 1945.[94] The U.S. Island Command on New Caledonia had introduced regulations in July 1944 whereby all animal introductions had to be quarantined by the chief army veterinarian and finally, in February 1945, instructed that all animal imports had to be cleared with the civil administration. This was the first effective recognition of French authority.[95]

But it was a case of shutting the stable door after the horse had bolted—and with it, *Boophilus microplus*. The American investigation, conducted by parasitologist Lieut. C. G. Fredine, was exceptionally thorough. Fredine carried out interviews in, or obtained reports from, areas as far apart as Panama and Victoria, Australia. He gleaned evidence from shippers, horse dealers, hide importers, Australian customs officers, senior scientific personnel, and army liaison officers as well as the French authorities and farmers in New Caledonia. His confidential report of January 1945 concluded that although ticks may have come in on mules from Panama, the length of the twenty-six-day voyage and the tick life cycle largely precluded that possibility; that the ticks came from Australia, probably Brisbane, on the untreated imported horses; that the ticks were not in New Caledonia before this; and that no tick fever was present in association with the tick.[96]

As the war neared its end and the cost of dealing with the spreading tick infestation mounted, the more radical political parties in New Caledonia, including the Communists, were critical of the Americans and pressured the government to act more decisively.[97] Verges had long felt the same. He had been involved in evaluating all manner of damage to the agricultural and pastoral sector of New Caledonia done by the American forces as well as trying to maintain the meat supply and control the tick infestation.[98] The French administration laid the blame for the tick problem squarely on the Americans and wanted an indemnity. They could trace back the assertion of their claim almost to the time of the initial infestation: first, to Sebree in June 1942, then to Rose in October 1944, and to Barnett in April 1945. In the last letter, Governor Tallec demanded compensation for damages both to the government for all the money expended in tick control and to the cattle farmers who had lost cattle from tick worry.[99]

Brigadier Barnett, commanding U.S. forces in April 1945, advised Governor Tallec that any claims would have to go to the U.S. Foreign Claims Commission and "it is believed that it will be difficult to establish the necessary proximate cause to justify payment."[100] Barnett was prevaricating, for the Fredine report of January that year left no doubt that the American army had been responsible for the tick importation. Legally, the French weakened their case to some extent by admitting in their October 1944 protest to Rose that the initial U.S. disregard of their requests for observance of the quarantine laws in June 1942 could be seen as one of military necessity at a time when it had been possible the Japanese might push out of the Solomons into New Caledonia. Moreover the local newspaper, *La France Australe,* reported on 19 February 1945 that the colony's council general stated that the U.S. considered that "military necessity did not permit of taking account of the warnings and protestations of the French authorities" and that responsibility for the introduction had not been established.[101] Barnett picked up on this and America's decisive role in the Pacific conflict, telling Tallec, "If the damage you complain of was caused by the United States Armed Forces, it happened at a critical time, when exigencies of the situation were such as to indicate that it was most important to the allied cause that men and equipment should reach this island as expeditiously as possible and fortunately in this case, we did not arrive with too little, too late."

Barnett went on to cite the overall agreement that had been signed between the French and United States governments when the war broke out, stating that the "French government will pay war damage claims of French citizens against the United States Forces as a reciprocal aid service under a 'mutual forbearance provision barring claims of one government against the other.' "[102]

There were, however, other considerations. The Americans were not in occupation of an enemy country, but of an ally. Moreover, if the French government were forced to bow to the general principle enunciated by Barnett, this did not include claims brought by individuals for loss.[103] And the government could have levied the cattle farmers for measures to control the tick and the farmers, in turn, could have claimed this from the U.S.[104] The Americans had paid many claims for other forms of civilian loss here and in other allied dependencies where it could be proven that loss had not occurred directly as a result of battle.[105] The French government received Barnett's interpretation coolly, in part because even as late as 1944 when there was not the slightest threat to U.S. forces in New Caledonia, the Americans, while no longer bringing in horses, still were ignoring the quarantine regulations, defiantly importing pet dogs, cats, parrots, and a range of other birds which might have carried numerous diseases, including rabies in dogs and cats.[106] The losses to cattle farmers mounted as the pest spread into new areas that still lacked dips and treatment facilities. In mid 1944, they suffered another blow when both the Sydney buyer and the Australian Department of Health complained of signs of tick infestation on hides imported from New Caledonia.[107]

• *Other irritating invaders*

All this was happening against a broader canvas of increasing disenchantment with the American presence. Although relieved that the Americans were their defenders and relishing the profits from their spending, the people of New Caledonia had been less pleased with examples of U.S. theft of cattle and damage to fencing. These did not occur in isolation. There were also many incidents of the U.S. forces' drunkenness, brawling, vandalism, and involvement in the manufacture and trade of illicit alcohol, as well as disrespect for, and even rapes of, civilian women—all predictable occurrences among such a huge agglomeration of young military males a long away from home, but nonetheless galling.[108] The U.S. forces also had made huge demands on urban housing as well as on Kanaka and Asian labour, draining off the supply from farmers and the administration by the offer of better wages and conditions, often in the face of official French protest.[109] The U.S. used its PX stores to sell items that undercut local prices, avoided paying tax to the local authorities, and encouraged the "French girls" to work there in return for better wages and cheaper goods than local storekeepers could offer.[110] In the midst of the controversy regarding the U.S. disregard for regulations concerning animal importation, the U.S. army decided in mid 1943 that the French quarantine-station buildings were necessary to expand the operations of the marine railway, including the removal of the fences. Directed by his superiors to assist, an indignant Verges insisted on the provision of alternative quarantine buildings.[111] It is not surprising then that by early 1944, American intelligence noted that at an official street parade the small contingents of the New Zealand and Australian forces drew more appreciative remarks and applause from the people of Noumea than the Americans.[112] Irritation with the U.S. sprang in part from American clumsiness in some of its handling of inevitable disputes with civilians, but this was magnified when matters such as quarantine issues appeared to undermine French sovereignty on the island.[113]

The animosity of French settlers was further inflamed by rumors emanating from some of the subordinates of the commander of the American land forces, Alexander Patch, in 1942 that the U.S. would take over New Caledonia after the war. An article that had appeared in the *Chicago Tribune,* and was reprinted in the Australian *Sydney Morning Herald* the following year, suggesting that the French should surrender their islands to the occupying forces, received a very cool reception in New Caledonia. Although a few weeks later Major General Lincoln took great care in a public broadcast to disabuse the French on this, they were concerned.[114] These were signs of the desires of various powerful interest groups in the USA.

Even before the war, President Franklin Roosevelt had believed some form of U.S. control of the island would be vital for American monopoly of proposed airplane routes for Pan American Air Lines into Australia and New Zealand. At the Cairo conference in November 1943—where there was no French, Australian, or New Zealand representation—Roosevelt and Stalin agreed that France, tainted by Vichy, had no right to her former colonies. Roosevelt specifically indicated that New Caledonia should be a trust of the new United Nations and thus more likely to acquiesce in U.S. dominance of the skies. The U.S. naval lobby, unconcerned with civilian aviation, but with an eye to future security, also wanted the several U.S. bases on Pacific islands to remain in American hands.

The strategic resources of New Caledonia made it particularly attractive. New Caledonia had a valuable mineral industry with significant nickel mines, making it a prime economic prize during the war when minerals like nickel and chromium were highly strategic.[115] A visiting U.S. Senate committee emphasized this, reflecting the view that U.S. blood and treasure needed recompense. When the local paper, *La France Australe,* reported that some U.S. senators proposed that New Caledonia be taken by the U.S. to wipe off the Lend Lease debt of France, the local reaction was of total revulsion. In 1944-45, New Caledonia's neighbors, Australia and New Zealand, themselves feeling left out of the war councils of the U.S. in the Pacific, worked in tandem to reject any notion of U.S. blanket control south of the equator. Though U.S. opinion was to shift by late 1945 with reduced naval budgets in peacetime, the emergence of the Soviet threat, and Roosevelt's death, it had seemed to many in the war years that the U.S. in the South Pacific might never go home.[116]

- *Disposals and costs*

These fears that the U.S. might stay after the war had come to nothing, though it became the trustee for the former Japanese territory of Micronesia in the north. Still, the future of the installations the U.S. forces had built had to be decided. The base and materials in New Caledonia had cost the U.S. over 21 million dollars.[117] What to do with them became more problematic as the war wound down; there was only so much equipment that could be transshipped home or more commonly to U.S. bases such as Guam and then, after the end of the war, to Japan for the American occupation. Moreover, the cost of maintaining base equipment and plant was high. To do this and keep the maintenance crews housed, fed, and healthy cost the U.S. 1.5 million dollars a month.[118] With some exceptions, the policy became to dispose of equipment for the best price locally or to use it to settle civilian claims. Failing this, it was to be dumped. On paper and via the French metropolitan government, New Caledonia owed vastly more to the U.S. on lend-lease than the U.S. owed it. By agreement, in May 1946, the U.S. government and the French government used lend-lease accounting to absorb the cost of outstanding claims, including the tick infestation.[119] At the time, it was an arrangement that suited both parties.

Of course, it seemed that New Caledonia had done very well; tons of plant had been sold at bargain-basement prices and the road, port, and airfield infrastructure, worth 3 million U.S. dollars, had been handed over by the Americans. No one, however, had accounted for all the decades of cost that the control of the tick through regular application of chemicals has necessitated. For example, between 1944 and 1953 alone, the tick-control campaign cost the government of New Caledonia about 11.5 million francs C. F. P. or about 2.3 million U.S. dollars.[120] To reduce reliance on tickcides that inevitably induce resistance to a particular chemical, and the cost involved in dipping, the industry today could introduce African or Indian cattle (*Bos indicus*) such as the Zebu to cross with established breeds to increase natural tick resistance in the progeny. Such programs are long term and beyond the resources of small island governments. This has been done in other countries including nearby Australia, but conservative New Caledonian farmers fear such crossbreeding would lead to reduced meat quality and a decrease in docility. An option of purchasing established *Bos* breeds such as Droughtmaster and Belmont Red, based on crossing with *Bos indicus*, also has not been tried nationally in New Caledonia. While antipathy to utilizing *Bos indicus* genes continues, the cost of the 1942 tick introduction to New Caledonia continues to mount.[121]

Boundaries Defended and Lost

Wartime events and mobility left an enduring legacy for the South Pacific. The feared extension of the domain of malaria-carrying *Anopheles* into the more southerly regions of Australia and eastwards into the islands of eastern Melanesia and Polynesia did not eventuate. Within the exigencies of prosecuting the war, most of the authorities concerned acted as expeditiously as possible to guarantee this. Yet wartime traffic from malarial zones into the malaria-free areas generally was not carefully screened for mosquitoes until well into 1943. It seems more likely that the failure of the vector and the parasites to find new homes was because they simply could not thrive outside their original habitat and in areas where there were few host humans carrying the malarial parasites. Buxton's line remained intact as a boundary. The possibility of *Anopheles* colonization, however, dominated postwar medical and entomological opinion, so that quarantine safeguards were maintained.

Unlike malaria-carrying *Anopheles,* the cattle tick was able to continue its eastward expansion out of Asia into Australia and then into a Pacific island that it could never have reached unaided. As it came on horseback, its three common parasites—*Babesia bovis, Babesia bigemina,* and *Anaplasma marginale*—involved in causing tick fever, so often fatal to cattle, thankfully failed to make the journey. The tick, *Boophilus microplus,* however, found a perfect home in New Caledonia, yet one that seemed unfavorable as a habitat for the *Anopheles* variety common to the islands nearest the eastern boundary of Buxton's line. For the human species too, New Caledonia seemed an ideal environment for American colonization. Of all the South Pacific islands, New Caledonia was the most valuable in terms of then-known resources. During the war it was in essence a fort on America's western front, with Americans in occupation. Peace, global politics, and the Cold War, however, induced America to retreat from the southwest Pacific to its prewar boundaries. It needed to keep its old allies in Europe and Australasia. There was to be no such retreat forced on the cattle tick. Aided by the U.S. army, this tiny insect and scourge of the cattle industry had invaded and colonized New Caledonia. Today many people there fondly remember the U.S. defenders' military presence and its boost to the modernization of the economy. Few recall the slights to property and person. Yet many technical articles as well as government documents about the tick in New Caledonia are prefaced by the statement "introduced by the Americans"[122] and Jean Verges' biographer has praised him for his valiant efforts to preserve the colony's cattle in the face of American intransigence.[123] The tick's presence is an enduring legacy of "the Americans' war," providing a less pleasing reminder of their brief invasion of New Caledonia.

Notes

I thank Tony Sweeney and Margaret Spencer for their comments on a draft of the first section, Bill Callow for his on the second section, and Ian Campbell for his on the whole article. Any errors are mine. I thank the University of Otago, Dunedin, New Zealand, for its continuing support of this research. Thanks too go to Ismet Kurtovich, archivist, for his help and that of his staff at the Archives

Territoriales de Nouvelle-Calédonie, Nouméa. Véronique Paullic of the Library at the Centre IRD de Nouméa kindly provided copies of rare French publications. I also thank the Australian National University for a joint Visiting Fellowship with the Resource Management in Asia-Pacific Project and the Division of Pacific and Asian History during December 2001 and January 2002, when I was able to complete this aspect of my current research in the Australian archives. Further discussion of this and related themes will be forthcoming in my planned book, *South Pacific Environment: Natives and Invaders in World War Two.*

1 Geoffrey Irwin, *The Prehistoric Exploration and Colonization of the Pacific* (Cambridge, U.K.: Cambridge University Press, 1992); Patrick Vinton Kirch, *The Lapita Peoples: Ancestors of the Oceanic World*, (Cambridge, MA: Blackwell Publishers, 1997); Patrick D. Nunn, *Environmental Change in the Pacific Basin* (Chichester, U.K.: Wiley, 1999), 288-90.
2 In the late nineteenth and twentieth centuries, Japan too became involved in the Pacific trade and, following World War I, effectively became a colonial power in Micronesia.
3 See, for example, A. Grenfell Price, *The Western Invasion of the Pacific and its Continents: A Study of Moving Frontiers and Changing Landscapes, 1513-1938* (Oxford, U.K.: Oxford University Press, 1963) and A. H. Clark, *The Invasion of New Zealand by People, Plants and Animals: The South Island* (New Brunswick, NJ: Rutgers University Press, 1949).
4 To the south and east of Buxton's line, at 20 degrees south and 170 degrees east, malaria-carrying *Anopheles* were not found. There are anophelines (the tribe that includes *Bironella* and *Anopheles*) outside this zone, for example in southern Australia, but these are not considered to be significant carriers of malaria. See L. W. Hackett, "Distribution of Malaria," in *Malariology: A Comprehensive Survey of all Aspects of this Group of Diseases from a Global Standpoint* Vol. I, ed. Mark F. Boyd (Philadelphia, PA, and London: W. B. Saunders Company, 1949), 725; Mandayam Osuri Tirunarayana Iyengar, *Distribution of Mosquitoes in the South Pacific Region: Distribution Geographique des Moustiques dans la Region du Pacifique Sud* (Noumea, New Caledonia: South Pacific Commission, 1955), 5-6. There are other *Anopheles* varieties that can carry dengue fever.
5 Les. M. Groube, "Contradictions and Malaria in Melanesian and Australian Prehistory," in *A Community of Culture: The People and Prehistory of the Pacific*, ed. Matthew Spriggs et al. (Canberra: Dept. of Prehistory, Research School of Pacific Studies, Australian National University, 1993), 16-86; Philip Houghton, *People of the Great Ocean: Aspects of Human Biology of the Early Pacific* (Cambridge, U.K.: Cambridge University Press, 1996), 88-89, 169, 217.
6 See for example, Stewart Firth, *New Guinea under the Germans* (Melbourne, Australia: Melbourne University Press, 1982), 114.
7 Mark F. Boyd, "Historical Review," in *Malariology*, Vol. I, 16.
8 S. T. Darling, M. A. Barber, H. P. Hacker, *Hookworm and Malaria Research in Malaya, Java, and the Fiji Islands: Report of the Uncinariasis Commission of the Orient, 1915-1917* (New York: Rockefeller Foundation, 1929), 81-82. There are over one hundred fifty species of *Anopheles*, and about seventy of these are potential vectors of malaria. "War Medicine and Surgery," *Medical Journal of Australia* 21: 7 Supplement (Aug. 1943), 82.
9 P. A. Buxton, *Researches in Polynesia and Melanesia:An Account of Investigations in Samoa, Tonga, the Ellice Group, and the New Hebrides, in 1924, 1925* Parts I-IV (London: London School of Hygiene and Tropical

Medicine, 1927); S. M. Lambert, *A Doctor in Paradise* (London: J. M. Dent & Sons, Ltd, 1942).

10 Buxton, *Researches*, 67, 72.

11 Legislative Council of Fiji, 1939, Annual Report of Medical Department, 1938, Council Paper (hereafter CP) no. 40. The common vector for dengue fever, now established in much of the western Pacific, was *Aedes aegypti*, that could also transmit yellow fever.

12 WPHC 2040/39: Director of Medical Services to Sec. of WPHC, 12 June 1939.

13 Legislative Council of Fiji, 1941, Annual Report of Medical Department, 1940, CP no. 6.

14 See John Robertson, *Australia at War* (Melbourne, Australia: William Heinemann, 1981), 68-105, 133; Carl Bridge, "Australia, New Zealand and Allied Grand Strategy, 1941-1943" in *Kia Kaha: New Zealand in the Second World War*, ed. John Crawford (Auckland, New Zealand: Oxford University Press, 2000), 49-63.

15 Legislative Council of Fiji, Supply and Production Board, 1944, CP no. 1; W. E. H. Stanner, *The South Seas in Transition: A Study of Postwar Rehabilitation and Reconstruction in Three British Pacific Dependencies* (Sydney, Australia: Australasian Publishing Co., 1953), 197-98.

16 Judith A. Bennett, "War, Emergency and the Environment: Fiji, 1939-1946," *Environment and History* 7 (2001), 255-87.

17 Legislative Council of Fiji, 1939, Annual Report of Medical Department, 1938, CP no. 40.

18 Public Records Office, Kew, U.K., Colonial Office records (hereafter PRO CO), 83/238/85448: Buxton to Smart, 20 Jan. 1942; Smart to Buxton, 28 Jan. 1942; Smart to McGusty, 9 Feb. 1942.

19 Certain war surplus provided an ideal haven for mosquitoes. In 1945, *Aedes hebrideus*, a dengue vector, was found along with various other mosquito larvae in tires from Finschafen and Biak, New Guinea, landed at Terminal Island, California (National Archives and Records Administration, College Park, MD [hereafter NARA] RG 52 : File Mosquitoes 1940-1948, Dicke to Carter, 11 June 1945, and enclosures).

20 NARA, RG 338: Port Operations, Fiji Islands, June 1942-Jan. 1944.

21 Allan S. Walker, *Clinical Problems of War* (Canberra: Australian War Memorial, 1952, third reprint 1962), 77-80.

22 Ibid., 84-88; PRO CO 83/238/85448: Fairley, Malaria in the Western Pacific, 22 Dec. 1942. In late 1943, Fairley, through tests on Australian army volunteers, was responsible for finding the correct prophylactic dose of atebrine at 100 mgs daily to prevent overt attacks of malaria. The same year, he was appointed chairman of an inter-allied committee to establish regulations and protocols for malaria control among the allied forces. See United States Army Medical Service, *Preventive Medicine in World War II*, Vol. VI, (Washington DC: Office of the Surgeon General, Dept. of the Army, 1963), 7, 541; Walker, *Clinical Problems*, 99; Robert J. T. Joy, "Malaria in American Troops in the South and Southwest Pacific in World War II," *Medical History* 43 (1999), 200, 204; Anthony W. Sweeney, "The Possibility of an 'X' Factor. The First Documented Drug Resistance of Human Malaria," *International Journal for Parasitology*, 26:10 (1996), 1036-39; "The Malaria Frontline: Pioneering Malaria Research by the Australian Army in World War II," *Medical Journal of Australia* 166 (17 Mar. 1997), 316-19; Mary Ellen Condon-Rall, "The Role of the U.S. Army in the Fight against Malaria, 1940-1944," *War and Society* 13:2 (Oct 1995), 99-105. Both Sweeney and Condon-Rall also highlight the work in

this area of American researchers, particularly a group headed by Dr. James A. Shannon.

23 For example, see NARA RG 112: Entry 54A: Malaria at Cairns, 19 Dec. 1942; RG 112: Entry 1012: Schopick, Malaria and Endemic Diseases, South Pacific Area, n. d., c. 1945.

24 K. Buckley and K. Klugman, *The Australian Presence in the Pacific: Burns Philp 1914-1946* (Sydney, Australia: George Allen & Unwin, 1983), 352-53.

25 British Consul, Tonga, Foreign and Commonwealth Office, Milton Keynes, U.K. (hereafter BCT) MP 65/1942: Port Director, Suva to British Consul, 29 July 1942; High Commissioner to Consul, 29 July 1942. I am very grateful to Dr. Ian Campbell who kindly took the time to make notes of these records in the BCT series for me in December 2000.

26 Charles W. Weeks, "The United States Occupation of Tonga, 1942-1945: the Social and Economic Impact," *Pacific Historical Review* (1987), 402-5; I. C. Campbell, *Island Kingdom: Tonga Ancient and Modern* (Christchurch, New Zealand: Canterbury University Press, 1992), 156-58; Elizabeth Wood-Ellem, "Behind the Battle Lines: Tonga in World War II," in *Echoes of Pacific War*, ed. Deryck Scarr, Niel Gunson, Jennifer Terrell (Canberra, Australia: Target Oceania, 1998), 12-15.

27 BCT MP 65/1942: Armstrong to Tyner and Olsen, 30 July 1942.

28 BCT MP 65/1942: Consul to High Commissioner, 30 July 1942.

29 BCT MP 65/1942: High Commissioner to Commander, South Pacific, 11 Aug. 1942.

30 NARA, RG 313: Entry 179 Sopac: Dearing to Chief of Staff, 11 Sept.1942.

31 BCT MP 65/1942: High Commissioner to Commander, South Pacific, 11 Aug. 1942; Ghormley to High Commissioner, 4 Oct. 1942; see also NARA, RG 313: Entry 179.

32 PRO CO 83/238/85448: Mitchell to Sec. of S., 23 Sept. 1942.

33 PRO CO 83/238/85448: Mitchell to Sec. of S., 23 Sept. 1942; Mitchell to Sec. of S., 2 Oct. 1942; Smart to Anderson, 9 Dec. 1942; A. A. S to ? A. H., 14 Dec. 1942; Anderson to Burston, 14 Dec. 1942; Fairley, Malaria in the Western Pacific, 22 Dec. 1942.

34 United States Army Medical Service, *Preventive Medicine,* 6-7, 404, 421-41, 513-15, 536-37; Joy, "Malaria," 192-200. General Douglas MacArthur was the Supreme Commander of Allied Forces in both southern areas.

35 Walker, *Clinical Problems*, pp. 88-89; PRO CO 83/238/85448: Sawyer to Smith, 12 Nov. 1942; Mitchell to Sec. of S., 2 Oct. 1942; S. of S. to Mitchell, 2 Feb 1943.

36 NARA, RG 218: Decimal series: Magee and McIntyre to Somerville, 1 Nov. 1942.

37 Walker, *Clinical Problems*, 83-89; PRO CO 83/238/85448: Fairley, Report, Malaria in the Western Pacific, 22 Dec. 1942; Anderson to Smart, 15 Jan. 1943 ; Acting Sec. to Governor , Memo, 30 Jan. 1943; NARA, RG 218: Decimal series: Leahy to Land, 24 Nov. 1942; War Shipping Administration, Operations Regulation 24. Re French territories, see also PRO CO 83/238/85448: Thomson to Smart, 27 Oct. 1942; Smart to Thompson, 26 Nov. 1942; Sec. of S. to Mitchell, 5 Dec. 1942. It seems Fairley gave advice to Mitchell on these matters during a stopover on his return to Australia from discussions in Washington. See PRO CO 83/238/85448: Smart to Anderson, 9 Dec. 1942.

38 NARA RG 112: Entry 1012: Schopick, Malaria and Endemic Diseases, South Pacific Area, n. d., c. 1945; Joy, "Malaria," 200.

39 Joy, "Malaria," 199; United States Army Medical Service, *Preventive Medicine*, 435-7; PRO CO 83/238/85448: Mitchell to Sec. of S., 5 Mar. 1943, telegrams 131 and 132.

40 PRO CO 83/238/85448: Sec. of S. to Mitchell, 2 Feb., 27 Mar., 25 May, 21 July 1943. The funding was to fall within the Colonial Development and Welfare Fund and amounted to over £71,000. Legislative Council of Fiji, 1944, Post war reconstruction: Fiji and the Western Pacific, CP 2.

41 Legislative Council of Fiji, 1944, Annual Report of Medical Department, 1943, CP 17; *Fiji Times*, 7 Apr. 1943

42 NARA, RG 313: Entry 179: Magath to Commander, SoPac, 31 Mar. 1943; NARA, San Bruno, California, RG 313-58-3440: Tutuila: Manual of Advanced Base Development, July 1943, 79; RG 313-58-3150, SoPac confidential letter #9=44, 10 Nov. 1944; Legislative Council of Fiji, 1944, M. H. Watt and M. I. Lambie, Report on the Public Health and Medical Services in the Colony of Fiji, CP 3. There is a tantalising mention of one case diagnosed in New Caledonia of a radio operator from San Diego, USA developing malaria in the Magenta area near Noumea in March 1943. He had not been in a malarial area. Investigations seem not to have found any malaria vectors in the region, but it is possible one came in on a vessel, injected the parasite, and then died. Similar cases have been reported in Australia in the early 1990s and mosquitoes lurking in planes are thought to have been the cause. See NARA RG 313: Entry 179: Goldman, Memo to Officer in Charge, Malaria Control, South Pacific, 12 Mar. 1943.

43 NARA RG 52: Entry 1005: Parner, memo for Carter, 28 Mar. 1945; RG 112: Entry 1012: Schopick, Malaria and Endemic diseases, South Pacific Area, n.d., c. Feb. 1945; RG 313: Entry 178: Goldman and Eads, Dengue Fever on a South Pacific Base, c. 1945; San Bruno, RG 313-58-3401: Newsletter, Malaria and Epidemic Control, South Pacific Area, March 1944; United States Army Medical Service, *Preventive Medicine*, 406, 441, 473; William J. Perry, "The Mosquitoes and Mosquito-borne Diseases on New Caledonia, an Historic Account: 1885-1946," *American Journal of Tropical Medicine*, 30:1 (1950), 104-10.

44 Dorothy Shineberg, *The People Trade: Pacific Island Laborers and New Caledonia, 1865-1930* (Honolulu: University of Hawaii Press, 1999), 29-30, 239-40.

45 Marshall Laird, *Studies of Mosquitoes and Freshwater Ecology in the South Pacific* (Wellington: Royal Society of New Zealand, 1956), 189-190; Perry, "The Mosquitoes," 104. I am grateful to Dr. Dorothy Shineberg for information regarding ports of entry in the nineteenth century.

46 R. C. Retard, "Epidemiology of malaria in the New Hebrides," *Tropical Doctor* 9 (Oct. 1979), 215-16; Willem J. M. Martens, Theo H. Jetten, and Dana A. Focks, "Sensitivity of malaria, schistosomiasis and dengue to global warming," *Climatic Change* 35 (1997), 147; H. C. Brookfield with Doreen Hart, *Rainfall in the Tropical Southwest Pacific* (Canberra: Dept. of Geography, Research School of Pacific Studies, Australian National University, 1966), maps 4(b), 6(b), 7(b), 8 (b); H. C. Brookfield with Doreen Hart, *Melanesia: A Geographical Interpretation of an Island World* (London: Methuen, 1971), 19; Robert H. Black, "The Geographical Distribution of Malaria in the South-west Pacific," *Australian Geographer* 6 (1955), 32-35. This is not to say that some other variety of *Anopheles* suited to this climate may not thrive, as was the case with the introduction of *Anopheles gambiae* to Brazil and the postwar (in about 1948) introduction to Guam of *Anopheles indefinitus*, thought to be the vector in 1969 of several cases of malaria there. The mosquito was thought to have come in

on landing barges or with the Japanese from the Dutch Indies. See Wesley R. Nowell, "Vector Introduction and Malaria Infection on Guam," *Journal of the American Mosquito Control Association* (June 1987), 259-65; National Archives of Fiji, Suva, Colonial Secretary series F 48/82/20: Inspector General to Colonial Secretary, 16 June 1948. It seems possible too that with global warming and periodic El Niño events malaria's range in the Pacific will extend beyond Buxton's line. See David J. Rogers and Sarah E. Randolph, "The Global Spread of Malaria in a Future Warmer World," *Science* 289 (2000), 1763-66; R. Sari Kovats, "El Niño and Human Health," *Bulletin of the World Health Organization* 78 (2000), 1127-35.

47 Dr. Tony Sweeney, pers. comm., 9 Oct. 2001. This species, however, survives in similar rainfall conditions in parts of northern Australia.

48 Retard, "Epidemiology."

49 "War Medicine and Surgery," *Medical Journal of Australia* 21: 7 Supplement (Aug. 1943), 81-84.

50 Lambert worked for the Rockefeller Foundation on yaws and hookworm campaigns in the islands in the 1920s and 1930s. He died in 1947. His book, *A Yankee Doctor in Paradise* (Boston, MA: Little Brown and Co, 1941), published also as *A Doctor in Paradise*, outlines his work in the Pacific.

51 F. H. Taylor cited in Sylvester M. Lambert, "Malaria incidence in Australia and the South Pacific," in Boyd, *Malariolog* Vol. II, 827.

52 Ibid., 828. Another with long experience in the western Pacific, the entomologist R. J. A. W. Lever, also shared this view. See "The Anopheline Mosquitoes of Melanesia," *Transactions of the Royal Society of Tropical Medicine and Hygiene* 38:6 (July 1945), 501. Laird echoes this. Laird, *Studies of Mosquitoes*, 5-12.

53 NARA RG 112: Entry 1012: Activities of the Army Veterinary Service in Pacific Ocean areas, 7 Dec. 1941-30 June 1945. Most of the animals of the 112th were handed over to the Quartermaster Squadron Remount Station, but the 97th took nine hundred horses and mules with them to Guadalcanal. Their fate is unknown. Eventually the horses of the 112th went to India, shipment being completed in September 1944.

54 Archives Territoriales de Nouvelle-Calédonie, Nouméa (hereafter ATNC): 44 W 514, Sautot to Colonel Burgheim, 2 Apr. 1942.

55 Born in Noumea in 1899, Verges studied in France at the veterinary schools at Lyon and Alfort and subsequently in the faculty of medicine in Paris. In 1927 he returned to New Caledonia and established the Veterinary Service. See Patrick O'Reilly, *Calédoniens: Repertoire bio-bibliographique de la Nouvelle-Calédonie* (Paris, France: The Society, 1980), 396.

56 ATNC 44 W 709 (212): Verges à Gouverneur, 24 Juin1942; Bourgeau à Sebree, 26 Juin 1942.

57 ATNC 44 W 367: Arrêté No. 1000, 10 Août 1946.

58 ATNC 107 W: Verges, Rapport, 7 Avr. 1944. Three pathogens or blood parasites are transmitted by *Boophilus microplus*: *Babesia bovis*, *Anaplasma marginale*, and *Babesia bigemina*. The first causes more than 80 percent of clinical tick fever in Australia. L. L. (Bill) Callow, pers. comm., 13 Feb. 2001.

59 The tick had come into northern Australia in 1829 on Banteng cattle (*Bos sundaicus*) from Timor. This herd subsequently mixed with *Bos taurus* herds brought in from New South Wales, establishing a zone of infection that radiated out from Darwin in the Northern Territory. By 1906 ticks

were rife on the east coast of Australia, south beyond Brisbane to the
Queensland-New South Wales border. See Beverley Angus, *The Cattle Tick
and Tick Fever in Australia* (Brisbane, Australia: Dept. of Primary
Industries, Queensland, 1998), 8-11, 43.

60 See, for example, Western Pacific High Commission Archives, Foreign and
Commonwealth Office, Milton Keynes, U.K., (here after WPHC) 659/19:
Woodford to HC, 11 Mar. 1918; WPHC 2582/18: Lucas to Workman, 18
Oct 1918 and encl.; WPHC 105/20: Lucas to Greene, 19 Dec. 1919, and
encl.; WPHC 806/29: Tothill to High Commissioner, 13 June 1930 and
encls. There was ample evidence for lack of *Boophilus microplus* in New
Caledonia at the time. For example, the French had exported cattle hides to
Sydney to the same company since about 1914; it was only in early 1944
the company first noted the presence of *Boophilus*. See NARA RG 313:
Entry 178: Manager, Commonwealth Wool and Produce Co. to Fredine,
17 Nov. 1944

61 WPHC 3146/29: Stuchbery to Superintendent of Agriculture, 18 Oct.
1929.

62 See Arrêté No. 242, 15 Fev. 1930, Actes du Gouvernement local, *Journal
Officiel* (29 Mars 1930), 212-13; NARA RG 313: Entry 178: English
translation of extract from *La France Australe*, 1 Mar. 1945. Australian
customs officials testified that, prior to the army horses, no animals of any
kind had passed through the port of Brisbane for New Caledonia, since
about 1934. Few had left Sydney for New Caledonia since the Pacific War
began and these were certified free of diseases and tick-free by a demanding
procedure. See NARA RG 313: Entry 178: Fredine, Report on the
Investigation of Cattle Ticks in New Caledonia, 13 Jan. 1945.

63 NARA RG 313: Entry 178: Fredine, Report on the Investigation of Cattle
Ticks in New Caledonia, 13 Jan. 1945.

64 ATNC 44 W 709 (212): Sebree to Bourgeau, 26 June 1942.

65 ATNC 44 W 514: Bourgeau à Verges, 7 Juil. 1942. No effective vaccine
existed to prevent cattle tick infection at the time.

66 ATNC 44 W 709 (212): Tallec à Rose, 28 Oct. 1944.

67 "All precautions were takenby the relevant [U.S.] officials in order to
protect their livestock." ATNC 107W: Verges, Rapport, 7 Avr. 1944.

68 NARA RG 313: Entry 178: Fredine, Report on the Investigation of Cattle
Ticks in New Caledonia, 13 Jan. 1945; Legg, Memo to Director-General of
Health, 28 July 1944; Baker to USASOS HG, 4 Nov. 1944; National
Archives of Australia, Canberra, (hereafter NAA) A989, item 1944/610/
11/1: Cumpston to Secretary, Dept. of External Affairs, 11 July 1944. The
Australian government experienced similar difficulties with convincing the
U.S. forces that Australian quarantine regulations also applied to them
when the Americans tried to import their horses to Australia.

69 NARA RG 313: Entry 178: Legg, Memo to Director-General of Health,
28 July 1944; Fredine, Report on the Investigation of Cattle Ticks, 13 Jan.
1945. Prior to being yarded at Brisbane, the horses "from surrounding
areas" were concentrated at Toowoomba, inland from Brisbane. See NARA
RG 313: Entry 178: Adams to Shute, 18 June 1942.

70 NARA RG 313: Entry 178: English translation of extract from *La France
Australe*, I Mar. 1945; RG 338: Entry 44463: Smith, Annex 2 to Political
Report No. 115, 10 Mar. 1945. With the fall of France, Pétain became the
leader of a Fascist regime dictated by the Germans, his government based at
Vichy.

71 J. Verges, *Les Tiques du bétail*, (Nouméa, New Caledonia: Imprimeries
Réunies, 1944), 5-6; L. L. (Bill) Callow, pers. comm. 13 Feb. 2001; ANC

107W: Verges, Rapport, 7 Avr. 1944; Marc Desquesnes, 'Boophilus Microplus, Biologie et Modes de Lutte, Applications à la Nouvelle-Calédonie, Thèse, Doctorat Vétérinaire, Ecole Nationale Vétérinaire d'Alfort, France 1988, p. 55.

72 James Cook, *The Journals of Captain James Cook on his Voyages of Discovery,* Vol. 2, ed. J. C. Beaglehole (Cambridge, U.K.: Cambridge University Press, 1961), 543.

73 L. O. Brun, J. T. Wilson and P. Daynes, "Ethion Resistance in the Cattle Tick (*Boophilus microplus*) in New Caledonia," *Tropical Pest Management* 29:1 (1983); 16-22, p. 16; Angus, *The Cattle Tick*, 89, 91; Desquesnes, "*Boophilus microplus*," 31, 257-58.

74 In Noumea there is a 6-degree difference between mean winter and summer temperatures. Mean winter temperatures for the island are around 18 degrees C and in summer there is no record of temperatures higher than 39 degrees C, with the mean around 30 degrees. On the plains in winter temperatures rarely fall below 10 degrees C. See Connell, *New Caledonia,* 7; Desquesnes, "*Boophilus microplus*," 257; Virginia Thompson and Richard Adloff, *The French Pacific Islands* (Berkeley, Los Angeles, London: University of California Press, 1971), 232. The smaller Gilbert and Ellice Protectorate, for example, produced about twice the weight of copra as New Caledonia. See R. W. Robson, *Pacific Islands Year book* (Sydney, Australia: Pacific Publications, 1942), 160.

75 ATNC 37 W 542: Raw statistics on herds and crops, 1937-1945; John Connell, *New Caledonia or Kanaky? The Political History of a French Colony* (Canberra: National Centre for Development Studies, Australian National University, 1987), 98-123; NARA RG 313: Entry 6303: Historical sketch US Naval Advanced Base, Noumea, c. 1 Dec. 1945; Thompson and Adloff, *The French Pacific Islands*, 395-96; Olivier Gargominy, *Les introductions d'especes animales et vegetales en Nouvelle-Calédonie* (Rennes, France: Ecole Nationale Superieure Agronomique et ORSTROM, 1993), 33; Desquesnes, "*Boophilus microplus*," 31.

76 ATNC 107 W: Verges, Rapport, 7 Avr. 1944. By early 1943, Verges had been called in as consultant veterinarian for the U.S. horses. (ATNC 44 W 518: Montchamp à Sec. Général, 5 Jan. 1943).

77 Brun, Wilson, and Daynes, "Ethion Resistance," 17; NARA RG 313: Entry 178: Fredine, Report on the Investigation of Cattle Ticks in New Caledonia, 13 Jan. 1945.

78 ATNC 44 W 365: Arrêté No. 399, 3 Mai 1944.

79 ATNC 44 W 682: Guindon à Gouverneur, 26 Oct. 1942

80 NARA RG 112: Entry 1012: Hodgson to Veterinarian, 10 Mae. 1945; ANTC 44 W 709: Patch to Montchamp, 29 Oct. 1942; Verges to Governor, 19 Nov. 1942; Lavoye, Rapport, Août. 1942; Lincoln to Governor, 11 Feb 1942; ATNC 44 W 718: Montchamp, Rapport au Conseil d'administration, 7 Dec 1942; ANTC 44 W 366: Arrêté, No. 537, 31 Mai 1945.

81 ATNC 44 W 718: Conseil d'administration, 16 Dec. 1943. The U.S. military fed their forces meat twenty-one times a week. Sidney W. Mintz, *Tasting Food, Tasting Freedom: Excursions into Eating, Culture and the Past* (Boston, MA: Beacon Press, 1996), 2.

82 ATNC 44 W 718: Montchamp, Rapport au Conseil d'administration, 7 Dec. 1942; ATNC 44 W 709: Dubusson à Gouverneur, 28 Dec. 1942.

83 ATNC 44 W 707 (211): [Illegible], Pour la Sociéte de Muéo, à Verges, 28 Juin 1944. Wandering cattle and poor fencing long had been a way the French extended their grazing areas beyond their official boundaries into

the reserves of the Kanaks. It seems likely this also contributed to the spread of the tick.

84 ATNC 44 W 718: Tallec, Rapport au Conseil d'administration, 7 Juil. 1944.

85 ATNC 44 W 514: Le Gouverneur à ?, 23 Dec. 1942; NARA RG 313: Entry 178: Map of tick infestation; Fredine, Report on the Investigation of Cattle Ticks, 13 Jan. 1945; RG 338, Entry 44463: Smith, Annex No. 1 to Economic Reports, Nos, 75, 83, 84, 85, 100, 101.

86 ATNC 44 W 516: Tallec to Rose, 18 Nov. 1944.

87 NARA RG 313: Entry 178: Verges, Report to the Governor, 30 May 1944 (English translation); see also L. O. Brun et P. M. Tronc, "La Tique du Bétail, 1942," *Bulletin de l'UPRA Bovines Nouvelle-Calédonie* (4 Août 1984), 36-40.

88 *Pacific Islands Monthly* (Aug. 1944), 8. See also July 1945, 27.

89 ATNC 44 W 707 (212): Verges, Rapport à Monsieur le Gouverneur, 26 Avr. 1944.

90 NAA A989, item 1944/610/11/1: Cumpston to Secretary, Dept. of External Affairs, 5 Sept. 1944; NAA A6445, item 36/1946: Forsyth to Australian Representative, 11 Sept. 1944; ATNC, 107W: Verges, Rapport, 12 Avr. 1944; Tallec à Commandant Supérieur des troopes, 19 Avr. 1944; ATNC Cote S J 29: Registre copie des correspondence de la bregade de gendameries de La Foa, 1944-1948; ATNC 44 W 718: Tallec, Rapport au Conseil d'administration, 10 Juil. 1944; Verges, *Les Tiques du bétail*; NARA RG 338: Entry 44463: Smith, Annex to Economic Report No. 85, 12 Aug. 1944; Smith, Annex to Economic Report No. 83, 5 Aug. 1944. Arsenical tickcides were not completely effective and resistance soon built up in the ticks. In about 1947, Rucide (DDT-based) began to be used and by the 1950s other chlorinated hydrocarbons. In 1973, the organic phosphate ethion was the main chemical used. L. L. (Bill) Callow, pers. comm., 13 Feb. 2001; Brun, Wilson, and Daynes, "Ethion Resistance," 17; Desquesnes, "*Boophilus microplus,*" 32.

91 NARA RG 313: Entry 178: Whitehead to Surgeon, Services Command, 9 June 1944.

92 NARA RG 112: Entry 1012: Activities of the Army Veterinary Service Pacific Ocean Area, 7 Dec. 1941-30 Jun. 1945; see encl., Kester, Inspection of Veterinary Service in the SPBC, 12 Nov. 1944.

93 See, for example in relation to the tick, NARA RG 388: Entry 44463: Smith, Annex No. 1 to Economic Reports, Nos, 75, 83, 84, 85, 100, 101; Annex No. 2 to Political Reports, Nos 82, 104, 112, 115.

94 NARA RG 313: Entry 178: Fredine, Report on the Investigation of Cattle Ticks, 13 Jan. 1945; ATNC Fonds de la Commune de Houailou: Fredine to Gabillon, 12 Sept. 1944.

95 NARA RG313: Entry 179:Island Command, Base Memo No. 28, Importation of Animals, 10 July 1949; NARA RG 313, Entry 178: Island Command, Base Memo No. 1, Importation of Animals, 11 Feb. 1945. The neighboring New Hebrides introduced the same July prohibition. WPHC New Hebrides series MP 58/29: Reynolds, Restriction in landing of animals, 2 July 1944 and encls.

96 NARA RG 313: Entry 178: Fredine, Report on the Investigation of Cattle Ticks, 13 Jan. 1945. In 1944, tests on specimens from New Caledonia conducted in Australia showed that there were no pathogens transmitted by *Boophilus microplus,* such as *Babesia bovis.* See NARA RG 313, Entry 178: Legg to Ferdine, 28 Oct. 1944.

97　NARA RG 388: Entry 44463: Smith, Annex No. 2 to the Political Reports, Nos 104, 112, 115. For the growth of the Communist Party, see Ismet Kurtovich, "A Communist Party in New Caledonia (1941-1948)," *Journal of Pacific History*, 35:2 (2000), 163-79.

98　The French colonial government wanted a joint commission of their own officials, including Verges, to sit with the U.S. assessors. The Americans refused, though there was such a joint commission in Tonga, for example. See ATNC 44 W 709: Patch to Montchamp, 30 Oct. 1942; Montchamp à Lincoln, 3 Dec. 1942; Verges à Gouverneur, 25 Mai 1943; 44 W 520:Tallec à Barnett, 13 Avr. 1945. For Tonga, see WPHC Secret File 9/31/1 Vol. 1.

99　ATNC 44 W 707 (212): Bourgeau à Sebree, 26 Juin 1942; ATNC 44 W 707 (212): Tallec à Rose, 26 Oct. 1944; ATNC 44 W 520:Tallec à Barnett, 13 Avr. 1945

100　ATNC 107 W: Barnett to Tallec, 27 Apr. 1945.

101　NARA RG 313: Entry 178: McColm to Commander South Pacific Area, 6 Mar. 1945 and extract from *La France Australe* (1 Mar. 1945) (English translation).

102　ATNC 107 W: Barnett to Tallec, 27 Apr. 1945

103　NARA RG 313, Entry 178: McColm to Commander South Pacific Area, 6 Mar. 1945.

104　One political party, the Caledonian Committee, held that there were precedents for this in World War I when the U.S. forces brought in a form of meningitis via their horses to France. This carried off large numbers of cattle. In this case the U.S. paid an indemnity to the farmers of Normandy. (NARA RG 338: Entry 44463: Smith Annex No. 2, Political Report 104, 23 Dec. 1944.)

105　See for example, NARA San Bruno, RG 313-58-3394: Clark to Commanding Officer, Tongatapu, 18 June 1943.

106　ATNC 44 W 707 (212): Tallec à Rose, 26 Oct. 1944; NARA RG 112: Entry 1012: Kester to the Surgeon, 12 Nov. 1944.

107　ATNC 145 W 18: Process-verbal de la Chambre de Commerce, 12 Juil. 1944; NAA A6445, item 36/1946: Forsyth to Australian Representative, 11 Sept. 1944. See also NARA RG 313: Entry 178 : Manager, Commonwealth Wool and Produce Co. to Fredine, 17 Nov. 1944.

108　ATNC 44 W 707 (212): Lincoln to Henriot, 31 Aug. 1943; Field to Lamont, 28 Oct. 1943; See throughout 44 W 702, 1943; 44 W 709: Lavage, Rapport, Aout 1942; NARA RG 313: Entry 183, Massoubre to Halsey, 26 Feb. 1943; NAA A981/4, Item New C9: The growth of anti-American feeling in New Caledonia, 1 Oct. 1942; Stephen Henningham, "The French administration, the local population and the American presence in New Caledonia, 1943-44," *Journal de la Société des Océanistes* 1 (1994), 25-27, 32-34.

109　ATNC 44 W 707 (212): Tallec à Barnett, 6 Jan. 1945; Henningham, "The French administration," 27-32.

110　ATNC 44 W 718: Conseil d'administration, 16 Dec. 1943; ATNC 44 W 520: Tallec à Barnett, 10 Fev. 1945; Henningham, "The French administration," 21-41.

111　ATNC 44 W 707 : Thatcher to Verges, 15 May 1943; Verges à Gouverneur, 25 Mai 1943; ATNC 44 W 518: Bourgeau à Lincoln, 8 Juin, 1943

112　NARA RG 313: Entry 183, Memo re French-American Relations, New Caledonia, 26 Feb. 1944.

113　For several other examples see, Henningham, "The French administration," 35-39.

114 NARA RG 313: Entry 183: Lincoln, radio address, 12 Mar. 1943; Daly 29 Mar 1943 (Parcel 17); Charles J. Weeks, "An hour of temptation: American interests in New Caledonia," *Australian Journal of Politics and History* 35:2 (1989), 198.

115 In part, this explains Australian intervention in New Caledonian politics to bolster the ascendancy of the Free French (mainly descendants of French settlers, who supported Charles de Gaulle) over the minority Vichy-ites (mainly metropolitan French who supported Pétain) in early 1940, long before the Americans entered the conflict. The fear was that Japan, facilitated by the Vichy government, would obtain access to these strategic minerals. See John Lawrey, *The Cross of Lorraine in the South Pacific: Australia and the Free French Movement 1940-1942* (Canberra, Australia: Journal of Pacific History, 1982). The settler descendants were known as "colons" or "Caldoches," the metropolitan French as "metros." In 1936 the population consisted of about 22 percent Caldoches, 5 percent metros, 58 percent Melanesians (Kanaks or Kanakas) and 12 percent Asians. See R. W. Robson, *Pacific Islands Year book* (Sydney, Australia: Pacific Publications, 1950), 423.

116 Weeks, "An hour of temptation," 185-200; NAA, A989/1, Hodgson to Ballard, 16 July 1943 and enclosures; Roger J. Bell, *Unequal Allies: Australian American Relations and the Pacific War* (Melbourne, Australia: Melbourne University Press, 1977), 144-72.

117 NARA RG 313: Entry 178: Historical sketch, U.S. Naval Advanced Base, Noumea, c. 1 Dec. 1945.

118 NARA RG 59: Entry 400, Report of the Field Commander, Noumea, 22 Oct. 1946.

119 NARA RG 59: Entry 400: Agreement for transfer of surplus property, 28 May 1946. U.S. lend-lease "aid" to the Free French worldwide was at least twenty times the value of goods and services provided by the French in New Caledonia. The French colonial treasury was not necessarily out of pocket for this amount because much of this material was distributed to civilians and they had to pay the government. NARA RG 338: Entry 44463: History of SOS SPA, c. Mar. 1944.

120 J.-P. Faivre, J. Poirier, and P. Routhier, *La Nouvelle-Calédonie: Géographie et histoire economie, demographie* (Paris, France: Nouvelles editions latines, 1955), 175; Thompson and Adloff, *The French Pacific*, 276, 476. C. F. P. = Colonies Françaises du Pacifique. In 1944, 50 francs C. F. P = one American dollar; 200 francs C. F. P. = one pound sterling.

121 L. O. Brun, J. T. Wilson and J. Nolan, "Patterns of resistance in five samples of Ethion resistant cattle tick (*Boophilus microplus*) from New Caledonia," *Tropical Pest Management* 30:3 (1984), 296-301, 300; Brun et Tronc, "La Tique," 39-40; Angus, *The Cattle Tick*, 265-325; Desquesnes, "*Boophilus microplus*," 95-100. In the late 1980s, the annual cost was 21 million francs C. F. P. (1,555 million French francs) out of the veterinary department's budget of 100 million (Desquesnes, "*Boophilus microplus*," 59).

122 See for example, ATNC 12 W 45: Rapport à l'Assemblée Territoriale, No. 40-86/sgcg/AT/65, 22 Nov. 1965; Thomson and Aldoff, *The French Pacific Islands*, 395; ORSTROM, *Atlas de la Nouvelle Caledonie et dépendances* (Paris:Edition de l'Office de la Reserche Scientifique et Technique outre-mer, 1981), 21: *Les Nouvelles Calédoniennes*, 7 Dec. 2000.

123 O'Reilly, *Calédoniens*, 396.

Compromising on Conservation: World War II and American Leadership in Whaling Diplomacy

Kurk Dorsey

As World War II came to a close, the governments of the United Kingdom and the United States found themselves bargaining over a series of issues that they had postponed in the darker years of the war, such as postwar economic structures, decolonization, and relations with other powers. While they were rarely on the same page, they were almost always at least in the same chapter; both parties recognized that the United States would emerge from the war with vast power and therefore have to take a more active leadership role in global affairs, and both implicitly agreed that the differences between them were not so great as to wreck what historians and politicians often call "the special relationship."

This unusually cordial rivalry extended to the regulation of whaling on the high seas, particularly in the Antarctic, through the creation of the International Whaling Commission. Great Britain and the United States had different ideas about whaling, but they also had a history of cooperation on the topic. Britain had been one of the major whaling powers in the world before World War II, while the United States had basically no whaling industry in the twentieth century. With no industry to speak of, the Americans had been more consistently interested in conservation measures, but the British had done more to make tangible advances in conservation, even while protecting the interests of their whalers. When war broke out in 1939, the differences between the allies on this issue were magnified, with disagreements emerging over such questions as the impact of military action on whale populations and the necessity of honoring prewar whaling treaties. American whaling experts and diplomats concluded that British whaling interests were so powerful that London would never lead the way to creating a permanent commission that would use science to promote conservation of whales. These Americans resolved, then, to take the lead themselves.

As the war ended and the transition to peacetime began, the sparring between Great Britain and the United States became more complex. British leaders increasingly emphasized the need to hunt whales in order to alleviate the global fat shortage, and Americans began to admit that it made sense to lift some restrictions under the circumstances. At the same time, American diplomats began to see the establishment of a whaling commission not as an end in itself but rather as part of an effort to build global institutions to maintain peace. In the end, British and American officials found themselves able to compromise. A relatively weak whaling commission—one born in Washington but based in London, one that emphasized the role of science but had a mission to promote the industry, and one that protected national sovereignty in the interests of obtaining global membership rather than prioritizing conservation as the first goal— met the postwar needs of both Great Britain and the United States.

Until the twentieth century, whaling had largely bypassed the Antarctic seas, where huge blue whales, too large and fast for Captain Ahab to catch, roamed the ice fields. But a series of technological developments made killing these behemoths and rendering their flesh into oil significantly easier, and by 1905 whalers had begun to work the waters below 40° south latitude. There they were largely free from any law because, by the 1920s, they could operate for months without calling at any port. A government that regulated them too strictly might well see the whalers change to a flag of convenience.[1]

The industry focused on the production of whale oil, the animals' accumulated fat rendered into liquid form. Into the 1920s, this oil was just "an inferior industrial fat." But then scientists invented new ways to refine whale oil so that it could be processed into quality soap and palatable margarine for the European market, attracting the attention of such large firms as Unilever and Procter and Gamble.[2] Margarine came to be easily the largest end product from whaling, and the market for it expanded so rapidly that the whaling industry grew from thirteen expeditions—each comprising a floating factory surrounded by a small flotilla of catcher vessels—in 1924-25 to forty-one in 1930-31. The catch followed suit, from ten thousand in the former season to more than forty thousand in the latter.[3] It soon became apparent that regulating these whalers would take a complex advance in diplomacy.

Alarm at the whalers' increasing catch turned into action very slowly. Before 1914, the British government and scientists had contemplated a conference on whaling, but World War I ended that move. The expansion of the catch in the 1920s brought renewed calls from scientists for international cooperation. In response, the League of Nations, in an unusual fit of action, produced a convention to regulate whaling in 1931. Twenty-seven countries, including landlocked Switzerland, signed on to this weak opening step, which protected the nearly extinct right whales, compelled whalers to turn in accurate statistics to the Bureau for International Whaling Statistics in Norway, outlawed some of the more wasteful practices, and banned the hunting of calves and lactating females.[4]

While officially a League convention, the 1931 treaty went only as far as the governments of Norway and the United Kingdom desired. Businesses in these two countries controlled the vast majority of the world's whaling, especially in the Antarctic. Especially in time of depression, neither government was anxious to place stiff restrictions on its businesses, which might encourage competition from other countries. At the same time, whaling in the south seas was directly tied to efforts to control Antarctica. Several nations had laid claim to the icy continent, and the presence of whaling vessels flying those nations' flags could only reinforce those claims.[5]

The statistics that alarmed the League of Nations had the same effect on the captains of the whaling industry. The forty thousand whales killed in the 1930-31 season were far more than a depressed global economy could consume, forcing down the price for whale oil and leaving tons of the liquid to age in storage tanks. Whale oil that had sold for as much as £100/ton during World War I had slipped to £25/ton. With whaling companies facing bankruptcy, industry leaders generally agreed that a cartel was necessary to control production and ensure a higher price for their commodity. In the summer of 1931 they decided to keep the fleet at home for the next season in an attempt to reduce the supply of whale oil. Where forty-one factory vessels had sailed in the fall of 1930, only five went to sea in the fall of 1931. For the next few years, whalers tried to regulate themselves by setting quotas for each company.[6]

But things continued to get worse. The effort to raise prices failed; whale oil bottomed out in 1932 at barely £13/ton and brought a mere £17/ton in 1937. British and Norwegian whaling companies sent out fewer expeditions than they had before the depression, but they were investing in newer and bigger vessels in an effort to stay competitive. Even worse, at least from the standpoint of the British and Norwegians, Germany embarked on a national whaling campaign in 1934, and Japan followed the next year. By 1936-37 the number of expeditions had climbed back to thirty and the total catch had once again passed thirty-four thousand whales. Equally troubling, the catch of blue whales—the most valuable species because of their great size— had declined from a peak of twenty-nine thousand in 1930-31 to fewer than fifteen thousand. And now any international effort to corral whaling would have to include two nations that were openly dedicated to challenging the status quo in global relations.

Scared by this international game of chicken, the Norwegian and British governments organized a second whaling conference for May 1937, with invitations going to Germany, Japan, Portugal, the United States, and the various dominions of the British Empire. Norwegian and British scientists, diplomats, and whalers hoped to bring all of the actual and potential whaling nations into a general agreement on rules for the hunt. These rules, in theory, would assure that there would always be blue and fin whales to support the industry. The most obvious problems for the industry were the shift from blue whales to the smaller fin whales and the decline in the yield of oil produced per catcher boat employed in the hunt.[7] No rational person attending the meetings in the summer of 1937 could have been optimistic about the fate of the blue whale and its fellow Antarctic cetaceans.

The London convention failed to blunt the tide of destruction, in part because the Japanese chose not to attend the meetings, and in part because the delegates were unable to grasp the magnitude of the whales' decline. And with Japanese whalers not participating, Germany, Britain, and Norway were hesitant to force their own whalers to abide by drastic regulations. In fact, the diplomats, especially the British, seemed unfazed by the doom and gloom coming from the scientists. In the end, the 1937 convention set an open season from 8 December to 7 March and established minimum sizes for taking each whale species. These rules would expire after the next season unless signatory nations chose to extend them.[8]

The inadequacy of the 1937 convention was obvious even as the delegates signed it. The size limits turned out to be so low as to allow killing of immature whales, and the open season was almost identical to the one that nature had set through weather, daylight, and the whales' migratory patterns. Before December, whales were too thin to yield much oil; later in March the weather became so bad that crews sometimes simply refused to serve.[9] In addition, the temporary nature of the rules meant that delegations would have to convene again to draft a new agreement and then go through the ratification process each year.

In 1938 and 1939 the United Kingdom and Norway called three more conferences to improve the 1937 agreement. Despite their efforts, the Japanese still held out, the price of whale oil remained around £15/ton, the number of whales taken rose to about forty-six thousand in the 1937-38 season, and the average size per whale continued to decline.[10] Thus, by the outbreak of the war in 1939, diplomatic efforts to regulate whaling were failing from any standpoint, whether environmental, political, or economic. The British and Norwegian initiatives had brought neither true conservation nor stability to the industry.

By comparison to the prewar slaughter, then, the war actually seemed to promise something of a reprieve for Antarctic whales. The number of active whaling vessels dropped quickly, beginning in the fall of 1939 with the inability of the German whaling fleet to leave blockaded ports. By the summer of 1940, so many British and Norwegian vessels had been sunk or requisitioned for military uses that the British decided not to send any expeditions south that year. And the next year, after Pearl Harbor, Japanese whalers became prime targets for the United States Navy. In addition, catcher boats were perfect for antisubmarine and minesweeping duties, and the floating factories, with their large deck spaces and ability to carry oil, were pressed in to convoy duty by both the Japanese and the Allies. By the end of the war, all that was left of the international fleet of forty-five floating factories were five damaged German ships and three older Norwegian vessels that had escaped to the United States, as well as two Norwegian vessels that had ridden out the war in Norway.[11]

But that did not mean that whalers were correct when they spoke of a six-year holiday for whales, which was part of their campaign to justify increased postwar whaling efforts. Whaling continued sporadically during the war, so that the U.S. government could issue press releases urging people to try whale meat, which had the benefit of being unrationed. In 1941, 1942, and 1943, U.S. officials encouraged refugee Norwegian whalers to catch sperm whales off Peru in a bid to increase stocks of sperm whale oil, a valuable industrial lubricant.[12] In addition, of course, the war against submarines in both oceans certainly resulted in the depth-charging of many whales by anxious sailors. As early as July 1942, British scientists felt compelled to dispel the notion that war would bring a resurgence of whale stocks. Considering that the use of whales for target practice might well have been common and the recent evidence that underwater noises can have deadly effects on cetaceans, it is hard to conclude that the years of war for people were years of peace for whales.

The holiday claim, though, was an important part of the whalers' position that regulations could be suspended for a time after the war because whales had had six years to rebuild their numbers. This position required not only blinders about the direct impact of the war on whales, but also a willful ignorance of whales' breeding behavior and biology. Like most large mammals, whales usually have one calf at a time. In addition, they take several years to reach breeding age and usually reproduce only every two years. With natural mortality added to the mix, there was no reason for whalers—who had firsthand experience with whales' biology—to assume at the end of the war that the south seas had been replenished. [13]

These debates influenced the decision by U.S. leaders to move from observers to leaders in whaling matters. With responsibility for less than 3 percent of the world's catch, the United States had had the luxury of being a disinterested and limited participant throughout the 1930s. For the 1931 convention, the U.S. government spent less time contemplating the merits of the subject than it did worrying about the political and financial implications of sending a delegate all the way to Geneva to work with the suspect League of Nations. The instructions to the U.S. delegates to the 1937 conference are striking in their brevity, barely a page long. Their content was simple—the American goal was to "prevent excessive and wasteful exploitation."[14] By 1939, the American whaling expert, Dr. Remington Kellogg, was confiding to a Norwegian colleague: "I doubt if the U.S.A. will ever take the initiative in requesting [a] conference." Kellogg added that the problem was that "these agreements rest solely on the good faith of the contracting governments," which was insufficient to guarantee true compliance.[15] In sum, Americans were willing to let Europeans take the lead—even if they led poorly—while they clamored for conservation from the back bench.

All of that changed with the outbreak of the war. At one level, the decision to take a leadership role in whaling diplomacy was a matter of national security. The goal of the 1943 sperm whale expedition, after all, was to procure a vital wartime commodity. Likewise, baleen whale oil could be made into glycerine, which could in turn be used to make explosives.[16] And of course, whales played a role as food. In other words, whaling had become a part of total war. But on another level, Kellogg and American diplomats concluded during the war that the British authorities would only pay lip service to conservation, and of course occupied Norway was in no position to lead. Even before the war, Kellogg had worried that the British government was unduly interested in the opinion of British industry in matters cetacean, but during the war he and American diplomats became convinced that the British were willing to bring about the blue whale's extinction as part of their efforts to avoid their own.

As it turned out, that was the position of many influential Britons. On 5 September 1939, H. L. French of the Ministry of Food made it clear that a war that lasted into 1940 would increase demands for whale oil; he concluded that it would be helpful "if some definite arrangement could be made for brushing the provisions of the Convention aside" for a season. In November, French reported that industry representatives were calling for the government to denounce the 1937 convention, although he acknowledged that probably "the whalers are really thinking of their own interests."[17] The recipient of this unwelcome advice was Alban Dobson, the Fisheries Secretary, who included whaling matters in his duties. For the next several years, he found himself battling to save the prewar whaling conventions from the whalers' flensing knife.

His job was complicated by the fact that he disliked some of the leading whalers but agreed with many of their points. The most outspoken whaling captain was Harald Salvesen, whom Dobson characterized as an "autocrat," "a very difficult member of society," and a person whose advice was based on his own financial interest and therefore had "to be treated with reserve, if not scepticism." But Dobson's job was to protect British whaling interests. When Salvesen noted that the outbreak of the war would delay British whalers from reaching the southern seas, Dobson agreed that the solution was to seek an extension of the end of the whaling season, which would require approval from the other signatories of the 1937 convention.[18]

This effort to extend the first season was the equivalent of a spring training game—it did not mean much, but it gave the various players a chance to hone their skills for the real contests.[19] The British wanted an extra day at the end of the season for each day lost at the beginning due to exigencies of the war. As Dobson noted, this would mean taking perhaps six hundred more whales, which was small change compared to the five thousand that the Germans would normally take. Besides, this was war against Hitler, and some sacrifices would have to be made. The Americans countered with sympathy but a general position that one cannot bend a convention just because it is inconvenient. And that sympathy extended only to Dobson's predicament, not to the British whaling industry; some Americans suspected that there was no dire emergency, just a desire by British whalers to reap extra profits at a time of crisis. In the end, they refused to acquiesce in changing the deadline, but they agreed to turn a blind eye to any violations if the British kept them to a minimum.[20]

What Americans did not know in 1942 and 1943 was that a debate was raging inside His Majesty's Government over the future of whaling. Salvesen took up the refrain of "starving Europe," and positioned the whaling industry as the knights in slightly corroded armor, ready to procure the fat that the victims of the Nazis so badly needed. The only impediment was the set of prewar conventions regulating whaling, which Salvesen thought ought to be abolished for the duration of the crisis. He found allies in the Ministry of Food and Ministry of War Transport, who argued that the prewar agreements should "not be considered sacrosanct." The Ministry of Agriculture and Fisheries was home to the holdouts, who argued forcefully that the agreements had to be maintained or strengthened. Late in 1942, Dobson told Salvesen and others that abrogating the treaties would be a retrograde step. By July of 1943 he was threatening to call Salvesen in and "give him a gentle reading of the Riot Act." One of his assistants went even further and called for an intensification of the regulations, especially a restriction on the number of floating factories allowed at sea. As he saw it, the end of the war would provide the perfect opportunity for a global agreement to severely restrict whaling.[21]

The U.S. government got its first insight into this struggle in March 1943, when Viscount Halifax, the British Ambassador in Washington, passed along to the State Department a proposal for a conference of British, Norwegian, American, and other allied delegates to amend the 1937 agreement in preparation for resumption of whaling as soon as possible. In particular, the British proposed lengthening the whaling season to as much as eight months, even though that would mean taking whales well before they had a chance to put on their layer of blubber. It was clear that Dobson had been forced to compromise, although it is possible that he acceded to the proposal with the certainty that the Americans would never agree to it. At the very least, he was confident that "the delay that inevitably occurs in securing the concurrence of the U.S.A." would prevent any snap decisions. [22] After much haggling over timing and agendas, the conference was finally scheduled for January 1944 in London.

Two confidential memoranda from November 1943 show that the American and British governments had chosen different paths. In that month, an official of the British Ministry of Agriculture and Fisheries admitted to Canadian diplomats that the whaling industry had suggested much of the agenda for the 1944 meeting, even though the government had disagreed with many parts of it, including the idea of an eight-month open season. The writer reported that industry officials "have even urged that the United Kingdom should denounce the [1937] Agreement ..., without prejudice to its resuscitation as soon as opportunity offers." He feared that delay would only increase pressure to denounce the convention, and therefore he urged the pursuit of "maximum supplies of whale oil." [23]

On the 20th of November, Kellogg addressed a letter to the State Department advocating a new, aggressive position in whaling diplomacy. He opened by arguing that the United States needed to send a strong delegation to London, or else the British and their dominions would dominate the discussions. Then he made it clear that previous efforts had failed to give "regulatory status to sound principles of conservation of existing whale stocks," and he placed the blame squarely on the United Kingdom and Norway. Conservation "had been compromised in the past by pressure exerted by local interests," including the British Board of Trade and the Norwegian Whaling Association. The only solution was to hold the first postwar whaling conference in Washington, where delegates could emphasize conservation without distraction from those local interests. Lest there be doubts that this issue was important, Kellogg mentioned that whale oil had strategic value. Kellogg's call found supporters in the State Department, and this time Hull's instructions to American delegates totaled twelve pages.[24]

Kellogg was the crucial link in this story, because he had remarkable credibility within the State Department. He had received his Ph.D. in 1928 from the University of California, writing his dissertation on paleo-cetaceans. His previous years of work with the U.S. Department of Agriculture not only helped to pay for graduate school but also prepared him for a government position, and he quickly landed a job as a mammalogist at the Smithsonian. Kellogg proved to be an adept, if somewhat gruff, administrator (known to some colleagues as "the abominable no man"), and he climbed the ranks until he became the second-ranking official in the institution in the 1950s. Given his degree and his position, Kellogg started with a certain amount of respect and prestige, but his ability to tame his temper in tight situations, follow orders, and meet diplomats half way made him very popular in Foggy Bottom.[25] By 1943, the State Department would not make a move on whaling without consulting Kellogg, appointing him to lead the delegation, and then giving him instructions that restated what he had written in the first place. Kellogg's influence was in part testimony to his own skills, but it also reflected both previous fruitful relations between scientists and diplomats in the United States and an innate sympathy toward conservation among the group of people who tended to become Foreign Service officers.[26]

Kellogg's ideas about conservation were straight out of the Progressive era. Whales were a resource. If properly managed, they would provide meat, fat, vitamins, bone meal, and a range of other products indefinitely. If improperly managed, they would be squandered. More than anything, Kellogg hated the idea that the world's whales would be squandered in a short-sighted frenzy, whether motivated by the whaling industry's greed or the desperation of a foreign government. In the grand scheme, he believed that three groups had to play a role in whaling. Unbiased scientists had to determine how many whales could be taken; bureaucrats had to enforce those limits; and whalers had to catch the animals and process them with maximum efficiency. It was the whalers who usually failed, both by taking too many and wasting what they caught. Kellogg seemed especially suspicious of Salvesen, the most powerful and outspoken whaler in Great Britain, who believed that industry should be left to its own devices because it had an obvious interest in seeing that the supply of whales did not run out.[27]

Once the delegates convened in January 1944, the differences between the American and British positions came into the open. John Maud of the British Ministry of Food argued that the world was facing a shortage of fats and oils likely to reach 1.1 million tons. He admitted that His Majesty's Government was "anxious not to kill the goose that laid the golden eggs," but he still demanded maximum production of whale oil within the 1937 treaty's limits. An American agricultural attaché, Loyd Steere, replied that conservation had to be the first goal, although the United States would consider allowances for temporary emergency production.[28] British and American delegates, then, were in agreement that the two highest priorities were the contradictory goals of alleviating the food shortage and conserving the whale stocks, but they could not agree on the order of priority.

The final results of the 1944 conference demonstrated that the United States was now asserting some leadership in regulating a natural resource that few Americans pursued or utilized. The protocol that emerged created a longer open season of 24 November to 24 March as a means to satisfy in part Maud's call for increased fat production. In exchange, the Americans demanded safeguards to prevent a return to the unrestrained prewar hunting, leading to acceptance of a Norwegian proposal to set a whaling quota for southern waters of sixteen thousand blue whale units (BWU), estimated to be twenty thousand whales.[29] Both of these changes would apply only to the first year of whaling, which most assumed would be 1944-45, although they later agreed that it would be 1945-46. Finally, Steere announced the intention of the United States to call its own whaling conference at "the earliest favorable opportunity," a choice of words and timing that Kellogg admitted was meant to forestall a similar British invitation. The British graciously agreed.[30]

In a confidential memorandum after the conference, Kellogg reported that current and former British fisheries officials admitted that their whaling industry had far too much power. One noted fisheries expert, whom Kellogg did not name, even suggested that the fats crisis had been blown out of proportion to the benefit of the whaling industry. Another showed Kellogg his office files, which revealed that whaling companies or those that used whale oil controlled the whaling branch of the Ministry of Food.[31] Such information simply reinforced the Americans' certainty that conservation depended on their leadership. Of course, it also suggested a remarkable admission on the part of British fisheries officials that their best hope to contain Salvesen lay in Washington.

The Americans, though, were taken by surprise in May 1945 when the British government announced that it would host another conference on whaling in the autumn of 1945 to plan long-term regulations. Privately, State Department officials admitted that they did not yet have an agenda for a conference in Washington, but they also termed the British action an "unusual procedure" and briefly considered rejecting the British invitation. In the end, the British and Americans agreed that the 1945 meeting in London would focus on rules for the 1946-47 season, with possible "ventilation" of proposals for long-term solutions.[32] Neither government was willing to disrupt greater diplomatic initiatives because of a disagreement about whaling, but each was also determined to lead in the way it saw fit.

The delegates assembled again in London on 20 November 1945 to hear one last British attempt to frame international whaling policy. Dobson opened the meeting with a request to focus on the fat and oil shortage. A. R. W. Harrison, of the Ministry of Food, gave the welcoming address, beginning by saying, "I was very gratified to hear you refer to whales as food, because that is the aspect of them which appeals most strongly to the Ministry of Food." He continued that the first priority of the British housewife was to have more fat available, and "the housewife is the person in whom the Minister of Food is most interested." Given this political pressure, Harrison made clear that "from our point of view it would be a tragedy if any international machinery were to get in the way of that increased production." To emphasize the point, the British passed out a report showing that the world faced a shortfall of at least 2.4 million tons of fats and edible oils.[33]

Dobson followed by laying out a rationale for two major changes to the rules. First, he asked for an extension of the 1946-47 hunting season; instead of closing on March 7, it would close on 24 April. He suggested that the shortage of factory vessels meant that whalers would need the extra time to reach the global quota of sixteen thousand BWU. Dobson and Salvesen then laid out a proposal to raise the catch limit to twenty thousand BWU; even though they did not anticipate hitting the target that year, they wanted to be prepared. Dobson suggested that this measure would be temporary, lasting just long enough to get the fat situation under control. Finally, he launched a preemptive strike against the Americans, from whom he certainly was anticipating a sharp response. He noted accurately that the 1944 Protocol had not yet come into force because the U.S. delegates had insisted that the Senate had to give consent first. He scolded the Americans for sticking to this "strictly legal position" in a time of crisis, suggesting not too subtly that American obstructionism was the greatest problem in whaling diplomacy. He did attempt to soften his comments by saying, "I do not want to put all of the onus on the United States of America," at which point he blamed Ireland, which had not sent any delegates.[34]

Dobson's sharp comments reflected his own growing frustration with the United States, which may have been equal to his frustration with Salvesen. Since 1940 he had been thwarted at every turn by the American way of doing business. He liked Kellogg and agreed with him on the key points, particularly his distrust of Salvesen, but he had no use for the delay and confusion that always seemed to accompany U.S. diplomacy. As early as November 1943 he was expressing "great puzzlement" at U.S. behavior in regards to a fisheries agreement, going so far as to say later that "we now seem to be up against them in some indefinable way in connection with what we regard as rather a trifling matter."[35] One may conclude that he saw these delays as playing into the hands of the whalers, who had so much power that he now found himself selling a set of ideas that he had privately dismissed only days before.

The conference quickly got down to business. The Americans made clear that they would not accept the twenty-thousand-BWU quota, which they feared might become the baseline for future years. The conferees settled on 7 April as the closing date for the whaling season, although only after much grumbling about the principle of the matter. They then turned to ventilating new ideas. Ira Gabrielson, the director of the U.S. Fish and Wildlife Service, pushed hard for reinstatement of a sanctuary for whales in Antarctic waters, but Dobson unilaterally swatted away that idea as unfeasible given the food shortage. Kellogg called for an embargo on the sale of whaling equipment to nations that had not ratified the 1944 or 1945 agreements, but Dobson also rejected that idea by saying that Parliament was simply too busy to consider such a motion. Finally, the U.S. delegates hinted that the British were exaggerating the magnitude of the fat shortage, which of course suggested that the very basis of the British position was unsound.[36] The differences between the United States and the United Kingdom could not have been more clear.

Although it did not generate much discussion at the 1945 meeting, one American proposal carried unusual long-term significance. Admitting that it was inconvenient to go to the Senate each year with a new whaling protocol, the United States proposed the establishment of a permanent commission of experts who would propose regulations based on scientific research. Such a commission would be limited to administering certain specified terms of the agreement and offering recommendations, but those recommendations would need the approval of the various signatory powers. The committee would not be limited to the major whaling nations—which the United States was not—but would be "composed of the persons best qualified to act in the interests of all countries concerned for the conservation and best utilization of the resource."[37] In other words, the selfish whaling nations that had created this mess before the war would have to yield to true conservationists, presumably from the United States. Although these ideas received only cursory attention in 1945, a year later they would be embodied in the International Whaling Commission.

As 1946 opened, American whaling experts believed that they had the last chance to place whaling on a rational basis. British actions in the previous three years had simply confirmed American suspicions that the whaling industry had compelled the United Kingdom to advocate short-sighted measures and unsustainable practices. British and Norwegian companies were rebuilding their whaling fleets rapidly. Even more worrisome, companies in or the governments of the United States, Japan, the Soviet Union, Argentina, the Netherlands, Australia, and a few other countries were making efforts to get back into whaling. Rising demand had driven whale oil to £71.5/ton. Kellogg believed that the pressure would be on to return to the unregulated killing of the years before 1937, and he warned that "No sound evidence has as yet been brought forth to indicate that the whale stocks can withstand such killing."[38]

But Kellogg was losing his grip on whaling diplomacy. The first signs of this development came in August 1946, as U.S. diplomats were discussing the rationale for hosting a whaling conference later that year. Diplomat William Flory laid out a comprehensive justification, which included conservation of whale stocks as an important goal. But he also argued that one goal had to be keeping the seas open to all who desired to whale, which was not only "in accord with our general economic foreign policy but is a matter of national interest." In other words, conservation would have to be squared with freedom of the seas and the U.S. market for sperm whale oil.[39]

That position revealed how U.S. whaling diplomacy had changed. Throughout 1945, regulating whaling had been an interesting, largely isolated issue, kept active mainly by Kellogg's personal leadership. The United States government had been willing to establish a permanent system of regulating whaling based on the conservationists' and consumers' interest that whale oil would be available indefinitely. American leaders sought to create a system that would protect the stock of whales and secondarily allow the development of the industry. That interest was still there, but now it was being trumped by a greater interest, the desire to build a cooperative global system that would maintain peace and bring prosperity to the United States and the world. The most prominent institutions had come together in 1944 with the meetings at Bretton Woods and Dumbarton Oaks, setting up the World Bank, International Monetary Fund, the International Trade Organization, and the United Nations. Now it was becoming clear that the proposed whaling commission had a role to play in this effort.

There was still room for conservation, and in fact the new commission would represent an advance over the 1937 agreement and its protocols in that regard. But there was more room for compromise. Instead of facing sanctions for not following agreed-upon protocols, nations were free to decide their own trade policies. In place of an independent organization established in the United States, far from the meddling of the whalers, the IWC was housed in the offices of the Ministry of Agriculture and Fisheries in London, and the two key offices were held by Norwegian Birger Bergersen and Alban Dobson, the very men whose inability to deal with the whaling industry had so disappointed Kellogg before. Rather than write tough rules to limit the number of whaling expeditions, the Americans argued that the seas were free to all, a reasonable position but one certainly influenced by a greater world vision. Finally, members of this new organization would be given the right to veto any new rule no matter its scientific justification, which fit the pattern of a nation seeking to maintain its freedom of action.[40]

This new spirit of compromise became evident during two speeches during the November 1946 meeting that led to the creation of the IWC. In a speech best remembered for the line describing whales as "wards of the entire world," Acting Secretary of State Dean Acheson placed his emphasis on "international cooperative efforts in whale conservation" and "increasing cooperation among nations in the solution of international conservation problems." Just as telling was a speech by C. Girard Davidson, the Assistant Secretary of the Interior, who was there to recount past U.S. successes in conservation diplomacy. But first he told delegates: "The world today has accepted the principle that the various nations must get together and work out their problems in cooperation and for their mutual welfare. The success of this principle depends upon its practical application to specific problems ... Each of you must feel proud to know that your work here is contributing to the vitality and health of international good-will."[41] Cooperation was the goal; conservation was just the means. The most striking symbol of that compromise was the system for amending the commission's regulations, which effectively required unanimity. The whaling commission would operate by consensus, even if conservation suffered.

These compromises did not necessarily weaken the effectiveness of the IWC. In fact, it might be argued that they were necessary to the creation of such a commission. Ultimately, the American interest in protecting sovereignty won praise from both the French and Dutch delegates, and it seems quite likely that the Soviets would not have joined a commission that they deemed too powerful.[42] In other words, a strong commission based in the United States and run by scientists like Kellogg might well have failed to win support from the assembled delegates in November, 1946. And no commission was certainly worse than a weak one.

In the end, then, the war had provided an opportunity to change the way pelagic whaling was restricted, but it had also overwhelmed the conservationist impulse. Two of the whaling nations, Germany and Japan, had been driven out of the business; the whaling fleets of Norway and Great Britain had been badly damaged; and the United States had resolved to promote effective conservation of the world's whales. Yet at the same time the global food crisis had undercut the argument for rigid conservation, and the American commitment to international leadership had made it impossible to look at whaling issues on their own merits. Just as the efforts of British conservationists had been derailed by the whaling industry, so too had the American efforts been altered by the U.S. global agenda.

Notes

1   The best comprehensive source on the history of whaling is J. N. Tønnessen and A. O. Johnsen, *The History of Modern Whaling* (Berkeley: University of California Press, 1982).
2   Karl Brandt, *Whaling and Whale Oil During and After World War II* (Palo Alto, CA: Food Research Institute, Stanford University, June 1948), 1.
3   All statistics for prewar whaling come from an undated table entitled "The Antarctic Whaling," found in the United States National Archives, Washington, D.C., Record Group 59, General Records of the Department of State (hereafter RG 59), File 562.8F3. This table likely was based on data from the International Bureau for Whaling Statistics in Norway, which compiled very accurate data on the global whale catch both before and after the war.
4   L. Fletcher, British Museum of Natural History, to the Colonial Office, 27 Oct. 1911; Lord Harcourt, Colonial Office, to the Duke of Connaught, Governor General of Canada, 11 March 1914, both, National Archives of Canada, Record Group 25, Records of the Department of External Affairs (hereafter RG 25), vol. 1125, File 787; Memorandum on the Proposed Expert Committee ... to Consider the Control of Whaling Operations, Ottawa, 20 May 1929, RG 25, vol. 1543, File 455, pt. 1.
5   Tønnessen and Johnsen, *History of Modern Whaling*, 178-82.
6   Tønnessen and Johnsen, *History of Modern Whaling*, 367-407.
7   The Minutes of the 1937 conference can be found at RU 7165 International Whaling Conferences and International Whaling Commission Records, 1930-68, Box 3, File London—Int'l Whaling Conference, 1937, Smithsonian Institution Archives, Washington.
8   The text of the agreement can be found at http://www.oceanlaw.net/texts/whales37.htm.
9   Hull to Franklin Roosevelt, 29 July 1937, RG 59, File 562.8F2.
10 H. Paulsen to Kellogg, 19 January 1940, RG 59, File 562.8F2; minutes of 1938 and 1939 meetings can be found in RG 59, File 562.8F3.
11 Mr. Lowe, note for files, 26 November 1942, Public Record Office, London, Records of the Ministry of Agriculture and Fisheries (henceforth MAF), MAF 41/1332 FGB 1576; R. Humphreys, Ministry of War Transport, to Mr. Lowe, 29 June 1945, MAF 41/1334 FGB 3616.
12 Tønnessen and Johnsen report that the *Thorshammer* took 8,559 sperm whales over those three seasons. *History of Modern Whaling*, 483.
13 Discovery Committee, Scientific Subcommittee, memo 14 July 1942, MAF 41/1332 FGB 1576; for whales' biology, see Peter G. H. Evans, *The Natural History of Whales and Dolphins* (New York: Facts on File Publications, 1987), Chapter 8.
14 Hull to Kellogg, 10 May 1937, RG 59, File 562.8F2.
15 Kellogg to Birger Bergersen, 15 April 1939, Remington Kellogg Papers, RU 7434, Entry 7170, File Bea-Bes, Smithsonian Institution Archives.
16 Resumé of Operations of Norwegian Whaling Ship, *Thorshammer*, 2 June 1944, RU 7165, Box 9; H. Earle Russel to Hull, 31 August 1937, RG 59 File 562.8F2.

17 French to Dobson, 5 September and 29 November 1939, MAF 41/1330 FGB 148.
18 Dobson to Hill, 2 July 1943, MAF 41/1333 FGB 2407.
19 "Spring training" is a term from American professional baseball. Every spring, teams play a series of exhibition games as part of their preparation, or training, for the regular season. The results of these games are unofficial and of interest only to the most rabid of fans (such as the author).
20 Dobson note, 12 March 1940, MAF 41/1330 FGB 148; Memorandum, 22 November 1939, RG 59, File 562.8F2.
21 See MAF 41/1332 FGB 1576 for the full exchange.
22 Viscount Halifax to Hull, 31 March 1943, RG 59, File 562.8F3; Dobson to Weston, 8 February 1943, MAF 41/1332 FGB 1576.
23 Note on the International Whaling Agreement, 1937, Nov. 1943, enclosed with a telegram from Stuart MacLeod to the Secretary of State for External Affairs, 23 December 1943, RG 25, Vol. 3263, File 6120-40.
24 Kellogg to Sturgeon, 20 Nov. 1943, RG 59, File 562.8F4/25; Hull to Kellogg, 23 December 1943, RG 59, File 562.8F4/51.
25 The U.S. State Department is located in a section of Washington known as Foggy Bottom.
26 More on this topic can be found in Kurkpatrick Dorsey, *The Dawn of Conservation Diplomacy: U.S.-Canadian Wildlife Diplomacy in the Progressive Era* (Seattle: University of Washington Press, 1998).
27 Kellogg's papers can be found in the Smithsonian Institution Archives, and Salvesen's are in the University of Edinburgh Library.
28 Minutes of First Meeting, 6 Jan. 1944, RG 25, vol. 3263, File 6120-40.
29 A blue whale unit was either one blue whale, two fin whales, two and a half humpbacks, or six sei whales. The idea was to draw rough equivalencies in oil production, so one could also think of a BWU as roughly one hundred barrels of oil.
30 Kellogg and Steere to Hull, 2 Feb. 1944, RG 59, File 562.8F4.
31 Memorandum by Dr. Remington Kellogg, 8 Feb. 1944, RG 59, File 562.8F4.
32 Sturgeon to Flory, 4 May 1945, RG 43, Entry 241, Subject File, 1937-48, File 1944 Protocol (II); Acting High Commissioner to External Affairs, 18 Oct. 1945, RG 25, vol. 3263, File 6120-40.
33 IWC No. 6, Opening Session, 20 Nov. 1945, RG 25, vol. 3263, File 6120-40.
34 IWC No. 11, Minutes of the Sixth and Seventh Sessions, 23 Nov. 1945, RG 25, vol. 3263, File 6120-40.
35 Dobson to Coote, 1 November and 9 December 1943, MAF 41/1333 FGB 2407.
36 IWC No. 10, Minutes of the Fourth and Fifth Sessions, 22 Nov. 1945; U.S. No. 3, 21 Nov. 1945, Memorandum on the Proposal for a Whaling Season of Indeterminate Length, RG 25, vol. 3263, File, 6120-40.
37 US No. 5, 21 Nov. 1945, Establishment of Permanent Commission, RG 25, vol. 3263, File 6120-40.
38 Karl Brandt to Kellogg, 8 Oct. 1946, and Kellogg's reply 15 Oct. 1946, RU 7165, Box 9, File Washington—International Whaling Conv, 1946.
39 Flory to Mr. Breese, 21 August 1946, RG 43, File 1946 Meeting I.
40 The final text of the International Convention for the Regulation of Whaling can be found at http://www.iwcoffice.org/Convention.htm.
41 Acheson's speech is document IWC/11 and Davidson's is IWC/42, both in the USNA, RG 43.
42 USNA, RG 43 contains the full minutes of the 1946 meeting.

Authors

Judith A. Bennett is Associate Professor of History and Associate Dean of Graduate Studies (Humanities) at the University of Otago, New Zealand. She is researching the impact of World War Two on the South Pacific Islands' environment and the forest history of the Melanesian Islands. She is the author of *Pacific Forest: A History of Resource Control and Contest in Solomon Islands, c. 1800-1997* (Brill and White Horse Press, 2000), and several articles on the environmental history of the Pacific.

Kurk Dorsey is associate professor of history at the University of New Hampshire. His 1998 book, *The Dawn of Conservation Diplomacy: US-Canadian Wildlife Protection Treaties in the Progressive Era* (University of Washington Press), was co-winner of the Stuart Bernath Prize from the Society for Historians of American Foreign Relations.

Mark Fiege is associate professor of history at Colorado State University in Fort Collins, where he teaches American environmental history. He is author of *Irrigated Eden: The Making of an Agricultural Landscape in the American West* (University of Washington Press, 1999). He is working on an environmental history of the United States.

Stewart Gordon is an independent scholar and a visiting professor at the Center for South Asian Studies, University of Michigan. He studies society and warfare in pre-colonial India and is the author of *The Marathas, 1600-1818*, a volume of the New Cambridge History of India (1993), and two edited volumes on courtly ceremony in Asia.

Simo Laakkonen is a researcher of environmental history at the University of Helsinki, Finland. He has written and edited books on the environmental history of the City of Helsinki in the nineteenth and twentiethth century. His main interest is, however, the history of degradation and protection of the Baltic Sea.

Roger Levine is an assistant professor of African and environmental history at the University of the South, Sewanee, Tennessee. His research interests center on the cultural and environmental history of the eastern frontier of South Africa during the colonial era, and he is currently revising his Yale University dissertation, a microhistory of an African cultural intermediary on the frontier, for publication.

Edmund Russell is associate professor of science, technology, and society and history at the University of Virginia. His work has focused on the historical relationship between war and environmental change and on the role of evolution (of nonhuman species) in human history. He is the author of *War and Nature: Fighting Humans and Insects with Chemicals from World War I to Silent Spring* (Cambridge University Press, 2001), which won the Edelstein Prize of the Society for the History of Technology.

William M. Tsutsui is associate professor of history at the University of Kansas. A specialist in the business and social history of modern Japan, he is the author of *Manufacturing Ideology: Scientific Management in Twentieth-Century Japan* (Princeton University Press, 1998) and *Godzilla on My Mind* (Palgrave Macmillan, 2004).

Richard P. Tucker is Adjunct Professor of Natural Resources at the University of Michigan, and Professor Emeritus of History at Oakland University. He writes on the history of forest degradation and wildlife management in India and across the colonial and tropical world. His most recent book is *Insatiable Appetite: The United States and the Ecological Degradation of the Tropical World* (University of California Press, 2000).

Index